Apache Spark 2.x Machine Learning Cookbook

Over 100 recipes to simplify machine learning model implementations with Spark

Siamak Amirghodsi
Meenakshi Rajendran
Broderick Hall
Shuen Mei

BIRMINGHAM - MUMBAI

Apache Spark 2.x Machine Learning Cookbook

Copyright © 2017 Packt Publishing

All rights reserved. No part of this book may be reproduced, stored in a retrieval system, or transmitted in any form or by any means, without the prior written permission of the publisher, except in the case of brief quotations embedded in critical articles or reviews.

Every effort has been made in the preparation of this book to ensure the accuracy of the information presented. However, the information contained in this book is sold without warranty, either express or implied. Neither the authors, nor Packt Publishing, and its dealers and distributors will be held liable for any damages caused or alleged to be caused directly or indirectly by this book.

Packt Publishing has endeavored to provide trademark information about all of the companies and products mentioned in this book by the appropriate use of capitals. However, Packt Publishing cannot guarantee the accuracy of this information.

First published: September 2017

Production reference: 1200917

Published by Packt Publishing Ltd.
Livery Place
35 Livery Street
Birmingham
B3 2PB, UK.
ISBN 978-1-78355-160-6

www.packtpub.com

Credits

Authors
Siamak Amirghodsi
Meenakshi Rajendran
Broderick Hall
Shuen Mei

Reviewers
Sumit Pal
Mohammad Guller

Commissioning Editor
Ashwin Nair

Acquisition Editor
Vinay Argekar

Content Development Editor
Nikhil Borkar

Technical Editor
Madhunikita Sunil Chindarkar

Copy Editor
Safis Editing

Project Coordinator
Sheejal Shah

Proofreader
Safis Editing

Indexer
Rekha Nair

Graphics
Kirk D'Penha

Production Coordinator
Melwyn Dsa

About the Authors

Siamak Amirghodsi (**Sammy**) is a world-class senior technology executive leader with an entrepreneurial track record of overseeing big data strategies, cloud transformation, quantitative risk management, advanced analytics, large-scale regulatory data platforming, enterprise architecture, technology road mapping, multi-project execution, and organizational streamlining in Fortune 20 environments in a global setting.

Siamak is a hands-on big data, cloud, machine learning, and AI expert, and is currently overseeing the large-scale cloud data platforming and advanced risk analytics build out for a tier-1 financial institution in the United States. Siamak's interests include building advanced technical teams, executive management, Spark, Hadoop, big data analytics, AI, deep learning nets, TensorFlow, cognitive models, swarm algorithms, real-time streaming systems, quantum computing, financial risk management, trading signal discovery, econometrics, long-term financial cycles, IoT, blockchain, probabilistic graphical models, cryptography, and NLP.

Siamak is fully certified on Cloudera's big data platform and follows Apache Spark, TensorFlow, Hadoop, Hive, Pig, Zookeeper, Amazon AWS, Cassandra, HBase, Neo4j, MongoDB, and GPU architecture, while being fully grounded in the traditional IBM/Oracle/Microsoft technology stack for business continuity and integration.

Siamak has a PMP designation. He holds an advanced degree in computer science and an MBA from the University of Chicago (ChicagoBooth), with emphasis on strategic management, quantitative finance, and econometrics.

Meenakshi Rajendran is a hands-on big data analytics and data governance manager with expertise in large-scale data platforming and machine learning program execution on a global scale. She is experienced in the end-to-end delivery of data analytics and data science products for leading financial institutions. Meenakshi holds a master's degree in business administration and is a certified PMP with over 13 years of experience in global software delivery environments. She not only understands the underpinnings of big data and data science technology but also has a solid understanding of the human side of the equation as well.

Meenakshi's favorite languages are Python, R, Julia, and Scala. Her areas of research and interest are Apache Spark, cloud, regulatory data governance, machine learning, Cassandra, and managing global data teams at scale. In her free time, she dabbles in software engineering management literature, cognitive psychology, and chess for relaxation.

Broderick Hall is a hands-on big data analytics expert and holds a master's degree in computer science with 20 years of experience in designing and developing complex enterprise-wide software applications with real-time and regulatory requirements at a global scale. He has an extensive experience in designing and building real-time financial applications for some of the largest financial institutions and exchanges in USA. He is a deep learning early adopter and is currently working on a large-scale cloud-based data platform with deep learning net augmentation.

Broderick has extensive experience working in healthcare, travel, real estate, and data center management. Broderick also enjoys his role as an adjunct professor, instructing courses in Java programming and object-oriented programming. He is currently focused on delivering real-time big data mission-critical analytics applications in the financial services industry.

Broderick has been actively involved with Hadoop, Spark, Cassandra, TensorFlow, and deep learning since the early days, while actively pursuing machine learning, cloud architecture, data platforms, data science, and practical applications in cognitive sciences. He enjoys programming in Scala, Python, R, Java, and Julia.

Shuen Mei is a big data analytic platforms expert with 15+ years of experience in the financial services industry. He is experienced in designing, building, and executing large-scale, enterprise-distributed financial systems with mission-critical low-latency requirements. He is certified in the Apache Spark, Cloudera Big Data platform, including Developer, Admin, and HBase.

Shuen is also a certified AWS solutions architect with emphasis on peta-byte range real-time data platform systems. Shuen is a skilled software engineer with extensive experience in delivering infrastructure, code, data architecture, and performance tuning solutions in trading and finance for Fortune 100 companies.

Shuen holds a master's degree in MIS from the University of Illinois. He actively follows Spark, TensorFlow, Hadoop, Spark, Cloud Architecture, Apache Flink, Hive, HBase, Cassandra, and related systems. He is passionate about Scala, Python, Java, Julia, cloud computing, machine learning algorithms, and deep learning at scale.

About the Reviewer

Sumit Pal, who has authored *SQL on Big Data - Technology, Architecture, and Innovations* by *Apress*, has more than 22 years of experience in the software industry in various roles, spanning companies from startups to enterprises.

Sumit is an independent consultant working with big data, data visualization, and data science, and he is a software architect building end-to-end data-driven analytic systems.

Sumit has worked for Microsoft (SQL server development team), Oracle (OLAP development team), and Verizon (big data analytics team) in a career spanning 22 years. Currently, he works for multiple clients advising them on their data architectures and big data solutions, and does hands-on coding with Spark, Scala, Java, and Python.

Sumit has spoken at the following Big Data Conferences:

- Data Summit NY, May 2017
- Big Data Symposium Boston, May 2017
- Apache Linux Foundation, May 2016, Vancouver, Canada,
- Data Center World, March 2016, Las Vegas
- Chicago, Nov 2015
- Big Data Conferences in Global Big Data Conference in Boston, Aug 2015

Sumit has also developed a Big Data Analyst Training course for Experfy, more details of which can be found at `https://www.experfy.com/training/courses/big-data-analyst`.

Sumit has an extensive experience in building scalable systems across the stack from middle tier and data tier to visualization for analytics applications, using big data and NoSQL DB. He has deep expertise in database internals, data warehouses, dimensional modeling, data science with Java and Python, and SQL.

Sumit started his career as a part of the SQL Server Development Team at Microsoft in 1996-97 and then as a core server engineer for Oracle Corporation at their OLAP Development team in Burlington, MA.

Sumit has also worked at Verizon as an Associate Director for big data architecture, where he strategized, managed, architected, and developed platforms and solutions for analytics and machine learning applications. He has also served as a chief architect at ModelN/LeapfrogRX (2006-2013), where he architected the middle-tier core analytics platform with open source OLAP engine (Mondrian) on J2EE and solved some complex Dimensional ETL, Modeling, and performance optimization problems.

Sumit has MS and BS in computer science. He hiked to the Mt. Everest Base camp in Oct, 2016.

www.PacktPub.com

For support files and downloads related to your book, please visit `www.PacktPub.com`.

Did you know that Packt offers eBook versions of every book published, with PDF and ePub files available? You can upgrade to the eBook version at `www.PacktPub.com` and as a print book customer, you are entitled to a discount on the eBook copy. Get in touch with us at `service@packtpub.com` for more details.

At `www.PacktPub.com`, you can also read a collection of free technical articles, sign up for a range of free newsletters and receive exclusive discounts and offers on Packt books and eBooks.

`https://www.packtpub.com/mapt`

Get the most in-demand software skills with Mapt. Mapt gives you full access to all Packt books and video courses, as well as industry-leading tools to help you plan your personal development and advance your career.

Why subscribe?

- Fully searchable across every book published by Packt
- Copy and paste, print, and bookmark content
- On demand and accessible via a web browser

Customer Feedback

Thanks for purchasing this Packt book. At Packt, quality is at the heart of our editorial process. To help us improve, please leave us an honest review on this book's Amazon page at `https://www.amazon.com/dp/1783551607`.

If you'd like to join our team of regular reviewers, you can email us at `customerreviews@packtpub.com`. We award our regular reviewers with free eBooks and videos in exchange for their valuable feedback. Help us be relentless in improving our products!

Table of Contents

Preface

Education is not the learning of facts,

but the training of the mind to think.

- Albert Einstein

Data is the new silicon of our age, and machine learning, coupled with biologically inspired cognitive systems, serves as the core foundation to not only enable but also accelerate the birth of the fourth industrial revolution. This book is dedicated to our parents, who through extreme hardship and sacrifice, made our education possible and taught us to always practice kindness.

The *Apache Spark 2.x Machine Learning Cookbook* is crafted by four friends with diverse background, who bring in a vast experience across multiple industries and academic disciplines. The team has immense experience in the subject matter at hand. The book is as much about friendship as it is about the science underpinning Spark and Machine Learning. We wanted to put our thoughts together and write a book for the community that not only combines Spark's ML code and real-world data sets but also provides context-relevant explanation, references, and readings for a deeper understanding and promoting further research. This book is a reflection of what our team would have wished to have when we got started with Apache Spark.

My own interest in machine learning and artificial intelligence started in the mid eighties when I had the opportunity to read two significant artifacts that happened to be listed back to back in *Artificial Intelligence, An International Journal*, Volume 28, Number 1, February 1986. While it has been a long journey for engineers and scientists of my generation, fortunately, the advancements in resilient distributed computing, cloud computing, GPUs, cognitive computing, optimization, and advanced machine learning have made the dream of long decades come true. All these advancements have become accessible for the current generation of ML enthusiasts and data scientists alike.

We live in one of the rarest periods in history--a time when multiple technological and sociological trends have merged at the same point in time. The elasticity of cloud computing with built-in access to ML and deep learning nets will provide a whole new set of opportunities to create and capture new markets. The emergence of Apache Spark as the *lingua franca* or the *common language* of near real-time resilient distributed computing and data virtualization has provided smart companies the opportunity to employ ML techniques at a scale without a heavy investment in specialized data centers or hardware.

The *Apache Spark 2.x Machine Learning Cookbook* is one of the most comprehensive treatments of the Apache Spark machine learning API, with selected subcomponents of Spark to give you the foundation you need before you can master a high-end career in machine learning and Apache Spark. The book is written with the goal of providing clarity and accessibility, and it reflects our own experience (including reading the source code) and learning curve with Apache Spark, which started with Spark 1.0.

The *Apache Spark 2.x Machine Learning Cookbook* lives at the intersection of Apache Spark, machine learning, and Scala for developers, and data scientists through a practitioner's lens who not only has to understand the code but also the details, theory, and inner workings of a given Spark ML algorithm or API to establish a successful career in the new economy.

The book takes the cookbook format to a whole new level by blending downloadable ready-to-run Apache Spark ML code recipes with background, actionable theory, references, research, and real-life data sets to help the reader understand the *what*, *how* and the *why* behind the extensive facilities offered by Spark for the machine learning library. The book starts by laying the foundations needed to succeed and then rapidly evolves to cover all the meaningful ML algorithms available in Apache Spark.

What this book covers

Chapter 1, *Practical Machine Learning with Spark Using Scala*, covers installing and configuring a real-life development environment with machine learning and programming with Apache Spark. Using screenshots, it walks you through downloading, installing, and configuring Apache Spark and IntelliJ IDEA along with the necessary libraries that would reflect a developer's desktop in a real-world setting. It then proceeds to identify and list over 40 data repositories with real-world data sets that can help the reader in experimenting and advancing even further with the code recipes. In the final step, we run our first ML program on Spark and then provide directions on how to add graphics to your machine learning programs, which are used in the subsequent chapters.

Chapter 2, *Just Enough Linear Algebra for Machine Learning with Spark*, covers the use of linear algebra (vector and matrix), which is the foundation of some of the most monumental works in machine learning. It provides a comprehensive treatment of the DenseVector, SparseVector, and matrix facilities available in Apache Spark, with the recipes in the chapter. It provides recipes for both local and distributed matrices, including RowMatrix, IndexedRowMatrix, CoordinateMatrix, and BlockMatrix to provide a detailed explanation of this topic. We included this chapter because mastery of the Spark and ML/MLlib was only possible by reading most of the source code line by line and understanding how the matrix decomposition and vector/matrix arithmetic work underneath the more course-grain algorithm in Spark.

Chapter 3, *Spark's Three Data Musketeers for Machine Learning - Perfect Together*, provides an end-to-end treatment of the three pillars of resilient distributed data manipulation and wrangling in Apache spark. The chapter comprises detailed recipes covering RDDs, DataFrame, and Dataset facilities from a practitioner's point of view. Through an exhaustive list of 17 recipes, examples, references, and explanation, it lays out the foundation to build a successful career in machine learning sciences. The chapter provides both functional (code) as well as non-functional (SQL interface) programming approaches to solidify the knowledge base reflecting the real demands of a successful Spark ML engineer at tier 1 companies.

Chapter 4, *Common Recipes for Implementing a Robust Machine Learning System*, covers and factors out the tasks that are common in most machine learning systems through 16 short but to-the-point code recipes that the reader can use in their own real-world systems. It covers a gamut of techniques, ranging from normalizing data to evaluating the model output, using best practice metrics via Spark's ML/MLlib facilities that might not be readily visible to the reader. It is a combination of recipes that we use in our day-to-day jobs in most situations but are listed separately to save on space and complexity of other recipes.

Chapter 5, *Practical Machine Learning with Regression and Classification in Spark 2.0 - Part I*, is the first of two chapters exploring classification and regression in Apache Spark. This chapter starts with Generalized Linear Regression (GLM) extending it to Lasso, Ridge with different types of optimization available in Spark. The chapter then proceeds to cover Isotonic regression, Survival regression with multi-layer perceptron (neural networks) and One-vs-Rest classifier.

Chapter 6, *Practical Machine Learning with Regression and Classification in Spark 2.0 - Part II*, is the second of the two regression and classification chapters. This chapter covers RDD-based regression systems, ranging from Linear, Logistic, and Ridge to Lasso, using Stochastic Gradient Decent and L_BFGS optimization in Spark. The last three recipes cover Support Vector Machine (SVM) and Naïve Bayes, ending with a detailed recipe for ML pipelines that are gaining a prominent position in the Spark ML ecosystem.

Chapter 7, *Recommendation Engine that Scales with Spark,* covers how to explore your data set and build a movie recommendation engine using Spark's ML library facilities. It uses a large dataset and some recipes in addition to figures and write-ups to explore the various methods of recommenders before going deep into collaborative filtering techniques in Spark.

Chapter 8, *Unsupervised Clustering with Apache Spark 2.0,* covers the techniques used in unsupervised learning, such as KMeans, Mixture, and Expectation (EM), Power Iteration Clustering (PIC), and Latent Dirichlet Allocation (LDA), while also covering the why and how to help the reader to understand the core concepts. Using Spark Streaming, the chapter commences with a real-time KMeans clustering recipe to classify the input stream into labeled classes via unsupervised means.

Chapter 9, *Optimization - Going Down the Hill with Gradient Descent,* is a unique chapter that walks you through optimization as it applies to machine learning. It starts from a closed form formula and quadratic function optimization (for example, cost function), to using Gradient Descent (GD) in order to solve a regression problem from scratch. The chapter helps to look underneath the hood by developing the reader's skill set using Scala code while providing in-depth explanation of how to code and understand Stochastic Descent (GD) from scratch. The chapter concludes with one of Spark's ML API to achieve the same concepts that we code from scratch.

Chapter 10, *Building Machine Learning Systems with Decision Tree and Ensemble Models,* covers the Tree and Ensemble models for classification and regression in depth using Spark's machine library. We use three real-world data sets to explore the classification and regression problems using Decision Tree, Random Forest Tree, and Gradient Boosted Tree. The chapter provides an in-depth explanation of these methods in addition to plug-and-play code recipes that explore Apache Spark's machine library step by step.

Chapter 11, *The Curse of High-Dimensionality in Big Data,* demystifies the art and science of dimensionality reduction and provides a complete coverage of Spark's ML/MLlib library, which facilitates this important concept in machine learning at scale. The chapter provides sufficient and in-depth coverage of the theory (the what and why) and then proceeds to cover two fundamental techniques available (the how) in Spark for the readers to use. The chapter covers Single Value Decomposition (SVD), which relates well with the second chapter and then proceeds to examine the Principal Component Analysis (PCA) in depth with code and write ups.

Chapter 12, *Implementing Text Analytics with Spark 2.0 ML Library*, covers the various techniques available in Spark for implementing text analytics at scale. It provides a comprehensive treatment by starting from the basics, such as Term Frequency (TF) and similarity techniques, such as Word2Vec, and moves on to analyzing a complete dump of Wikipedia for a real-life Spark ML project. The chapter concludes with an in-depth discussion and code for implementing Latent Semantic Analysis (LSA) and Topic Modeling with Latent Dirichlet Allocation (LDA) in Spark.

Chapter 13, *Spark Streaming and Machine Learning Library*, starts by providing an introduction to and the future direction of Spark streaming, and then proceeds to provide recipes for both RDD-based (DStream) and structured streaming to establish a baseline. The chapter then proceeds to cover all the available ML streaming algorithms in Spark at the time of writing this book. The chapter provides code and shows how to implement streaming DataFrame and streaming data sets, and then proceeds to cover queueStream for debugging before it goes into Streaming KMeans (unsupervised learning) and streaming linear models such as Linear and Logistic regression using real-world datasets.

What you need for this book

Please use the details from the software list document.

To execute the recipes in this book, you need a system running Windows 7 and above, or Mac 10, with the following software installed:

- Apache Spark 2.x
- Oracle JDK SE 1.8.x
- JetBrain IntelliJ Community Edition 2016.2.X or later version
- Scala plug-in for IntelliJ 2016.2.x
- Jfreechart 1.0.19
- breeze-core 0.12
- Cloud9 1.5.0 JAR
- Bliki-core 3.0.19
- hadoop-streaming 2.2.0
- Jcommon 1.0.23
- Lucene-analyzers-common 6.0.0
- Lucene-core-6.0.0
- Spark-streaming-flume-assembly 2.0.0
- Spark-streaming-kafka-assembly 2.0.0

The hardware requirements for this software are mentioned in the software list provided with the code bundle of this book.

Who this book is for

This book is for Scala developers with a fairly good exposure to and understanding of machine learning techniques, but who lack practical implementations with Spark. A solid knowledge of machine learning algorithms is assumed, as well as some hands-on experience of implementing ML algorithms with Scala. However, you do not need to be acquainted with the Spark ML libraries and the ecosystem.

Sections

In this book, you will find several headings that appear frequently (Getting ready, How to do it…, How it works…, There's more…, and See also). To give clear instructions on how to complete a recipe, we use these sections as follows:

Getting ready

This section tells you what to expect in the recipe, and describes how to set up any software or any preliminary settings required for the recipe.

How to do it…

This section contains the steps required to follow the recipe.

How it works…

This section usually consists of a detailed explanation of what happened in the previous section.

There's more…

This section consists of additional information about the recipe in order to make the reader more knowledgeable about the recipe.

See also

This section provides helpful links to other useful information for the recipe.

Conventions

In this book, you will find a number of text styles that distinguish between different kinds of information. Here are some examples of these styles and an explanation of their meaning. Code words in text, database table names, folder names, filenames, file extensions, pathnames, dummy URLs, user input, and Twitter handles are shown as follows: "Mac users note that we installed Spark 2.0 in the `/Users/USERNAME/spark/spark-2.0.0-bin-hadoop2.7/` directory on a Mac machine."

A block of code is set as follows:

```
object HelloWorld extends App {
   println("Hello World!")
 }
```

Any command-line input or output is written as follows:

```
mysql -u root -p
```

New terms and **important words** are shown in bold. Words that you see on the screen, for example, in menus or dialog boxes, appear in the text like this: "Configure **Global Libraries**. Select **Scala SDK** as your global library."

Warnings or important notes appear like this.

Tips and tricks appear like this.

Reader feedback

Feedback from our readers is always welcome. Let us know what you think about this book-what you liked or disliked. Reader feedback is important for us as it helps us develop titles that you will really get the most out of. To send us general feedback, simply e-mail feedback@packtpub.com, and mention the book's title in the subject of your message. If there is a topic that you have expertise in and you are interested in either writing or contributing to a book, see our author guide at www.packtpub.com/authors.

Customer support

Now that you are the proud owner of a Packt book, we have a number of things to help you to get the most from your purchase.

Downloading the example code

You can download the example code files for this book from your account at http://www.packtpub.com. If you purchased this book elsewhere, you can visit http://www.packtpub.com/support and register to have the files e-mailed directly to you. You can download the code files by following these steps:

1. Log in or register to our website using your e-mail address and password.
2. Hover the mouse pointer on the **SUPPORT** tab at the top.
3. Click on **Code Downloads & Errata**.
4. Enter the name of the book in the **Search** box.
5. Select the book for which you're looking to download the code files.
6. Choose from the drop-down menu where you purchased this book from.
7. Click on **Code Download**.

You can also download the code files by clicking on the **Code Files** button on the book's webpage at the Packt Publishing website. This page can be accessed by entering the book's name in the **Search** box. Please note that you need to be logged in to your Packt account. Once the file is downloaded, please make sure that you unzip or extract the folder using the latest version of:

- WinRAR / 7-Zip for Windows
- Zipeg / iZip / UnRarX for Mac
- 7-Zip / PeaZip for Linux

The code bundle for the book is also hosted on GitHub at
`https://github.com/PacktPublishing/Apache-Spark-2x-Machine-Learning-Cookbook`.
We also have other code bundles from our rich catalog of books and videos available at
`https://github.com/PacktPublishing/`. Check them out!

Errata

Although we have taken every care to ensure the accuracy of our content, mistakes do happen. If you find a mistake in one of our books-maybe a mistake in the text or the code- we would be grateful if you could report this to us. By doing so, you can save other readers from frustration and help us improve subsequent versions of this book. If you find any errata, please report them by visiting `http://www.packtpub.com/submit-errata`, selecting your book, clicking on the **Errata Submission Form** link, and entering the details of your errata. Once your errata are verified, your submission will be accepted and the errata will be uploaded to our website or added to any list of existing errata under the Errata section of that title. To view the previously submitted errata, go to `https://www.packtpub.com/books/content/support` and enter the name of the book in the search field. The required information will appear under the **Errata** section.

Piracy

Piracy of copyrighted material on the Internet is an ongoing problem across all media. At Packt, we take the protection of our copyright and licenses very seriously. If you come across any illegal copies of our works in any form on the Internet, please provide us with the location address or website name immediately so that we can pursue a remedy. Please contact us at `copyright@packtpub.com` with a link to the suspected pirated material. We appreciate your help in protecting our authors and our ability to bring you valuable content.

Questions

If you have a problem with any aspect of this book, you can contact us at `questions@packtpub.com`, and we will do our best to address the problem.

1
Practical Machine Learning with Spark Using Scala

In this chapter, we will cover:

- Downloading and installing the JDK
- Downloading and installing IntelliJ
- Downloading and installing Spark
- Configuring IntelliJ to work with Spark and run Spark ML sample codes
- Running a sample ML code from Spark
- Identifying data sources for practical machine learning
- Running your first program using Apache Spark 2.0 with the IntelliJ IDE
- How to add graphics to your Spark program

Introduction

With the recent advancements in cluster computing coupled with the rise of big data, the field of machine learning has been pushed to the forefront of computing. The need for an interactive platform that enables data science at scale has long been a dream that is now a reality.

The following three areas together have enabled and accelerated interactive data science at scale:

- **Apache Spark**: A unified technology platform for data science that combines a fast compute engine and fault-tolerant data structures into a well-designed and integrated offering
- **Machine learning**: A field of artificial intelligence that enables machines to mimic some of the tasks originally reserved exclusively for the human brain
- **Scala**: A modern JVM-based language that builds on traditional languages, but unites functional and object-oriented concepts without the verboseness of other languages

First, we need to set up the development environment, which will consist of the following components:

- Spark
- IntelliJ community edition IDE
- Scala

The recipes in this chapter will give you detailed instructions for installing and configuring the IntelliJ IDE, Scala plugin, and Spark. After the development environment is set up, we'll proceed to run one of the Spark ML sample codes to test the setup.

Apache Spark

Apache Spark is emerging as the de facto platform and trade language for big data analytics and as a complement to the **Hadoop** paradigm. Spark enables a data scientist to work in the manner that is most conducive to their workflow right out of the box. Spark's approach is to process the workload in a completely distributed manner without the need for **MapReduce** (**MR**) or repeated writing of the intermediate results to a disk.

Spark provides an easy-to-use distributed framework in a unified technology stack, which has made it the platform of choice for data science projects, which more often than not require an iterative algorithm that eventually merges toward a solution. These algorithms, due to their inner workings, generate a large amount of intermediate results that need to go from one stage to the next during the intermediate steps. The need for an interactive tool with a robust native distributed **machine learning library** (**MLlib**) rules out a disk-based approach for most of the data science projects.

Spark has a different approach toward cluster computing. It solves the problem as a technology stack rather than as an ecosystem. A large number of centrally managed libraries combined with a lightning-fast compute engine that can support fault-tolerant data structures has poised Spark to take over Hadoop as the preferred big data platform for analytics.

Spark has a modular approach, as depicted in the following diagram:

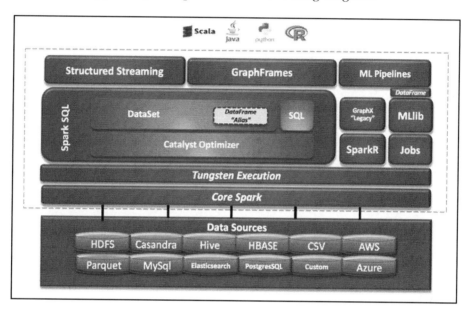

Machine learning

The aim of machine learning is to produce machines and devices that can mimic human intelligence and automate some of the tasks that have been traditionally reserved for a human brain. Machine learning algorithms are designed to go through very large data sets in a relatively short time and approximate answers that would have taken a human much longer to process.

The field of machine learning can be classified into many forms and at a high level, it can be classified as supervised and unsupervised learning. Supervised learning algorithms are a class of ML algorithms that use a training set (that is, labeled data) to compute a probabilistic distribution or graphical model that in turn allows them to classify the new data points without further human intervention. Unsupervised learning is a type of machine learning algorithm used to draw inferences from datasets consisting of input data without labeled responses.

Out of the box, Spark offers a rich set of ML algorithms that can be deployed on large datasets without any further coding. The following figure depicts Spark's MLlib algorithms as a mind map. Spark's MLlib is designed to take advantage of parallelism while having fault-tolerant distributed data structures. Spark refers to such data structures as **Resilient Distributed Datasets** or **RDDs**:

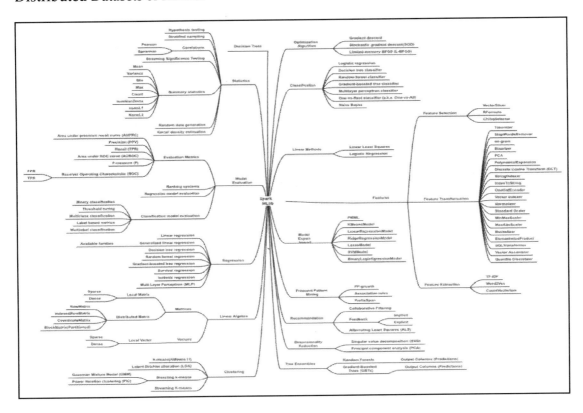

Scala

Scala is a modern programming language that is emerging as an alternative to traditional programming languages such as **Java** and **C++**. Scala is a JVM-based language that not only offers a concise syntax without the traditional boilerplate code, but also incorporates both object-oriented and functional programming into an extremely crisp and extraordinarily powerful type-safe language.

Scala takes a flexible and expressive approach, which makes it perfect for interacting with Spark's MLlib. The fact that Spark itself is written in Scala provides a strong evidence that the Scala language is a full-service programming language that can be used to create sophisticated system code with heavy performance needs.

Scala builds on Java's tradition by addressing some of its shortcomings, while avoiding an all-or-nothing approach. Scala code compiles into Java bytecode, which in turn makes it possible to coexist with rich Java libraries interchangeably. The ability to use Java libraries with Scala and vice versa provides continuity and a rich environment for software engineers to build modern and complex machine learning systems without being fully disconnected from the Java tradition and code base.

Scala fully supports a feature-rich functional programming paradigm with standard support for lambda, currying, type interface, immutability, lazy evaluation, and a pattern-matching paradigm reminiscent of Perl without the cryptic syntax. Scala is an excellent match for machine learning programming due to its support for algebra-friendly data types, anonymous functions, covariance, contra-variance, and higher-order functions.

Here's a hello world program in Scala:

```
object HelloWorld extends App {
   println("Hello World!")
 }
```

Compiling and running `HelloWorld` in Scala looks like this:

```
Siamaks-MBP:~ Siamak$ scalac HelloWorld.scala
Siamaks-MBP:~ Siamak$ scala HelloWorld
Hello World!
Siamaks-MBP:~ Siamak$ ▌
```

The Apache Spark Machine Learning Cookbook takes a practical approach by offering a multi-disciplinary view with the developer in mind. This book focuses on the interactions and cohesiveness of **machine learning, Apache Spark**, and **Scala**. We also take an extra step and teach you how to set up and run a comprehensive development environment familiar to a developer and provide code snippets that you have to run in an interactive shell without the modern facilities that an IDE provides:

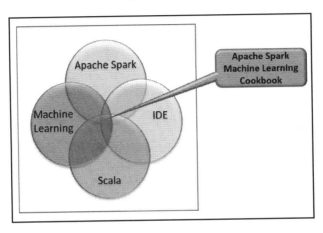

Software versions and libraries used in this book

The following table provides a detailed list of software versions and libraries used in this book. If you follow the installation instructions covered in this chapter, it will include most of the items listed here. Any other JAR or library files that may be required for specific recipes are covered via additional installation instructions in the respective recipes:

Core systems	Version
Spark	2.0.0
Java	1.8
IntelliJ IDEA	2016.2.4
Scala-sdk	2.11.8

Miscellaneous JARs that will be required are as follows:

Miscellaneous JARs	Version
`bliki-core`	3.0.19
`breeze-viz`	0.12
`Cloud9`	1.5.0
`Hadoop-streaming`	2.2.0
`JCommon`	1.0.23
`JFreeChart`	1.0.19
`lucene-analyzers-common`	6.0.0
`Lucene-Core`	6.0.0
`scopt`	3.3.0
`spark-streaming-flume-assembly`	2.0.0
`spark-streaming-kafka-0-8-assembly`	2.0.0

We have additionally tested all the recipes in this book on Spark 2.1.1 and found that the programs executed as expected. It is recommended for learning purposes you use the software versions and libraries listed in these tables.

To stay current with the rapidly changing Spark landscape and documentation, the API links to the Spark documentation mentioned throughout this book point to the latest version of Spark 2.x.x, but the API references in the recipes are explicitly for Spark 2.0.0.

All the Spark documentation links provided in this book will point to the latest documentation on Spark's website. If you prefer to look for documentation for a specific version of Spark (for example, Spark 2.0.0), look for relevant documentation on the Spark website using the following URL:

```
https://spark.apache.org/documentation.html
```

We've made the code as simple as possible for clarity purposes rather than demonstrating the advanced features of Scala.

Downloading and installing the JDK

The first step is to download the JDK development environment that is required for Scala/Spark development.

Getting ready

When you are ready to download and install the JDK, access the following link:

```
http://www.oracle.com/technetwork/java/javase/downloads/index.html
```

How to do it...

After successful download, follow the on-screen instructions to install the JDK.

Downloading and installing IntelliJ

IntelliJ Community Edition is a lightweight IDE for Java SE, Groovy, Scala, and Kotlin development. To complete setting up your machine learning with the Spark development environment, the IntelliJ IDE needs to be installed.

Getting ready

When you are ready to download and install IntelliJ, access the following link:

```
https://www.jetbrains.com/idea/download/
```

How to do it...

At the time of writing, we are using IntelliJ version 15.x or later (for example, version 2016.2.4) to test the examples in the book, but feel free to download the latest version. Once the installation file is downloaded, double-click on the downloaded file (.exe) and begin to install the IDE. Leave all the installation options at the default settings if you do not want to make any changes. Follow the on-screen instructions to complete the installation:

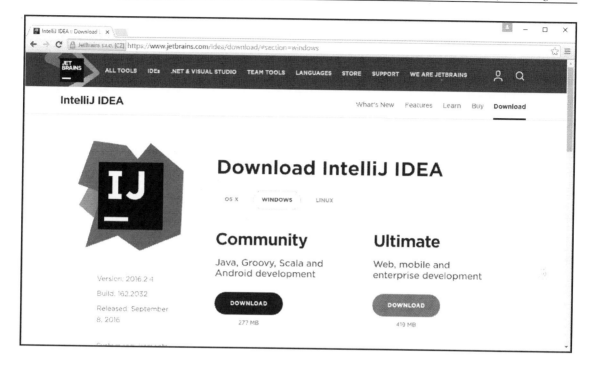

Downloading and installing Spark

We now proceed to download and install Spark.

Getting ready

When you are ready to download and install Spark, access the Apache website at this link:

`http://spark.apache.org/downloads.html`

How to do it...

Go to the Apache website and select the required download parameters, as shown in this screenshot:

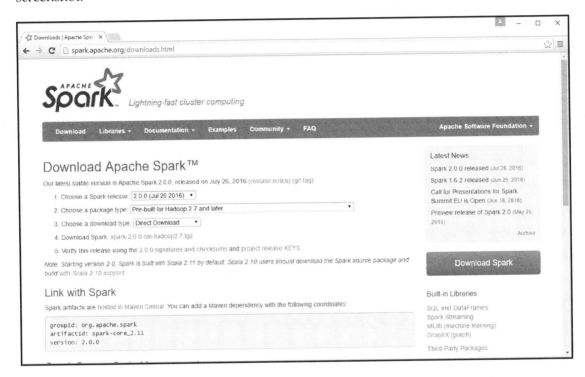

Make sure to accept the default choices (click on **Next**) and proceed with the installation.

Configuring IntelliJ to work with Spark and run Spark ML sample codes

We need to run some configurations to ensure that the project settings are correct before being able to run the samples that are provided by Spark or any of the programs listed this book.

Getting ready

We need to be particularly careful when configuring the project structure and global libraries. After we set everything up, we proceed to run the sample ML code provided by the Spark team to verify the setup. Sample code can be found under the Spark directory or can be obtained by downloading the Spark source code with samples.

How to do it...

The following are the steps for configuring IntelliJ to work with Spark MLlib and for running the sample ML code provided by Spark in the examples directory. The examples directory can be found in your home directory for Spark. Use the Scala samples to proceed:

1. Click on the **Project Structure...** option, as shown in the following screenshot, to configure project settings:

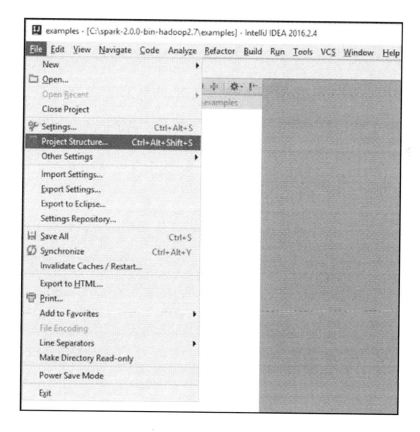

2. Verify the settings:

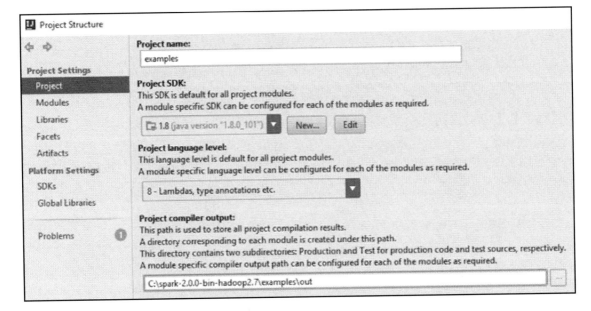

3. Configure **Global Libraries**. Select **Scala SDK** as your global library:

4. Select the JARs for the new Scala SDK and let the download complete:

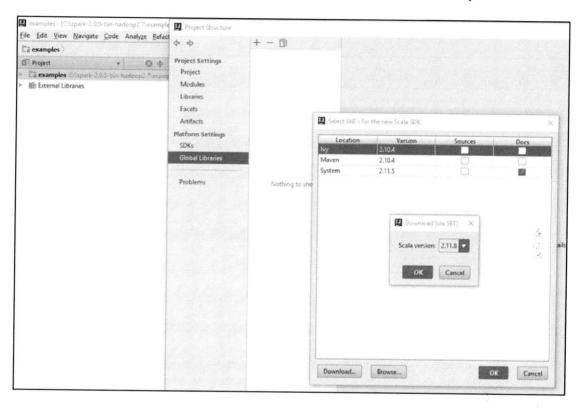

5. Select the project name:

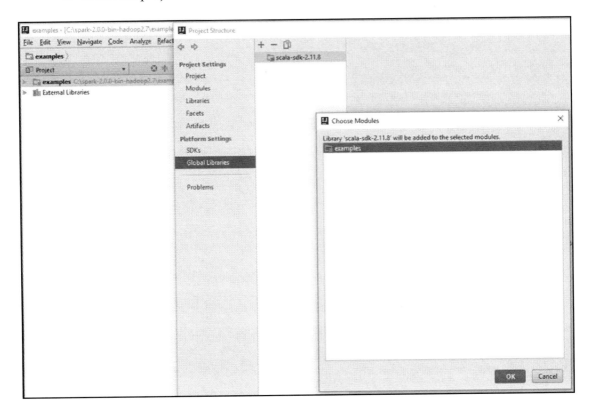

6. Verify the settings and additional libraries:

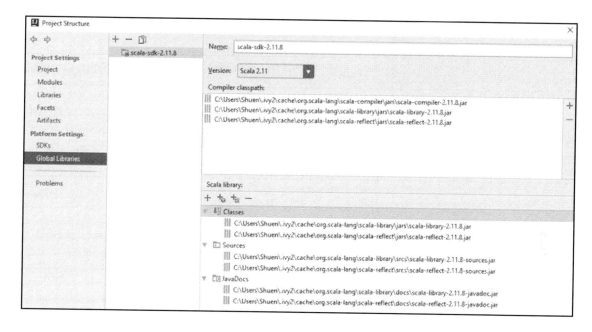

7. Add dependency JARs. Select modules under the **Project Settings** in the left-hand pane and click on dependencies to choose the required JARs, as shown in the following screenshot:

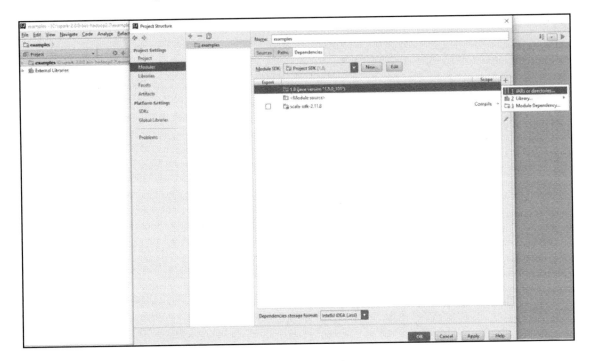

8. Select the JAR files provided by Spark. Choose Spark's default installation directory and then select the `lib` directory:

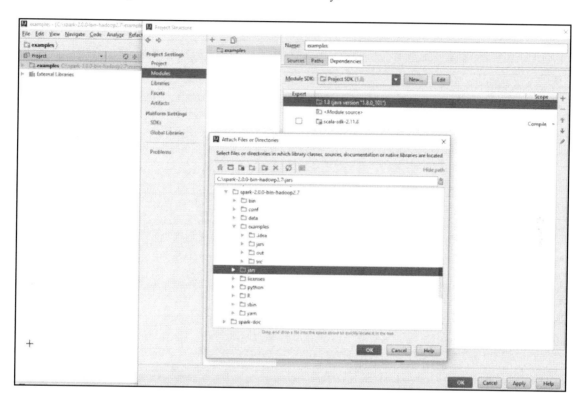

9. We then select the JAR files for examples that are provided for Spark out of the box.

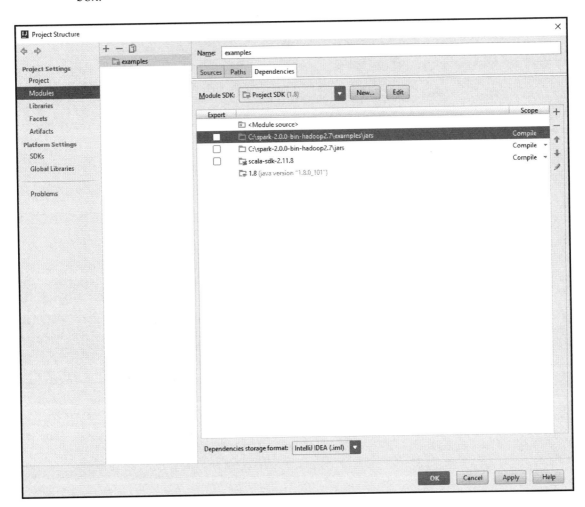

10. Add required JARs by verifying that you selected and imported all the JARs listed under `External Libraries` in the the left-hand pane:

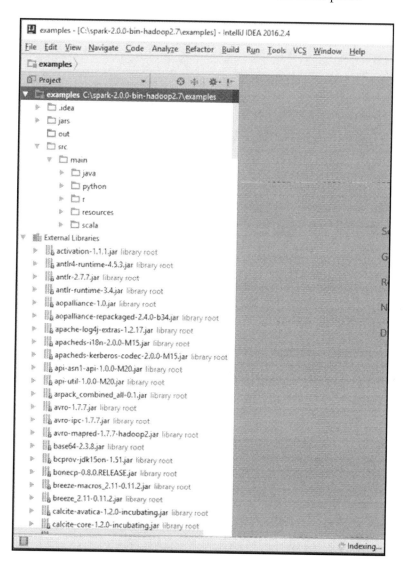

11. Spark 2.0 uses Scala 2.11. Two new streaming JARs, Flume and Kafka, are needed to run the examples, and can be downloaded from the following URLs:

- `https://repo1.maven.org/maven2/org/apache/spark/spark-streaming-flume-assembly_2.11/2.0.0/spark-streaming-flume-assembly_2.11-2.0.0.jar`

- `https://repo1.maven.org/maven2/org/apache/spark/spark-streaming-kafka-0-8-assembly_2.11/2.0.0/spark-streaming-kafka-0-8-assembly_2.11-2.0.0.jar`

The next step is to download and install the Flume and Kafka JARs. For the purposes of this book, we have used the Maven repo:

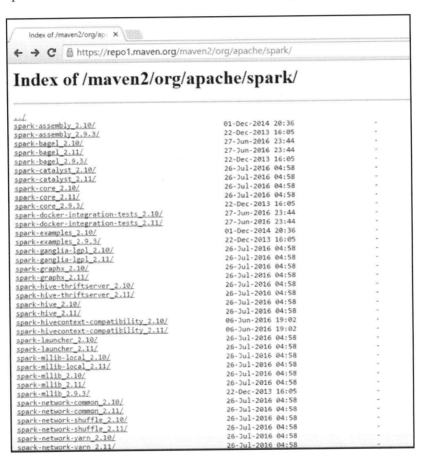

12. Download and install the Kafka assembly:

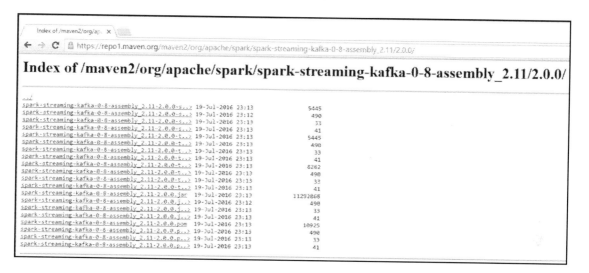

13. Download and install the Flume assembly:

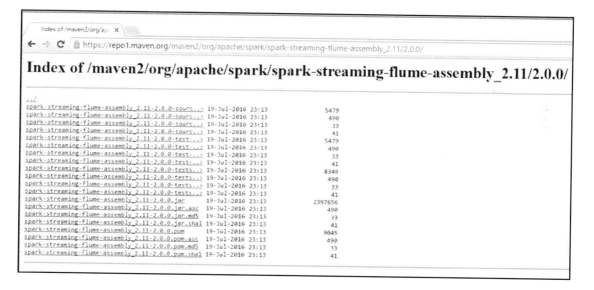

14. After the download is complete, move the downloaded JAR files to the `lib` directory of Spark. We used the `C` drive when we installed Spark:

15. Open your IDE and verify that all the JARs under the `External Libraries` folder on the left, as shown in the following screenshot, are present in your setup:

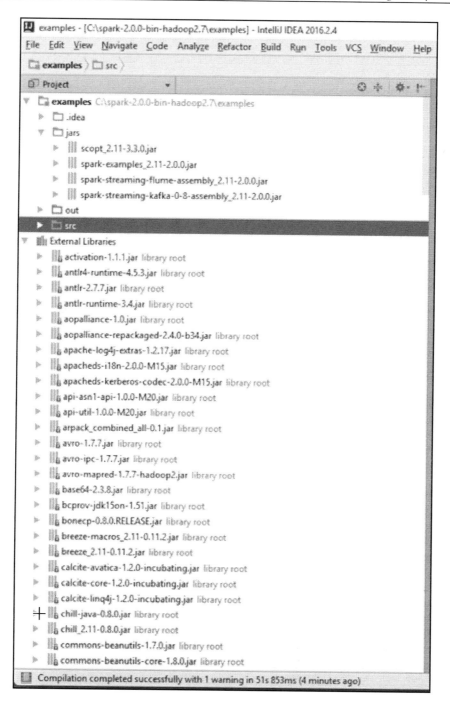

16. Build the example projects in Spark to verify the setup:

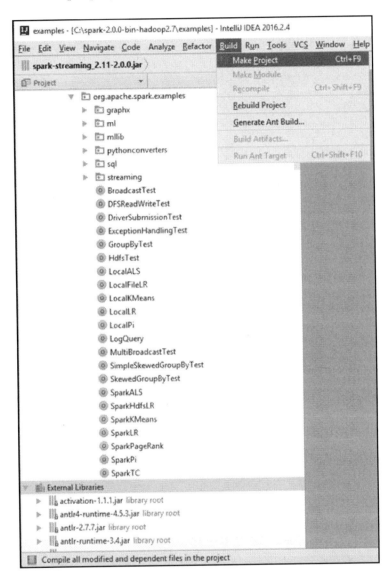

17. Verify that the build was successful:

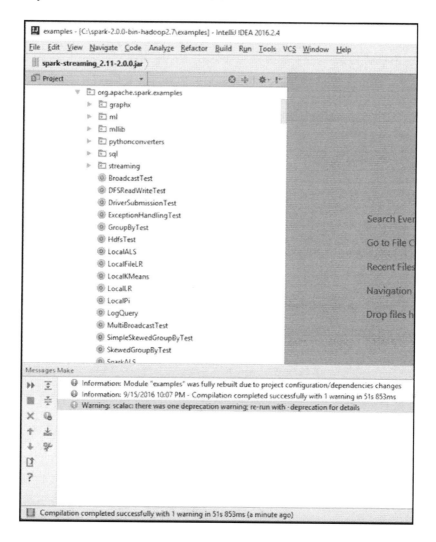

There's more...

Prior to Spark 2.0, we needed another library from Google called **Guava** for facilitating I/O and for providing a set of rich methods of defining tables and then letting Spark broadcast them across the cluster. Due to dependency issues that were hard to work around, Spark 2.0 no longer uses the Guava library. Make sure you use the Guava library if you are using Spark versions prior to 2.0 (required in version 1.5.2). The Guava library can be accessed at the following URL:

```
https://github.com/google/guava/wiki
```

You may want to use Guava version 15.0, which can be found here:

```
https://mvnrepository.com/artifact/com.google.guava/guava/15.0
```

If you are using installation instructions from previous blogs, make sure to exclude the Guava library from the installation set.

See also

If there are other third-party libraries or JARs required for the completion of the Spark installation, you can find those in the following Maven repository:

```
https://repo1.maven.org/maven2/org/apache/spark/
```

Running a sample ML code from Spark

We can verify the setup by simply downloading the sample code from the Spark source tree and importing it into IntelliJ to make sure it runs.

Getting ready

We will first run the logistic regression code from the samples to verify installation. In the next section, we proceed to write our own version of the same program and examine the output in order to understand how it works.

How to do it...

1. Go to the source directory and pick one of the ML sample code files to run. We've selected the logistic regression example.

If you cannot find the source code in your directory, you can always download the Spark source, unzip, and then extract the examples directory accordingly.

2. After selecting the example, select **Edit Configurations...**, as shown in the following screenshot:

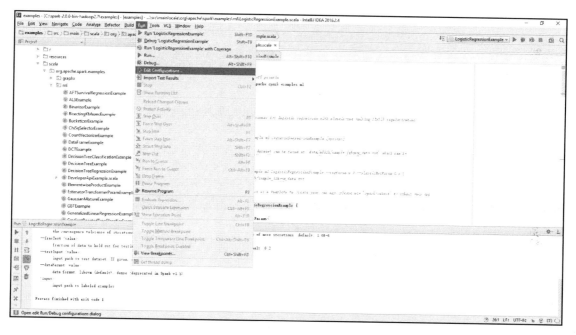

3. In the **Configurations** tab, define the following options:
   - **VM options**: The choice shown allows you to run a standalone Spark cluster
   - **Program arguments**: What we are supposed to pass into the program

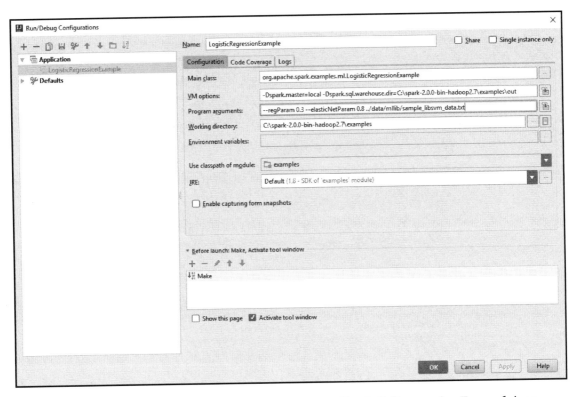

4. Run the logistic regression by going to **Run 'LogisticRegressionExample'**, as shown in the following screenshot:

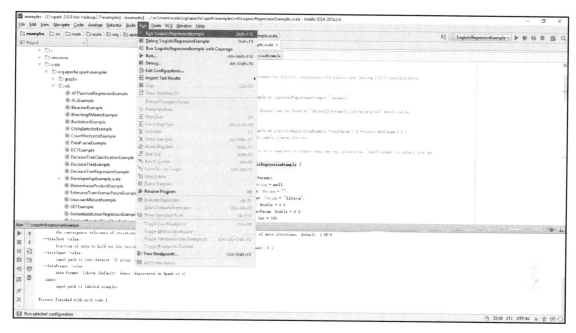

5. Verify the exit code and make sure it is as shown in the following screenshot:

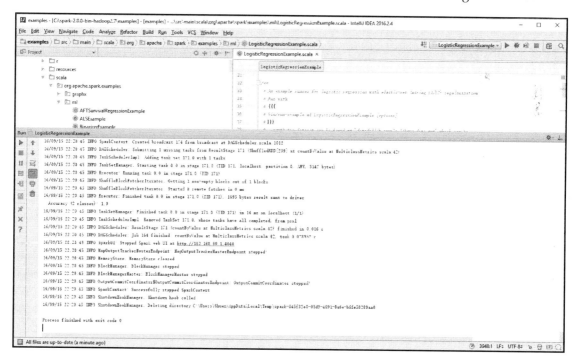

Identifying data sources for practical machine learning

Getting data for machine learning projects was a challenge in the past. However, now there is a rich set of public data sources specifically suitable for machine learning.

Getting ready

In addition to the university and government sources, there are many other open sources of data that can be used to learn and code your own examples and projects. We will list the data sources and show you how to best obtain and download data for each chapter.

How to do it...

The following is a list of open source data worth exploring if you would like to develop applications in this field:

- *UCI machine learning repository*: This is an extensive library with search functionality. At the time of writing, there were more than 350 datasets. You can click on the `https://archive.ics.uci.edu/ml/index.html` link to see all the datasets or look for a specific set using a simple search (*Ctrl + F*).
- *Kaggle datasets*: You need to create an account, but you can download any sets for learning as well as for competing in machine learning competitions. The `https://www.kaggle.com/competitions` link provides details for exploring and learning more about Kaggle, and the inner workings of machine learning competitions.
- *MLdata.org*: A public site open to all with a repository of datasets for machine learning enthusiasts.
- *Google Trends*: You can find statistics on search volume (as a proportion of total search) for any given term since 2004 on `http://www.google.com/trends/explore`.
- *The CIA World Factbook*: The `https://www.cia.gov/library/publications/the-world-factbook/` link provides information on the history, population, economy, government, infrastructure, and military of 267 countries.

See also

Other sources for machine learning data:

- SMS spam data: `http://www.dt.fee.unicamp.br/~tiago/smsspamcollection/`
- Financial dataset from Lending Club
  `https://www.lendingclub.com/info/download-data.action`
- Research data from Yahoo `http://webscope.sandbox.yahoo.com/index.php`
- Amazon AWS public dataset `http://aws.amazon.com/public-data-sets/`
- Labeled visual data from Image Net `http://www.image-net.org`
- Census datasets `http://www.census.gov`
- Compiled YouTube dataset `http://netsg.cs.sfu.ca/youtubedata/`
- Collected rating data from the MovieLens site
  `http://grouplens.org/datasets/movielens/`
- Enron dataset available to the public `http://www.cs.cmu.edu/~enron/`
- Dataset for the classic book elements of statistical learning
  `http://statweb.stanford.edu/~tibs/ElemStatLearn/data.htmlIMDB`
- Movie dataset `http://www.imdb.com/interfaces`
- Million Song dataset `http://labrosa.ee.columbia.edu/millionsong/`
- Dataset for speech and audio `http://labrosa.ee.columbia.edu/projects/`
- Face recognition data `http://www.face-rec.org/databases/`
- Social science data `http://www.icpsr.umich.edu/icpsrweb/ICPSR/studies`
- Bulk datasets from Cornell University `http://arxiv.org/help/bulk_data_s3`
- Project Guttenberg datasets
  `http://www.gutenberg.org/wiki/Gutenberg:Offline_Catalogs`
- Datasets from World Bank `http://data.worldbank.org`
- Lexical database from World Net `http://wordnet.princeton.edu`
- Collision data from NYPD `http://nypd.openscrape.com/#/`
- Dataset for congressional row calls and others `http://voteview.com/dwnl.htm`
- Large graph datasets from Stanford
  `http://snap.stanford.edu/data/index.html`
- Rich set of data from datahub `https://datahub.io/dataset`
- Yelp's academic dataset `https://www.yelp.com/academic_dataset`
- Source of data from GitHub
  `https://github.com/caesar0301/awesome-public-datasets`
- Dataset archives from Reddit `https://www.reddit.com/r/datasets/`

There are some specialized datasets (for example, text analytics in Spanish, and gene and IMF data) that might be of some interest to you:

- Datasets from Colombia (in Spanish):
  `http://www.datos.gov.co/frm/buscador/frmBuscador.aspx`
- Dataset from cancer studies
  `http://www.broadinstitute.org/cgi-bin/cancer/datasets.cgi`
- Research data from Pew `http://www.pewinternet.org/datasets/`
- Data from the state of Illinois/USA `https://data.illinois.gov`
- Data from freebase.com `http://www.freebase.com`
- Datasets from the UN and its associated agencies `http://data.un.org`
- International Monetary Fund datasets `http://www.imf.org/external/data.htm`
- UK government data `https://data.gov.uk`
- Open data from Estonia
  `http://pub.stat.ee/px-web.2001/Dialog/statfile1.asp`
- Many ML libraries in R containing data that can be exported as CSV
  `https://www.r-project.org`
- Gene expression datasets `http://www.ncbi.nlm.nih.gov/geo/`

Running your first program using Apache Spark 2.0 with the IntelliJ IDE

The purpose of this program is to get you comfortable with compiling and running a recipe using the Spark 2.0 development environment you just set up. We will explore the components and steps in later chapters.

We are going to write our own version of the Spark 2.0.0 program and examine the output so we can understand how it works. To emphasize, this short recipe is only a simple RDD program with Scala sugar syntax to make sure you have set up your environment correctly before starting to work with more complicated recipes.

How to do it...

1. Start a new project in IntelliJ or in an IDE of your choice. Make sure that the necessary JAR files are included.

2. Download the sample code for the book, find the `myFirstSpark20.scala` file, and place the code in the following directory.

   We installed Spark 2.0 in the `C:\spark-2.0.0-bin-hadoop2.7\` directory on a Windows machine.

3. Place the `myFirstSpark20.scala` file in the `C:\spark-2.0.0-bin-hadoop2.7\examples\src\main\scala\spark\ml\cookbook\chapter1` directory:

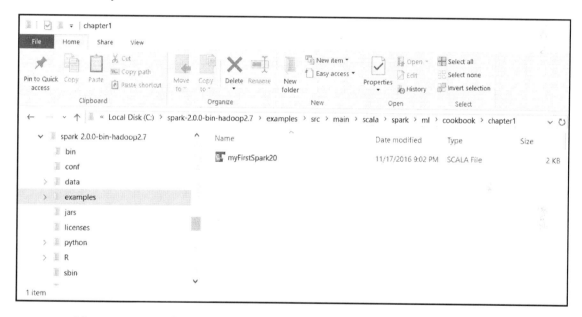

   Mac users note that we installed Spark 2.0 in the `/Users/USERNAME/spark/spark-2.0.0-bin-hadoop2.7/` directory on a Mac machine.

   Place the `myFirstSpark20.scala` file in the `/Users/USERNAME/spark/spark-2.0.0-bin-hadoop2.7/examples/src/main/scala/spark/ml/cookbook/chapter1` directory.

4. Set up the package location where the program will reside:

```
package spark.ml.cookbook.chapter1
```

5. Import the necessary packages for the Spark session to gain access to the cluster and log4j.Logger to reduce the amount of output produced by Spark:

```
import org.apache.spark.sql.SparkSession
import org.apache.log4j.Logger
import org.apache.log4j.Level
```

6. Set output level to ERROR to reduce Spark's logging output:

```
Logger.getLogger("org").setLevel(Level.ERROR)
```

7. Initialize a Spark session by specifying configurations with the builder pattern, thus making an entry point available for the Spark cluster:

```
val spark = SparkSession
.builder
.master("local[*]")
 .appName("myFirstSpark20")
.config("spark.sql.warehouse.dir", ".")
.getOrCreate()
```

The myFirstSpark20 object will run in local mode. The previous code block is a typical way to start creating a SparkSession object.

8. We then create two array variables:

```
val x =
Array(1.0,5.0,8.0,10.0,15.0,21.0,27.0,30.0,38.0,45.0,50.0,64.0)
val y =
Array(5.0,1.0,4.0,11.0,25.0,18.0,33.0,20.0,30.0,43.0,55.0,57.0)
```

9. We then let Spark create two RDDs based on the array created before:

```
val xRDD = spark.sparkContext.parallelize(x)
val yRDD = spark.sparkContext.parallelize(y)
```

10. Next, we let Spark operate on the RDD; the zip() function will create a new RDD from the two RDDs mentioned before:

```
val zipedRDD = xRDD.zip(yRDD)
zipedRDD.collect().foreach(println)
```

In the console output at runtime (more details on how to run the program in the IntelliJ IDE in the following steps), you will see this:

```
(1.0,5.0)
(5.0, 1.0)
(8.0,4.0)
(10.0,11.0)
(15.0,25.0)
(21.0,18.0)
(27.0,33.0)
(30.0,20.0)
(38.0,30.0)
(45.0,43.0)
(50.0,55.0)
(64.0,57.0)
```

11. Now, we sum up the value for xRDD and yRDD and calculate the new zipedRDD sum value. We also calculate the item count for zipedRDD:

```
val xSum = zipedRDD.map(_._1).sum()
val ySum = zipedRDD.map(_._2).sum()
val xySum= zipedRDD.map(c => c._1 * c._2).sum()
val n= zipedRDD.count()
```

12. We print out the value calculated previously in the console:

```
println("RDD X Sum: " +xSum)
println("RDD Y Sum: " +ySum)
println("RDD X*Y Sum: "+xySum)
println("Total count: "+n)
```

Here's the console output:

```
RDD X Sum: 314.0
RDD Y Sum: 302.0
RDD X*Y Sum: 11869.0
Total count: 12
```

13. We close the program by stopping the Spark session:

```
spark.stop()
```

14. Once the program is complete, the layout of `myFirstSpark20.scala` in the IntelliJ project explorer will look like the following:

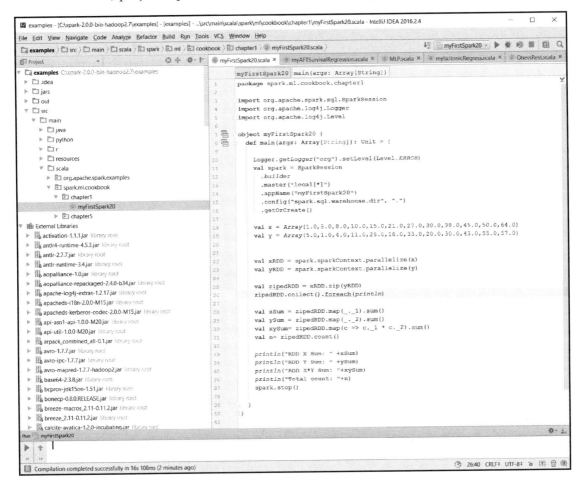

15. Make sure there is no compiling error. You can test this by rebuilding the project:

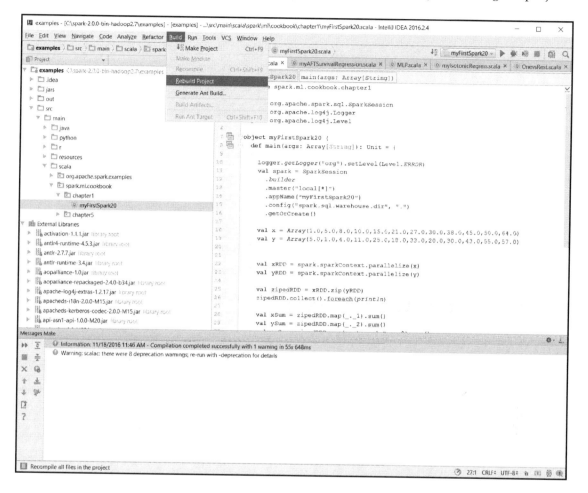

Once the rebuild is complete, there should be a build completed message on the console:

```
Information: November 18, 2016, 11:46 AM - Compilation completed
successfully with 1 warning in 55s 648ms
```

16. You can run the previous program by right-clicking on the myFirstSpark20 object in the project explorer and selecting the context menu option (shown in the next screenshot) called Run myFirstSpark20.

You can also use the **Run** menu from the menu bar to perform the same action.

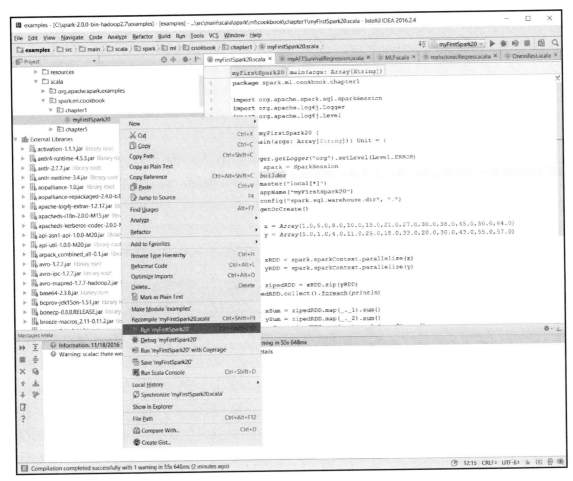

17. Once the program is successfully executed, you will see the following message:

```
Process finished with exit code 0
```

This is also shown in the following screenshot:

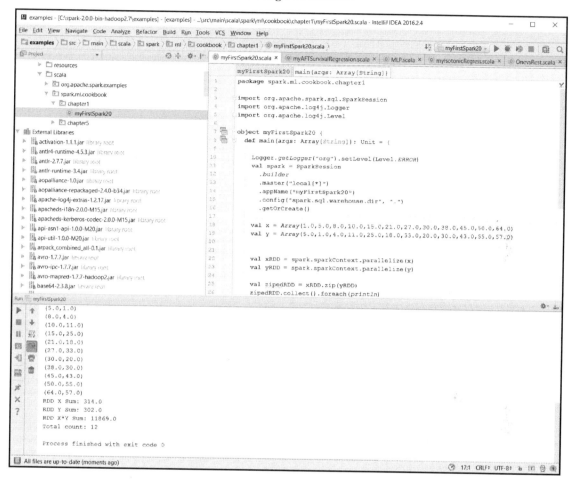

18. Mac users with IntelliJ will be able to perform this action using the same context menu.

 Place the code in the correct path.

How it works...

In this example, we wrote our first Scala program, `myFirstSpark20.scala`, and displayed the steps to execute the program in IntelliJ. We placed the code in the path described in the steps for both Windows and Mac.

In the `myFirstSpark20` code, we saw a typical way to create a `SparkSession` object and how to configure it to run in local mode using the `master()` function. We created two RDDs out of the array objects and used a simple `zip()` function to create a new RDD.

We also did a simple sum calculation on the RDDs that were created and then displayed the result in the console. Finally, we exited and released the resource by calling `spark.stop()`.

There's more...

Spark can be downloaded from `http://spark.apache.org/downloads.html`.

Documentation for Spark 2.0 related to RDD can be found at `http://spark.apache.org/docs/latest/programming-guide.html#rdd-operations`.

See also

- More information about JetBrain IntelliJ can be found at `https://www.jetbrains.com/idea/`.

How to add graphics to your Spark program

In this recipe, we discuss how to use JFreeChart to add a graphic chart to your Spark 2.0.0 program.

How to do it...

1. Set up the JFreeChart library. JFreeChart JARs can be downloaded from the `https://sourceforge.net/projects/jfreechart/files/` site.

2. The JFreeChart version we have covered in this book is JFreeChart 1.0.19, as can be seen in the following screenshot. It can be downloaded from the `https://sourceforge.net/projects/jfreechart/files/1.%20JFreeChart/1.0.19/jfreechart-1.0.19.zip/download` site:

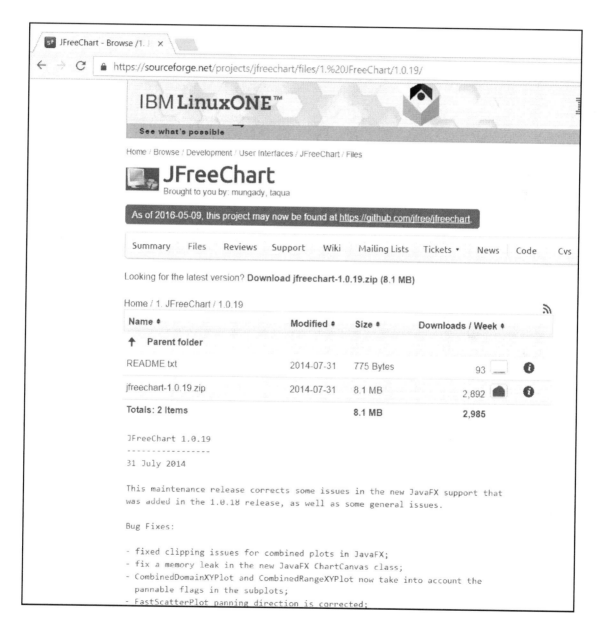

3. Once the ZIP file is downloaded, extract it. We extracted the ZIP file under C:\ for a Windows machine, then proceed to find the lib directory under the extracted destination directory.

4. We then find the two libraries we need (JFreeChart requires JCommon), JFreeChart-1.0.19.jar and JCommon-1.0.23:

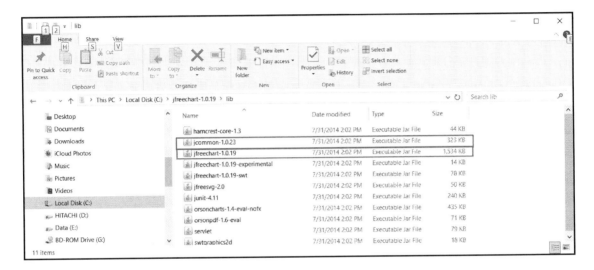

5. Now we copy the two previously mentioned JARs into the C:\spark-2.0.0-bin-hadoop2.7\examples\jars\ directory.

6. This directory, as mentioned in the previous setup section, is in the classpath for the IntelliJ IDE project setting:

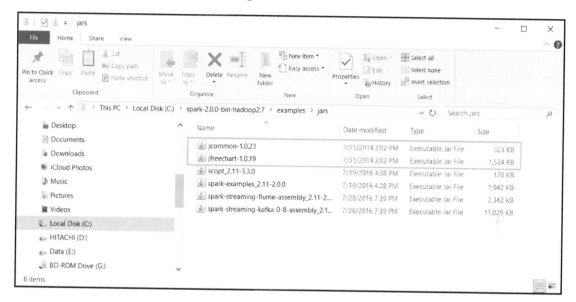

 In macOS, you need to place the previous two JARs in the /Users/USERNAME/spark/spark-2.0.0-bin-hadoop2.7/examples\jars\ directory.

7. Start a new project in IntelliJ or in an IDE of your choice. Make sure that the necessary JAR files are included.
8. Download the sample code for the book, find MyChart.scala, and place the code in the following directory.
9. We installed Spark 2.0 in the C:\spark-2.0.0-bin-hadoop2.7\ directory in Windows. Place MyChart.scala in the C:\spark-2.0.0-bin-hadoop2.7\examples\src\main\scala\spark\ml\cookbook\chapter1 directory.
10. Set up the package location where the program will reside:

```
package spark.ml.cookbook.chapter1
```

11. Import the necessary packages for the Spark session to gain access to the cluster and `log4j.Logger` to reduce the amount of output produced by Spark.

12. Import necessary JFreeChart packages for the graphics:

```
import java.awt.Color
import org.apache.log4j.{Level, Logger}
import org.apache.spark.sql.SparkSession
import org.jfree.chart.plot.{PlotOrientation, XYPlot}
import org.jfree.chart.{ChartFactory, ChartFrame, JFreeChart}
import org.jfree.data.xy.{XYSeries, XYSeriesCollection}
import scala.util.Random
```

13. Set the output level to ERROR to reduce Spark's logging output:

```
Logger.getLogger("org").setLevel(Level.ERROR)
```

14. Initialize a Spark session specifying configurations with the builder pattern, thus making an entry point available for the Spark cluster:

```
val spark = SparkSession
   .builder
   .master("local[*]")
   .appName("myChart")
   .config("spark.sql.warehouse.dir", ".")
   .getOrCreate()
```

15. The `myChart` object will run in local mode. The previous code block is a typical start to creating a `SparkSession` object.

16. We then create an RDD using a random number and ZIP the number with its index:

```
val data = spark.sparkContext.parallelize(Random.shuffle(1 to
15).zipWithIndex)
```

17. We print out the RDD in the console:

```
data.foreach(println)
```

Here is the console output:

```
(14,10)
(6,2)
(7,7)
(8,12)
(13,5)
(15,13)
(10,8)
(4,3)
(3,11)
(1,0)
(2,4)
(11,9)
(12,14)
(9,6)
(5,1)
```

18. We then create a data series for JFreeChart to display:

```
val xy = new XYSeries("")
data.collect().foreach{ case (y: Int, x: Int) => xy.add(x,y) }
val dataset = new XYSeriesCollection(xy)
```

19. Next, we create a chart object from JFreeChart's `ChartFactory` and set up the basic configurations:

```
val chart = ChartFactory.createXYLineChart(
  "MyChart",   // chart title
  "x",                 // x axis label
  "y",                  // y axis label
  dataset,                 // data
  PlotOrientation.VERTICAL,
  false,                 // include legend
  true,                  // tooltips
  false                  // urls
)
```

20. We get the plot object from the chart and prepare it to display graphics:

```
val plot = chart.getXYPlot()
```

21. We configure the plot first:

```
configurePlot(plot)
```

22. The configurePlot function is defined as follows; it sets up some basic color schema for the graphical part:

```
def configurePlot(plot: XYPlot): Unit = {
  plot.setBackgroundPaint(Color.WHITE)
  plot.setDomainGridlinePaint(Color.BLACK)
  plot.setRangeGridlinePaint(Color.BLACK)
  plot.setOutlineVisible(false)
}
```

23. We now show the chart:

```
show(chart)
```

24. The show() function is defined as follows. It is a very standard frame-based graphic-displaying function:

```
def show(chart: JFreeChart) {
  val frame = new ChartFrame("plot", chart)
  frame.pack()
  frame.setVisible(true)
}
```

25. Once `show(chart)` is executed successfully, the following frame will pop up:

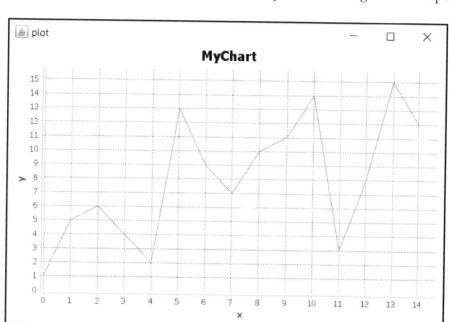

26. We close the program by stopping the Spark session:

```
spark.stop()
```

How it works...

In this example, we wrote `MyChart.scala` and saw the steps for executing the program in IntelliJ. We placed code in the path described in the steps for both Windows and Mac.

In the code, we saw a typical way to create the `SparkSession` object and how to use the `master()` function. We created an RDD out of an array of random integers in the range of 1 to 15 and zipped it with the Index.

We then used JFreeChart to compose a basic chart that contains a simple *x* and *y* axis, and supplied the chart with the dataset we generated from the original RDD in the previous steps.

We set up the schema for the chart and called the `show()` function in JFreeChart to show a Frame with the *x* and *y* axes displayed as a linear graphical chart.

Finally, we exited and released the resource by calling `spark.stop()`.

There's more...

More about JFreeChart can be found here:

- `http://www.jfree.org/jfreechart/`
- `http://www.jfree.org/jfreechart/api/javadoc/index.html`

See also

Additional examples about the features and capabilities of JFreeChart can be found at the following website:

`http://www.jfree.org/jfreechart/samples.html`

2
Just Enough Linear Algebra for Machine Learning with Spark

In this chapter, we will cover the following recipes:

- Package imports and initial setup for vectors and matrices
- Creating DenseVector and setup with Spark 2.0
- Creating SparseVector and setup with Spark 2.0
- Creating DenseMatrix and setup with Spark 2.0
- Using sparse local matrices with Spark 2.0
- Performing vector arithmetic using Spark 2.0
- Performing matrix arithmetic with Spark 2.0
- Distributed matrices in Spark 2.0 ML library
- Exploring RowMatrix in Spark 2.0
- Exploring distributed IndexedRowMatrix in Spark 2.0
- Exploring distributed CoordinateMatrix in Spark 2.0
- Exploring distributed BlockMatrix in Spark 2.0

Introduction

Linear algebra is the cornerstone of **machine learning** (**ML**) and **mathematical programming** (**MP**). When dealing with Spark's machine library, one must understand that the Vector/Matrix structures provided by Scala (imported by default) are different from the Spark ML, MLlib Vector, Matrix facilities provided by Spark. The latter, powered by RDDs, is the desired data structure if you are going to use Spark (that is, parallelism) out of the box for large-scale matrix/vector computation (for example, SVD implementation alternatives with more numerical accuracy, desired in some cases for derivatives pricing and risk analytics). The Scala Vector/Matrix libraries provide a rich set of linear algebra operations such as dot product, additions, and so on, that still have their own place in an ML pipeline. In summary, the key difference between using Scala Breeze and Spark or Spark ML is that the Spark facility is backed by RDDs which allows for simultaneous distributed, concurrent computing, and resiliency without requiring any additional concurrency module or extra effort (for example, Akka + Breeze).

Almost all machine learning algorithms use some form of classification or regression mechanism (not necessarily linear) to train a model and then proceed to minimize errors by comparing the training output to the actual output. For example, any implementation of a recommendation system in Spark will heavily rely on matrix decomposition, factorization, approximation, or **Single Value Decomposition** (**SVD**). Another machine learning area of interest dealing with dimensionality reduction for big datasets is **Principal Component Analysis** (**PCA**), which relies heavily on linear algebra, factorization, and matrix manipulation.

When we examined the Spark ML and MLlib algorithms' source code for the first time in Spark 1.x.x, we quickly noticed that Vectors and Matrices use RDDs as the base for many prominent algorithms.

When we revisited the source code for Spark 2.0 and machine learning libraries, we noticed some interesting changes that need to be considered going forward. Here is an example of such changes from Spark 1.6.2 to Spark 2.0.0 that impacted some of our linear algebra code with Spark:

- In the previous version (Spark 1.6.x), you can convert the `DenseVector` or `SparseVector` (refer to `https://spark.apache.org/docs/1.5.2/api/java/org/apache/spark/mllib/linalg/Vectors.html`) directly by using the `toBreeze()` function, as shown in the following code base:

  ```
  val w3 = w1.toBreeze // spark 1.6.x code
  val w4 = w2.toBreeze //spark 1.6.x code
  ```

- In Spark 2.0, the `toBreeze()` function has not only been changed to `asBreeze()`, but it has also been demoted to a private function
- To remedy this, use one of the following code snippets to convert the preceding vector to the commonly used `BreezeVector` instance:

```
val w3 = new BreezeVector(x.toArray) //x.asBreeze, spark 2.0
val w4 = new BreezeVector(y.toArray) //y.asBreeze, spark 2.0
```

Scala is a concise language in which both object-oriented and functional programming paradigms can coexist without conflict. While in the machine learning paradigm, functional programming is preferred, there is nothing wrong with using the object-oriented approach for initial data collection and presentation at a later stage.

In terms of large-scale distributed matrices, our experience shows that when approaching large matrix sets 10^9 to 10^{13} to 10^{27}, and so on, you have to take a deeper look at the resulting network operation and shuffling that are inherent in a distributed operation. Based on our experience, the combination of local and distributed matrix/vector operations (for example, dot product, multiplication, and so on) work best when you operate at scale.

The following figure depicts the categorization of available Spark vectors and matrices:

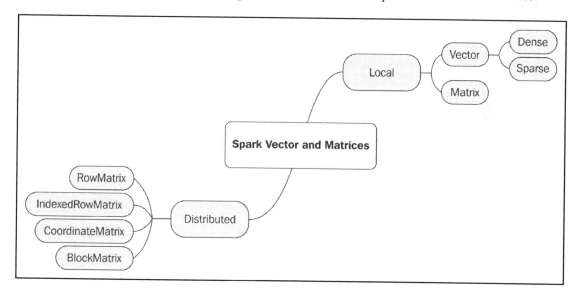

Package imports and initial setup for vectors and matrices

Before we can program in Spark or use vector and matrix artifacts, we need to first import the right packages and then set up `SparkSession` so we can gain access to the cluster handle.

In this short recipe, we highlight a comprehensive number of packages that can cover most of the linear algebra operations in Spark. The individual recipes that follow will include the exact subset required for the specific program.

How to do it...

1. Start a new project in IntelliJ or in an IDE of your choice. Make sure that the necessary JAR files are included.

2. Set up the package location where the program will reside:

   ```
   package spark.ml.cookbook.chapter2
   ```

3. Import the necessary packages for vector and matrix manipulation:

   ```
   import org.apache.spark.mllib.linalg.distributed.RowMatrix
   import org.apache.spark.mllib.linalg.distributed.{IndexedRow,
   IndexedRowMatrix}
   import org.apache.spark.mllib.linalg.distributed.{CoordinateMatrix,
   MatrixEntry}
   import org.apache.spark.sql.{SparkSession}
   import org.apache.spark.rdd._
   import org.apache.spark.mllib.linalg._
   import breeze.linalg.{DenseVector => BreezeVector}
   import Array._
   import org.apache.spark.mllib.linalg.DenseMatrix
   import org.apache.spark.mllib.linalg.SparseVector
   ```

4. Import the packages for setting up the logging level for `log4j`. This step is optional, but we highly recommend it (change the level appropriately as you move through the development cycle):

   ```
   import org.apache.log4j.Logger
   import org.apache.log4j.Level
   ```

5. Set up the logging level to warning and error to cut down on output. See the previous step for the package requirement:

```
Logger.getLogger("org").setLevel(Level.ERROR)
Logger.getLogger("akka").setLevel(Level.ERROR)
```

6. Set up the Spark context and application parameters so Spark can run:

```
val spark = SparkSession
 .builder
 .master("local[*]")
 .appName("myVectorMatrix")
 .config("spark.sql.warehouse.dir", ".")
 .getOrCreate()
```

There's more...

Prior to Spark 2.0, the SparkContext and SQLContext had to be initialized separately. Refer to the following code snippet if you plan to run the code in previous versions of Spark.

Set up the application parameters so Spark can run (using Spark 1.5.2 or Spark 1.6.1):

```
val conf = new
SparkConf().setMaster("local[*]").setAppName("myVectorMatrix").setS
parkHome("C:\\spark-1.5.2-bin-hadoop2.6")
 val sc = new SparkContext(conf)
 val sqlContext = new SQLContext(sc)
```

See also

SparkSession is the new entry point into the cluster in Spark 2.x.x and above. SparkSession unifies access entry to the cluster and all things data. It unifies access to SparkContext, SQLContext, or HiveContext, while making it easier to work with the DataFrame and Dataset APIs. We will revisit the SparkSession with a dedicated recipe in Chapter 4, *Common Recipes for Implementing a Robust Machine Learning System*.

See the following figure for reference:

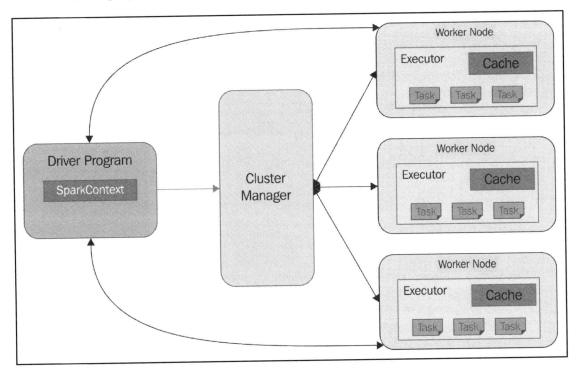

The documentation for method calls can be seen
at `https://spark.apache.org/docs/2.0.0/api/scala/#org.apache.spark.sql.SparkSess`
`ion`.

Creating DenseVector and setup with Spark 2.0

In this recipe, we explore `DenseVectors` using the Spark 2.0 machine library.

Spark provides two distinct types of vector facilities (dense and sparse) for storing and manipulating feature vectors that are going to be used in machine learning or optimization algorithms.

How to do it...

1. In this section, we examine `DenseVector` examples that you would most likely use for implementing/augmenting existing machine learning programs. These examples also help to better understand Spark ML or MLlib source code and the underlying implementation (for example, Single Value Decomposition).

2. Here we look at creating an ML vector feature (with independent variables) from arrays, which is a common use case. In this case, we have three almost fully populated Scala arrays corresponding to customer and product feature sets. We convert these arrays to the corresponding `DenseVectors` in Scala:

```
val CustomerFeatures1: Array[Double] =
Array(1,3,5,7,9,1,3,2,4,5,6,1,2,5,3,7,4,3,4,1)
 val CustomerFeatures2: Array[Double] =
Array(2,5,5,8,6,1,3,2,4,5,2,1,2,5,3,2,1,1,1,1)
 val ProductFeatures1: Array[Double]  =
Array(0,1,1,0,1,1,1,0,0,1,1,1,1,0,1,2,0,1,1,0)
```

Set the variables to create the vectors from the array. Convert from the array to the `DenseVector`:

```
val x = Vectors.dense(CustomerFeatures1)
 val y = Vectors.dense(CustomerFeatures2)
 val z = Vectors.dense(ProductFeatures1)
```

3. The next step is to create a `DenseVector` and to assign values via initialization.

This is the most cited case and is often used in class constructors that deal with batch input:

```
val denseVec2 = Vectors.dense(5,3,5,8,5,3,4,2,1,6)
```

4. The following is another example to show on-the-fly conversion from a string to a double during the initialization. Here we start with a string and invoke `toDouble` inline:

```
val xyz = Vectors.dense("2".toDouble, "3".toDouble, "4".toDouble)
 println(xyz)
```

The output is as follows:

```
[2.0,3.0,4.0]
```

How it works...

1. The signature for this method constructor is:

   ```
   DenseVector (double[] values)
   ```

2. The method inherits from the following which makes its concrete methods available to all routines:

   ```
   interface class java.lang.Object
   interface org.apache.spark.mllib.linalg. Vector
   ```

3. There are several method calls that are of interest:
   1. Make a deep copy of the vector:

      ```
      DenseVector copy()
      ```

   2. Convert to the `SparseVector`. You will do this if your vector is long and the density decreases after a number of operations (for example, zero out non-contributing members):

      ```
      SparseVector toSparse()
      ```

   3. Find the number of non-zero elements. This is useful so you can convert on-the-fly to the SparseVector if the density ID is low:

      ```
      Int numNonzeros()
      ```

   4. Convert the vector to the array. This is often necessary when dealing with distributed operations that require close interactions with RDDs or proprietary algorithms that use Spark ML as a subsystem:

      ```
      Double[] toArray()
      ```

There's more...

One must be careful not to mix vector facilities provided by the `Breeze` library with Spark ML vectors. To work with ML library algorithms, you are required to use its native data structures, but you can always convert from ML vectors to `Breeze`, do all your math operations, and then convert to Spark's desired data structure when using the ML library algorithms (for example, ALS or SVD).

We need the vector and matrix import statements so we can work with the ML library itself, otherwise the Scala vector and matrix will be used by default. This is the source of much confusion when the programs fail to scale on cluster.

The following figure depicts a pictorial view which should help clarify the subject:

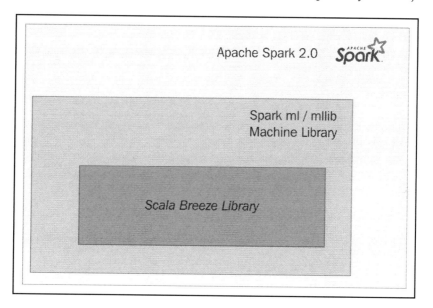

See also

- Documentation for constructor is available at
  `https://spark.apache.org/docs/latest/api/java/org/apache/spark/mllib/l inalg/DenseVector.html#constructor_summary`

- Documentation for method calls is available
  at `https://spark.apache.org/docs/latest/api/java/org/apache/spark/mllib /linalg/DenseVector.html#method_summary`

Creating SparseVector and setup with Spark

In this recipe, we examine several types of `SparseVector` creation. As the length of the vector increases (millions) and the density remains low (few non-zero members), then sparse representation becomes more and more advantageous over the `DenseVector`.

How to do it...

1. Start a new project in IntelliJ or in an IDE of your choice. Make sure that the necessary JAR files are included.

2. Import the necessary packages for vector and matrix manipulation:

```
import org.apache.spark.sql.{SparkSession}
import org.apache.spark.mllib.linalg._
import breeze.linalg.{DenseVector => BreezeVector}
import Array._
import org.apache.spark.mllib.linalg.SparseVector
```

3. Set up the Spark context and application parameters so Spark can run. See the first recipe in this chapter for more details and variations:

```
val spark = SparkSession
  .builder
  .master("local[*]")
  .appName("myVectorMatrix")
  .config("spark.sql.warehouse.dir", ".")
  .getOrCreate()
```

4. Here we look at creating a ML SparseVector that corresponds to its equivalent DenseVector. The call consists of three parameters: Size of the vector, indexes to non-zero data, and finally, the data itself.

In the following example, we can compare the dense versus SparseVector creation. As you can see, the four elements that are non-zero (5, 3, 8, 9) correspond to locations (0, 2, 18, 19) while the number 20 indicates the total size:

```
val denseVec1 =
Vectors.dense(5,0,3,0,0,0,0,0,0,0,0,0,0,0,0,0,0,0,8,9)
val sparseVec1 = Vectors.sparse(20, Array(0,2,18,19), Array(5, 3,
8,9))
```

5. To understand the data structure better, we compare the output and some of the important attributes that help us, especially with dynamic programming using vectors.

First we take a look at the printout for the DenseVector to see its representation:

```
println(denseVec1.size)
println(denseVec1.numActives)
println(denseVec1.numNonzeros)
println("denceVec1 presentation = ",denseVec1)
```

The output is as follows:

```
denseVec1.size = 20

denseVec1.numActives = 20
denseVec1.numNonzeros = 4
(denseVec1 presentation = ,[5.0,0.0,3.0,0.0,0.0,
0.0,0.0,0.0,0.0,0.0,0.0,0.0,0.0,0.0,0.0,0.0,0.0,0.0,8.0,9.0])
```

6. Next, we take a look at the printout for the SparseVector to see its internal representation:

```
println(sparseVec1.size)
println(sparseVec1.numActives)
println(sparseVec1.numNonzeros)
println("sparseVec1 presentation = ",sparseVec1)
```

If we compare and contrast the internal representation and the number of elements versus active and non-zero, you will see that the SparseVector only stores non-zero elements and indexes to reduce storage requirement.

The output is as follows:

```
denseVec1.size = 20
println(sparseVec1.numActives)= 4
sparseVec1.numNonzeros = 4
   (sparseVec1 presentation = ,(20,[0,2,18,19],[5.0,3.0,8.0,9.0]))
```

7. We can convert back and forth between sparse and DenseVectors as needed. The reason that you might want to do this is that external math and linear algebra do not conform to Spark's internal representation. We made the variable type explicit to make the point, but you can eliminate that extra declaration in actual practice:

```
val ConvertedDenseVect : DenseVector= sparseVec1.toDense
 val ConvertedSparseVect : SparseVector= denseVec1.toSparse
println("ConvertedDenseVect =", ConvertedDenseVect)
 println("ConvertedSparseVect =", ConvertedSparseVect)
```

The output is as follows:

```
(ConvertedDenseVect =,[5.0,0.0,3.0,0.0,0.0,0.0,0.0,0.0,
0.0,0.0,0.0,0.0,0.0,0.0,0.0,0.0,0.0,0.0,8.0,9.0])
(ConvertedSparseVect =,(20,[0,2,18,19],[5.0,3.0,8.0,9.0]))
```

How it works...

1. The signature for this method constructor is:

```
SparseVector(int size, int[] indices, double[] values)
```

The method inherits from the following which makes its concrete methods available to all routines:

```
interface class java.lang.Object
```

There are several method calls related to vectors that are of interest:

1. Make a deep copy of the vector:

```
SparseVector Copy()
```

2. Convert to the SparseVector. You will do this if your vector is long and the density decreases after a number of operations (for example, zero out non-contributing members):

```
DenseVector toDense()
```

3. Find the number of non-zero elements. This is useful so you can convert on-the-fly to the SparseVector if the density ID is low.

```
Int numNonzeros()
```

4. Convert the vector to an array. This is often necessary when dealing with distributed operations that require 1:1 interactions with RDDs or proprietary algorithms that use Spark ML as a subsystem:

```
Double[] toArray()
```

There's more...

1. One must remember that the dense and SparseVectors are local vectors and they must not be confused with the distributed facilities (for example, distributed matrices such as the RowMatrix class).
2. The underlying math operations for the vectors on a local machine will be provided by two libraries:

   - **Breeze**: http://www.scalanlp.org/
   - **JBLAS**: http://jblas.org/

There is another data structure related directly to Vectors called LabeledPoint, which we covered in Chapter 4, *Common Recipes for Implementing a Robust Machine Learning System*. In short, it is a data structure corresponding to LIBSVM and LIBLINEAR formats for storing ML data consisting of a feature vector plus a label (for example, independent and dependent variables in a regression):

- **LIBSVM**: http://www.csie.ntu.edu.tw/~cjlin/libsvm/

- **LIBLINEAR**: http://www.csie.ntu.edu.tw/~cjlin/liblinear/

See also

- Documentation for constructor is available
  at https://spark.apache.org/docs/latest/api/java/org/apache/spark/mllib/linalg/SparseVector.html#constructor_summary

- Documentation for method calls is available
  at https://spark.apache.org/docs/latest/api/java/org/apache/spark/mllib/linalg/SparseVector.html#method_summary

Creating dense matrix and setup with Spark 2.0

In this recipe, we explore matrix creation examples that you most likely would need in your Scala programming and while reading the source code for many of the open source libraries for machine learning.

Spark provides two distinct types of local matrix facilities (dense and sparse) for storage and manipulation of data at a local level. For simplicity, one way to think of a matrix is to visualize it as columns of Vectors.

Getting ready

The key to remember here is that the recipe covers local matrices stored on one machine. We will use another recipe, *Distributed matrices in the Spark2.0 ML library*, covered in this chapter, for storing and manipulating distributed matrices.

How to do it...

1. Start a new project in IntelliJ or in an IDE of your choice. Make sure that the necessary JAR files are included.

2. Import the necessary packages for vector and matrix manipulation:

```
import org.apache.spark.sql.{SparkSession}
import org.apache.spark.mllib.linalg._
import breeze.linalg.{DenseVector => BreezeVector}
import Array._
import org.apache.spark.mllib.linalg.SparseVector
```

3. Set up the Spark session and application parameters so Spark can run:

```
val spark = SparkSession
 .builder
 .master("local[*]")
 .appName("myVectorMatrix")
 .config("spark.sql.warehouse.dir", ".")
 .getOrCreate()
```

4. Here we look at creating an ML vector feature from Scala arrays. Let us define a 2x2 dense matrix and instantiate it with an array:

```
val MyArray1= Array(10.0, 11.0, 20.0, 30.3)
val denseMat3 = Matrices.dense(2,2,MyArray1)
```

The output is as follows:

```
DenseMat3=
10.0  20.0
11.0  30.3
```

Constructing a dense matrix and assigning values via initialization in a single step:

Construct a dense local matrix directly by defining the array inline. This is an array of 3x3 and has nine members. You can think of it as three columns of three vectors (3x3):

```
val denseMat1 = Matrices.dense(3,3,Array(23.0, 11.0, 17.0, 34.3, 33.0,
24.5, 21.3,22.6,22.2))
```

The output is as follows:

denseMat1=
23.0 34.3 21.3
11.0 33.0 22.6
17.0 24.5 22.2

This is another example to show inline instantiation of a dense local matrix with vectors. This is a common case in which you collect vectors into a matrix (column order) and then perform an operation on the entire set. The most common case is to collect the vectors and then use a distributed matrix to do distributed parallel operation.

In Scala, we use the ++ operator with arrays to achieve concatenation:

```
val v1 = Vectors.dense(5,6,2,5)
 val v2 = Vectors.dense(8,7,6,7)
 val v3 = Vectors.dense(3,6,9,1)
 val v4 = Vectors.dense(7,4,9,2)

 val Mat11 = Matrices.dense(4,4,v1.toArray ++ v2.toArray ++ v3.toArray ++
v4.toArray)
 println("Mat11=\n", Mat11)
```

The output is as follows:

Mat11=
5.0 8.0 3.0 7.0
6.0 7.0 6.0 4.0
2.0 6.0 9.0 9.0
5.0 7.0 1.0 2.0

How it works...

1. The signatures for this method constructor are (Column-major dense matrix):

```
DenseMatrix(int numRows, int numCols, double[] values)
DenseMatrix(int numRows, int numCols, double[] values, boolean
isTransposed)
```

2. The method inherits from the following which makes their concrete methods available to all routines:
    - interface class java.lang.Object

    - java.io.Serializable

    - Matrix

3. There are several method calls that are of interest:
    1. Generate the diagonal matrix from the supplied values in the vector:

       ```
       static DenseMatrix(Vector vector)
       ```

    2. Create an identity matrix. An identity matrix is a matrix that has diagonals as 1 and any other element as 0:

       ```
       static eye(int n)
       ```

    3. Keep track of whether the matrix is transposed:

       ```
       boolean isTransposed()
       ```

4. Create a matrix with a set of random numbers - drawn from uniform distribution:

```
static DenseMatrix rand(int numRows, int numCols,
java.util.Random rng)
```

5. Create a matrix with a set of random numbers - drawn from gaussian distribution:

```
static DenseMatrix randn(int numRows, int numCols,
java.util.Random rng)
```

6. Transpose the matrix:

```
DenseMatrix transpose()
```

7. Make a deep copy of the vector:

```
DenseVector Copy()
```

8. Convert to a SparseVector. You will do this if your vector is long and the density decreases after a number of operations (for example, zero out non-contributing members):

```
SparseVector toSparse()
```

9. Find the number of non-zero elements. This is useful so you can convert on-the-fly to a SparseVector if the density ID is low:

```
Int numNonzeros()
```

10. Get all the values stored in Matrix:

```
Double[] Values()
```

There's more...

The most difficult part of working with matrices in Spark is to getting used to column order versus row order. It is key to remember that Spark ML uses underlying libraries that work better with column stored mechanisms. Here is an example to demonstrate:

1. Given a matrix definition which defines a 2x2 matrix:

   ```
   val denseMat3 = Matrices.dense(2,2, Array(10.0, 11.0, 20.0, 30.3))
   ```

2. The matrix is actually stored as :

   ```
   10.0  20.0
   11.0 30.3
   ```

   You move from left to right in the value set and then from column to column for the placement in the Matrix.

3. As you can see, the assumption that the matrix is stored row wise is not in alignment with the Spark approach. The following order is not correct from Spark's perspective:

   ```
   10.0  11.0
   20.0 30.3
   ```

See also

- Documentation for constructor is available
  at https://spark.apache.org/docs/latest/api/java/org/apache/spark/mllib/linalg/DenseMatrix.html#constructor_summary

- Documentation For method calls is available
  at https://spark.apache.org/docs/latest/api/java/org/apache/spark/mllib/linalg/DenseMatrix.html#method_summary

Using sparse local matrices with Spark 2.0

In this recipe, we concentrate on SparseMatrix creation. In the previous recipe, we saw how a local dense matrix is declared and stored. A good number of machine learning problem domains can be represented as a set of features and labels within the matrix. In large-scale machine learning problems (for example, progression of a disease through large population centers, security fraud, political movement modeling, and so on), a good portion of the cells will be 0 or null (for example, the current number of people with a given disease versus the healthy population).

To help with storage and efficient operation in real time, sparse local matrices specialize in storing the cells efficiently as a list plus an index, which leads to faster loading and real time operations.

How to do it...

1. Start a new project in IntelliJ or in an IDE of your choice. Make sure that the necessary JAR files are included.

2. Import the necessary packages for vector and matrix manipulation:

```
import org.apache.spark.mllib.linalg.distributed.RowMatrix
import org.apache.spark.mllib.linalg.distributed.{IndexedRow,
IndexedRowMatrix}
import
org.apache.spark.mllib.linalg.distributed.{CoordinateMatrix,
MatrixEntry}
import org.apache.spark.sql.{SparkSession}
import org.apache.spark.mllib.linalg._
import breeze.linalg.{DenseVector => BreezeVector}
import Array._
import org.apache.spark.mllib.linalg.DenseMatrix
import org.apache.spark.mllib.linalg.SparseVector
```

3. Set up the Spark context and application parameters so Spark can run - See the first recipe in this chapter for more details and variations:

```
val spark = SparkSession
 .builder
 .master("local[*]")
 .appName("myVectorMatrix")
 .config("spark.sql.warehouse.dir", ".")
 .getOrCreate()
```

4. The creation of a SparseMatrix is a little bit more complicated due to the way we store the sparse presentation as Compressed Column Storage (CCS), also referred to as the Harwell-Boeing SparseMatrix format. Please see, *How it works...* for a detailed explanation.

We declare and create a local 3x2 SparseMatrix with only three non-zero members:

```
val sparseMat1= Matrices.sparse(3,2 ,Array(0,1,3), Array(0,1,2),
Array(11,22,33))
```

Let's examine the output so we fully understand what is happening at a lower level. The three values will be placed at (0,0),(1,1),(2,1):

```
println("Number of Columns=",sparseMat1.numCols)
println("Number of Rows=",sparseMat1.numRows)
println("Number of Active elements=",sparseMat1.numActives)
println("Number of Non Zero elements=",sparseMat1.numNonzeros)
println("sparseMat1 representation of a sparse matrix and its
value=\n",sparseMat1)
```

The output is as follows:

(Number of Columns=,2)
(Number of Rows=,3)
(Number of Active elements=,3)
(Number of Non Zero elements=,3)
sparseMat1 representation of a sparse matrix and its value= 3 x 2 CSCMatrix
(0,0) 11.0
(1,1) 22.0
(2,1) 33.0

To clarify further, here is the code for the SparseMatrix that is illustrated on Spark's documentation pages of the SparseMatrix (see following section titled *See also*). This is a 3x3 Matrix with six non-zero values. Note that the order of the declaration is: Matrix Size, Column Pointers, Row Indexes, and the Value as the last member:

```
/* from documentation page
1.0 0.0 4.0
0.0 3.0 5.0
2.0 0.0 6.0
*
*/
//[1.0, 2.0, 3.0, 4.0, 5.0, 6.0], rowIndices=[0, 2, 1, 0, 1, 2],
colPointers=[0, 2, 3, 6]
val sparseMat33= Matrices.sparse(3,3 ,Array(0, 2, 3, 6) ,Array(0,
```

```
2, 1, 0, 1, 2),Array(1.0, 2.0, 3.0, 4.0, 5.0, 6.0))
  println(sparseMat33)
```

The output is as follows:

```
3 x 3 CSCMatrix
(0,0)  1.0
(2,0)  2.0
(1,1)  3.0
(0,2)  4.0
(1,2)  5.0
(2,2)  6.0
```

- Column Pointers = [0,2,3,6]
- Row Indexes = [0,2,1,0,1,2]
- Non-Zero Values = [1.0,2.0,3.0,4.0,5.0,6.0]

How it works...

In our experience, most of the difficulties with SparseMatrices come from a lack of understanding of the difference between **Compressed Row Storage** (**CRS**) and **Compressed Column Storage** (**CCS**). We highly recommend that the reader researches this topic in depth to clearly understand the differences.

In short, the CCS format is used by Spark for the transposed target matrix:

1. There are two distinct signatures for this method call constructor:

   - SparseMatrix (int numRows, int numCols, int[] colPtrs, int[] rowIndices, double[] values)
   - SparseMatrix(int numRows, int numCols, int[] colPtrs, int[] rowIndices, double[] values, boolean isTransposed)

   In option number two, we are indicating that the matrix is declared as transposed already, so the matrix will be treated differently.

2. The method inherits from the following which makes their concrete methods available to all routines:
   - interface class java.lang.Object
   - java.io.Serializable
   - Matrix

3. There are several method calls that are of interest:
   - Generate the diagonal matrix from the supplied values in the vector:

   ```
   static SparseMatrix spdiag(Vector vector)
   ```

   - Create an identity matrix. An identity matrix is a matrix that has diagonals as 1 and any other element as 0:

   ```
   static speye(int n)
   ```

   - Keep track of whether the matrix is transposed:

   ```
   boolean isTransposed()
   ```

   - Create a matrix with a set of random numbers - drawn from uniform distribution:

   ```
   static SparseMatrix sprand(int numRows, int numCols,
   java.util.Random rng)
   ```

   - Create a matrix with a set of random numbers - drawn from gaussian distribution:

   ```
   static SparseMatrix sprandn(int numRows, int numCols,
   java.util.Random rng)
   ```

   - Transpose the matrix:

   ```
   SparseMatrix transpose()
   ```

   - Make a deep copy of the vector

   ```
   SparseMatrix Copy()
   ```

   - Convert to a SparseVector. You will do this if your vector is long and the density decreases after a number of operations (for example, zero out non-contributing members):

   ```
   DenseMatrix toDense()
   ```

   - Find the number of non-zero elements. This is useful so you can convert on-the-fly to the SparseVector if the density ID is low:

   ```
   Int numNonzeros()
   ```

- Get all the values stored in the Matrix:

```
Double[] Values()
```

- There are other calls corresponding to the specific operation for the SparseMatrix. The following is a sample, but we strongly recommend that you familiarize yourself with the manual pages (see the *There's more...* section):

    1. Get Row Indexes: `int rowIndices()`
    2. Check for transposition: `booleanisTransposed()`
    3. Get Column pointers: `int[]colPtrs()`

There's more...

To reiterate, in a lot of machine learning applications, you end up dealing with sparsity due to the large dimensional nature of the feature space that is not linearly distributed. To illustrate, we take the simplest case in which we have 10 customers indicating their affinity for four themes in the product line:

	Theme 1	Theme 2	Theme 3	Theme 4
Cust 1	1	0	0	0
Cust 2	0	0	0	1
Cust 3	0	0	0	0
Cust 4	0	1	0	0
Cust 5	1	1	1	0
Cust 6	0	0	0	0
Cust 7	0	0	1	0
Cust 8	0	0	0	0
Cust 9	1	0	1	1
Cust 10	0	0	0	0

As you can see, most of the elements are 0 and storing them as a dense matrix is not desirable while we increase the number of customers and themes to tens of millions (M x N). The SparseVector and matrix help with the storage and operation of these sparse structures in an efficient way.

See also

- Documentation for constructor is available
  at `https://spark.apache.org/docs/latest/api/java/org/apache/spark/mllib/linalg/SparseMatrix.html#constructor_summary`

- Documentation for method calls is available
  at `https://spark.apache.org/docs/latest/api/java/org/apache/spark/mllib/linalg/SparseMatrix.html#method_summary`

Performing vector arithmetic using Spark 2.0

In this recipe, we explore vector addition in the Spark environment using the `Breeze` library for underlying operations. Vectors allow us to collect features and then manipulate them via linear algebra operations such as add, subtract, transpose, dot product, and so on.

How to do it...

1. Start a new project in IntelliJ or in an IDE of your choice. Make sure that the necessary JAR files are included.

2. Import the necessary packages for vector and matrix manipulation:

```
import org.apache.spark.mllib.linalg.distributed.RowMatrix
import org.apache.spark.mllib.linalg.distributed.{IndexedRow,
IndexedRowMatrix}
import
org.apache.spark.mllib.linalg.distributed.{CoordinateMatrix,
MatrixEntry}
import org.apache.spark.sql.{SparkSession}
import org.apache.spark.mllib.linalg._
import breeze.linalg.{DenseVector => BreezeVector}
import Array._
import org.apache.spark.mllib.linalg.DenseMatrix
import org.apache.spark.mllib.linalg.SparseVector
```

3. Set up the Spark session and application parameters so Spark can run:

```
val spark = SparkSession
  .builder
  .master("local[*]")
  .appName("myVectorMatrix")
  .config("spark.sql.warehouse.dir", ".")
  .getOrCreate()
```

4. We create the Vectors:

```
val w1 = Vectors.dense(1,2,3)
val w2 = Vectors.dense(4,-5,6)
```

5. We convert the vectors from the Spark public interface to a `Breeze` (library) artifact so we can use a rich set of operators provided for Vector manipulation:

```
val w1 = Vectors.dense(1,2,3)
val w2 = Vectors.dense(4,-5,6)
val w3 = new BreezeVector(w1.toArray) //w1.asBreeze
val w4=  new BreezeVector(w2.toArray) // w2.asBreeze
println("w3 + w4 =",w3+w4)
println("w3 - w4 =",w3+w4)
println("w3 * w4 =",w3.dot(w4))
```

6. Let's look at the output and understand the results. For an operational understanding of vector addition, subtraction, and multiplication, see the *How it works...* section in this recipe.

   The output is as follows:

```
w3 + w4 = DenseVector(5.0, -3.0, 9.0)
w3 - w4 = DenseVector(5.0, -3.0, 9.0)
w3 * w4 =12.0
```

7. Vector operations using both sparse and dense vectors with the Breeze library conversion are:

```
val sv1 = Vectors.sparse(10, Array(0,2,9), Array(5, 3, 13))
val sv2 = Vectors.dense(1,0,1,1,0,0,1,0,0,13)
println("sv1 - Sparse Vector = ",sv1)
println("sv2 - Dense Vector = ",sv2)
println("sv1 * sv2 =", new
BreezeVector(sv1.toArray).dot(new
BreezeVector(sv2.toArray)))
```

This is an alternate way, but it has the drawback of using a private function (see the actual source code for Spark 2.x.x itself). We recommend the method presented previously:

```
println("sv1  * sve2  =", sv1.asBreeze.dot(sv2.asBreeze))
```

We take a look at the output:

```
sv1 - Sparse Vector =  (10,[0,2,9],[5.0,3.0,13.0])
sv2 - Dense  Vector = [1.0,0.0,1.0,1.0,0.0,0.0,1.0,0.0,0.0,13.0]
sv1 * sv2 = 177.0
```

How it works...

Vectors are mathematical artifacts that allow us to express magnitude and direction. In machine learning, we collect object/user preferences into vectors and matrices in order to take advantage of distributed operations at scale.

Vectors are tuples of numbers usually corresponding to some attributes collected for machine learning algorithms. The vectors are usually real numbers (measured values), but many times we use binary values to show the presence or absence of a preference or bias for a particular topic.

A vector can be thought of as either a row vector or a column vector. The column vector presentation is more suitable for ML thinking. The column vector is represented as follows:

$$\mathbf{x} = \begin{pmatrix} x_1 \\ \vdots \\ x_n \end{pmatrix}$$

The row vector is represented as follows:

$$\mathbf{x}^\mathrm{T} = \begin{pmatrix} x_1 & \cdots & x_n \end{pmatrix}$$

Vector addition is represented as follows:

$$x + y = \begin{pmatrix} x_1 \\ x_2 \\ \vdots \\ x_n \end{pmatrix} + \begin{pmatrix} y_1 \\ y_2 \\ \vdots \\ y_n \end{pmatrix} = \begin{pmatrix} x_1 + y_1 \\ x_2 + y_2 \\ \vdots \\ x_n + y_n \end{pmatrix}$$

Vector subtraction is represented as follows:

$$x - y = \begin{pmatrix} x_1 \\ x_2 \\ \vdots \\ x_n \end{pmatrix} - \begin{pmatrix} y_1 \\ y_2 \\ \vdots \\ y_n \end{pmatrix} = \begin{pmatrix} x_1 - y_1 \\ x_2 - y_2 \\ \vdots \\ x_n - y_n \end{pmatrix}$$

Vector multiplication or "dot" product is represented as follows:

$$\mathbf{a} \cdot \mathbf{b} = \mathbf{a}^T \mathbf{b} = \begin{bmatrix} a_1 & a_2 & a_3 \end{bmatrix} \begin{bmatrix} b_1 \\ b_2 \\ b_3 \end{bmatrix} = a_1 b_1 + a_2 b_2 + a_3 b_3$$

$$W = X = \sum_{i=1}^{n} w_i x_i = W^T X$$

There's more...

The public interfaces offered by the Spark ML and MLlib library, whether used for sparse or dense vectors, currently lacks the necessary operators to do full vector arithmetic. We must convert our local vectors to the Breeze library vector to have the operators available for linear algebra.

Prior to Spark 2.0, the method for conversion to Breeze (toBreeze) was available to use, but now the method has changed to asBreeze() and made private! A quick read of the source code is necessary to understand the new paradigm. Perhaps the change reflects Spark's core developers' desire to have less dependency on an underlying Breeze library.

If you are using any version of Spark prior to Spark 2.0 (Spark 1.5.1 or 1.6.1), use the following code snippets for conversion.
Pre-Spark 2.0 example 1:

```
val w1 = Vectors.dense(1,2,3)
 val w2 = Vectors.dense(4,-5,6)
 val w3 = w1.toBreeze
 val w4= w2.toBreeze
 println("w3 + w4 =",w3+w4)
 println("w3 - w4 =",w3+w4)
 println("w3 * w4 =",w3.dot(w4))
```

Pre-spark 2.0 example 2:

```
println("sv1 - Sparse Vector = ",sv1)
 println("sv2 - Dense Vector = ",sv2)
 println("sv1 * sv2 =", sv1.toBreeze.dot(sv2.toBreeze))
```

See also

- Breeze library documentation is available
  at http://www.scalanlp.org/api/breeze/#breeze.package

- Linalg library documentation is available
  at https://spark.apache.org/docs/latest/api/java/allclasses-noframe.htm
  l

Performing matrix arithmetic using Spark 2.0

In this recipe, we explore matrix operations such as addition, transpose, and multiplication in Spark. The more complex operations such as inverse, SVD, and so on, will be covered in future sections. The native sparse and dense matrices for the Spark ML library provide multiplication operators so there is no need to convert to Breeze explicitly.

Matrices are the workhorses of distributed computing. ML features that are collected can be arranged in a matrix configuration and operated at scale. Many of the ML methods such as **ALS (Alternating Least Square)** and **SVD (Singular Value Decomposition)** rely on efficient matrix and vector operations to achieve large-scale machine learning and training.

How to do it...

1. Start a new project in IntelliJ or in an IDE of your choice. Make sure that the necessary JAR files are included.

2. Import the necessary packages for vector and matrix manipulation:

```
import org.apache.spark.mllib.linalg.distributed.RowMatrix
import org.apache.spark.mllib.linalg.distributed.{IndexedRow,
IndexedRowMatrix}
import
org.apache.spark.mllib.linalg.distributed.{CoordinateMatrix,
MatrixEntry}
import org.apache.spark.sql.{SparkSession}
import org.apache.spark.mllib.linalg._
import breeze.linalg.{DenseVector => BreezeVector}
import Array._
import org.apache.spark.mllib.linalg.DenseMatrix
import org.apache.spark.mllib.linalg.SparseVector
```

3. Set up the Spark session and application parameters so Spark can run:

```
val spark = SparkSession
.builder
.master("local[*]")
.appName("myVectorMatrix")
.config("spark.sql.warehouse.dir", ".")
.getOrCreate()
```

4. We create the matrices:

```
val sparseMat33= Matrices.sparse(3,3 ,Array(0, 2, 3, 6) ,Array(0,
2, 1, 0, 1, 2),Array(1.0, 2.0, 3.0, 4.0, 5.0, 6.0))
val denseFeatureVector= Vectors.dense(1,2,1)
val denseVec13 = Vectors.dense(5,3,0)
```

5. Multiply the matrix and vector and print the results. This is an extremely useful operation which becomes a common theme in most Spark ML cases. We use a `SparseMatrix` to demonstrate the fact that the Dense, Sparse, and Matrix are interchangeable and only the density (for example, the percent of non-zero elements) and performance should be the criteria for selection:

```
val result0 = sparseMat33.multiply(denseFeatureVector)
println("SparseMat33 =", sparseMat33)
 println("denseFeatureVector =", denseFeatureVector)
  println("SparseMat33 * DenseFeatureVector =", result0)
```

The output is as follows:

```
(SparseMat33 =,3 x 3 CSCMatrix
(0,0)  1.0
(2,0)  2.0
(1,1)  3.0
(0,2)  4.0
(1,2)  5.0
(2,2)  6.0)
denseFeatureVector =,[1.0,2.0,1.0]
SparseMat33 * DenseFeatureVector = [5.0,11.0,8.0]
```

6. Multiplying a `DenseMatrix` with `DenseVector`.

   This is provided for completeness and will help the user to follow the matrix and vector multiplication more easily without worrying about sparsity:

```
println("denseVec2 =", denseVec13)
println("denseMat1 =", denseMat1)
val result3= denseMat1.multiply(denseVec13)
println("denseMat1 * denseVect13 =", result3)
```

   The output is as follows:

denseVec2 =,[5.0,3.0,0.0]
denseMat1 = 23.0 34.3 21.3
         11.0 33.0 22.6
         17.0 24.5 22.2
denseMat1 * denseVect13 =,[217.89,154.0,158.5]

7. We demonstrate the transposing of a Matrix, which is an operation to swap rows with columns. It is an important operation and used almost on a daily basis if you are involved in Spark ML or data engineering.

Here we demonstrate two steps:

1. Transposing a `SparseMatrix` and examining the new resulting matrix via the output:

```
val transposedMat1= sparseMat1.transpose
 println("transposedMat1=\n",transposedMat1)
```

The output is as follows:

Original sparseMat1 =,3 x 2 CSCMatrix
(0,0) 11.0
(1,1) 22.0
(2,1) 33.0)

(transposedMat1=,2 x 3 CSCMatrix
(0,0) 11.0
(1,1) 22.0
(1,2) 33.0)

1.0 4.0 7.0
2.0 5.0 8.0
3.0 6.0 9.0

2. Demonstrating that the transpose of a transpose yields the original matrix:

```
val transposedMat1= sparseMat1.transpose
println("transposedMat1=\n",transposedMat1)
println("Transposed twice", denseMat33.transpose.transpose)
// we get the original back
```

The output is as follows:

Matrix transposed twice=
1.0 4.0 7.0
2.0 5.0 8.0
3.0 6.0 9.0

Transposing a dense matrix and examining the new resulting matrix via the output:

This makes it easier to see how row and column indexes are swapped:

```
val transposedMat2= denseMat1.transpose
 println("Original sparseMat1 =", denseMat1)
 println("transposedMat2=" ,transposedMat2)
```

```
Original sparseMat1 =
23.0   34.3   21.3
11.0   33.0   22.6
17.0   24.5   22.2
transposedMat2=
23.0   11.0   17.0
34.3   33.0   24.5
21.3   22.6   22.2
```

3. We now look at matrix multiplication and how it would look in code.

We declare two 2x2 Dense Matrices:

```
// Matrix multiplication
 val dMat1: DenseMatrix= new DenseMatrix(2, 2, Array(1.0,
3.0, 2.0, 4.0))
 val dMat2: DenseMatrix = new DenseMatrix(2, 2,
Array(2.0,1.0,0.0,2.0))

 println("dMat1 * dMat2 =", dMat1.multiply(dMat2)) //A x B
 println("dMat2 * dMat1 =", dMat2.multiply(dMat1)) //B x A
not the same as A xB
```

The output is as follows:

dMat1 =,1.0 2.0
3.0 4.0
dMat2 =,2.0 0.0
1.0 2.0
dMat1 * dMat2 =,4.0 4.0
10.0 8.0
//Note: A x B is not the same as B x A
dMat2 * dMat1 = 2.0 4.0
7.0 10.0

How it works...

A matrix can be thought of as columns of vectors. Matrices are the power tools for distributed computation involving linear algebra transformation. A variety of attributes or feature representation can be collected and operated upon via matrices.

In short, matrices are two-dimensional *m x n* arrays of numbers (usually real numbers) whose elements can be referenced using a two-element subscript, *i* and *j*:

A matrix is represented as follows:

$$\begin{pmatrix} a_{11} & a_{12} & \cdots & a_{1n} \\ a_{21} & a_{22} & \cdots & a_{2n} \\ \vdots & \vdots & \ddots & \vdots \\ a_{m1} & a_{m2} & \cdots & a_{mn} \end{pmatrix}$$

A matrix transpose is represented as follows:

$$A = \begin{bmatrix} 111 & 222 \\ 333 & 444 \\ 555 & 666 \end{bmatrix} \qquad A' = \begin{bmatrix} 111 & 333 & 555 \\ 222 & 444 & 666 \end{bmatrix}$$

Matrix multiplication is represented as follows:

$$\begin{pmatrix} a_{11} & a_{12} & a_{13} \\ a_{21} & a_{22} & a_{23} \\ a_{31} & a_{32} & a_{33} \end{pmatrix} \begin{pmatrix} b_{11} & b_{12} \\ b_{21} & b_{22} \\ b_{31} & b_{32} \end{pmatrix} = \begin{pmatrix} a_{11}b_{11} + a_{12}b_{21} + a_{13}b_{31} & a_{11}b_{12} + a_{12}b_{22} + a_{13}b_{32} \\ a_{21}b_{11} + a_{22}b_{21} + a_{23}b_{31} & a_{21}b_{12} + a_{22}b_{22} + a_{23}b_{32} \\ a_{31}b_{11} + a_{32}b_{21} + a_{33}b_{31} & a_{31}b_{12} + a_{32}b_{22} + a_{33}b_{32} \end{pmatrix}$$

Vector matrix multiplication or "dot" product is represented as follows:

$$\mathbf{a} \cdot \mathbf{b} = \mathbf{a}^{\mathsf{T}}\mathbf{b} = \begin{bmatrix} a_1 & a_2 & a_3 \end{bmatrix} \begin{bmatrix} b_1 \\ b_2 \\ b_3 \end{bmatrix} = a_1b_1 + a_2b_2 + a_3b_3$$

$$W = X = \sum_{i=1}^{n} w_i x_i = W^T X$$

Distributed matrices in the Spark 2.0 ML library: In the next four recipes, we will cover the four types of distributed matrices in Spark. Spark provides full support for distributed matrices baked by RDDs right out of the box. The fact that Spark supports distributed computing does not relieve the developer from planning their algorithms with parallelism in mind.

The underlying RDDs provide full parallelism and fault tolerance over the underlying data that is stored in the matrix. Spark is bundled with MLLIB and LINALG, which jointly provide a public interface and support for matrices that are not local and need full cluster support due to their size or complexity of chained operations.

Spark ML provides four types of distributed matrices to support parallelism: RowMatrix, IndexedRowMatrix, CoordinateMatrix, and BlockMatrix:

- RowMatrix: Represents a row-oriented distributed matrix compatible with ML library
- IndexedRowMatrix: Similar to RowMatrix with one additional benefit of indexing the rows. This is a specialized version of RowMatrix in which the matrix itself is created from the RDD of IndexedRow (Index, Vector) data structure. To visualize it, imagine a matrix where each row is a pair (long, RDD) and the work of pairing them (zip function) is done for you. This will allow you to carry the Index together with the RDD along its computational path in a given algorithm (matrix operations at scale)
- CoordinateMatrix: A very useful format which is used for coordinates (for example, *x*, *y*, *z* coordinates in a projection space)
- BlockMatrix: A distributed matrix made of blocks of locally maintained matrices

We cover the creation of the four types in a brief recipe and then quickly move to a more complicated (code and concept) use case involving RowMatrix which is a typical ML use case involving a massively parallel distributed matrix operation (for example, multiplication) with a local matrix.

If you plan to code or design large matrix operations, you must dig into the Spark internals such as core Spark and how staging, pipelining, and shuffling works in each version of Spark (continuous improvement and optimization in each version).

We also recommend the following before embarking on a large-scale matrix and optimization journey:

The source for matrix computations and optimization in Apache Spark is available at http://www.kdd.org/kdd2016/papers/files/adf0163-bosagh-zadehAdoi.pdf and https://pdfs.semanticscholar.org/a684/fc37c79a3276af12a21c1af1ebd8d47f2d6a.pdf.

The source for efficient large scale distributed matrix computation with Spark is available at https://www.computer.org/csdl/proceedings/big-data/2015/9926/00/07364023.pdf and http://dl.acm.org/citation.cfm?id=2878336&preflayout=flat

The source for exploring matrix dependency for efficient distributed matrix computation is available at `http://net.pku.edu.cn/~cuibin/Papers/2015-SIGMOD-DMac.pdf` and `http://dl.acm.org/citation.cfm?id=2723712`

Exploring RowMatrix in Spark 2.0

In this recipe, we explore the `RowMatrix` facility that is provided by Spark. `RowMatrix`, as the name implies, is a row-oriented matrix with the catch being the lack of an index that can be defined and carried through the computational life cycle of a `RowMatrix`. The rows are RDDs which provide distributed computing and resiliency with fault tolerance.

The matrix is made of rows of local vectors that are parallelized and distributed via RDDs. In short, each row will be an RDD, but the total number of columns will be limited by the maximum size of a local vector. This is not an issue in most cases, but we felt we should mention it for completion.

How to do it...

1. Start a new project in IntelliJ or in an IDE of your choice. Make sure that the necessary JAR files are included.

2. Import the necessary packages for vector and matrix manipulation:

```
import org.apache.spark.mllib.linalg.distributed.RowMatrix
import org.apache.spark.mllib.linalg.distributed.{IndexedRow,
IndexedRowMatrix}
import
org.apache.spark.mllib.linalg.distributed.{CoordinateMatrix,
MatrixEntry}
import org.apache.spark.sql.{SparkSession}
import org.apache.spark.mllib.linalg._
import breeze.linalg.{DenseVector => BreezeVector}
import Array._
import org.apache.spark.mllib.linalg.DenseMatrix
import org.apache.spark.mllib.linalg.SparseVector
```

3. Set up the Spark context and application parameters so Spark can run. See the first recipe in the chapter for more details and variations:

```
val spark = SparkSession
  .builder
  .master("local[*]")
  .appName("myVectorMatrix")
  .config("spark.sql.warehouse.dir", ".")
  .getOrCreate()
```

4. The amount and timing of warning statements returned as output varies due to the nature of distributed computing (non-sequential) with distributed matrices. The interlacing of messages with actual output varies depending on the execution path and that results in hard to read output. In the following statements, we elevate the `log4j` messages from warning (WARN - out of the box) to errors (ERROR) for clarity. We suggest that the developer follows the warning messages in detail to grasp the parallel nature of these operations and to fully understand the concept of an RDD:

```
import Log4J logger and the level
import org.apache.log4j.Logger
 import org.apache.log4j.Level
```

Set the level to error:

```
Logger.getLogger("org").setLevel(Level.ERROR)
Logger.getLogger("akka").setLevel(Level.ERROR)
```

Originally comes out the box like this

```
Logger.getLogger("org").setLevel(Level.WARN)
Logger.getLogger("akka").setLevel(Level.WARN)
```

5. We define two sequence data structures of dense vectors.

A Scala sequence of dense local vectors which will be the data for the distributed `RowMatrix`:

```
val dataVectors = Seq(
   Vectors.dense(0.0, 1.0, 0.0),
   Vectors.dense(3.0, 1.0, 5.0),
   Vectors.dense(0.0, 7.0, 0.0)
 )
```

A Scala sequence of dense local vectors which will be the data for the local identity matrix. A quick check of linear algebra shows that any matrix multiplied by an identity matrix will yield the same original matrix (that is, $A \times I = A$). We like to use the identity matrix to prove that the multiplication worked and the original statistic computed over the original matrix is the same as the original x identity:

```scala
val identityVectors = Seq(
   Vectors.dense(1.0, 0.0, 0.0),
   Vectors.dense(0.0, 1.0, 0.0),
   Vectors.dense(0.0, 0.0, 1.0)
 )
```

6. Create our first distributed matrix by parallelizing the underlying dense vectors to RDDs.

Going forward, our dense vectors are now rows in the new distributed vectors backed by RDD (that is, all RDD operations are fully supported!).

Take the original Sequences (made of vectors) and turn them into RDDs. We will cover RDDs in detail in the next chapter. In this single statement, we have turned a local data structure to a distributed artifact:

```scala
val distMat33 = new RowMatrix(sc.parallelize(dataVectors))
```

We calculate some basic statistics to verify that the `RowMatrix` is constructed properly. The point to remember is that the dense vectors are now rows and not columns (which is the source of much confusion):

```scala
println("distMatt33 columns - Count =",
distMat33.computeColumnSummaryStatistics().count)
 println("distMatt33 columns - Mean =",
distMat33.computeColumnSummaryStatistics().mean)
 println("distMatt33 columns - Variance =",
distMat33.computeColumnSummaryStatistics().variance)
 println("distMatt33 columns - CoVariance =",
distMat33.computeCovariance())
```

The output is as follows:

The statistics calculated (mean, variance, min, max, and so on) are for each column and not the entire matrix. This is the reason you see three numbers for mean and variance which corresponds to each column.

distMatt33 columns - Count =	3	
distMatt33 columns - Mean =	[1.0, 3.0, 1.66]	
(distMatt33 columns - Variance =	[3.0,12.0,8.33]	
(distMatt33 columns - CoVariance =	3.0 -3.0 5.0	
	-3.0 12.0 -5.0	
	5.0 -5.0 8.33	

7. In this step, we create our local matrix from the identity vector's data structure. The point to remember is that the multiplication requires a local matrix and not a distributed one. Please see the call signature for verification. We use the `map`, `toArray`, and `flatten` operators to create a Scala flattened array data structure that can be used as one of the parameters to create a local matrix as shown in the next step:

```
val flatArray = identityVectors.map(x => x.toArray).flatten.toArray
dd.foreach(println(_))
```

8. We create the local matrix as an identity matrix so we can verify the multiplication $A * I = A$:

```
val dmIdentity: Matrix = Matrices.dense(3, 3, flatArray)
```

9. We multiply the distributed matrix by the local one and create a new distributed matrix. This is a typical use case in which you end up multiplying a tall and skinny local matrix with a large-scale distributed matrix to achieve scale and the inherited dimensionality reduction of the resulting matrix:

```
val distMat44 = distMat33.multiply(dmIdentity)
 println("distMatt44 columns - Count =",
distMat44.computeColumnSummaryStatistics().count)
 println("distMatt44 columns - Mean =",
distMat44.computeColumnSummaryStatistics().mean)
 println("distMatt44 columns - Variance =",
distMat44.computeColumnSummaryStatistics().variance)
 println("distMatt44 columns - CoVariance =",
distMat44.computeCovariance())
```

10. Comparing step 7 and 8, we see that in fact the operation proceeded correctly and we can verify via descriptive statistics and the co-variance matrix that $A \times I = A$ using a distributed and local matrix.

The output is as follows:

```
distMatt44 columns - Count = 3
distMatt44 columns - Mean = [ 1.0, 3.0, 1.66 ]
distMatt44 columns - Variance = [ 3.0,12.0,8.33 ]
distMatt44 columns - CoVariance = 3.0 -3.0 5.0
                                 -3.0 12.0 -5.0
                                  5.0 -5.0 8.33
```

How it works...

1. The signatures for this method constructor are:
   - `RowMatrix(RDD<Vector> rows)`
   - `RowMatrix(RDD<Vector>, long nRows, Int nCols)`

2. The method inherits from the following which makes their concrete methods available to all routines:
   - interface class java.lang.Object
   - Implements the following interfaces:
     - Logging
     - Distributed matrix

3. There are several method calls that are of interest:
   - Calculate descriptive statistics such as mean, min, max, variance, and so on:

     - `MultivariateStatisticalSummary`
     - `computeColumnSummaryStatistics()`
   - Compute the co-variance matrix from the original:
     - `Matrix computeCovariance()`
   - Compute the Gramian matrix, also referred to as the Gram Matrix ($A^T A$):
     - `Matrix computeGramianMatrix()`

- Calculate the PCA components:
  - `Matrix computePrincipalComponents(int k)`

  k is the number of principal components

- Calculate the SVD decomposition of the original matrix:
  - `SingularValueDecomposition<RowMatrix, Matrix> computeSVD(int k, boolean compute, double rCond)`

  k is the number of leading singular values to keep $(0<k<=n)$.

  - Multiply:

    - `RowMatrix Multiply(Matrix B)`

- Rows:
  - `RDD<Vector> rows()`

- Calculate the QR decomposition:
  - `QRDecomposition<RowMatrix, Matrix> tallSkinnyQR(boolean computeQ))`

- Find the number of non-zero elements. This is useful so you can convert on-the-fly to the SparseVector if the density ID is low:
  - `Int numNonzeros()`

- Get all the values stored in the matrix:
  - `Double[] Values()`

- Others:

  - Calculate the column similarities (very useful in document analysis). There are two methods available which are covered in the `Chapter 12`, *Implementing Text Analytics with Spark 2.0 ML Library*

  - Number of columns and number of rows which we find useful for dynamic programming

There's more...

There are some additional factors to consider when you use sparse or dense elements (vectors or block matrices). Multiplying by a local matrix is usually preferable since it doesn't require expensive shuffling.

While simplicity and control is preferred when dealing with large matrices, the four types of distributed matrices simplify the setup and operation. Each of the four types has advantages and disadvantages that have to be considered and weighed against these three criteria:

- Sparsity or Density of underlying data
- Shuffling that will take place when using these facilities.
- Network capacity utilization when dealing with edge cases

For the reasons mentioned, and especially to reduce the shuffling (that is, a network bottleneck) required during a distributed matrix operation (for example, multiplication of two RowMatrixes), we prefer multiplication with a local matrix to reduce shuffle noticeably. While this seems a bit counter-intuitive at first, in practice it is fine for the cases we have encountered. The reason for this is because when we multiply a large matrix with a vector or tall and skinny matrix, the resulting matrix is small enough that fits into the memory.

The other point of caution will be that the returning information (a row or local matrix) has to be small enough so it can be returned to the driver.

For imports, we need both local and distributed vector and matrix imports so we can work with the ML library. Otherwise, the Scala vector and matrix will be used by default.

See also

- Documentation for constructor is available
  at https://spark.apache.org/docs/latest/api/java/org/apache/spark/mllib /linalg/distributed/RowMatrix.html#constructor_summary

- Documentation for method calls is available
  at https://spark.apache.org/docs/latest/api/java/org/apache/spark/mllib /linalg/distributed/RowMatrix.html#method_summary

Exploring Distributed IndexedRowMatrix in Spark 2.0

In this recipe, we cover the `IndexRowMatrix`, which is the first specialized distributed matrix that we cover in this chapter. The primary advantage of `IndexedRowMatrix` is that the index can be carried along with the row (RDD), which is the data itself.

In the case of `IndexRowMatrix`, we have an index defined by the developer which is permanently paired with a given row that is very useful for random access cases. The index not only helps with random access, but is also used for identifying the row itself when performing `join()` operations.

How to do it...

1. Start a new project in IntelliJ or in an IDE of your choice. Make sure that the necessary JAR files are included.

2. Import the necessary packages for vector and matrix manipulation:

```
import org.apache.spark.mllib.linalg.distributed.RowMatrix
import org.apache.spark.mllib.linalg.distributed.{IndexedRow,
IndexedRowMatrix}
import org.apache.spark.mllib.linalg.distributed.{CoordinateMatrix,
MatrixEntry}
import org.apache.spark.sql.{SparkSession}
import org.apache.spark.mllib.linalg._
import breeze.linalg.{DenseVector => BreezeVector}
import Array._
import org.apache.spark.mllib.linalg.DenseMatrix
import org.apache.spark.mllib.linalg.SparseVector
```

3. Set up the Spark context and application parameters so Spark can run. See the first recipe in the chapter for more details and variations:

```
val spark = SparkSession
 .builder
 .master("local[*]")
 .appName("myVectorMatrix")
 .config("spark.sql.warehouse.dir", ".")
 .getOrCreate()
```

4. We start with our original data vectors and then proceed to construct an appropriate data structure (that is, RowIndex) to house the index and vector.

5. We then proceed to construct the `IndexedRowMatrix` and show the access. For those of you who have worked with LIBSVM, this format is close to label and vector artifacts with a twist that labels are now indexes (that is, long).

6. Start with a sequence of vectors as the base data structure for `IndexedRowMatrix`:

```
val dataVectors = Seq(
   Vectors.dense(0.0, 1.0, 0.0),
   Vectors.dense(3.0, 1.0, 5.0),
   Vectors.dense(0.0, 7.0, 0.0)
 )
```

7. Start with a sequence of vectors as the base data structure for `IndexedRowMatrix`:

```
val distInxMat1
 = sc.parallelize( List( IndexedRow( 0L, dataVectors(0)),
IndexedRow( 1L, dataVectors(1)), IndexedRow( 1L, dataVectors(2))))
println("distinct elements=", distInxMat1.distinct().count())
```

The output is as follows:

(distinct elements=,3)

How it works...

The index is a long data structure which provides a meaningful row index corresponding to each row of the `IndexedRowMatrix`. The horsepower underneath the implementation are the RDDs which offer all the advantages of a distributed resilient data structure in a parallel environment from the get go.

The primary advantage of `IndexedRowMatrix` is that the index can be carried along with the row (RDD) which is the data itself. The fact that we can define and carry along the index with the data (the actual row of matrix) is very useful when we have the `join()` operation that needs a key to select a specific row of data.

The following figure shows a pictorial view of the `IndexedRowMatrix` which should help clarify the subject:

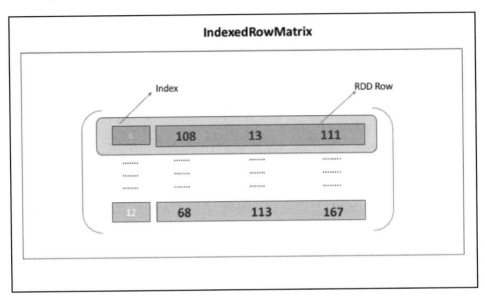

The definition may be unclear as you are required to repeatedly define the index and the data to compose the original matrix. The following code snippet shows the inner list with (index, Data) repetition for reference:

```
List( IndexedRow( 0L, dataVectors(0)), IndexedRow( 1L, dataVectors(1)),
IndexedRow( 1L, dataVectors(2)))
```

The other operations are similar to the `IndexRow` matrix that was covered in the previous recipe.

See also

- Documentation for constructor is available
  at `https://spark.apache.org/docs/latest/api/java/org/apache/spark/mllib/linalg/distributed/IndexedRowMatrix.html#constructor_summary`

- Documentation for method calls is available
  at `https://spark.apache.org/docs/latest/api/java/org/apache/spark/mllib/linalg/distributed/IndexedRowMatrix.html#method_summary`

Exploring distributed CoordinateMatrix in Spark 2.0

In this recipe, we cover the second form of specialized distributed matrix. This is very handy when dealing with ML implementations that need to deal with often large 3D coordinate systems (x, y, z). It is a convenient way to package the coordinate data structure into a distributed matrix.

How to do it...

1. Start a new project in IntelliJ or in an IDE of your choice. Make sure that the necessary JAR files are included.

2. Import the necessary packages for vector and matrix manipulation:

```
import org.apache.spark.mllib.linalg.distributed.RowMatrix
import org.apache.spark.mllib.linalg.distributed.{IndexedRow,
IndexedRowMatrix}
import
org.apache.spark.mllib.linalg.distributed.{CoordinateMatrix,
MatrixEntry}
import org.apache.spark.sql.{SparkSession}
import org.apache.spark.mllib.linalg._
import breeze.linalg.{DenseVector => BreezeVector}
import Array._
import org.apache.spark.mllib.linalg.DenseMatrix
import org.apache.spark.mllib.linalg.SparseVector
```

3. Set up the Spark context and application parameters so Spark can run. See the first recipe in the chapter for more details and variations:

```
val spark = SparkSession
 .builder
 .master("local[*]")
 .appName("myVectorMatrix")
 .config("spark.sql.warehouse.dir", ".")
 .getOrCreate()
```

4. We start with a SEQ of `MatrixEntry`, which corresponds to each coordinate and will be placed in the `CoordinateMatrix`. Note that the entries cannot be real numbers any more (they are x, y, z coordinates after all):

```
val CoordinateEntries = Seq(
    MatrixEntry(1, 6, 300),
    MatrixEntry(3, 1, 5),
    MatrixEntry(1, 7, 10)
)
```

5. We instantiate the call and construct the `CoordinateMatrix`. We need an additional step to create RDDs which we have shown in the constructor by using the Spark context for parallelization (that is, `sc.parallelize`):

```
val distCordMat1 = new CoordinateMatrix(
sc.parallelize(CoordinateEntries.toList))
```

6. We print the first `MatrixEntry` to verify the matrix elements. We will address RDDs in the next chapter, but note that `count()` is an action by itself and using `collect()` will be redundant:

```
println("First Row (MatrixEntry) =",distCordMat1.entries.first())
```

The output is as follows:

First Row (MatrixEntry) =,MatrixEntry(1,6,300.0)

How it works...

1. `CoordinateMatrix` is a specialized matrix in which each entry is a coordinate system or a tuple of three numbers (long, long, long corresponding to x, y, z coordinates). A related data structure is `MatrixEntry`, in which coordinates will be stored and then placed at a location in the `CoordinateMatrix`. The following code snippet demonstrates the use of `MaxEntry`, which seems to be a source of confusion in itself.

2. The following figure shows a pictorial view of the `CoordinateMatrix`, which should help clarify the subject:

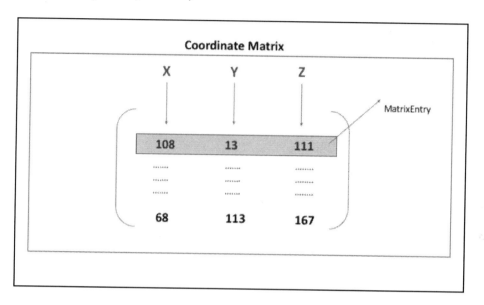

The code snippet which holds three coordinates is:

```
MatrixEntry(1, 6, 300), MatrixEntry(3, 1, 5), MatrixEntry(1, 7, 10)
```

`MaxEntry` is nothing but a required structure to hold the coordinate. Unless you need to modify the source code supplied by Spark (see GitHub `CoordinateMatrix.scala`) to define a more specialized container (compressed), there is no need to understand it any further:

- The `CoordinateMatrix` is also backed by RDDs which lets you leverage parallelism from the get go.
- You need to import `IndexedRow` as well so you can define the row with its index prior to instantiating the `IndexedRowMatrix`.
- This matrix can be converted to `RowMatrix`, `IndexedRowMatrix`, and `BlockMatrix`.

There is also an added benefit of efficient storage, retrieval, and operation that comes with a sparse coordinate system (for example, security threat matrix of all devices versus location).

See also

- Documentation for constructor is available
  at `https://spark.apache.org/docs/latest/api/java/org/apache/spark/mllib/linalg/distributed/CoordinateMatrix.html#constructor_summary`

- Documentation for method calls is available at `https://spark.apache.org/docs/latest/api/java/org/apache/spark/mllib/linalg/distributed/CoordinateMatrix.html#method_summary`

- Documentation for MaxEntry is available
  at `http://spark.apache.org/docs/latest/api/java/index.html`

Exploring distributed BlockMatrix in Spark 2.0

In this recipe, we explore `BlockMatrix`, which is a nice abstraction and a placeholder for the block of other matrices. In short, it is a matrix of other matrices (matrix blocks) which can be accessed as a cell.

We take a quick look at a simplified code snippet by converting the `CoordinateMatrix` to a `BlockMatrix` and then do a quick check for its validity and access one of its properties to show that it was set up properly. BlockMatrix code takes longer to set up and it needs a real life application (not enough space) to demonstrate and show its properties in action.

How to do it...

1. Start a new project in IntelliJ or in an editor of your choice and make sure all the necessary JAR files (Scala and Spark) are available to your application.
2. Import the necessary packages for vector and matrix manipulation:

```
import org.apache.spark.mllib.linalg.distributed.RowMatrix
 import org.apache.spark.mllib.linalg.distributed.{IndexedRow,
IndexedRowMatrix}
 import
org.apache.spark.mllib.linalg.distributed.{CoordinateMatrix,
MatrixEntry}
 import org.apache.spark.sql.{SparkSession}
 import org.apache.spark.mllib.linalg._
```

```
import breeze.linalg.{DenseVector => BreezeVector}
import Array._
import org.apache.spark.mllib.linalg.DenseMatrix
import org.apache.spark.mllib.linalg.SparseVector
```

3. Set up the Spark context and application parameters so Spark can run. See the first recipe in this chapter for more details and variations:

```
val spark = SparkSession
.builder
.master("local[*]")
.appName("myVectorMatrix")
.config("spark.sql.warehouse.dir", ".")
.getOrCreate()
```

4. Create a `CoordinateMatrix` quickly to use as a base for conversion:

```
val distCordMat1 = new CoordinateMatrix(
sc.parallelize(CoordinateEntries.toList))
```

5. We take the `CoordinateMatrix` and convert it into a `BlockMatrix`:

```
val distBlkMat1 =  distCordMat1.toBlockMatrix().cache()
```

6. This is a very useful call with this type of matrix. In real life, it is often necessary to check the setup before proceeding to compute:

```
distBlkMat1.validate()
println("Is block empty =", distBlkMat1.blocks.isEmpty())
```

The output is as follows:

Is block empty =,false

How it works...

A matrix block will be defined as a tuple of (int, int, Matrix). What is unique about this matrix is that it has `Add()` and `Multiply()` functions that can take another `BlockMatrix` as a second parameter to the distributed matrix. While setting it up is a bit confusing at first (especially on-the-fly as data arrives), there are helper functions that can help you verify your work and make sure the `BlockMatrix` is set up properly. This type of matrix can be converted to a local, `IndexRowMatrix`, and `CoordinateMatrix`. One of the most common use cases for the `BlockMatrix` is to have a `BlockMatrix` of `CoordinateMatrices`.

See also

- Documentation for constructor is available
  at https://spark.apache.org/docs/latest/api/java/org/apache/spark/mllib/linalg/distributed/BlockMatrix.html#constructor_summary

- Documentation for method calls is available
  at https://spark.apache.org/docs/latest/api/java/org/apache/spark/mllib/linalg/distributed/BlockMatrix.html#method_summary

3
Spark's Three Data Musketeers for Machine Learning - Perfect Together

In this chapter, we will cover the following recipes:

- Creating RDDs with Spark 2.0 using internal data sources
- Creating RDDs with Spark 2.0 using external data sources
- Transforming RDDs with Spark 2.0 using the filter() API
- Transforming RDDs with the super useful flatMap() API
- Transforming RDDs with set operation APIs
- RDD transformation/aggregation with groupBy() and reduceByKey()
- Transforming RDDs with the zip() API
- Join transformation with paired key-value RDDs
- Reduce and grouping transformation with paired key-value RDDs
- Creating DataFrames from Scala data structures
- Operating on DataFrames programmatically without SQL
- Loading DataFrames and setup from an external source
- Using DataFrames with standard SQL language - SparkSQL
- Working with the Dataset API using a Scala sequence
- Creating and using Datasets from RDDs and back again
- Working with JSON using the Dataset API and SQL together
- Functional programming with the Dataset API using domain objects

Introduction

The three workhorses of Spark for efficient processing of data at scale are RDD, DataFrames, and the Dataset API. While each can stand on its own merit, the new paradigm shift favors Dataset as the unifying data API to meet all data wrangling needs in a single interface.

The new Spark 2.0 Dataset API is a type-safe collection of domain objects that can be operated on via transformation (similar to RDDs' filter, `map`, `flatMap()`, and so on) in parallel using functional or relational operations. For backward compatibility, Dataset has a view called **DataFrame**, which is a collection of rows that are untyped. In this chapter, we demonstrate all three API sets. The figure ahead summarizes the pros and cons of the key components of Spark for data wrangling:

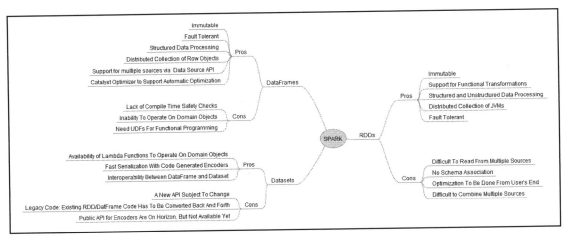

An advanced developer in machine learning must understand and be able to use all three API sets without any issues, for algorithmic augmentation or legacy reasons. While we recommend that every developer should migrate toward the high-level Dataset API, you will still need to know RDDs for programming against the Spark core system. For example, it is very common for investment banking and hedge funds to read leading journals in machine learning, mathematical programming, finance, statistics, or artificial intelligence and then code the research in low-level APIs to gain competitive advantage.

RDDs - what started it all...

The RDD API is a critical toolkit for Spark developers since it favors low-level control over the data within a functional programming paradigm. What makes RDDs powerful also makes it harder to work with for new programmers. While it may be easy to understand the RDD API and manual optimization techniques (for example, `filter()` before a `groupBy()` operation), writing advanced code would require consistent practice and fluency.

When data files, blocks, or data structures are converted to RDDs, the data is broken down into smaller units called **partitions** (similar to splits in Hadoop) and distributed among the nodes so they can be operated on in parallel at the same time. Spark provides this functionality right out of the box at scale without any additional coding. The framework will take care of all the details for you and you can concentrate on writing code without worrying about the data.

To appreciate the genius and yet the elegance of the underlying RDDs, one must read the original paper on this subject, which was deemed as the best work on this subject. The paper can be accessed here:

`https://www.usenix.org/system/files/conference/nsdi12/nsdi12-final138.pdf`

There are many types of RDDs in Spark that can simplify programming. The following mind map depicts a partial taxonomy of RDDs. It is suggested that a programmer on Spark know the types of RDDs available out of the box at minimum, even the less-known ones such as **RandomRDD** ,**VertexRDD**, **HadoopRDD**, **JdbcRDD**, and **UnionRDD**, in order to avoid unnecessary coding.

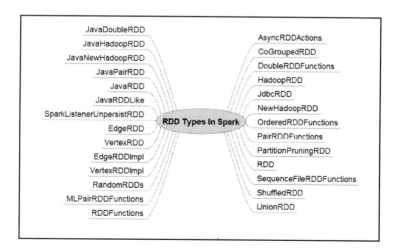

DataFrame - a natural evolution to unite API and SQL via a high-level API

The Spark developer community has always strived to provide an easy-to-use high-level API for the community starting from the AMPlab days at Berkley. The next evolution in the Data API materialized when Michael Armbrust gave the community the SparkSQL and Catalyst optimizer, which made data virtualization possible with Spark using a simple and well-understood SQL interface. The DataFrame API was a natural evolution to take advantage of SparkSQL by organizing data into named columns like relational tables.

The DataFrame API made data wrangling via SQL available to a multitude of data scientists and developers familiar with DataFrames in R (data.frame) or Python/Pandas (pandas.DataFrame).

Dataset - a high-level unifying Data API

A dataset is an immutable collection of objects which are modelled/mapped to a traditional relational schema. There are four attributes that distinguish it as the preferred method going forward. We particularly find the Dataset API appealing since we find it familiar to RDDs with the usual transformational operators (for example, `filter()`, `map()`, `flatMap()`, and so on). The Dataset will follow a lazy execution paradigm similar to RDD. The best way to try to reconcile DataFrames and Datasets is to think of a DataFrame as an alias that can be thought of as `Dataset[Row]`.

- **Strong type safety**: We now have both compile-time (syntax errors) and runtime safety in a unified Data API, which helps the ML developer not only during development, but can also help guard against mishaps during runtime. Developers hit by unexpected runtime errors using DataFrame or RDD Lambda either in Scala or Python (due to flaws in data) will better understand and appreciate this new contribution from the Spark community and Databricks (`https://databricks.com`).

- **Tungsten Memory Management enabled**: Tungsten brings Apache Spark closer to bare metal (that is, leveraging the `sun.misc.Unsafe interface`). The encoders facilitate mapping of JVM objects to tabular format (see the following figure). If you use the Dataset API, Spark will map the JVM objects to internal Tungsten off-heap binary format, which is more efficient. While the details of Tungsten internals are beyond the scope of a cookbook on machine learning, it is worth mentioning that the benchmarking shows significant improvement using off-head memory management versus JVM objects. It is noteworthy to mention that the concept of off-heap memory management has always been intrinsic in Apache Flink before it became available in Spark. Spark developers realized the importance of project Tungsten since Spark 1.4, 1.5, and 1.6 to its current state in Spark 2.0+. Again, we emphasize that even though DataFrame will be supported as of writing this, and has been covered in detail (most prod systems are still pre-Spark 2.0), we encourage you to start thinking in the Dataset paradigm. The following figure shows how RDD, DataFrame, and DataSet relate to the project Tungsten evolutionary roadmap:

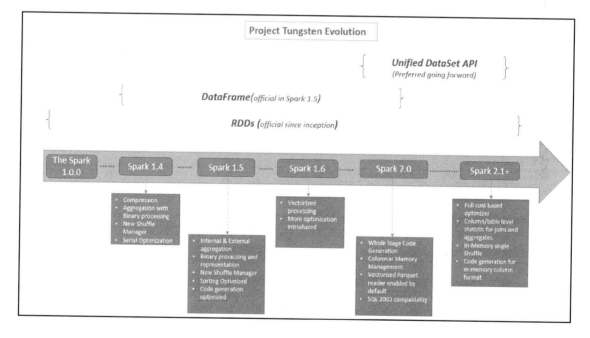

- **Encoders**: Encoders are Spark's serialization and deserialization (that is, SerDe) framework in Spark 2.0. Encoders seamlessly handle the mapping of JVM objects to tabular format that you can get under the cover and modify if desired (expert level).

  - Unlike standard Java serialization and other serialization schemes (for example, Kryo), the encoders do not use runtime reflection to discover object internals to serialize on the fly. Instead, encoder code is generated and compiled during compile time to bytecode for a given object, which will result in much faster operation (no reflection is used) to serialize and de-serialize the object. The reflection at runtime for object internals (for example, lookup of fields and their format) imposes extra overhead that is not present using Spark 2.0. The ability to use Kryo, standard java serialization, or any other serialization technique still remains an option (edge cases and backward compatibility) if needed.

  - The encoders for standard data types and objects (made of standard data types) are available in Tungsten out of the box. Using a quick informal program benchmark, serializing objects back and forth using Kryo serialization, which is popular with Hadoop MapReduce developers, versus encoders, revealed a significant 4x to 8x improvement. When we looked at the source code and probed under the covers, we realized that the encoders actually use runtime code generation (at bytecode level!) to pack and unpack objects. For completeness, we mention that the objects also seemed to be smaller, but further details and the reasons as to why it is so, is beyond the scope of this book.

  - The Encoder[T] is an internal artifact made of the DataSet[T], which is just a schema of records. You can create your own custom encoders as needed in Scala using tuples of underlying data (for example, Long, Double, and Int). Before you embark on the custom encoder journey (for example, want to store custom objects in DataSet[T]), make sure you take a look at `Encoders.scala` and `SQLImplicits.scala` in Spark's source directory. The plan and strategic direction for Spark is to provide a public API in future releases.

- **Catalyst optimizer friendly**: Using Catalyst, the API gestures are translated into logical query plans which use a catalog (user-defined functions) and ultimately translate the logical plan to a physical plan, which is often much more efficient than proposed by the original scheme (even if you try to put `groupBy()` before `filter()`, it is smart enough to arrange it the other way around). For better clarity, see the following figure:

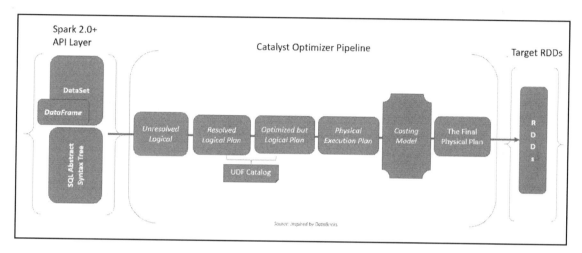

Noteworthy for pre-Spark 2.0 users:

- `SparkSession` is now the single entry point into the system. SQLContext and HiveContext are replaced by SparkSession.
- For Java users, be sure to replace DataFrame with `Dataset<Row>`
- Use the new catalog interface via `SparkSession` to execute `cacheTable()`, `dropTempView()`, `createExternalTable()`, `ListTable()`, and so on.
- DataFrame and DataSet API:
    - `unionALL()` is deprecated; you should use now `union()`
    - `explode()` should be replaced by `functions.explode()` plus `select()` or `flatMap()`
    - `registerTempTable` has been deprecated and replaced by `createOrReplaceTempView()`

Creating RDDs with Spark 2.0 using internal data sources

There are four ways to create RDDs in Spark. They range from the `parallelize()` method for simple testing and debugging within the client driver code to streaming RDDs for near-realtime responses. In this recipe, we provide you with several examples to demonstrate RDD creation using internal sources. The streaming case will be covered in the streaming Spark example in `Chapter 13`, *Streaming Machine Learning System*, so we can address it in a meaningful way.

How to do it...

1. Start a new project in IntelliJ or in an IDE of your choice. Make sure the necessary JAR files are included.

2. Set up the package location where the program will reside:

   ```
   package spark.ml.cookbook.chapter3
   ```

3. Import the necessary packages:

   ```
   import breeze.numerics.pow
   import org.apache.spark.sql.SparkSession
   import Array._
   ```

4. Import the packages for setting up logging level for `log4j`. This step is optional, but we highly recommend it (change the level appropriately as you move through the development cycle).

   ```
   import org.apache.log4j.Logger
   import org.apache.log4j.Level
   ```

5. Set up the logging level to warning and error to cut down on output. See the previous step for package requirements.

   ```
   Logger.getLogger("org").setLevel(Level.ERROR)
   Logger.getLogger("akka").setLevel(Level.ERROR)
   ```

6. Set up the Spark context and application parameter so Spark can run:

```
val spark = SparkSession
  .builder
  .master("local[*]")
  .appName("myRDD")
  .config("Spark.sql.warehouse.dir", ".")
  .getOrCreate()
```

7. We declare two local data structures to hold the data prior to using any distributed RDDs. It should be noted that the data here will be held in the driver's heap space via local data structures. We make an explicit mention here, due to the multitude of problems programmers encounter when using large data sets for testing using the `parallelize()` technique. Ensure that you have enough space to hold the data locally in the driver if you use this technique.

```
val SignalNoise: Array[Double] =
Array(0.2,1.2,0.1,0.4,0.3,0.3,0.1,0.3,0.3,0.9,1.8,0.2,3.5,0.5,0.3,0
.3,0.2,0.4,0.5,0.9,0.1)
val SignalStrength: Array[Double] =
Array(6.2,1.2,1.2,6.4,5.5,5.3,4.7,2.4,3.2,9.4,1.8,1.2,3.5,5.5,7.7,9
.3,1.1,3.1,2.1,4.1,5.1)
```

8. We use the `parallelize()` function to take the local data and distribute it across the cluster.

```
val parSN=spark.sparkContext.parallelize(SignalNoise) //
parallelized signal noise RDD
val parSS=spark.sparkContext.parallelize(SignalStrength)  //
parallelized signal strength
```

9. Let's take a look at the difference between the two data structures as seen by Spark. This can be done by printing the two data structure handles: a local array and a cluster parallel collection (that is, RDD).

The output will be as follows:

```
Signal Noise Local Array , [D@2ab0702e)
RDD Version of Signal Noise on the cluster
,ParallelCollectionRDD[0] at parallelize at myRDD.scala:45)
```

10. Spark tries to set the number of partitions (that is, splits in Hadoop) itself based on the configuration of the cluster, but there are times when we need to set the number of partitions manually. The `parallelize()` function offers a second parameter that allows you to set the number of partitions manually.

```
val parSN=spark.sparkContext.parallelize(SignalNoise) //
parallelized signal noise RDD set with default partition
val parSS=spark.sparkContext.parallelize(SignalStrength)  //
parallelized signal strength set with default partition
val parSN2=spark.sparkContext.parallelize(SignalNoise,4) //
parallelized signal noise set with 4 partition
val parSS2=spark.sparkContext.parallelize(SignalStrength,8)   //
parallelized signal strength set with 8 partition
println("parSN partition length ", parSN.partitions.length )
println("parSS partition length ", parSS.partitions.length )
println("parSN2 partition length ",parSN2.partitions.length )
println("parSS2 partition length ",parSS2.partitions.length )
```

The output will be as follows:

```
parSN partition length ,2
parSS partition length ,2
parSN2 partition length ,4
parSS2 partition length ,8
```

In the first two lines, Spark has chosen two partitions by default, and, in the next two lines, we have set the number of partitions to 4 and 8, respectively.

How it works...

The data held in the client driver is parallelized and distributed across the cluster using the number of portioned RDDs (the second parameter) as the guideline. The resulting RDD is the magic of Spark that started it all (refer to Matei Zaharia's original white paper).

The resulting RDDs are now fully distributed data structures with fault tolerance and lineage that can be operated on in parallel using Spark framework.

We read a text file `A Tale of Two Cities by Charles Dickens` from `http://www.gutenberg.org/` into Spark RDDs. We then proceed to split and tokenize the data and print the number of total words using Spark's operators (for example, `map`, `flatMap()`, and so on).

Creating RDDs with Spark 2.0 using external data sources

In this recipe, we provide you with several examples to demonstrate RDD creation using external sources.

How to do it...

1. Start a new project in IntelliJ or in an IDE of your choice. Make sure the necessary JAR files are included.

2. Set up the package location where the program will reside:

   ```
   package spark.ml.cookbook.chapter3
   ```

3. Import the necessary packages:

   ```
   import breeze.numerics.pow
   import org.apache.spark.sql.SparkSession
   import Array._
   ```

4. Import the packages for setting up logging level for log4j. This step is optional, but we highly recommend it (change the level appropriately as you move through the development cycle).

   ```
   import org.apache.log4j.Logger
   import org.apache.log4j.Level
   ```

5. Set up the logging level to warning and error to cut down on output. See the previous step for package requirements.

   ```
   Logger.getLogger("org").setLevel(Level.ERROR)
   Logger.getLogger("akka").setLevel(Level.ERROR)
   ```

6. Set up the Spark context and application parameter so Spark can run.

   ```
   val spark = SparkSession
     .builder
     .master("local[*]")
     .appName("myRDD")
     .config("Spark.sql.warehouse.dir", ".")
     .getOrCreate()
   ```

7. We obtain the data from the Gutenberg project. This is a great source for accessing actual text, ranging from the complete works of *Shakespeare* to *Charles Dickens*.

8. Download the text from the following sources and store it in your local directory:
   - Source: `http://www.gutenberg.org`
   - Selected book: *A Tale of Two Cities by Charles Dickens*
   - URL: `http://www.gutenberg.org/cache/epub/98/pg98.txt`

9. Once again, we use `SparkContext`, available via `SparkSession`, and its function `textFile()` to read the external data source and parallelize it across the cluster. Remarkably, all the work is done for the developer behind the scenes by Spark using one single call to load a wide variety of formats (for example, text, S3, and HDFS), which parallelizes the data across the cluster using the `protocol:filepath` combination.

10. To demonstrate, we load the book, which is stored as ASCII, text using the `textFile()` method from `SparkContext` via `SparkSession`, which, in turn goes to work behind the scenes and creates portioned RDDs across the cluster.

```
val book1 =
spark.sparkContext.textFile("../data/sparkml2/chapter3/a.txt")
```

The output will be as follows:

```
Number of lines = 16271
```

11. Even though we have not covered the Spark transformation operator, we'll look at a small code snippet which will break the file into words using blanks as a separator. In a real-life situation, a regular expression will be needed to cover all the edge cases with all the whitespace variations (refer to the *Transforming RDDs with Spark using filter() APIs* recipe in this chapter).
    - We use a lambda function to receive each line as it is read and split it into words using blanks as separator.
    - We use a flatMap to break the array of lists of words (that is, each group of words from a line corresponds to a distinct array/list for that line). In short, what we want is a list of words and not a list of a list of words for each line.

```
val book2 = book1.flatMap(l => l.split(" "))
println(book1.count())
```

The output will be as follows:

```
Number of words = 143228
```

How it works...

We read a text file `A Tale of Two Cities by Charles Dickens` from `http://www.gutenberg.org/` into an RDD and then proceed to tokenize the words by using whitespace as the separator in a lambda expression using `.split()` and `.flatmap()` of RDD itself. We then proceed to use the `.count()` method of RDDs to output the total number of words. While this is simple, you have to bear in mind that the operation takes place using the distributed parallel framework of Spark with only a couple of lines.

There's more...

Creating RDDs with external data sources, whether it is a text file, Hadoop HDFS, sequence file, Casandra, or Parquet file is remarkably simple. Once again, we use `SparkSession` (`SparkContext` prior to Spark 2.0) to get a handle to the cluster. Once the function (for example, textFile Protocol: file path) is executed, the data is broken into smaller pieces (partitions) and automatically flows to the cluster, which becomes available to the computations as fault-tolerant distributed collections that can be operated on in parallel.

1. There are a number of variations that one must consider when working with real-life situations. The best advice based on our own experience is to consult the documentation before writing your own functions or connectors. Spark either supports your data source right out of the box, or the vendor has a connector that can be downloaded to do the same.

2. Another situation that we often see is many small files that are generated (usually within `HDFS` directories) that need to be parallelized as RDDs for consumption. `SparkContext` has a method named `wholeTextFiles()` which lets you read a directory containing multiple files and returns each of them as (filename, content) key-value pairs. We found this to be very useful in multi-stage machine learning situations using lambda architecture, where the model parameters are calculated as a batch and then updated in Spark every day.

In this example, we read multiple files and then print the first file for examination.

The `spark.sparkContext.wholeTextFiles()` function is used to read a large number of small files and present them as (K,V), or key-value:

```
val dirKVrdd =
spark.sparkContext.wholeTextFiles("../data/sparkml2/chapter3/*.txt") //
place a large number of small files for demo
println ("files in the directory as RDD ", dirKVrdd)
println("total number of files ", dirKVrdd.count())
println("Keys ", dirKVrdd.keys.count())
println("Values ", dirKVrdd.values.count())
dirKVrdd.collect()
println("Values ", dirKVrdd.first())
```

On running the previous code, you will get the following output:

```
files in the directory as RDD ,../data/sparkml2/chapter3/*.txt
WholeTextFileRDD[10] at wholeTextFiles at myRDD.scala:88)
total number of files 2
Keys ,2
Values ,2
Values ,(file:/C:/spark-2.0.0-bin-
hadoop2.7/data/sparkml2/chapter3/a.txt,
The Project Gutenberg EBook of A Tale of Two Cities,
by Charles Dickens
```

See also

Spark documentation for the `textFile()` and `wholeTextFiles()` functions:

```
http://spark.apache.org/docs/latest/api/scala/index.html#org.apache.spark.Spark
Context
```

The `textFile()` API is a single abstraction for interfacing to external data sources. The formulation of protocol/path is enough to invoke the right decoder. We'll demonstrate reading from an ASCII text file, Amazon AWS S3, and HDFS with code snippets that the user would leverage to build their own system.

- The path can be expressed as a simple path (for example, local text file) to a complete URI with the required protocol (for example, s3n for AWS storage buckets) to complete resource path with server and port configuration (for example, to read HDFS file from a Hadoop cluster).
- The `textFile()` method supports full directories, regex wildcards, and compressed formats as well. Take a look at this example code:

```
val book1 = spark.sparkContext.textFile("C:/xyz/dailyBuySel/*.tif")
```

- The `textFile()` method has an optional parameter at the end that defines the minimum number of partitions required by RDDs.

For example, we explicitly direct Spark to break the file into 13 partitions:

```
val book1 = spark.sparkContext.textFile("../data/sparkml2/chapter3/a.txt",
13)
```

You also have the option of specifying a URI to read and create RDDs from other sources such as HDFS, and S3 by specifying a complete URI (protocol:path). The following examples demonstrate the point:

1. Reading and creating files from Amazon S3 buckets. A word of caution is that the AWS inline credentials in the URI will break if the AWS secret key has a forward slash. See this sample file:

```
spark.sparkContext.hadoopConfiguration.set("fs.s3n.awsAccessKeyId",
"xyz")
spark.sparkContext.hadoopConfiguration.set("fs.s3n.awsSecretAccessK
ey", "....xyz...")
S3Rdd = spark.sparkContext.textFile("s3n://myBucket01/MyFile01")
```

2. Reading from HDFS is very similar. In this example, we are reading from a local Hadoop cluster, but, in a real-world situation, the port number will be different and set by administrator.

```
val hdfsRDD =
spark.sparkContext.textFile("hdfs:///localhost:9000/xyz/top10Vector
s.txt")
```

Transforming RDDs with Spark 2.0 using the filter() API

In this recipe, we explore the `filter()` method of RDD which is used to select a subset of the base RDD and return a new filtered RDD. The format is similar to `map()`, but a lambda function selects which members are to be included in the resulting RDD.

How to do it...

1. Start a new project in IntelliJ or in an IDE of your choice. Make sure the necessary JAR files are included.

2. Set up the package location where the program will reside:

   ```
   package spark.ml.cookbook.chapter3
   ```

3. Import the necessary packages:

   ```
   import breeze.numerics.pow
   import org.apache.spark.sql.SparkSession
   import Array._
   ```

4. Import the packages for setting up logging level for `log4j`. This step is optional, but we highly recommend it (change the level appropriately as you move through the development cycle).

   ```
   import org.apache.log4j.Logger
   import org.apache.log4j.Level
   ```

5. Set up the logging level to warning and error to cut down on output. See the previous step for package requirements.

   ```
   Logger.getLogger("org").setLevel(Level.ERROR)
   Logger.getLogger("akka").setLevel(Level.ERROR)
   ```

6. Set up the Spark context and application parameter so Spark can run.

   ```
   val spark = SparkSession
     .builder
     .master("local[*]")
     .appName("myRDD")
     .config("Spark.sql.warehouse.dir", ".")
     .getOrCreate()
   ```

7. Add the following lines for the examples to compile. The `pow()` function will allow us to raise any number to any power (for example, square the number):

   ```
   import breeze.numerics.pow
   ```

8. We create some data and `parallelize()` it to get our base RDD. We also use `textFile()` to create the initial (for example, base RDD) from our text file that we downloaded earlier from the `http://www.gutenberg.org/cache/epub/98/pg98.txt` link:

```
val num : Array[Double] = Array(1,2,3,4,5,6,7,8,9,10,11,12,13)
  val numRDD=sc.parallelize(num)
  val book1 =
spark.sparkContext.textFile("../data/sparkml2/chapter3/a.txt")
```

9. We apply the `filter()` function to the RDDs to demonstrate the `filter()` function transformation. We use the `filter()` function to select the odd members from the original RDD.

10. The `filter()` function iterates (in parallel) through members of the RDD and applies the mod function (%) and compares it to 1. In short, if there is a reminder after dividing by 2, then it must be an odd number.

```
val myOdd= num.filter( i => (i%2) == 1)
```

This is a second variation of the previous line, but here we demonstrate the use of _ (underscore), which acts as a wildcard. We use this notation in Scala to abbreviate the obvious:

```
val myOdd2= num.filter(_ %2 == 1) // 2nd variation using scala
notation
myOdd.take(3).foreach(println)
```

On running the previous code, you will get the following output:

```
1.0
3.0
5.0
```

11. Another example combines map and filter together. This code snippet first squares every number and then applies the `filter` function to select the odd numbers from the original RDD.

```
val myOdd3= num.map(pow(_,2)).filter(_ %2 == 1)
myOdd3.take(3).foreach(println)
```

The output will be as follows:

```
1.0
9.0
25.0
```

12. In this example, we use the `filter()` method to identify the lines that are fewer than 30 characters. The resulting RDD will only contain the short lines. A quick examination of counts and output verify the results. The RDD transformation functions can be chained together, as long as the format complies with the function syntax.

```
val shortLines = book1.filter(_.length < 30).filter(_.length > 0)
   println("Total number of lines = ", book1.count())
   println("Number of Short Lines = ", shortLines.count())
   shortLines.take(3).foreach(println)
```

On running the previous code, you will get the following output:

```
(Total number of lines = 16271)
(Number of Short Lines = 1424)
Title: A Tale of Two Cities
Author: Charles Dickens
Language: English
```

13. In this example we use the `contain()` method to filter out sentences that contain the word `two` in any upper/lowercase combination. We use several methods chained together to find the desired sentences.

```
val theLines =
book1.map(_.trim.toUpperCase()).filter(_.contains("TWO"))
println("Total number of lines = ", book1.count())
println("Number of lines with TWO = ", theLines.count())
theLines.take(3).foreach(println)
```

How it works...

The `filter()` API is demonstrated using several examples. In the first example we went through an RDD and output odd numbers by using a lambda expression `.filter ( i => (i%2) == 1)` which takes advantage of the mod (modulus) function.

In the second example we made it a bit interesting by mapping the result to a square function using a lambda expression `num.map(pow(_,2)).filter(_ %2 == 1)`.

In the third example, we went through the text and filtered out short lines (for example, lines under 30 character) using the lambda expression `.filter(_.length < 30).filter(_.length > 0)` to print short versus total number of lines (`.count()`) as output.

There's more...

The `filter()` API walks through the parallelized distributed collection (that is, RDDs) and applies the selection criteria supplied to `filter()` as a lambda in order to include or exclude the element from the resulting RDD. The combination uses `map()`, which transforms each element and `filter()`, which selects a subset is a powerful combination in Spark ML programming.

We will see later with the `DataFrame` API how a similar `Filter()` API can be used to achieve the same effect using a higher-level framework used in R and Python (pandas).

See also

- Documentation for `.filter()`, which is a method call of RDD, is available at `http://spark.apache.org/docs/latest/api/scala/index.html#org.apache.spark.api.java.JavaRDD`.
- Documentation for `BloomFilter()`--for the sake of completeness, be aware that there is also a bloom filter function already in existence and it is suggested that you avoid coding this yourselves. We will tackle this in chapter 13, *Spark Streaming and Machine Learning Library*, to match Spark's view and layout. The link for this same is `http://spark.apache.org/docs/latest/api/scala/index.html#org.apache.spark.util.sketch.BloomFilter`.

Transforming RDDs with the super useful flatMap() API

In this recipe, we examine the `flatMap()` method which is often a source of confusion for beginners; however, on closer examination we demonstrate that it is a clear concept that applies the lambda function to each element just like map, and then flattens the resulting RDD as a single structure (rather than having a list of lists, we create a single list made of all sublist with sublist elements).

How to do it...

1. Start a new project in IntelliJ or in an IDE of your choice. Make sure the necessary JAR files are included.

2. Set up the package location where the program will reside

   ```
   package spark.ml.cookbook.chapter3
   ```

3. Import the necessary packages

   ```
   import breeze.numerics.pow
   import org.apache.spark.sql.SparkSession
   import Array._
   ```

4. Import the packages for setting up logging level for `log4j`. This step is optional, but we highly recommend it (change the level appropriately as you move through the development cycle).

   ```
   import org.apache.log4j.Logger
   import org.apache.log4j.Level
   ```

5. Set up the logging level to warning and error to cut down on output. See the previous step for package requirements.

   ```
   Logger.getLogger("org").setLevel(Level.ERROR)
   Logger.getLogger("akka").setLevel(Level.ERROR)
   ```

6. Set up the Spark context and application parameter so Spark can run.

   ```
   val spark = SparkSession
     .builder
     .master("local[*]")
     .appName("myRDD")
     .config("Spark.sql.warehouse.dir", ".")
     .getOrCreate()
   ```

7. We use `textFile()` function to create the initial (that is, base RDD) from our text file that we downloaded earlier from
   `http://www.gutenberg.org/cache/epub/98/pg98.txt`:

   ```
   val book1 =
     spark.sparkContext.textFile("../data/sparkml2/chapter3/a.txt")
   ```

8. We apply the map function to the RDDs to demonstrate the `map()` function transformation. To start with, we are doing it the wrong way to make a point: we first attempt to separate all the words based on the regular expression *[\s\W]+]* using just `map()` to demonstrate that the resulting RDD is a list of lists in which each list corresponds to a line and the tokenized word within that line. This example demonstrates what could cause confusion for beginners when using `flatMap()`.

9. The following line trims each line and then splits the line into words. The resulting RDD (that is, wordRDD2) will be a list of lists of words rather than a single list of words for the whole file.

```
val wordRDD2 = book1.map(_.trim.split("""[\s\W]+""")
).filter(_.length > 0)
wordRDD2.take(3) foreach(println(_))
```

On running the previous code, you will get the following output.

```
[Ljava.lang.String;@1e60b459
[Ljava.lang.String;@717d7587
[Ljava.lang.String;@3e906375
```

10. We use the `flatMap()` method to not only map, but also flatten the list of lists so we end up with an RDD which is made of words themselves. We trim and split the words (that is, tokenize) and then filter for words greater than zero and then map it to upper case.

```
val wordRDD3 = book1.flatMap(_.trim.split("""[\s\W]+""")
).filter(_.length > 0).map(_.toUpperCase())
println("Total number of lines = ", book1.count())
println("Number of words = ", wordRDD3.count())
```

In this case, after flattening the list using `flatMap()`, we can get a list of the words back as expected.

```
wordRDD3.take(5) foreach(println(_))
```

The output is as follows:

```
Total number of lines = 16271
Number of words = 141603
THE
PROJECT
GUTENBERG
EBOOK
OF
```

How it works...

In this short example, we read a text file and then split the words (that is, tokenize it) using the `flatMap(_.trim.split("""[\s\W]+""")` lambda expression to have a single RDD with the tokenized content. Additionally we use the `filter ()` API `filter(_.length > 0)` to exclude the empty lines and the lambda expression `.map(_.toUpperCase())` in a `.map()` API to map to uppercase before outputting the results.

There are cases where we do not want to get a list back for every element of base RDD (for example, get a list for words corresponding to a line). We sometimes prefer to have a single flattened list that is flat and corresponds to every word in the document. In short, rather than a list of lists, we want a single list containing all the elements.

There's more...

The function `glom()` is a function that lets you model each partition in the RDD as an array rather than a row list. While it is possible to produce the results in most cases, `glom()` allows you to reduce the shuffling between partitions.

While at the surface, both method 1 and 2 mentioned in the text below look similar for calculating the minimum numbers in an RDD, the `glom()` function will cause much less data shuffling across the network by first applying `min()` to all the partitions, and then sending over the resulting data. The best way to see the difference is to use this on 10M+ RDDs and watch the IO and CPU usage accordingly.

- The first method is to find the minimum value without using `glom()`:

```
val minValue1= numRDD.reduce(_ min _)
println("minValue1 = ", minValue1)
```

On running the preceding code, you will get the following output:

minValue1 = 1.0

- The second method is to find the minimum value using `glom(`, which causes a local application of the min function to a partition and then sends the results across via a shuffle.

```
val minValue2 = numRDD.glom().map(_.min).reduce(_ min _)
println("minValue2 = ", minValue2)
```

On running the preceding code, you will get the following output:

```
minValue1 = 1.0
```

See also

- Documentation for `flatMap()`, `PairFlatMap()`, and other variations under RDD is available
  at `http://spark.apache.org/docs/latest/api/scala/index.html#org.apache.spark.api.java.JavaRDD`
- Documentation for the `FlatMap()` function under RDD is available
  at `http://spark.apache.org/docs/latest/api/scala/index.html#org.apache.spark.api.java.function.FlatMapFunction`
- Documentation for the `PairFlatMap()` function - very handy variation for paired data elements is available
  at `http://spark.apache.org/docs/latest/api/scala/index.html#org.apache.spark.api.java.function.PairFlatMapFunction`
- The `flatMap()` method applies the supplied function (lambda or named function via def) to every element, flattens the structure, and produces a new RDD.

Transforming RDDs with set operation APIs

In this recipe, we explore set operations on RDDs, such as `intersection()`, `union()`, `subtract()`, and `distinct()` and `Cartesian()`. Let's implement the usual set operations in a distributed manner.

How to do it...

1. Start a new project in IntelliJ or in an IDE of your choice. Make sure the necessary JAR files are included.

2. Set up the package location where the program will reside

```
package spark.ml.cookbook.chapter3
```

3. Import the necessary packages

```
import breeze.numerics.pow
import org.apache.spark.sql.SparkSession
import Array._
```

4. Import the packages for setting up logging level for `log4j`. This step is optional, but we highly recommend it (change the level appropriately as you move through the development cycle).

```
import org.apache.log4j.Logger
import org.apache.log4j.Level
```

5. Set up the logging level to warning and error to cut down on output. See the previous step for package requirements.

```
Logger.getLogger("org").setLevel(Level.ERROR)
Logger.getLogger("akka").setLevel(Level.ERROR)
```

6. Set up the Spark context and application parameter so Spark can run.

```
val spark = SparkSession
  .builder
  .master("local[*]")
  .appName("myRDD")
  .config("Spark.sql.warehouse.dir", ".")
  .getOrCreate()
```

7. Set up the data structures and RDD for the example:

```
val num : Array[Double]   = Array(1,2,3,4,5,6,7,8,9,10,11,12,13)
val odd : Array[Double]   = Array(1,3,5,7,9,11,13)
val even : Array[Double]  = Array(2,4,6,8,10,12)
```

8. We apply the `intersection()` function to the RDDs to demonstrate the transformation:

```
val intersectRDD = numRDD.intersection(oddRDD)
```

On running the previous code, you will get the following output:

```
1.0
3.0
5.0
```

9. We apply the `union()` function to the RDDs to demonstrate the transformation:

```
val unionRDD = oddRDD.union(evenRDD)
```

On running the previous code, you will get the following output:

```
1.0
2.0
3.0
4.0
```

10. We apply the `subract()` function to the RDDs to demonstrate the transformation:

```
val subtractRDD = numRDD.subtract(oddRDD)
```

On running the previous code, you will get the following output:

```
2.0
4.0
6.0
8.0
```

11. We apply the `distinct()` function to the RDDs to demonstrate the transformation:

```
val namesRDD = spark.sparkContext.parallelize(List("Ed","Jain",
"Laura", "Ed"))
val ditinctRDD = namesRDD.distinct()
```

On running the previous code, you will get the following output:

```
"ED"
"Jain"
"Laura"
```

12. We apply the `distinct()` function to the RDDs to demonstrate the transformation

```
val cartesianRDD = oddRDD.cartesian(evenRDD)
cartesianRDD.collect.foreach(println)
```

On running the previous code, you will get the following output:

```
(1.0,2.0)
(1.0,4.0)
(1.0,6.0)
(3.0,2.0)
(3.0,4.0)
(3.0,6.0)
```

How it works...

In this example, we started with three sets of number Arrays (odd, even, and their combo) and then proceeded to pass them as parameters into the set operation API. We covered how to use `intersection()`, `union()`, `subtract()`, `distinct()`, and `cartesian()` RDD operators.

See also

While the RDD set operators are easy to use, one must be careful with the data shuffling that Spark has to perform in the background to complete some of these operations (for example, intersection).

It is worth nothing that the union operator does not remove duplicates from the resulting RDD set.

RDD transformation/aggregation with groupBy() and reduceByKey()

In this recipe, we explore the `groupBy()` and `reduceBy()` methods, which allow us to group values corresponding to a key. It is an expensive operation due to internal shuffling. We first demonstrate `groupby()` in more detail and then cover `reduceBy()` to show the similarity in coding these while stressing the advantage of the `reduceBy()` operator.

How to do it...

1. Start a new project in IntelliJ or in an IDE of your choice. Make sure the necessary JAR files are included.

2. Set up the package location where the program will reside:

   ```
   package spark.ml.cookbook.chapter3
   ```

3. Import the necessary packages:

   ```
   import breeze.numerics.pow
   import org.apache.spark.sql.SparkSession
   import Array._
   ```

4. Import the packages for setting up logging level for `log4j`. This step is optional, but we highly recommend it (change the level appropriately as you move through the development cycle):

   ```
   import org.apache.log4j.Logger
   import org.apache.log4j.Level
   ```

5. Set up the logging level to warning and error to cut down on output. See the previous step for package requirements.

   ```
   Logger.getLogger("org").setLevel(Level.ERROR)
   Logger.getLogger("akka").setLevel(Level.ERROR)
   ```

6. Set up the Spark context and application parameter so Spark can run:

   ```
   val spark = SparkSession
     .builder
     .master("local[*]")
     .appName("myRDD")
     .config("Spark.sql.warehouse.dir", ".")
     .getOrCreate()
   ```

7. Set up the data structures and RDD for the example. In this example we create an RDD using range facilities and divide them into three partitions (that is, explicit parameter set). It simply creates numbers 1 through 12 and puts them into 3 partitions.

   ```
   val rangeRDD=sc.parallelize(1 to 12,3)
   ```

8. We apply the `groupBy()` function to the RDDs to demonstrate the transformation. In the example, we take the partitioned RDD of ranges and label them as odd/even using the `mod` function.

```
val groupByRDD= rangeRDD.groupBy( i => {if (i % 2 == 1) "Odd"
  else "Even"}).collect
groupByRDD.foreach(println)
```

On running the previous code, you will get the following output:

```
groupByRDD=
(Odd, CompactBuffer (1, 3, 5, 7, 9, 11))
(Even, CompactBuffer (2, 4, 6, 8, 10, 12))
```

9. Now that we have seen how to code `groupBy()`, we switch gears and demonstrate `reduceByKey()`.

10. To see the difference in coding, while producing the same output more efficiently, we set up an array with two letters (that is, a and b) so we can show aggregation by summing them up.

```
val alphabets = Array("a", "b", "a", "a", "a", "b") // two type
only to make it simple
```

11. In this step, we use a Spark context to produce a parallelized RDD:

```
val alphabetsPairsRDD =
spark.sparkContext.parallelize(alphabets).map(alphabets =>
(alphabets, 1))
```

12. We apply the `groupBy()` function first using the usual Scala syntax (_+_) to traverse the RDD and sum up, while aggregating by the type of alphabet (that is, considered key):

```
val countsUsingGroup = alphabetsPairsRDD.groupByKey()
  .map(c => (c._1, c._2.sum))
  .collect()
```

13. We apply the `reduceByKey()` function first using the usual Scala syntax (_+_) to traverse the RDD and sum up while aggregating by type of alphabet (that is, considered key)

```
val countsUsingReduce = alphabetsPairsRDD
  .reduceByKey(_ + _)
  .collect()
```

14. We output the results:

```
println("Output for  groupBy")
countsUsingGroup.foreach(println(_))
println("Output for  reduceByKey")
countsUsingReduce.foreach(println(_))
```

On running the previous code, you will get the following output:

```
Output for groupBy
(b,2)
(a,4)
Output for reduceByKey
(b,2)
(a,4)
```

How it works...

In this example, we created numbers one through twelve and placed them in three partitions. We then proceeded to break them into odd/even using a simple mod operation while. The `groupBy()` is used to aggregate them into two groups of odd/even. This is a typical aggregation problem that should look familiar to SQL users. Later in this chapter we revisit this operation using `DataFrame` which also takes advantage of the better optimization techniques provided by the SparkSQL engine. In the later part, we demonstrate the similarity of `groupBy()` and `reduceByKey()`. We set up an array of alphabets (that is, `a` and `b`) and then convert them into RDD. We then proceed to aggregate them based on key (that is, unique letters - only two in this case) and print the total in each group.

There's more...

Given the direction for Spark which favors the Dataset/DataFrame paradigm over low level RDD coding, one must seriously consider the reasoning for doing `groupBy()` on an RDD. While there are legitimate situations for which the operation is needed, the readers are advised to reformulate their solution to take advantage of the SparkSQL subsystem and its optimizer called **Catalyst**.

The Catalyst optimizer takes into account Scala's powerful features such as **pattern matching** and **quasiquotes** while building an optimized query plan.

- The documentation on Scala pattern matching is available
  at `http://docs.scala-lang.org/tutorials/tour/pattern-matching.html`
- The documentation on Scala quasiquotes is available
  at `http://docs.scala-lang.org/overviews/quasiquotes/intro.html`

Runtime efficiency consideration: The `groupBy()` function groups data by keys. The operation causes internal shuffling which can explode the execution time; one must always prefer to use the `reduceByKey()` family of operations to a straight `groupBy()` method call. The `groupBy()` method is an expensive operation due to shuffling. Each group is made of keys and items that belong to that key. The ordering of values corresponding to the key will not be guaranteed by Spark.

For an explanation of the two operations, see the Databricks knowledge base blog:

`https://databricks.gitbooks.io/databricks-Spark-knowledge-base/content/best_practices/prefer_reducebykey_over_groupbykey.html`

See also

Documentation for `groupBy()` and `reduceByKey()` operations under RDD:

`http://spark.apache.org/docs/latest/api/scala/index.html#org.apache.spark.api.java.JavaRDD`

Transforming RDDs with the zip() API

In this recipe we explore the `zip()` function. For those of us working in Python or Scala, `zip()` is a familiar method that lets you pair items before applying an inline function. Using Spark, it can be used to facilitate RDD arithmetic between pairs. Conceptually, it combines the two RDDs in such a way that each member of one RDD is paired with the second RDD that occupies the same position (that is, it lines up the two RDDs and makes pairs out of the members).

How to do it...

1. Start a new project in IntelliJ or in an IDE of your choice. Make sure the necessary JAR files are included.

2. Set up the package location where the program will reside

   ```
   package spark.ml.cookbook.chapter3
   ```

3. Import the necessary packages

   ```
   import org.apache.spark.sql.SparkSession
   ```

4. Import the packages for setting up logging level for log4j. This step is optional, but we highly recommend it (change the level appropriately as you move through the development cycle).

   ```
   import org.apache.log4j.Logger
   import org.apache.log4j.Level
   ```

5. Set up the logging level to warning and error to cut down on output. See the previous step for package requirements.

   ```
   Logger.getLogger("org").setLevel(Level.ERROR)
   Logger.getLogger("akka").setLevel(Level.ERROR)
   ```

6. Set up the Spark context and application parameter so Spark can run.

   ```
   val spark = SparkSession
   .builder
   .master("local[*]")
   .appName("myRDD")
   .config("Spark.sql.warehouse.dir", ".")
   .getOrCreate()
   ```

7. Set up the data structures and RDD for the example. In this example we create two RDDs from `Array[]` and let Spark decide on the number of partitions (that is, the second parameter in the `parallize()` method is not set).

   ```
   val SignalNoise: Array[Double] =
   Array(0.2,1.2,0.1,0.4,0.3,0.3,0.1,0.3,0.3,0.9,1.8,0.2,3.5,0.5,0.3,0
   .3,0.2,0.4,0.5,0.9,0.1)
   val SignalStrength: Array[Double] =
   Array(6.2,1.2,1.2,6.4,5.5,5.3,4.7,2.4,3.2,9.4,1.8,1.2,3.5,5.5,7.7,9
   .3,1.1,3.1,2.1,4.1,5.1)
   ```

```
val parSN=spark.sparkContext.parallelize(SignalNoise) //
parallelized signal noise RDD
val parSS=spark.sparkContext.parallelize(SignalStrength)  //
parallelized signal strength
```

8. We apply the `zip()` function to the RDDs to demonstrate the transformation. In the example, we take the partitioned RDD of ranges and label them as odd/even using the mod function. We use the `zip()` function to pair elements from the two RDDs (SignalNoiseRDD and SignalStrengthRDD) so we can apply a `map()` function and compute their ratio (noise to signal ratio). We can use this technique to perform almost all types of arithmetic or non-arithmetic operations involving individual members of two RDDs.

9. The pairing of two RDD members act as a tuple or a row. The individual members of the pair created by `zip()` can be accessed by their position (for example, `._1` and `._2`)

```
val zipRDD= parSN.zip(parSS).map(r => r._1 / r._2).collect()
println("zipRDD=")
zipRDD.foreach(println)
```

On running the previous code, you will get the following output:

```
zipRDD=
0.03225806451612903
1.0
0.08333333333333334
0.0625
0.05454545454545454
```

How it works...

In this example, we first set up two arrays representing signal noise and signal strength. They are simply a set of measured numbers that we could have received from the IoT platform. We then proceeded to pair the two separate arrays so each member looks like they have been input originally as a pair of (x, y). We then proceed to divide the pair and produce the noise to signal ratio using the following code snippet:

```
val zipRDD= parSN.zip(parSS).map(r => r._1 / r._2)
```

The `zip()` method has many variations that involve partitions. The developers should familiarize themselves with variations of the `zip()` method with partition (for example, `zipPartitions`).

See also

- Documentation for `zip()` and `zipPartitions()` operations under RDD is available

  at http://spark.apache.org/docs/latest/api/scala/index.html#org.apache.
  spark.api.java.JavaRDD

Join transformation with paired key-value RDDs

In this recipe, we introduce the `KeyValueRDD` pair RDD and the supporting join operations such as `join()`, `leftOuterJoin` and `rightOuterJoin()`, and `fullOuterJoin()` as an alternative to the more traditional and more expensive set operations available via the set operation API, such as `intersection()`, `union()`, `subtraction()`, `distinct()`, `cartesian()`, and so on.

We'll demonstrate `join()`, `leftOuterJoin` and `rightOuterJoin()`, and `fullOuterJoin()`, to explain the power and flexibility of key-value pair RDDs.

```
println("Full Joined RDD = ")
val fullJoinedRDD = keyValueRDD.fullOuterJoin(keyValueCity2RDD)
fullJoinedRDD.collect().foreach(println(_))
```

How to do it...

1. Set up the data structures and RDD for the example:

```
val keyValuePairs =
List(("north",1),("south",2),("east",3),("west",4))
val keyValueCity1 =
List(("north","Madison"),("south","Miami"),("east","NYC"),("west","
SanJose"))
val keyValueCity2 = List(("north","Madison"),("west","SanJose"))
```

2. Turn the List into RDDs:

```
val keyValueRDD = spark.sparkContext.parallelize(keyValuePairs)
val keyValueCity1RDD =
spark.sparkContext.parallelize(keyValueCity1)
val keyValueCity2RDD =
spark.sparkContext.parallelize(keyValueCity2)
```

3. We can access the `keys` and `values` inside a pair RDD.

```
val keys=keyValueRDD.keys
val values=keyValueRDD.values
```

4. We apply the `mapValues()` function to the pair RDDs to demonstrate the transformation. In this example we use the map function to lift up the value by adding 100 to every element. This is a popular technique to introduce noise to the data (that is, jittering).

```
val kvMappedRDD = keyValueRDD.mapValues(_+100)
kvMappedRDD.collect().foreach(println(_))
```

On running the previous code, you will get the following output:

```
(north,101)
(south,102)
(east,103)
(west,104)
```

5. We apply the `join()` function to the RDDs to demonstrate the transformation. We use `join()` to join the two RDDs. We join the two RDDs based on keys (that is, north, south, and so on).

```
println("Joined RDD = ")
val joinedRDD = keyValueRDD.join(keyValueCity1RDD)
joinedRDD.collect().foreach(println(_))
```

On running the previous code, you will get the following output:

```
(south, (2,Miami))
(north, (1,Madison))
(west, (4,SanJose))
(east, (3,NYC))
```

6. We apply the `leftOuterJoin()` function to the RDDs to demonstrate the transformation. The `leftOuterjoin` acts like a relational left outer join. Spark replaces the absence of a membership with `None` rather than `NULL`, which is common in relational systems.

```
println("Left Joined RDD = ")
val leftJoinedRDD = keyValueRDD.leftOuterJoin(keyValueCity2RDD)
leftJoinedRDD.collect().foreach(println(_))
```

On running the previous code, you will get the following output:

```
(south, (2, None))
(north, (1, Some(Madison)))
(west, (4, Some(SanJose)))
(east, (3, None))
```

7. We'll apply `rightOuterJoin()` to the RDDs to demonstrate the transformation. This is similar to a right outer join in relational systems.

```
println("Right Joined RDD = ")
val rightJoinedRDD = keyValueRDD.rightOuterJoin(keyValueCity2RDD)
rightJoinedRDD.collect().foreach(println(_))
```

On running the previous code, you will get the following output:

```
(north, (Some(1), Madison))
(west, (Some(4), SanJose))
```

8. We then apply the `fullOuterJoin()` function to the RDDs to demonstrate the transformation. This is similar to full outer join in relational systems.

```
val fullJoinedRDD = keyValueRDD.fullOuterJoin(keyValueCity2RDD)
fullJoinedRDD.collect().foreach(println(_))
```

On running the previous code, you will get the following output:

```
Full Joined RDD =
(south, (Some(2), None))
(north, (Some(1), Some(Madison)))
(west, (Some(4), Some(SanJose)))
(east, (Some(3), None))
```

How it works...

In this recipe, we declared three lists representing typical data available in relational tables, which could be imported using a connector to Casandra or RedShift (not shown here to simplify the recipe). We used two of the three lists representing city names (that is, data tables) and joined them with the first list, which represents directions (for example, defining tables). The first step is to define three lists of paired values. We then parallelized them into key-value RDDs so we can perform join operations between the first RDD (that is, directions) and the other two RDDs representing city names. We applied the join function to the RDDs to demonstrate the transformation.

We demonstrated `join()`, `leftOuterJoin` and `rightOuterJoin()`, and `fullOuterJoin()` to show the power and flexibility when combined with key-value pair RDDs.

There's more...

Documentation for `join()` and its variations under RDD is available at `http://spark.apache.org/docs/latest/api/scala/index.html#org.apache.spark.api.java.JavaRDD`.

Reduce and grouping transformation with paired key-value RDDs

In this recipe, we explore reduce and group by key. The `reduceByKey()` and `groupbyKey()` operations are much more efficient and preferred to `reduce()` and `groupBy()` in most cases. The functions provide convenient facilities to aggregate values and combine them by key with less shuffling, which is problematic on large data sets.

How to do it...

1. Start a new project in IntelliJ or in an IDE of your choice. Make sure the necessary JAR files are included.

2. Set up the package location where the program will reside

```
package spark.ml.cookbook.chapter3
```

3. Import the necessary packages

```
import org.apache.spark.sql.SparkSession
```

4. Import the packages for setting up logging level for `log4j`. This step is optional, but we highly recommend it (change the level appropriately as you move through the development cycle).

```
import org.apache.log4j.Logger
import org.apache.log4j.Level
```

5. Set up the logging level to warning and error to cut down on output. See the previous step for package requirement:

```
Logger.getLogger("org").setLevel(Level.ERROR)
Logger.getLogger("akka").setLevel(Level.ERROR)
```

6. Set up the Spark context and application parameter so Spark can run.

```
val spark = SparkSession
  .builder
  .master("local[*]")
  .appName("myRDD")
  .config("Spark.sql.warehouse.dir", ".")
  .getOrCreate()
```

7. Set up the data structures and RDD for the example:

```
val signaltypeRDD =
spark.sparkContext.parallelize(List(("Buy",1000),("Sell",500),("Buy
",600),("Sell",800)))
```

8. We apply `groupByKey()` to demonstrate the transformation. In this example, we group all the buy and sell signals together while operating in a distributed setting.

```
val signaltypeRDD =
spark.sparkContext.parallelize(List(("Buy",1000),("Sell",500),("Buy
",600),("Sell",800)))
val groupedRDD = signaltypeRDD.groupByKey()
groupedRDD.collect().foreach(println(_))
```

On running the previous code, you will get the following output:

```
Group By Key RDD =
(Sell, CompactBuffer(500, 800))
(Buy, CompactBuffer(1000, 600))
```

9. We apply the `reduceByKey()` function to the pair of RDDs to demonstrate the transformation. In this example the function is to sum up the total volume for the buy and sell signals. The Scala notation of (`_+_`) simply denotes adding two members at the time and producing a single result from it. Just like `reduce()`, we can apply any function (that is, inline for simple functions and named functions for more complex cases).

```
println("Reduce By Key RDD = ")
val reducedRDD = signaltypeRDD.reduceByKey(_+_)
reducedRDD.collect().foreach(println(_))
```

On running the previous code, you will get the following output:

```
Reduce By Key RDD =
(Sell,1300)
(Buy,1600)
```

How it works...

In this example we declared a list of items as being sold or purchased and their corresponding price (that is, typical commercial transaction). We then proceeded to calculate the sum using Scala shorthand notation (`_+_`). In the last step, we provided the total for each key group (that is, `Buy` or `Sell`). The key-value RDD is a powerful construct that can reduce coding while providing the functionality needed to group paired values into aggregated buckets. The `groupByKey()` and `reduceByKey()` functions mimic the same aggregation functionality, while `reduceByKey()` is more efficient due to less shuffling of the data while final results are being assembled.

See also

Documentation for `groupByKey()` and `reduceByKey()` operations under RDD is available at `http://spark.apache.org/docs/latest/api/scala/index.html#org.apache.spark.api.java.JavaRDD`.

Creating DataFrames from Scala data structures

In this recipe, we explore the `DataFrame` API, which provides a higher level of abstraction than RDDs for working with data. The API is similar to R and Python data frame facilities (pandas).

`DataFrame` simplifies coding and lets you use standard SQL to retrieve and manipulate data. Spark keeps additional information about DataFrames, which helps the API to manipulate the frames with ease. Every `DataFrame` will have a schema (either inferred from data or explicitly defined) which allows us to view the frame like an SQL table. The secret sauce of SparkSQL and DataFrame is that the catalyst optimizer will work behind the scenes to optimize access by rearranging calls in the pipeline.

How to do it...

1. Start a new project in IntelliJ or in an IDE of your choice. Make sure the necessary JAR files are included.

2. Set up the package location where the program will reside:

   ```
   package spark.ml.cookbook.chapter3
   ```

3. Set up the imports related to DataFrames and the required data structures and create the RDDs as needed for the example:

   ```
   import org.apache.spark.sql._
   ```

4. Import the packages for setting up logging level for `log4j`. This step is optional, but we highly recommend it (change the level appropriately as you move through the development cycle).

   ```
   import org.apache.log4j.Logger
   import org.apache.log4j.Level
   ```

5. Set up the logging level to warning and error to cut down on output. See the previous step for package requirement.

   ```
   Logger.getLogger("org").setLevel(Level.ERROR)
   Logger.getLogger("akka").setLevel(Level.ERROR)
   ```

6. Set up the Spark context and application parameter so Spark can run.

```
val spark = SparkSession
  .builder
  .master("local[*]")
  .appName("myDataFrame")
  .config("Spark.sql.warehouse.dir", ".")
  .getOrCreate()
```

7. We set up the Scala data structures as two `List()` objects and a sequence (that is, `Seq()`). We then proceed to turn the `List` structures into RDDs for conversion to `DataFrames` for the next steps:

```
val signaltypeRDD =
spark.sparkContext.parallelize(List(("Buy",1000),("Sell",500),("Buy",600),("Sell",800)))
val numList = List(1,2,3,4,5,6,7,8,9)
val numRDD = spark.sparkContext.parallelize(numList)
val myseq = Seq(
("Sammy","North",113,46.0),("Sumi","South",110,41.0),
("Sunny","East",111,51.0),("Safron","West",113,2.0 ))
```

8. We take a list which is turned into an RDD using the `parallelize()` method and use the `toDF()` method of the RDD to turn it into a DataFrame. The `show()` method allows us to view the DataFrame, which is similar to a SQL table.

```
val numDF = numRDD.toDF("mylist")
numDF.show
```

On running the previous code, you will get the following output.:

```
+------+
|mylist|
+------+
|     1|
|     2|
|     3|
|     4|
|     5|
|     6|
|     7|
|     8|
|     9|
+------+
```

9. In the following code snippet, we take a generic Scala **Seq (Sequence)** data structure and use `createDataFrame()` explicitly to create a DataFrame while naming the columns at the same time.

```
val df1 =
spark.createDataFrame(myseq).toDF("Name","Region","dept","Hours")
```

10. In the next two steps, we use the `show()` method to see the contents and then proceed to use `printscheme()` to show the inferred scheme based on types. In this example, the DataFrame correctly identified the integer and double in the Seq as the valid type for the two columns of numbers.

```
df1.show()
df1.printSchema()
```

On running the previous code, you will get the following output:

```
+------+------+----+-----+
|  Name|Region|dept|Hours|
+------+------+----+-----+
| Sammy| North| 113| 46.0|
|  Sumi| South| 110| 41.0|
| Sunny|  East| 111| 51.0|
|Safron|  West| 113|  2.0|
+------+------+----+-----+

root
|-- Name: string (nullable = true)
|-- Region: string (nullable = true)
|-- dept: integer (nullable = false)
|-- Hours: double (nullable = false)
```

How it works...

In this recipe, we took two lists and a Seq data structure and converted them to DataFrame and used `df1.show()` and `df1.printSchema()` to display contents and schema for the table.

DataFrames can be created from both internal and external sources. Just like SQL tables, the DataFrames have schemas associated with them that can either be inferred or explicitly defined using Scala case classes or the `map()` function to explicitly convert while ingesting the data.

There's more...

To ensure completeness, we include the `import` statement that we used prior to Spark 2.0.0 to run the code (namely, Spark 1.5.2):

```
import org.apache.spark._
import org.apache.spark.rdd.RDD
import org.apache.spark.sql.SQLContext
import org.apache.spark.mllib.linalg
import org.apache.spark.util
import Array._
import org.apache.spark.sql._
import org.apache.spark.sql.types
import org.apache.spark.sql.DataFrame
import org.apache.spark.sql.Row;
import org.apache.spark.sql.types.{ StructType, StructField, StringType};
```

See also

Documentation for DataFrame is available
at `https://spark.apache.org/docs/latest/sql-programming-guide.html`.

If you see any issues with implicit conversion, double check to make sure you have included the implicits import statement.

Example code for Spark 2.0:

```
import sqlContext.implicits
```

Operating on DataFrames programmatically without SQL

In this recipe, we explore how to manipulate DataFrame with code and method calls only (without SQL). The DataFrames have their own methods that allow you to perform SQL-like operations using a programmatic approach. We demonstrate some of these commands such as `select()`, `show()`, and `explain()` to get the point across that the DataFrame itself is capable of wrangling and manipulating the data without using SQL.

How to do it...

1. Start a new project in IntelliJ or in an IDE of your choice. Make sure the necessary JAR files are included.

2. Set up the package location where the program will reside

   ```
   package spark.ml.cookbook.chapter3
   ```

3. Set up the imports related to DataFrames and the required data structures and create the RDDs as needed for the example

   ```
   import org.apache.spark.sql._
   ```

4. Import the packages for setting up logging level for log4j. This step is optional, but we highly recommend it (change the level appropriately as you move through the development cycle).

   ```
   import org.apache.log4j.Logger
   import org.apache.log4j.Level
   ```

5. Set up the logging level to warning and error to cut down on output. See the previous step for package requirement.

   ```
   Logger.getLogger("org").setLevel(Level.ERROR)
   Logger.getLogger("akka").setLevel(Level.ERROR)
   ```

6. Set up the Spark context and application parameter so Spark can run.

   ```
   val spark = SparkSession
     .builder
     .master("local[*]")
     .appName("myDataFrame")
     .config("Spark.sql.warehouse.dir", ".")
     .getOrCreate()
   ```

7. We are creating an RDD from an external source, which is a comma-separated text file:

   ```
   val customersRDD =
   spark.sparkContext.textFile("../data/sparkml2/chapter3/customers13.
   txt") //Customer file
   ```

8. Here is a quick look at what the customer data file would look like

```
Customer data file
1101,susan,nyc,23
1204,adam,chicago,76
1123,joe,london,65
1109,tiffany,chicago,20
```

9. After creating the RDD for the corresponding customer data file, we proceed to explicitly parse and convert the data types using a map() function from the RDD. In this example, we want to make sure the last field (that is, age) is represented as an integer.

```
val custRDD = customersRDD.map {
   line => val cols = line.trim.split(",")
      (cols(0).toInt, cols(1), cols(2), cols(3).toInt)
}
```

10. In the third step, we convert the RDD to a DataFrame using a toDF() call.

```
val custDF = custRDD.toDF("custid","name","city","age")
```

11. Once we have the DataFrame ready, we want to display the contents quickly for visual verification and also print and verify the schema.

```
custDF.show()
custDF.printSchema()
```

On running the previous code, you will get the following output:

```
+------+-------+-------+---+
|custid|   name|   city|age|
+------+-------+-------+---+
|  1101|  susan|    nyc| 23|
|  1204|   adam|chicago| 76|
|  1123|    joe| london| 65|
|  1109|tiffany|chicago| 20|
+------+-------+-------+---+
root
|-- custid: integer (nullable = false)
|-- name: string (nullable = true)
|-- city: string (nullable = true)
|-- age: integer (nullable = false)
```

12. Having the DataFrame ready and inspected, we proceed to demonstrate DataFrame access and manipulation via `show()`, `select()`, `sort()`, `groupBy()`, and `explain()` APIs.

13. We use the `filter()` method to list customers that are more than 25 years old:

```
custDF.filter("age > 25.0").show()
```

On running the previous code, you will get the following output:

```
+------+----+-------+---+
|custid|name|   city|age|
+------+----+-------+---+
|  1204|adam|chicago| 76|
|  1123| joe| london| 65|
+------+----+-------+---+
```

14. We use the `select()` method to display the names of customers.

```
custDF.select("name").show()
```

On running the previous code, you will get the following output.

```
+-------+
|   name|
+-------+
|  susan|
|   adam|
|    joe|
|tiffany|
+-------+
```

15. We use `select()` to list multiple columns:

```
custDF.select("name","city").show()
```

On running the previous code, you will get the following output:

```
+-------+-------+
|   name|   city|
+-------+-------+
|  susan|    nyc|
|   adam|chicago|
|    joe| london|
|tiffany|chicago|
+-------+-------+
```

16. We use an alternative syntax to display and refer to fields within the DataFrame:

```
custDF.select(custDF("name"),custDF("city"),custDF("age")).show()
```

On running the previous code, you will get the following output:

```
+-------+-------+---+
|   name|   city|age|
+-------+-------+---+
|  susan|    nyc| 23|
|   adam|chicago| 76|
|    joe| london| 65|
|tiffany|chicago| 20|
+-------+-------+---+
```

17. Using `select()` and a predicate, to list customers' name and city where the age is less than 50:

```
custDF.select(custDF("name"),custDF("city"),custDF("age")
<50).show()
```

On running the previous code, you will get the following output:

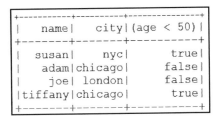

18. We use `sort()` and `groupBy()` to sort and group customers by their city of residence:

```
custDF.sort("city").groupBy("city").count().show()
```

On running the previous code, you will get the following output.

19. We can also ask for a plan of execution: this command will be more relevant with upcoming recipes in which we use SQL to access and manipulate the DataFrame.

```
custDF.explain()
```

On running the previous code, you will get the following output:

```
== Physical Plan ==
TungstenProject [_1#10 AS custid#14,_2#11 AS name#15,_3#12 AS
city#16,_4#13 AS age#17]
  Scan PhysicalRDD[_1#10,_2#11,_3#12,_4#13]
```

How it works...

In this example, we loaded data from a text file into an RDD and then converted it to a DataFrame structure using the `.toDF()` API. We then proceeded to mimic SQL queries using built-in methods such as `select()`, `filter()`, `show()`, and `explain()` that help us to programmatically explore the data (no SQL). The `explain()` command shows the query plan which can be awfully useful to remove the bottleneck.

DataFrames provide multiple approaches to data wrangling.

For those comfortable with the DataFrame API and packages from R (`https://cran.r-project.org`) like dplyr or an older version, we have a programmatic API with an extensive set of methods that lets you do all your data wrangling via the API.

For those more comfortable with SQL, you can simply use SQL to retrieve and manipulate data as if you were using Squirrel or Toad to query the database.

There's more...

To ensure completeness, we include the `import` statements that we used prior to Spark 2.0.0 to run the code (namely, Spark 1.5.2):

```
import org.apache.spark.

import org.apache.spark.rdd.RDD
import org.apache.spark.sql.SQLContext
import org.apache.spark.mllib.linalg._
import org.apache.spark.util._
import Array._
import org.apache.spark.sql._
import org.apache.spark.sql.types._
```

```
import org.apache.spark.sql.DataFrame
import org.apache.spark.sql.Row;
import org.apache.spark.sql.types.{ StructType, StructField, StringType};
```

See also

Documentation for DataFrame is available
at `https://spark.apache.org/docs/latest/sql-programming-guide.html`.

If you see any issues with implicit conversion, double check to make sure you have
included the implicits `import` statement.

Example `import` statement for Spark 2.0:

```
import sqlContext.implicits._
```

Loading DataFrames and setup from an external source

In this recipe, we examine data manipulation using SQL. Spark's approach to provide both
a pragmatic and SQL interface works very well in production settings in which we not only
require machine learning, but also access to existing data sources using SQL to ensure
compatibility and familiarity with existing SQL-based systems. DataFrame with SQL makes
for an elegant process toward integration in real-life settings.

How to do it...

1. Start a new project in IntelliJ or in an IDE of your choice. Make sure the necessary
   JAR files are included.

2. Set up the package location where the program will reside:

   ```
   package spark.ml.cookbook.chapter3
   ```

3. Set up the imports related to DataFrame and the required data structures and
   create the RDDs as needed for the example:

   ```
   import org.apache.spark.sql._
   ```

4. Import the packages for setting up logging level for `log4j`. This step is optional, but we highly recommend it (change the level appropriately as you move through the development cycle).

```
import org.apache.log4j.Logger
import org.apache.log4j.Level
```

5. Set up the logging level to warning and `Error` to cut down on output. See the previous step for package requirement:

```
Logger.getLogger("org").setLevel(Level.ERROR)
Logger.getLogger("akka").setLevel(Level.ERROR)
```

6. Set up the Spark context and application parameter so Spark can run.

```
val spark = SparkSession
 .builder
 .master("local[*]")
 .appName("myDataFrame")
 .config("Spark.sql.warehouse.dir", ".")
 .getOrCreate()
```

7. We create the DataFrame corresponding to the `customer` file. In this step, we first create an RDD and then proceed to use the `toDF()` to convert the RDD to DataFrame and name the columns.

```
val customersRDD =
spark.sparkContext.textFile("../data/sparkml2/chapter3/customers13.
txt") //Customer file


val custRDD = customersRDD.map {
   line => val cols = line.trim.split(",")
      (cols(0).toInt, cols(1), cols(2), cols(3).toInt)
}
val custDF = custRDD.toDF("custid","name","city","age")
```

Customer data contents for reference:

```
custDF.show()
```

On running the preceding code, you will get the following output:

```
+------+-------+-------+---+
|custid|  name|   city|age|
+------+-------+-------+---+
|  1101|  susan|    nyc| 23|
|  1204|   adam|chicago| 76|
|  1123|    joe| london| 65|
|  1109|tiffany|chicago| 20|
+------+-------+-------+---+
```

8. We create the DataFrame corresponding to the `product` file. In this step, we first create an RDD and then proceed to use the `toDF()` to convert the RDD to DataFrame and name the columns.

```
val productsRDD =
spark.sparkContext.textFile("../data/sparkml2/chapter3/products13.t
xt") //Product file
 val prodRDD = productsRDD.map {
     line => val cols = line.trim.split(",")
         (cols(0).toInt, cols(1), cols(2), cols(3).toDouble)
 }
```

9. We convert `prodRDD` to DataFrame:

```
val prodDF =
prodRDD.toDF("prodid","category","dept","priceAdvertised")
```

10. Using SQL select, we display contents of the table.

Product data contents:

```
prodDF.show()
```

On running the previous code, you will get the following output:

```
+------+--------+----+---------------+
|prodid|category|dept|priceAdvertised|
+------+--------+----+---------------+
|    11|    home|   2|          23.55|
|    12|  garden|   5|           11.3|
|    23|    home|   6|          67.34|
|    89|  garden|   2|           3.05|
|   101|ligthing|   3|          21.21|
|    11|    home|   6|           21.0|
|    12|  garden|   5|           66.9|
+------+--------+----+---------------+
```

11. We create the DataFrame corresponding to the `sales` file. In this step we first create an RDD and then proceed to use `toDF()` to convert the RDD to DataFrame and name the columns.

```
val salesRDD =
spark.sparkContext.textFile("../data/sparkml2/chapter3/sales13.txt"
) //Sales file
val saleRDD = salesRDD.map {
    line => val cols = line.trim.split(",")
        (cols(0).toInt, cols(1).toInt, cols(2).toDouble)
}
```

12. We convert the `saleRDD` to DataFrame:

```
val saleDF = saleRDD.toDF("prodid", "custid", "priceSold")
```

13. We use SQL select to display the table.

Sales data contents:

```
saleDF.show()
```

On running the previous code, you will get the following output:

```
+------+------+---------+
|prodid|custid|priceSold|
+------+------+---------+
|    11|  1204|    15.56|
|    12|  1204|     55.0|
|   101|  1109|    21.21|
|    11|  1109|     21.0|
|    89|  1123|     3.05|
|    89|  1204|      3.0|
|    23|  1101|    67.34|
|    23|  1101|    66.34|
+------+------+---------+
```

14. We print schemas for the customer, product, and sales DataFrames to verify schema after column definition and type conversion:

```
custDF.printSchema()
productDF.printSchema()
salesDF. printSchema()
```

On running the previous code, you will get the following output:

```
root
 |-- custid: integer (nullable = false)
 |-- name: string (nullable = true)
 |-- city: string (nullable = true)
 |-- age: integer (nullable = false)
root
 |-- prodid: integer (nullable = false)
 |-- category: string (nullable = true)
 |-- dept: string (nullable = true)
 |-- priceAdvertised: double (nullable = false)
root
 |-- prodid: integer (nullable = false)
 |-- custid: integer (nullable = false)
 |-- priceSold: double (nullable = false)
```

How it works...

In this example, we first loaded data into an RDD and then converted it into a DataFrame using the `toDF()` method. The DataFrame is very good at inferring types, but there are occasions that require manual intervention. We used the `map()` function after creating the RDD (lazy initialization paradigm applies) to massage the data either by type conversion or calling on more complicated user defined functions (referenced in the `map()` method) to do the conversion or data wrangling. Finally, we proceeded to examine the schema for each of the three DataFrames using `show()` and `printSchema()`.

There's more...

To ensure completeness, we include the `import` statements that we used prior to Spark 2.0.0 to run the code (namely, Spark 1.5.2):

```
import org.apache.spark._
import org.apache.spark.rdd.RDD
import org.apache.spark.sql.SQLContext
import org.apache.spark.mllib.linalg._
import org.apache.spark.util._
import Array._
import org.apache.spark.sql._
import org.apache.spark.sql.types._
import org.apache.spark.sql.DataFrame
import org.apache.spark.sql.Row;
import org.apache.spark.sql.types.{ StructType, StructField, StringType};
```

See also

Documentation for DataFrame is available at https://spark.apache.org/docs/latest/sql-programming-guide.html.

If you see any issues with implicit conversion, double check to make sure you have included the implicits `import` statement.

Example `import` statement for Spark 1.5.2:

```
import sqlContext.implicits._
```

Using DataFrames with standard SQL language - SparkSQL

In this recipe, we demonstrate how to use DataFrame SQL capabilities to perform basic CRUD operations, but there is nothing limiting you from using the SQL interface provided by Spark to any level of sophistication (that is, DML) desired.

How to do it...

1. Start a new project in IntelliJ or in an IDE of your choice. Make sure the necessary JAR files are included.

2. Set up the package location where the program will reside

```
package spark.ml.cookbook.chapter3
```

3. Set up the imports related to DataFrames and the required data structures and create the RDDs as needed for the example

```
import org.apache.spark.sql._
```

4. Import the packages for setting up logging level for `log4j`. This step is optional, but we highly recommend it (change the level appropriately as you move through the development cycle).

```
import org.apache.log4j.Logger
import org.apache.log4j.Level
```

5. Set up the logging level to warning and ERROR to cut down on output. See the previous step for package requirement.

```
Logger.getLogger("org").setLevel(Level.ERROR)
Logger.getLogger("akka").setLevel(Level.ERROR)
```

6. Set up the Spark context and application parameter so Spark can run.

```
val spark = SparkSession
 .builder
 .master("local[*]")
 .appName("myDataFrame")
 .config("Spark.sql.warehouse.dir", ".")
 .getOrCreate()
```

7. We will be using the DataFrames created in the previous recipe to demonstrate the SQL capabilities of DataFrames. You can refer to the previous steps for details.

```
a. customerDF with columns: "custid","name","city","age"
b. productDF with Columns:
"prodid","category","dept","priceAdvertised"
c. saleDF with columns:    "prodid", "custid", "priceSold"

val customersRDD =
spark.sparkContext.textFile("../data/sparkml2/chapter3/customers13.
txt") //Customer file

val custRDD = customersRDD.map {
    line => val cols = line.trim.split(",")
       (cols(0).toInt, cols(1), cols(2), cols(3).toInt)
}
val custDF = custRDD.toDF("custid","name","city","age")
val productsRDD =
spark.sparkContext.textFile("../data/sparkml2/chapter3/products13.t
xt") //Product file

val prodRDD = productsRDD.map {
      line => val cols = line.trim.split(",")
         (cols(0).toInt, cols(1), cols(2), cols(3).toDouble)        }

val prodDF =
prodRDD.toDF("prodid","category","dept","priceAdvertised")

val salesRDD =
spark.sparkContext.textFile("../data/sparkml2/chapter3/sales13.txt"
) //Sales file
```

```
val saleRDD = salesRDD.map {
    line => val cols = line.trim.split(",")
        (cols(0).toInt, cols(1).toInt, cols(2).toDouble)
    }
val saleDF = saleRDD.toDF("prodid", "custid", "priceSold")
```

8. Before we can use the DataFrame for queries via SQL, we have to register the DataFrame as a temp table so the SQL statements can refer to it without any Scala/Spark syntax. This step may cause confusion for many beginners as we are not creating any table (temp or permanent), but the call `registerTempTable()` (pre-Spark 2.0) and `createOrReplaceTempView()` (Spark 2.0+) creates a name in SQL land that the SQL statements can refer to without additional UDF or any domain-specific query language. In short, there is additional metadata that is kept by Spark in the background (`registerTempTable()` call), which facilitates querying in the execution phase.

9. Create the `CustDf` DataFrame as a name which SQL statements recognize as `customers`:

    ```
    custDF.createOrReplaceTempView("customers")
    ```

10. Create the `prodDf` DataFrame as a name which SQL statements recognize as `product`:

    ```
    prodDF.createOrReplaceTempView("products")
    ```

11. Create the `saleDf` DataFrame as a name which SQL statements recognize as `sales`:

    ```
    saleDF.createOrReplaceTempView("sales")
    ```

12. Now that everything is ready, let's demonstrate the power of DataFrames with standard SQL. For those who prefer not to work with SQL, the programmatic way is always at your fingertips.

13. In this example we see how to select a column from the customers table (it is not a SQL table underneath, but you can certainly abstract it as such).

    ```
    val query1DF = spark.sql ("select custid, name from customers")
    query1DF.show()
    ```

On running the previous code, you will get the following output.

```
+------+-------+
|custid|   name|
+------+-------+
|  1101|  susan|
|  1204|   adam|
|  1123|    joe|
|  1109|tiffany|
+------+-------+
```

14. Select multiple columns from the customer table:

```
val query2DF = spark.sql("select prodid, priceAdvertised from
products")
 query2DF.show()
```

On running the previous code, you will get the following output.

```
+------+---------------+
|prodid|priceAdvertised|
+------+---------------+
|    11|          23.55|
|    12|           11.3|
|    23|          67.34|
|    89|           3.05|
|   101|          21.21|
|    11|           21.0|
|    12|           66.9|
+------+---------------+
```

15. We print the schema for customer, product, and sales DataFrames to verify it after column definition and type conversion:

```
val query3DF = spark.sql("select sum(priceSold) as totalSold from
sales")
 query3DF.show()
```

On running the previous code, you will get the following output.

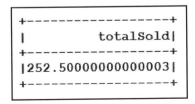

```
+-----------------+
|        totalSold|
+-----------------+
|252.50000000000003|
+-----------------+
```

16. In this example, we join the sales and product tables and list all the customers that have purchased a product at more than 20% discount. This SQL joins the sales and product tables and then uses a simple formula to find products that are sold at a deep discount. To reiterate, the key aspect of DataFrame is that we use standard SQL without any special syntax.

```
val query4DF = spark.sql("select custid, priceSold, priceAdvertised
from sales s, products p where (s.priceSold/p.priceAdvertised <
.80) and p.prodid = s.prodid")
query4DF.show()
```

On running the previous code, you will get the following output.

```
|custid|priceSold|priceAdvertised|
+------+---------+---------------+
|  1204|    15.56|          23.55|
|  1204|    15.56|           21.0|
+------+---------+---------------+
```

We can always use the `explain()` method to examine the physical query plan that Spark SQL used to execute the query.

```
query4DF.explain()
```

On running the previous code, you will get the following output:

```
== Physical Plan ==
TungstenProject [custid#30,priceSold#31,priceAdvertised#25]
 Filter ((priceSold#31 / priceAdvertised#25) < 0.8)
 SortMergeJoin [prodid#29], [prodid#22]
 TungstenSort [prodid#29 ASC], false, 0
 TungstenExchange hashpartitioning(prodid#29)
 TungstenProject [_1#26 AS prodid#29,_2#27 AS custid#30,_3#28 AS
priceSold#31]
 Scan PhysicalRDD[_1#26,_2#27,_3#28]
 TungstenSort [prodid#22 ASC], false, 0
 TungstenExchange hashpartitioning(prodid#22)
 TungstenProject [_4#21 AS priceAdvertised#25,_1#18 AS prodid#22]
 Scan PhysicalRDD[_1#18,_2#19,_3#20,_4#21]
```

How it works...

The basic workflow for DataFrame using SQL is to first populate the DataFrame either through internal Scala data structures or via external data sources first, and then use the `createOrReplaceTempView()` call to register the DataFrame as a SQL-like artifact.

When you use DataFrames, you have the benefit of additional metadata that Spark stores (whether API or SQL approach) which can benefit you during the coding and execution.

While RDDs are still the workhorses of core Spark, the trend is toward the DataFrame approach which has successfully shown its capabilities in languages such as Python/Pandas or R.

There's more...

There has been a change for registration of a DataFrame as a table. Refer to this:

- For versions prior to Spark 2.0.0: `registerTempTable()`
- For Spark version 2.0.0 and previous: `createOrReplaceTempView()`

Pre-Spark 2.0.0 to register a DataFrame as a SQL table like artifact:

Before we can use the DataFrame for queries via SQL, we have to register the DataFrame as a temp table so the SQL statements can refer to it without any Scala/Spark syntax. This step may cause confusion for many beginners as we are not creating any table (temp or permanent), but the call `registerTempTable()` creates a name in SQL land that the SQL statements can refer to without additional UDF or without any domain-specific query language.

- Register the `CustDf` DataFrame as a name which SQL statements recognize as `customers`:

    ```
    custDF.registerTempTable("customers")
    ```

- Register the `prodDf` DataFrame as a name which SQL statements recognize as `product`:

    ```
    custDF.registerTempTable("customers")
    ```

- Register the `saleDf` DataFrame as a name which SQL statements recognize as `sales`:

  ```
  custDF.registerTempTable("customers")
  ```

To ensure completeness, we include the `import` statements that we used prior to Spark 2.0.0 to run the code (namely, Spark 1.5.2):

```
import org.apache.spark._

import org.apache.spark.rdd.RDD
import org.apache.spark.sql.SQLContext
import org.apache.spark.mllib.linalg._
import org.apache.spark.util._
import Array._
import org.apache.spark.sql._
import org.apache.spark.sql.types._
import org.apache.spark.sql.DataFrame
import org.apache.spark.sql.Row;
import org.apache.spark.sql.types.{ StructType, StructField, StringType};
```

See also

Documentation for DataFrame is available at `https://spark.apache.org/docs/latest/sql-programming-guide.html`.

If you see any issues with implicit conversion, please double check to make sure you have included implicits `import` statement.

Example `import` statement for Spark 1.5.2

```
import sqlContext.implicits._
```

DataFrame is an extensive subsystem and deserves an entire book on its own. It makes complex data manipulation at scale available to SQL programmers.

Working with the Dataset API using a Scala Sequence

In this recipe, we examine the new Dataset and how it works with the *seq* Scala data structure. We often see a relationship between the LabelPoint data structure used with ML libraries and a Scala sequence (that is, seq data structure) that play nicely with dataset.

The Dataset is being positioned as a unifying API going forward. It is important to note that DataFrame is still available as an alias described as `Dataset[Row]`. We have covered the SQL examples extensively via DataFrame recipes, so we concentrate our efforts on other variations for dataset.

How to do it...

1. Start a new project in IntelliJ or in an IDE of your choice. Make sure the necessary JAR files are included.

2. Set up the package location where the program will reside

   ```
   package spark.ml.cookbook.chapter3
   ```

3. Import the necessary packages for a Spark session to get access to the cluster and `Log4j.Logger` to reduce the amount of output produced by Spark.

   ```
   import org.apache.log4j.{Level, Logger}
   import org.apache.spark.sql.SparkSession
   ```

4. Define a Scala `case class` to model data for processing, and the `Car` class will represent electric and hybrid cars.

   ```
   case class Car(make: String, model: String, price: Double,
   style: String, kind: String)
   ```

5. Let's create a Scala sequence and populate it with electric and hybrid cars.

   ```
   val carData =
   Seq(
   Car("Tesla", "Model S", 71000.0, "sedan","electric"),
   Car("Audi", "A3 E-Tron", 37900.0, "luxury","hybrid"),
   Car("BMW", "330e", 43700.0, "sedan","hybrid"),
   Car("BMW", "i3", 43300.0, "sedan","electric"),
   Car("BMW", "i8", 137000.0, "coupe","hybrid"),
   ```

```
Car("BMW", "X5 xdrive40e", 64000.0, "suv","hybrid"),
Car("Chevy", "Spark EV", 26000.0, "coupe","electric"),
Car("Chevy", "Volt", 34000.0, "sedan","electric"),
Car("Fiat", "500e", 32600.0, "coupe","electric"),
Car("Ford", "C-Max Energi", 32600.0, "wagon/van","hybrid"),
Car("Ford", "Focus Electric", 29200.0, "sedan","electric"),
Car("Ford", "Fusion Energi", 33900.0, "sedan","electric"),
Car("Hyundai", "Sonata", 35400.0, "sedan","hybrid"),
Car("Kia", "Soul EV", 34500.0, "sedan","electric"),
Car("Mercedes", "B-Class", 42400.0, "sedan","electric"),
Car("Mercedes", "C350", 46400.0, "sedan","hybrid"),
Car("Mercedes", "GLE500e", 67000.0, "suv","hybrid"),
Car("Mitsubishi", "i-MiEV", 23800.0, "sedan","electric"),
Car("Nissan", "LEAF", 29000.0, "sedan","electric"),
Car("Porsche", "Cayenne", 78000.0, "suv","hybrid"),
Car("Porsche", "Panamera S", 93000.0, "sedan","hybrid"),
Car("Tesla", "Model X", 80000.0, "suv","electric"),
Car("Tesla", "Model 3", 35000.0, "sedan","electric"),
Car("Volvo", "XC90 T8", 69000.0, "suv","hybrid"),
Car("Cadillac", "ELR", 76000.0, "coupe","hybrid")
)
```

6. Configure output level to ERROR to reduce Spark's logging output.

```
Logger.getLogger("org").setLevel(Level.ERROR)
Logger.getLogger("akka").setLevel(Level.ERROR)
```

7. Create a SparkSession yielding access to the Spark cluster, including the underlying session object attributes and functions.

```
val spark = SparkSession
.builder
.master("local[*]")
.appName("mydatasetseq")
.config("Spark.sql.warehouse.dir", ".")
.getOrCreate()
```

8. Import Spark implicits, therefore adding in behavior with only an import.

```
import spark.implicits._
```

9. Next, we will create a Dataset from the car data sequence utilizing the Spark session's createDataset() method.

```
val cars = spark.createDataset(MyDatasetData.carData)
// carData is put in a separate scala object MyDatasetData
```

10. Let's print out the results as confirmation that our method invocation transformed the sequence into a Spark Dataset by invoking the show method.

```
infecars.show(false)
+----------+--------------+--------+---------+--------+
|make |model |price |style |kind |
```

```
+---------+--------------+--------+---------+--------+
|Tesla    |Model S       |71000.0 |sedan    |electric|
|Audi     |A3 E-Tron     |37900.0 |luxury   |hybrid  |
|BMW      |330e          |43700.0 |sedan    |hybrid  |
|BMW      |i3            |43300.0 |sedan    |electric|
|BMW      |i8            |137000.0|coupe    |hybrid  |
|BMW      |X5 xdrive40e  |64000.0 |suv      |hybrid  |
|Chevy    |Spark EV      |26000.0 |coupe    |electric|
|Chevy    |Volt          |34000.0 |sedan    |electric|
|Fiat     |500e          |32600.0 |coupe    |electric|
|Ford     |C-Max Energi  |32600.0 |wagon/van|hybrid  |
|Ford     |Focus Electric|29200.0 |sedan    |electric|
|Ford     |Fusion Energi |33900.0 |sedan    |electric|
|Hyundai  |Sonata        |35400.0 |sedan    |hybrid  |
|Kia      |Soul EV       |34500.0 |sedan    |electric|
|Mercedes |B-Class       |42400.0 |sedan    |electric|
|Mercedes |C350          |46400.0 |sedan    |hybrid  |
|Mercedes |GLE500e       |67000.0 |suv      |hybrid  |
|Mitsubishi|i-MiEV       |23800.0 |sedan    |electric|
|Nissan   |LEAF          |29000.0 |sedan    |electric|
|Porsche  |Cayenne       |78000.0 |suv      |hybrid  |
+---------+--------------+--------+---------+--------+
only showing top 20 rows
```

11. Print out the Dataset's implied column names. We can now use class attribute names as column names.

```
cars.columns.foreach(println)
make
model
price
style
kind
```

12. Let's show the automatically generated schema, and validate inferred data types.

```
println(cars.schema)
StructType(StructField(make,StringType,true),
StructField(model,StringType,true),
StructField(price,DoubleType,false),
StructField(style,StringType,true),
StructField(kind,StringType,true))
```

13. Finally, we will filter the Dataset on price referring to the `Car` class attribute price as a column and show results.

```
cars.filter(cars("price") > 50000.00).show()
```

```
+--------+------------+--------+-----+--------+
|    make|       model|   price|style|    kind|
+--------+------------+--------+-----+--------+
|   Tesla|     Model S| 71000.0|sedan|electric|
|     BMW|          i8|137000.0|coupe|  hybrid|
|     BMW|X5 xdrive40e| 64000.0|  suv|  hybrid|
|Mercedes|     GLE500e| 67000.0|  suv|  hybrid|
| Porsche|     Cayenne| 78000.0|  suv|  hybrid|
| Porsche|  Panamera S| 93000.0|sedan|  hybrid|
|   Tesla|     Model X| 80000.0|  suv|electric|
|   Volvo|     XC90 T8| 69000.0|  suv|  hybrid|
|Cadillac|         ELR| 76000.0|coupe|  hybrid|
+--------+------------+--------+-----+--------+
```

14. We close the program by stopping the Spark session.

```
spark.stop()
```

How it works...

In this recipe, we introduced Spark's Dataset feature which first appeared in Spark 1.6 and which was further refined in subsequent releases. First, we created an instance of a Dataset from a Scala sequence with the help of the `createDataset()` method belonging to the Spark session. The next step was to print out meta information about the generated Datatset to establish that the creation transpired as expected. Finally, snippets of Spark SQL were used to filter the Dataset by the price column for any price greater than $50,000.00 and show the final results of execution.

There's more...

Dataset has a view called `DataFrame`, which is a Dataset of `rows` which is untyped. The Datatset still retains all the transformation abilities of RDD such as `filter()`, `map()`, `flatMap()`, and so on. This is one of the reasons we find Datasets easy to use if we have programmed in Spark using RDDs.

See also

- Documentation for Dataset can be found at `http://spark.apache.org/docs/latest/api/scala/index.html#org.apache.spark.sql.Dataset`.
- KeyValue grouped dataset can be found at `http://spark.apache.org/docs/latest/api/scala/index.html#org.apache.spark.sql.KeyValueGroupedDataset`
- Relational grouped dataset can be found at `http://spark.apache.org/docs/latest/api/scala/index.html#org.apache.spark.sql.RelationalGroupedDataset`

Creating and using Datasets from RDDs and back again

In this recipe, we explore how to use RDD and interact with Dataset to build a multi-stage machine learning pipeline. Even though the Dataset (conceptually thought of as RDD with strong type-safety) is the way forward, you still have to be able to interact with other machine learning algorithms or codes that return/operate on RDD for either legacy or coding reasons. In this recipe, we also explore how to create and convert from Dataset to RDD and back.

How to do it...

1. Start a new project in IntelliJ or in an IDE of your choice. Make sure the necessary JAR files are included.

2. Set up the package location where the program will reside:

   ```
   package spark.ml.cookbook.chapter3
   ```

3. Import the necessary packages for Spark session to get access to the cluster and `Log4j.Logger` to reduce the amount of output produced by Spark.

   ```
   import org.apache.log4j.{Level, Logger}
   import org.apache.spark.sql.SparkSession
   ```

4. Define a Scala case class to model data for processing.

```scala
case class Car(make: String, model: String, price: Double,
style: String, kind: String)
```

5. Let's create a Scala sequence and populate it with electric and hybrid cars.

```scala
val carData =
Seq(
Car("Tesla", "Model S", 71000.0, "sedan","electric"),
Car("Audi", "A3 E-Tron", 37900.0, "luxury","hybrid"),
Car("BMW", "330e", 43700.0, "sedan","hybrid"),
Car("BMW", "i3", 43300.0, "sedan","electric"),
Car("BMW", "i8", 137000.0, "coupe","hybrid"),
Car("BMW", "X5 xdrive40e", 64000.0, "suv","hybrid"),
Car("Chevy", "Spark EV", 26000.0, "coupe","electric"),
Car("Chevy", "Volt", 34000.0, "sedan","electric"),
Car("Fiat", "500e", 32600.0, "coupe","electric"),
Car("Ford", "C-Max Energi", 32600.0, "wagon/van","hybrid"),
Car("Ford", "Focus Electric", 29200.0, "sedan","electric"),
Car("Ford", "Fusion Energi", 33900.0, "sedan","electric"),
Car("Hyundai", "Sonata", 35400.0, "sedan","hybrid"),
Car("Kia", "Soul EV", 34500.0, "sedan","electric"),
Car("Mercedes", "B-Class", 42400.0, "sedan","electric"),
Car("Mercedes", "C350", 46400.0, "sedan","hybrid"),
Car("Mercedes", "GLE500e", 67000.0, "suv","hybrid"),
Car("Mitsubishi", "i-MiEV", 23800.0, "sedan","electric"),
Car("Nissan", "LEAF", 29000.0, "sedan","electric"),
Car("Porsche", "Cayenne", 78000.0, "suv","hybrid"),
Car("Porsche", "Panamera S", 93000.0, "sedan","hybrid"),
Car("Tesla", "Model X", 80000.0, "suv","electric"),
Car("Tesla", "Model 3", 35000.0, "sedan","electric"),
Car("Volvo", "XC90 T8", 69000.0, "suv","hybrid"),
Car("Cadillac", "ELR", 76000.0, "coupe","hybrid")
)
```

6. Set output level to ERROR to reduce Spark's logging output.

```scala
Logger.getLogger("org").setLevel(Level.ERROR)
Logger.getLogger("akka").setLevel(Level.ERROR)
```

7. Initialize a Spark session specifying configurations with the builder pattern, thus making an entry point available for the Spark cluster.

```
val spark = SparkSession
.builder
.master("local[*]")
.appName("mydatasetrdd")
.config("Spark.sql.warehouse.dir", ".")
.getOrCreate()
```

8. Next, we retrieve a reference to the Spark context from the Spark session, because we will need it later to generate an RDD.

```
val sc = spark.sparkContext
```

9. Import Spark implicits, therefore adding in behavior with only an import.

```
import spark.implicits._
```

10. Let's make an RDD from the car data sequence.

```
val rdd = spark.makeRDD(MyDatasetData.carData)
```

11. Next, we will create a Dataset from the RDD containing the car data by making use of Spark's session `createDataset()` method.

```
val cars = spark.createDataset(rdd)
```

12. Let's print out the Dataset to validate that creation happened as we would expect via the `show` method.

```
cars.show(false)
```

On running the previous code, you will get the following output.

```
+----------+---------------+--------+---------+--------+
|make      |model          |price   |style    |kind    |
+----------+---------------+--------+---------+--------+
|Tesla     |Model S        |71000.0 |sedan    |electric|
|Audi      |A3 E-Tron      |37900.0 |luxury   |hybrid  |
|BMW       |330e           |43700.0 |sedan    |hybrid  |
|BMW       |i3             |43300.0 |sedan    |electric|
|BMW       |i8             |137000.0|coupe    |hybrid  |
|BMW       |X5 xdrive40e   |64000.0 |suv      |hybrid  |
|Chevy     |Spark EV       |26000.0 |coupe    |electric|
|Chevy     |Volt           |34000.0 |sedan    |electric|
|Fiat      |500e           |32600.0 |coupe    |electric|
|Ford      |C-Max Energi   |32600.0 |wagon/van|hybrid  |
|Ford      |Focus Electric |29200.0 |sedan    |electric|
|Ford      |Fusion Energi  |33900.0 |sedan    |electric|
|Hyundai   |Sonata         |35400.0 |sedan    |hybrid  |
|Kia       |Soul EV        |34500.0 |sedan    |electric|
|Mercedes  |B-Class        |42400.0 |sedan    |electric|
|Mercedes  |C350           |46400.0 |sedan    |hybrid  |
|Mercedes  |GLE500e        |67000.0 |suv      |hybrid  |
|Mitsubishi|i-MiEV         |23800.0 |sedan    |electric|
|Nissan    |LEAF           |29000.0 |sedan    |electric|
|Porsche   |Cayenne        |78000.0 |suv      |hybrid  |
+----------+---------------+--------+---------+--------+
only showing top 20 rows
```

13. Next, we will print out the implied column names.

```
cars.columns.foreach(println)
make
model
price
style
kind
```

14. Let's show the automatically generated schema, and validate that the inferred data types are correct.

```
println(cars.schema)
StructType(StructField(make,StringType,true),
StructField(model,StringType,true),
StructField(price,DoubleType,false),
StructField(style,StringType,true),
StructField(kind,StringType,true))
```

15. Now, let's group the Dataset by make, and count the number of makes in our dataset.

```
cars.groupBy("make").count().show()
```

On running the previous code, you will get the following output.

16. The next step will use Spark's SQL on the Dataset, filtering by make for the value of Tesla, and transforming the resulting Dataset back into an RDD.

```
val carRDD = cars.where("make = 'Tesla'").rdd
Car(Tesla,Model X,80000.0,suv,electric)
Car(Tesla,Model 3,35000.0,sedan,electric)
Car(Tesla,Model S,71000.0,sedan,electric)
```

17. Finally, display the contents of the RDD, taking advantage of the foreach() method.

```
carRDD.foreach(println)
Car(Tesla,Model X,80000.0,suv,electric)
Car(Tesla,Model 3,35000.0,sedan,electric)
Car(Tesla,Model S,71000.0,sedan,electric)
```

18. We close the program by stopping the Spark session.

```
spark.stop()
```

How it works...

In this section, we transformed an RDD into a Dataset and finally transformed it back to an RDD. We began with a Scala sequence which was changed into an RDD. After the creation of the RDD, invocation of Spark's session createDataset() method occurred, passing the RDD as an argument while receiving a Dataset as the result.

Next, the Dataset was grouped by the make column, counting the existence of various makes of cars. The next step involved filtering the Dataset for makes of Tesla and transforming the results back to an RDD. Finally, we displayed the resulting RDD by way of the RDD `foreach()` method.

There's more...

The Dataset source file in Spark is only about 2500+ lines of Scala code. It is a very nice piece of code which can be leveraged for specialization under Apache license. We list the following URL and encourage you to at least scan the file and understand how buffering comes into play when using Dataset.

Source code for Datasets hosted on GitHub is available at `https://github.com/apache/spark/blob/master/sql/core/src/main/scala/org/apache/e/spark/sql/Dataset.scala`.

See also

- Documentation for Dataset can be found at `http://spark.apache.org/docs/latest/api/scala/index.html#org.apache.spark.sql.Dataset`
- KeyValue grouped Dataset can be found at `http://spark.apache.org/docs/latest/api/scala/index.html#org.apache.spark.sql.KeyValueGroupedDataset`
- Relational grouped Dataset can be found at `http://spark.apache.org/docs/latest/api/scala/index.html#org.apache.spark.sql.RelationalGroupedDataset`

Working with JSON using the Dataset API and SQL together

In this recipe, we explore how to use JSON with Dataset. The JSON format has rapidly become the de-facto standard for data interoperability in the last 5 years.

We explore how Dataset uses JSON and executes API commands like `select()`. We then progress by creating a view (that is, `createOrReplaceTempView()`) and then execute a SQL query to demonstrate how to query against a JSON file using API and SQL with ease.

How to do it...

1. Start a new project in IntelliJ or in an IDE of your choice. Make sure the necessary JAR files are included.

2. We will use a JSON data file named `cars.json` which has been created for this example:

```
{"make": "Telsa", "model": "Model S", "price": 71000.00, "style":
"sedan", "kind": "electric"}
{"make": "Audi", "model": "A3 E-Tron", "price": 37900.00, "style":
"luxury", "kind": "hybrid"}
{"make": "BMW", "model": "330e", "price": 43700.00, "style":
"sedan", "kind": "hybrid"}
```

3. Set up the package location where the program will reside

```
package spark.ml.cookbook.chapter3
```

4. Import the necessary packages for the Spark session to gain access to the cluster and `Log4j.Logger` to reduce the amount of output produced by Spark.

```
import org.apache.log4j.{Level, Logger}
import org.apache.spark.sql.SparkSession
```

5. Define a Scala `case class` to model data for processing.

```
case class Car(make: String, model: String, price: Double,
style: String, kind: String)
```

6. Set output level to ERROR to reduce Spark's logging output.

```
Logger.getLogger("org").setLevel(Level.ERROR)
Logger.getLogger("akka").setLevel(Level.ERROR)
```

7. Initialize a Spark session creating an entry point for access to the Spark cluster.

```
val spark = SparkSession
.builder
.master("local[*]")
.appName("mydatasmydatasetjsonetrdd")
.config("Spark.sql.warehouse.dir", ".")
.getOrCreate()
```

8. Import Spark implicits, therefore adding in behavior with only an import.

```
import spark.implicits._
```

9. Now, we will load the JSON data file into memory, specifying the class type as `Car`.

```
val cars =
spark.read.json("../data/sparkml2/chapter3/cars.json").as[Car]
```

10. Let's print out the data from our generated Dataset of type `Car`.

```
cars.show(false)
```

```
+--------+---------+--------------+--------+---------+
|kind    |make     |model         |price   |style    |
+--------+---------+--------------+--------+---------+
|electric|Telsa    |Model S       |71000.0 |sedan    |
|hybrid  |Audi     |A3 E-Tron     |37900.0 |luxury   |
|hybrid  |BMW      |330e          |43700.0 |sedan    |
|electric|BMW      |i3            |43300.0 |sedan    |
|hybrid  |BMW      |i8            |137000.0|coupe    |
|hybrid  |BMW      |X5 xdrive40e  |64000.0 |suv      |
|electric|Chevy    |Spark EV      |26000.0 |coupe    |
|electric|Chevy    |Volt          |34000.0 |sedan    |
|electric|Fiat     |500e          |32600.0 |coupe    |
|hybrid  |Ford     |C-Max Energi  |32600.0 |wagon/van|
|electric|Ford     |Focus Electric|29200.0 |sedan    |
|electric|Ford     |Fusion Energi |33900.0 |sedan    |
|hybrid  |Hyundai  |Sonata        |35400.0 |sedan    |
|electric|Kia      |Soul EV       |34500.0 |sedan    |
|electric|Mercedes |B-Class       |42400.0 |sedan    |
|hybrid  |Mercedes |C350          |46400.0 |sedan    |
|hybrid  |Mercedes |GLE500e       |67000.0 |suv      |
|electric|Mitsubishi|i-MiEV       |23800.0 |sedan    |
|electric|Nissan   |LEAF          |29000.0 |sedan    |
|hybrid  |Porsche  |Cayenne       |78000.0 |suv      |
+--------+---------+--------------+--------+---------+
only showing top 20 rows
```

11. Next, we will display column names of the Dataset to verify that the cars' JSON attribute names were processed correctly.

```
cars.columns.foreach(println)
make
model
price
style
kind
```

12. Let's see the automatically generated schema and validate the inferred data types.

```
println(cars.schema)
StructType(StructField(make,StringType,true),
StructField(model,StringType,true),
StructField(price,DoubleType,false),
StructField(style,StringType,true),
StructField(kind,StringType,true))
```

13. In this step, we will select the Dataset's `make` column, removing duplicates by applying the `distinct` method and showing the results.

```
cars.select("make").distinct().show()
```

```
+----------+
|      make|
+----------+
|Mitsubishi|
|       Kia|
|      Volvo|
|    Hyundai|
|      Audi|
|   Cadillac|
|   Mercedes|
|      Tesla|
|       BMW|
|      Telsa|
|      Chevy|
|    Porsche|
|     Nissan|
|       Fiat|
|       Ford|
+----------+
```

14. Next, create a view on the cars Dataset so we can execute a literal Spark SQL query string against the dataset.

```
cars.createOrReplaceTempView("cars")
```

15. Finally, we execute a Spark SQL query filtering the Dataset for electric cars, and returning only three of the defined columns.

```
spark.sql("select make, model, kind from cars where kind =
'electric'").show()
```

```
+----------+--------------+--------+
|     make |        model |  kind  |
+----------+--------------+--------+
|    Telsa |      Model S |electric|
|      BMW |           i3 |electric|
|    Chevy |     Spark EV |electric|
|    Chevy |         Volt |electric|
|     Fiat |         500e |electric|
|     Ford |Focus Electric|electric|
|     Ford | Fusion Energi|electric|
|      Kia |      Soul EV |electric|
|  Mercedes|      B-Class |electric|
|Mitsubishi|        i-MiEV|electric|
|   Nissan |         LEAF |electric|
|    Tesla |      Model X |electric|
|    Tesla |      Model 3 |electric|
+----------+--------------+--------+
```

16. We close the program by stopping the Spark session.

```
spark.stop()
```

How it works...

It is extremely straightforward to read a **JavaScript Object Notation (JSON)** data file and to transform it into a Dataset with Spark. JSON has become a widely used data format over the past several years and Spark's support for the format is substantial.

In the first part, we demonstrated loading JSON into a Dataset by means of built in JSON parsing functionality in Spark's session. You should take note of Spark's built-in functionality that transforms the JSON data into the car case class.

In the second part, we demonstrated Spark SQL being applied on the Dataset to wrangle the said data into a desirable state. We utilized the Dataset's select method to retrieve the `make` column and apply the `distinct` method for the removal of duplicates. Next, we set up a view on the cars Dataset, so we can apply SQL queries against it. Finally, we used the session's SQL method to execute a literal SQL query string against the Dataset, retrieving any items which are of kind electric.

There's more...

To fully understand and master the Dataset API, be sure to understand the concept of `Row` and `Encoder`.

Datasets follow the *lazy execution* paradigm, meaning that execution only occurs by invoking actions in Spark. When we execute an action, the Catalyst query optimizer produces a logical plan and generates a physical plan for optimized execution in a parallel distributed manner. See the figure in the introduction for all the detailed steps.

Documentation for `Row` is available
at `http://spark.apache.org/docs/latest/api/scala/index.html#org.apache.spark.sql.Dataset`

Documentation for `Encoder` is available
at `http://spark.apache.org/docs/latest/api/scala/index.html#org.apache.spark.sql.Encoder`

See also

- Documentation for Dataset is available
  at `http://spark.apache.org/docs/latest/api/scala/index.html#org.apache.spark.sql.Dataset`
- Documentation for KeyValue grouped Dataset is available
  at `http://spark.apache.org/docs/latest/api/scala/index.html#org.apache.spark.sql.KeyValueGroupedDataset`
- Documentation for relational grouped
  Dataset `http://spark.apache.org/docs/latest/api/scala/index.html#org.apache.spark.sql.RelationalGroupedDataset`

Again, be sure to download and explore the Dataset source file, which is about 2500+ lines from GitHub. Exploring the Spark source code is the best way to learn advanced programming in Scala, Scala Annotations, and Spark 2.0 itself.

Noteworthy for Pre-Spark 2.0 users:

- SparkSession is the single entry point into the system. SQLContext and HiveContext are replaced by SparkSession.
- For Java users, be sure to replace DataFrame with `Dataset<Row>`.
- Use the new catalog interface via SparkSession to execute `cacheTable()`, `dropTempView()`, `createExternalTable()`, and `ListTable()`, and so on.

- DataFrame and DataSet API
  - `unionALL()` is deprecated and you should now use `union()` instead.
  - `explode()` should be replaced by `functions.explode()` plus `select()` or `flatMap()`
  - `registerTempTable` has been deprecated and replaced by `createOrReplaceTempView()`
- The `Dataset()` API source code (that is, `Dataset.scala`) can be found via GitHub at `https://github.com/apache/spark/blob/master/sql/core/src/main/scala/org/apache/spark/sql/Dataset.scala`

Functional programming with the Dataset API using domain objects

In this recipe, we explore how functional programming works with Dataset. We use the Dataset and functional programming to separate the cars (domain object) by their models.

How to do it...

1. Start a new project in IntelliJ or in an IDE of your choice. Make sure the necessary JAR files are included.

2. Use package instruction to provide the right path

   ```
   package spark.ml.cookbook.chapter3
   ```

3. Import the necessary packages for Spark context to get access to the cluster and `Log4j.Logger` to reduce the amount of output produced by Spark.

   ```
   import org.apache.log4j.{Level, Logger}
   import org.apache.spark.sql.{Dataset, SparkSession}
   import spark.ml.cookbook.{Car, mydatasetdata}
   import scala.collection.mutable
   import scala.collection.mutable.ListBuffer
   import org.apache.log4j.{Level, Logger}
   import org.apache.spark.sql.SparkSession
   ```

4. Define a Scala case to contain our data for processing, and our car class will represent electric and hybrid cars.

```scala
case class Car(make: String, model: String, price: Double,
style: String, kind: String)
```

5. Let's create a `Seq` populated with electric and hybrid cars.

```scala
val carData =
Seq(
Car("Tesla", "Model S", 71000.0, "sedan","electric"),
Car("Audi", "A3 E-Tron", 37900.0, "luxury","hybrid"),
Car("BMW", "330e", 43700.0, "sedan","hybrid"),
Car("BMW", "i3", 43300.0, "sedan","electric"),
Car("BMW", "i8", 137000.0, "coupe","hybrid"),
Car("BMW", "X5 xdrive40e", 64000.0, "suv","hybrid"),
Car("Chevy", "Spark EV", 26000.0, "coupe","electric"),
Car("Chevy", "Volt", 34000.0, "sedan","electric"),
Car("Fiat", "500e", 32600.0, "coupe","electric"),
Car("Ford", "C-Max Energi", 32600.0, "wagon/van","hybrid"),
Car("Ford", "Focus Electric", 29200.0, "sedan","electric"),
Car("Ford", "Fusion Energi", 33900.0, "sedan","electric"),
Car("Hyundai", "Sonata", 35400.0, "sedan","hybrid"),
Car("Kia", "Soul EV", 34500.0, "sedan","electric"),
Car("Mercedes", "B-Class", 42400.0, "sedan","electric"),
Car("Mercedes", "C350", 46400.0, "sedan","hybrid"),
Car("Mercedes", "GLE500e", 67000.0, "suv","hybrid"),
Car("Mitsubishi", "i-MiEV", 23800.0, "sedan","electric"),
Car("Nissan", "LEAF", 29000.0, "sedan","electric"),
Car("Porsche", "Cayenne", 78000.0, "suv","hybrid"),
Car("Porsche", "Panamera S", 93000.0, "sedan","hybrid"),
Car("Tesla", "Model X", 80000.0, "suv","electric"),
Car("Tesla", "Model 3", 35000.0, "sedan","electric"),
Car("Volvo", "XC90 T8", 69000.0, "suv","hybrid"),
Car("Cadillac", "ELR", 76000.0, "coupe","hybrid")
)
```

6. Set output level to ERROR to reduce Spark's output.

```scala
Logger.getLogger("org").setLevel(Level.ERROR)
Logger.getLogger("akka").setLevel(Level.ERROR)
```

7. Create a SparkSession yielding access to the Spark cluster and underlying session object attributes such as the SparkContext and SparkSQLContext.

```
val spark = SparkSession
.builder
.master("local[*]")
.appName("mydatasetseq")
.config("spark.sql.warehouse.dir", ".")
.getOrCreate()
```

8. Import spark implicits, therefore adding in behavior with only an import.

```
import spark.implicits._
```

9. Now we will create a Dataset from the car data Seq utilizing the SparkSessions's `createDataset()` function.

```
val cars = spark.createDataset(MyDatasetData.carData)
```

10. Display the Dataset to understand how to transform data in subsequent steps.

```
cars.show(false)
```

On running the previous code, you will get the following output.

```
+---------+--------------+--------+---------+--------+
|make     |model         |price   |style    |kind    |
+---------+--------------+--------+---------+--------+
|Tesla    |Model S       |71000.0 |sedan    |electric|
|Audi     |A3 E-Tron     |37900.0 |luxury   |hybrid  |
|BMW      |330e          |43700.0 |sedan    |hybrid  |
|BMW      |i3            |43300.0 |sedan    |electric|
|BMW      |i8            |137000.0|coupe    |hybrid  |
|BMW      |X5 xdrive40e  |64000.0 |suv      |hybrid  |
|Chevy    |Spark EV      |26000.0 |coupe    |electric|
|Chevy    |Volt          |34000.0 |sedan    |electric|
|Fiat     |500e          |32600.0 |coupe    |electric|
|Ford     |C-Max Energi  |32600.0 |wagon/van|hybrid  |
|Ford     |Focus Electric|29200.0 |sedan    |electric|
|Ford     |Fusion Energi |33900.0 |sedan    |electric|
|Hyundai  |Sonata        |35400.0 |sedan    |hybrid  |
|Kia      |Soul EV       |34500.0 |sedan    |electric|
|Mercedes |B-Class       |42400.0 |sedan    |electric|
|Mercedes |C350          |46400.0 |sedan    |hybrid  |
|Mercedes |GLE500e       |67000.0 |suv      |hybrid  |
|Mitsubishi|i-MiEV       |23800.0 |sedan    |electric|
|Nissan   |LEAF          |29000.0 |sedan    |electric|
|Porsche  |Cayenne       |78000.0 |suv      |hybrid  |
+---------+--------------+--------+---------+--------+
only showing top 20 rows
```

11. Now we construct a functional sequence of steps to transform the original Dataset into data grouped by make with all various models attached.

```
val modelData = cars.groupByKey(_.make).mapGroups({
case (make, car) => {
val carModel = new ListBuffer[String]()
            car.map(_.model).foreach({
                c =>  carModel += c
          })
          (make, carModel)
        }
    })
```

12. Let's display results from our previous sequence of functional logic for validation.

```
modelData.show(false)
```

On running the previous code, you will get the following output.

```
+----------+-----------------------------------------------+
|_1        |_2                                             |
+----------+-----------------------------------------------+
|Mitsubishi|[i-MiEV]                                       |
|Kia       |[Soul EV]                                      |
|Volvo     |[XC90 T8]                                      |
|Hyundai   |[Sonata]                                       |
|Audi      |[A3 E-Tron]                                    |
|Cadillac  |[ELR]                                          |
|Mercedes  |[B-Class, C350, GLE500e]                       |
|Tesla     |[Model S, Model X, Model 3]                    |
|BMW       |[330e, i3, i8, X5 xdrive40e]                   |
|Chevy     |[Spark EV, Volt]                               |
|Porsche   |[Cayenne, Panamera S]                          |
|Nissan    |[LEAF]                                         |
|Fiat      |[500e]                                         |
|Ford      |[C-Max Energi, Focus Electric, Fusion Energi]  |
+----------+-----------------------------------------------+
```

13. We close the program by stopping the Spark session.

```
spark.stop()
```

How it works...

In this example, we use a Scala sequence data structure to hold the original data, which is a series of cars and their attributes. Using `createDataset()`, we create a DataSet and populate it. We then proceed to use the 'make' attribute with `groupBy` and `mapGroups()` to list cars by their models using a functional paradigm with DataSet. Using this form of functional programming with domain objects was not impossible before DataSet (for example, the case class with RDD or UDF with DataFrame), but the DataSet construct makes this easy and intrinsic.

There's more...

Be sure to include the `implicits` statement in all your DataSet coding:

```
import spark.implicits._
```

See also

The documentation for Datasets can be accessed at `http://spark.apache.org/docs/latest/api/scala/index.html#org.apache.spark.sql.Dataset`.

4
Common Recipes for Implementing a Robust Machine Learning System

In this chapter, we will cover:

- Spark's basic statistical API to help you build your own algorithms
- ML pipelines for real-life machine learning applications
- Normalizing data with Spark
- Splitting data for training and testing
- Common operations with the new Dataset API
- Creating and using RDD versus DataFrame versus Dataset from a text file in Spark 2.0
- LabeledPoint data structure for Spark ML
- Getting access to Spark cluster in Spark 2.0+
- Getting access to Spark cluster pre-Spark 2.0
- Getting access to SparkContext vis-a-vis SparkSession object in Spark 2.0
- New model export and PMML markup in Spark 2.0
- Regression model evaluation using Spark 2.0
- Binary classification model evaluation using Spark 2.0
- Multilabel classification model evaluation using Spark 2.0
- Multiclass classification model evaluation using Spark 2.0
- Using the Scala Breeze library to do graphics in Spark 2.0

Introduction

In every line of business ranging from running a small business to creating and managing a mission critical application, there are a number of tasks that are common and need to be included as a part of almost every workflow that is required during the course of executing the functions. This is true even for building robust machine learning systems. In Spark machine learning, some of these tasks range from splitting the data for model development (train, test, validate) to normalizing input feature vector data to creating ML pipelines via the Spark API. We provide a set of recipes in this chapter to enable the reader to think about what is actually required to implement an end-to-end machine learning system.

This chapter attempts to demonstrate a number of common tasks which are present in any robust Spark machine learning system implementation. To avoid redundant references these common tasks in every recipe covered in this book, we have factored out such common tasks as short recipes in this chapter, which can be leveraged as needed while reading the other chapters. These recipes can either stand alone or be included as pipeline subtasks in a larger system. Please note that these common recipes are emphasized in the larger context of machine learning algorithms in later chapters, while also including them as independent recipes in this chapter for completeness.

Spark's basic statistical API to help you build your own algorithms

In this recipe, we cover Spark's multivariate statistical summary (that is, *Statistics.colStats*) such as correlation, stratified sampling, hypothesis testing, random data generation, kernel density estimators, and much more, which can be applied to extremely large datasets while taking advantage of both parallelism and resiliency via RDDs.

How to do it...

1. Start a new project in IntelliJ or in an IDE of your choice. Make sure that the necessary JAR files are included.

2. Set up the package location where the program will reside:

```
package spark.ml.cookbook.chapter4
```

3. Import the necessary packages for the Spark session to gain access to the cluster and `log4j.Logger` to reduce the amount of output produced by Spark:

```
import org.apache.spark.mllib.linalg.Vectors
import org.apache.spark.mllib.stat.Statistics
import org.apache.spark.sql.SparkSession
import org.apache.log4j.Logger
import org.apache.log4j.Level
```

4. Set the output level to ERROR to reduce Spark's logging output:

```
Logger.getLogger("org").setLevel(Level.ERROR)
Logger.getLogger("akka").setLevel(Level.ERROR)
```

5. Initialize a Spark session specifying configurations with the builder pattern, thus making an entry point available for the Spark cluster:

```
val spark = SparkSession
.builder
.master("local[*]")
.appName("Summary Statistics")
.config("spark.sql.warehouse.dir", ".")
.getOrCreate()
```

6. Let's retrieve the Spark session underlying the SparkContext to use when generating RDDs:

```
val sc = spark.sparkContext
```

7. Now we create a RDD with the handcrafted data to illustrate usage of summary statistics:

```
val rdd = sc.parallelize(
  Seq(
    Vectors.dense(0, 1, 0),
    Vectors.dense(1.0, 10.0, 100.0),
    Vectors.dense(3.0, 30.0, 300.0),
    Vectors.dense(5.0, 50.0, 500.0),
    Vectors.dense(7.0, 70.0, 700.0),
    Vectors.dense(9.0, 90.0, 900.0),
    Vectors.dense(11.0, 110.0, 1100.0)
  )
)
```

8. We use Spark's statistics objects by invoking the method `colStats()` and passing the RDD as an argument:

```
val summary = Statistics.colStats(rdd)
```

The `colStats()` method will return a `MultivariateStatisticalSummary`, which contains the computed summary statistics:

```
println("mean:" + summary.mean)
println("variance:" +summary.variance)
println("none zero" + summary.numNonzeros)
println("min:" + summary.min)
println("max:" + summary.max)
println("count:" + summary.count)
mean:[5.142857142857142,51.57142857142857,514.2857142857142]
variance:[16.80952380952381,1663.952380952381,168095.2380952381]
none zero[6.0,7.0,6.0]
min:[0.0,1.0,0.0]
max:[11.0,110.0,1100.0]
count:7
```

9. We close the program by stopping the Spark session:

```
spark.stop()
```

How it works...

We created an RDD from dense vector data followed by the generation of summary statistics on it using the statistics object. Once the `colStats()` method returned, we retrieved summary statistics such as the mean, variance, minimum, maximum, and so on.

There's more...

It cannot be emphasized enough how efficient the statistical API is on large datasets. These APIs will provide you with basic elements to implement any statistical learning algorithm from scratch. Based on our research and experience with half versus full matrix factorization, we encourage you to first read the source code and make sure that there isn't an equivalent functionality already implemented in Spark before implementing your own.

While we only demonstrate a basic statistics summary here, Spark comes equipped out of the box with:

- Correlation: `Statistics.corr(seriesX, seriesY, "type of correlation")`:
  - Pearson (default)
  - Spearman
- Stratified sampling - RDD API:
  - With a replacement RDD
  - Without a replacement - requires an additional pass
- Hypothesis testing:
  - Vector - `Statistics.chiSqTest( vector )`
  - Matrix - `Statistics.chiSqTest( dense matrix )`
- **Kolmogorov-Smirnov (KS)** test for equality - one or two-sided:
  - `Statistics.kolmogorovSmirnovTest(RDD, "norm", 0, 1)`
- Random data generator - `normalRDD()`:
  - Normal - can specify a parameter
  - Lots of option plus `map()`s to generate any distribution
- Kernel density estimator - `KernelDensity().estimate( data )`

A quick reference to the *Goodness of fit* concept in statistics can be found at `https://en.wikipedia.org/wiki/Goodness_of_fit` link.

See also

Documentation for more multivariate statistical summary:

- `https://spark.apache.org/docs/latest/api/scala/index.html#org.apache.spark.mllib.stat.MultivariateStatisticalSummary`

ML pipelines for real-life machine learning applications

This is the first of two recipes which cover the ML pipeline in Spark 2.0. For a more advanced treatment of ML pipelines with additional details such as API calls and parameter extraction, see later chapters in this book.

In this recipe, we attempt to have a single pipeline that can tokenize text, use HashingTF (an old trick) to map term frequencies, run a regression to fit a model, and then predict which group a new term belongs to (for example, news filtering, gesture classification, and so on).

How to do it...

1. Start a new project in IntelliJ or in an IDE of your choice. Make sure that the necessary JAR files are included.

2. Set up the package location where the program will reside:

   ```
   package spark.ml.cookbook.chapter4
   ```

3. Import the necessary packages for the Spark session to gain access to the cluster and `log4j.Logger` to reduce the amount of output produced by Spark:

   ```
   import org.apache.spark.ml.Pipeline
   import org.apache.spark.ml.classification.LogisticRegression
   import org.apache.spark.ml.feature.{HashingTF, Tokenizer}
   import org.apache.spark.sql.SparkSession
   import org.apache.log4j.{Level, Logger}
   ```

4. Set the output level to ERROR to reduce Spark's logging output:

   ```
   Logger.getLogger("org").setLevel(Level.ERROR)
   Logger.getLogger("akka").setLevel(Level.ERROR)
   ```

5. Initialize a Spark session specifying configurations with the builder pattern, thus making an entry point available for the Spark cluster:

   ```
   val spark = SparkSession
   .builder
   .master("local[*]")
   .appName("My Pipeline")
   .config("spark.sql.warehouse.dir", ".")
   .getOrCreate()
   ```

6. Let's create a training set DataFrame with several random text documents:

```
val trainset = spark.createDataFrame(Seq(
  (1L, 1, "spark rocks"),
  (2L, 0, "flink is the best"),
  (3L, 1, "Spark rules"),
  (4L, 0, "mapreduce forever"),
  (5L, 0, "Kafka is great")
)).toDF("id", "label", "words")
```

7. Create a tokenizer to parse the text documents into individual terms:

```
val tokenizer = new Tokenizer()
  .setInputCol("words")
  .setOutputCol("tokens")
```

8. Create a HashingTF for transforming terms into feature vectors:

```
val hashingTF = new HashingTF()
  .setNumFeatures(1000)
  .setInputCol(tokenizer.getOutputCol)
  .setOutputCol("features")
```

9. Create a logistic regression class to generate a model to predict which group a new text document belongs to:

```
val lr = new LogisticRegression()
  .setMaxIter(15)
  .setRegParam(0.01)
```

10. Next, we construct a data pipeline with an array of three stages:

```
val pipeline = new Pipeline()
  .setStages(Array(tokenizer, hashingTF, lr))
```

11. Now, we train the model so we can make predictions later:

```
val model = pipeline.fit(trainset)
```

12. Let's create a test dataset to validate our trained model:

```
val testSet = spark.createDataFrame(Seq(
  (10L, 1, "use spark please"),
  (11L, 2, "Kafka")
)).toDF("id", "label", "words")
```

13. Finally, we transform the test set using the trained model, generating predictions:

```
model.transform(testSet).select("probability",
"prediction").show(false)
```

```
+------------------------------------------+----------+
|probability                               |prediction|
+------------------------------------------+----------+
|[0.1188495343876135,0.8811504656123865]   |1.0       |
|[0.6377057793949985,0.36229422060500155]  |0.0       |
+------------------------------------------+----------+
```

14. We close the program by stopping the Spark session:

```
spark.stop()
```

How it works...

In this section, we investigated constructing a simple machine learning pipeline with Spark. We began with creating a DataFrame comprised of two groups of text documents and then proceeded to set up a pipeline.

First, we created a tokenizer to parse text documents into terms followed by the creation of the HashingTF to convert the terms into features. Then, we created a logistic regression object to predict which group a new text document belongs to.

Second, we constructed the pipeline by passing an array of arguments to it, specifying three stages of execution. You will notice each subsequent stage provides the result as a specified column, while using the previous stage's output column as the input.

Finally, we trained the model by invoking `fit()` on the pipeline object and defining a set of test data for verification. Next, we transformed the test set with the model, producing which of the defined two groups the text documents in the test set belong to.

There's more...

The pipeline in Spark ML was inspired by scikit-learn in Python, which is referenced here for completeness:

```
http://scikit-learn.org/stable/
```

ML pipelines make it easy to combine multiple algorithms used to implement a production task in Spark. It would be unusual to see a use case in a real-life situation that is made of a single algorithm. Often a number of cooperating ML algorithms work together to achieve a complex use case. For example, in LDA-based systems (for example, news briefings) or human emotion detection, there are a number of steps before and after the core system to be implemented as a single pipe to produce any meaningful and production-worthy system. See the following link for a real-life use case requiring a pipeline to implement a robust system:

```
https://www.thinkmind.org/index.php?view=article&articleid=achi_2013_15_50_2024
1
```

See also

Documentation for more multivariate statistical summary:

- Pipeline docs are available at `https://spark.apache.org/docs/latest/api/scala/index.html#org.apache.spark.ml.Pipeline`
- Pipeline model that is useful when we load and save the `.load()`, `.save()` methods: `https://spark.apache.org/docs/latest/api/scala/index.html#org.apache.spark.ml.PipelineModel`
- Pipeline stage information is available at `https://spark.apache.org/docs/latest/api/scala/index.html#org.apache.spark.ml.PipelineStage`
- HashingTF, a nice old trick to map a sequence to their term frequency in text analytics is available at `https://spark.apache.org/docs/latest/api/scala/index.html#org.apache.spark.mllib.feature.HashingTF`

Normalizing data with Spark

In this recipe, we demonstrate normalizing (scaling) the data prior to importing the data into an ML algorithm. There are a good number of ML algorithms such as **Support Vector Machine (SVM)** that work better with scaled input vectors rather than with the raw values.

How to do it...

1. Go to the UCI Machine Learning Repository and download the `http://archive.ics.uci.edu/ml/machine-learning-databases/wine/wine.data` file.

2. Start a new project in IntelliJ or in an IDE of your choice. Make sure that the necessary JAR files are included.

3. Set up the package location where the program will reside:

   ```
   package spark.ml.cookbook.chapter4
   ```

4. Import the necessary packages for the Spark session to gain access to the cluster and `log4j.Logger` to reduce the amount of output produced by Spark:

   ```
   import org.apache.spark.sql.SparkSession
   import org.apache.spark.ml.linalg.{Vector, Vectors}
   import org.apache.spark.ml.feature.MinMaxScaler
   ```

5. Define a method to parse wine data into a tuple:

   ```
   def parseWine(str: String): (Int, Vector) = {
   val columns = str.split(",")
   (columns(0).toInt, Vectors.dense(columns(1).toFloat,
   columns(2).toFloat, columns(3).toFloat))
     }
   ```

6. Set the output level to ERROR to reduce Spark's logging output:

   ```
   Logger.getLogger("org").setLevel(Level.ERROR)
   Logger.getLogger("akka").setLevel(Level.ERROR)
   ```

7. Initialize a Spark session specifying configurations with the builder pattern, thus making an entry point available for the Spark cluster:

   ```
   val spark = SparkSession
   .builder
   .master("local[*]")
   .appName("My Normalize")
   .getOrCreate()
   ```

8. Import `spark.implicits`, therefore adding in behavior with only an `import`:

   ```
   import spark.implicits._
   ```

9. Let's load the wine data into memory, taking only the first four columns and converting the latter three into a new feature vector:

   ```
   val data =
   Spark.read.text("../data/sparkml2/chapter4/wine.data").as[String].m
   ap(parseWine)
   ```

10. Next, we generate a DataFrame with two columns:

    ```
    val df = data.toDF("id", "feature")
    ```

11. Now, we will print out the DataFrame schema and display data contained within the DataFrame:

    ```
    df.printSchema()
    df.show(false)
    ```

    ```
    root
     |-- id: integer (nullable = true)
     |-- feature: vector (nullable = true)

    +---+----------------------------------------------------------------+
    |id |feature                                                         |
    +---+----------------------------------------------------------------+
    |1  |[14.229999542236328,1.7100000381469727,2.430000066757202]       |
    |1  |[13.199999809265137,1.7799999713897705,2.140000104904175]       |
    |1  |[13.15999984741211,2.359999895095825,2.6700000762939453]        |
    |1  |[14.369999885559082,1.9500000476837158,2.5]                     |
    |1  |[13.239999771118164,2.5899999141693115,2.869999885559082]       |
    |1  |[14.199999809265137,1.7599999904632568,2.450000047683716]       |
    |1  |[14.39000034332754,1.8700000047683716,2.450000047683716]        |
    |1  |[14.0600004196167,2.1500000953674316,2.609999895095825]         |
    |1  |[14.829999923706055,1.6399999856948853,2.1700000762939453]      |
    |1  |[13.859999656677246,1.350000023841858,2.2699999809265137]       |
    |1  |[14.100000381469727,2.1600000858306885,2.299999952316284]       |
    |1  |[14.119999885559082,1.4800000190734863,2.319999933242798]       |
    |1  |[13.75,1.7300000190734863,2.4100000858306885]                   |
    |1  |[14.75,1.7300000190734863,2.390000104904175]                    |
    |1  |[14.380000114440918,1.8700000047683716,2.380000114440918]       |
    |1  |[13.630000114440918,1.809999942779541,2.700000047683716]        |
    |1  |[14.300000190734863,1.9199999570846558,2.7200000286102295]      |
    |1  |[13.829999923706055,1.5700000524520874,2.619999885559082]       |
    |1  |[14.1899995803833,1.590000033378601,2.4800000190734863]         |
    |1  |[13.640000343322754,3.0999999046325684,2.559999942779541]       |
    +---+----------------------------------------------------------------+
    only showing top 20 rows
    ```

12. Finally, we generate the scaling model and transform the feature into a common range between a negative and positive one displaying the results:

```
val scale = new MinMaxScaler()
        .setInputCol("feature")
        .setOutputCol("scaled")
        .setMax(1)
        .setMin(-1)
scale.fit(df).transform(df).select("scaled").show(false)
```

```
+----------------------------------------------------------------+
|scaled                                                          |
+----------------------------------------------------------------+
|[0.6842103413928011,-0.6166007929349322,0.1443850799183537]    |
|[0.14210524598647445,-0.5889328361222417,-0.165775306299344]   |
|[0.12105263554158285,-0.359683862626296277,0.40106958144216076]|
|[0.7578947289168343,-0.5217391324834041,0.21925131848980062]   |
|[0.16315785643136604,-0.26877476743705553,0.6149731202177233]  |
|[0.6684210090425888,-0.5968379666401532,0.1657754337959101]    |
|[0.7684212851061929,-0.5533597016733449,0.1657754337959101]    |
|[0.5947371234523811,-0.44268773306769926,0.3368982648163601]   |
|[1.0,-0.6442687968659172,-0.13368977548300953]                 |
|[0.4894735692940979,-0.7588932836122242,-0.02673800609522836]  |
|[0.6157897338972727,-0.43873516780874344,0.005347524721106112] |
|[0.6263157881528056,-0.7075098881275044,0.02673787859866228]   |
|[0.4315790160541024,-0.6086956624170206,0.12299472604079753]   |
|[0.9578947791102168,-0.6086956624170206,0.10160437216324114]   |
|[0.7631580070115136,-0.5533597016733449,0.09090919522446317]   |
|[0.36842118471942786,-0.5770751403453742,0.4331551122584951]   |
|[0.7210527861217304,-0.533596875378566,0.4545454661360515]     |
|[0.4736842369438856,-0.6719367536786077,0.34759344175513807]   |
|[0.6631577309479095,-0.6640316231606962,0.19786096461224445]   |
|[0.37368446281410694,-0.06719375075713208,0.28342238012246934] |
+----------------------------------------------------------------+
only showing top 20 rows
```

13. We close the program by stopping the Spark session:

```
spark.stop()
```

How it works...

In this example, we explored feature scaling which is a critical step in most machine learning algorithms such as **classifiers**. We started out by loading the wine data files, extracted an identifier, and used the next three columns to create a feature vector.

Then, we created a `MinMaxScaler` object, configuring a minimum and maximum range to scale our values into. We invoked the scaling model by executing the `fit()` method on the scaler class, and then we used the model to scale the values in our DataFrame.

Finally, we displayed the resulting DataFrame and we noticed feature vector values ranges are between negative 1 and positive 1.

There's more...

The roots of normalizing and scaling can be better understood by examining the concept of **unit vectors** in introductory linear algebra. Please see the following links for some common references for unit vectors:

- You can refer to unit vectors at `https://en.wikipedia.org/wiki/Unit_vector`
- For scalar, you can refer to `https://en.wikipedia.org/wiki/Scalar_(mathematics)`

In the case of input sensitive algorithms, such as SVM, it is recommended that the algorithm be trained on scaled values (for example, range from 0 to 1) of the features rather than the absolute values as represented by the original vector.

See also

Documentation for `MinMaxScaler` is available at `https://spark.apache.org/docs/latest/api/scala/index.html#org.apache.spark.ml.feature.MinMaxScaler`

We want to emphasize that `MinMaxScaler` is an extensive API that extends the `Estimator` (a concept from the ML pipeline) and when used correctly can lead to achieving coding efficiency and high accuracy results.

Splitting data for training and testing

In this recipe, you will learn to use Spark's API to split your available input data into different datasets that can be used for training and validation phases. It is common to use an 80/20 split, but other variations of splitting the data can be considered as well based on your preference.

How to do it...

1. Go to the UCI Machine Learning Repository and download the `http://archive.ics.uci.edu/ml/machine-learning-databases/00359/News AggregatorDataset.zip` file.

2. Start a new project in IntelliJ or in an IDE of your choice. Make sure that the necessary JAR files are included.

3. Set up the package location where the program will reside:

```
package spark.ml.cookbook.chapter4
```

4. Import the necessary packages for the Spark session to gain access to the cluster and `log4j.Logger` to reduce the amount of output produced by Spark:

```
import org.apache.spark.sql.SparkSession
import org.apache.log4j.{ Level, Logger}
```

5. Set the output level to ERROR to reduce Spark's logging output:

```
Logger.getLogger("org").setLevel(Level.ERROR)
Logger.getLogger("akka").setLevel(Level.ERROR)
```

6. Initialize a Spark session specifying configurations with the builder pattern, thus making an entry point available for the Spark cluster:

```
val spark = SparkSession
.builder
.master("local[*]")
.appName("Data Splitting")
.getOrCreate()
```

7. We begin with loading a data file by way of the Spark session's `csv()` method to parse and load data into a dataset:

```
val data =
spark.read.csv("../data/sparkml2/chapter4/newsCorpora.csv")
```

8. Now, we count how many items the CSV loader parsed and loaded into memory. We will need this value later to reconcile data splitting.

```
val rowCount = data.count()
println("rowCount=" + rowCount)
```

9. Next, we utilize the dataset's `randomSplit` method to split the data into two buckets with allocations of 80% and 20% of data each:

```
val splitData = data.randomSplit(Array(0.8, 0.2))
```

10. The `randomSplit` method returns an array with two sets of data, the first set with 80% of data being the training set and the next with 20% being the testing set:

```
val trainingSet = splitData(0)
val testSet = splitData(1)
```

11. Let's generate counts for both training and testing sets:

```
val trainingSetCount = trainingSet.count()
val testSetCount = testSet.count()
```

12. Now we reconcile the values, and notice that the original row count is 415606 and the final summation of the training and testing sets equals 415606:

```
println("trainingSetCount=" + trainingSetCount)
println("testSetCount=" + testSetCount)
println("setRowCount=" + (trainingSetCount+testSetCount))
rowCount=415606
trainingSetCount=332265
testSetCount=83341
setRowCount=415606
```

13. We close the program by stopping the Spark session:

```
spark.stop()
```

How it works...

We began by loading the data file `newsCorpora.csv` and then by way of the `randomSplit()` method attached to the dataset object, we split the dataset.

There's more...

To validate the result, we must set up a Delphi technique in which the test data is absolutely unknown to the model. See Kaggle competitions for details at https://www.kaggle.com/competitions.

Three types of datasets are needed for a robust ML system:

- **Training dataset**: This is used to fit a model to sample
- **Validation dataset**: This is used to estimate the delta or prediction error for the fitted model (trained by training set)
- **Test dataset**: This is used to assess the model generalization error once a final model is selected

See also

Documentation for `randomSplit()` is available at `https://spark.apache.org/docs/latest/api/scala/index.html#org.apache.spark.api.java.JavaRDD@randomSplit(weights:Array%5BDouble%5D):Array%5Borg.apache.spark.api.java.JavaRDD%5BT%5D%5D`.

The `randomSplit()` is a method call within an RDD. While the number of RDD method calls can be overwhelming, mastering this Spark concept and API is a must.

API signature is as follows:

```
def randomSplit(weights: Array[Double]): Array[JavaRDD[T]]
```

Randomly splits this RDD with the provided weights.

Common operations with the new Dataset API

In this recipe, we cover the Dataset API, which is the way forward for data wrangling in Spark 2.0 and beyond. In Chapter 3, *Spark's Three Data Musketeers for Machine Learning - Perfect Together* we covered three detailed recipes for dataset, and in this chapter we cover some of the common, repetitive operations that are required to work with these new API sets. Additionally, we demonstrate the query plan generated by the Spark SQL Catalyst optimizer.

How to do it...

1. Start a new project in IntelliJ or in an IDE of your choice. Make sure that the necessary JAR files are included.

2. We will use a JSON data file named `cars.json`, which has been created for this example:

   ```
   name,city
   Bears,Chicago
   Packers,Green Bay
   Lions,Detroit
   Vikings,Minnesota
   ```

3. Set up the package location where the program will reside:

   ```
   package spark.ml.cookbook.chapter4
   ```

4. Import the necessary packages for the Spark session to get access to the cluster and `log4j.Logger` to reduce the amount of output produced by Spark:

   ```
   import org.apache.spark.ml.Pipeline
   import org.apache.spark.ml.classification.LogisticRegression
   import org.apache.spark.ml.feature.{HashingTF, Tokenizer}
   import org.apache.spark.sql.SparkSession
   import org.apache.log4j.{Level, Logger}
   ```

5. Define a Scala `case class` to model the data:

   ```
   case class Team(name: String, city: String)
   ```

6. Set the output level to ERROR to reduce Spark's logging output:

   ```
   Logger.getLogger("org").setLevel(Level.ERROR)
   Logger.getLogger("akka").setLevel(Level.ERROR)
   ```

7. Initialize a Spark session specifying configurations with the builder pattern, thus making an entry point available for the Spark cluster:

   ```
   val spark = SparkSession
   .builder
   .master("local[*]")
   .appName("My Dataset")
   .config("spark.sql.warehouse.dir", ".")
   .getOrCreate()
   ```

8. Import `spark.implicits`, therefore adding in behavior with only an `import`:

```
import spark.implicits._
```

9. Let's create a dataset from a Scala list and print out the results:

```
val champs = spark.createDataset(List(Team("Broncos", "Denver"),
Team("Patriots", "New England")))
champs.show(false)
```

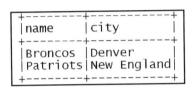

10. Next, we will load a CSV into memory and transform it into a dataset of type `Team`:

```
val teams = spark.read
  .option("Header", "true")
  .csv("../data/sparkml2/chapter4/teams.csv")
  .as[Team]

teams.show(false)
```

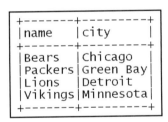

11. Now we demonstrate a transversal of the teams dataset by use of the `map` function, yielding a new dataset of city names:

```
val cities = teams.map(t => t.city)
cities.show(false)
```

```
+---------+
|value    |
+---------+
|Chicago  |
|Green Bay|
|Detroit  |
|Minnesota|
+---------+
```

12. Display the execution plan for retrieving city names:

```
cities.explain()
== Physical Plan ==
*SerializeFromObject [staticinvoke(class
org.apache.spark.unsafe.types.UTF8String, StringType, fromString,
input[0, java.lang.String, true], true) AS value#26]
+- *MapElements <function1>, obj#25: java.lang.String
+- *DeserializeToObject newInstance(class Team), obj#24: Team
+- *Scan csv [name#9,city#10] Format: CSV, InputPaths:
file:teams.csv, PartitionFilters: [], PushedFilters: [],
ReadSchema: struct<name:string,city:string>
```

13. Finally, we save the `teams` dataset to a JSON file:

```
teams.write
.mode(SaveMode.Overwrite)
.json("../data/sparkml2/chapter4/teams.json"){"name":"Bears","city"
:"Chicago"}
{"name":"Packers","city":"Green Bay"}
{"name":"Lions","city":"Detroit"}
{"name":"Vikings","city":"Minnesota"}
```

14. We close the program by stopping the Spark session:

```
spark.stop()
```

How it works...

First, we created a dataset from a Scala list and displayed the output to validate the creation of the dataset as expected. Second, we loaded a **comma-separated value (CSV)** file into memory, transforming it into a dataset of type `Team`. Third, we executed the `map()` function over our dataset to build a list of team city names and printed out the execution plan used to generate the dataset. Finally, we persisted the `teams` dataset we previously loaded into a JSON formatted file for future use.

There's more...

Please take a note of some interesting points on datasets:

- Datasets use *lazy* evaluation
- Datasets take advantage of the Spark SQL Catalyst optimizer
- Datasets take advantage of the tungsten off-heap memory management
- There are plenty of systems that will remain pre-Spark 2.0 for the next 2 year so you must still learn and master RDDs and DataFrame for practical reasons.

See also

Documentation for Dataset is available at `https://spark.apache.org/docs/latest/api/scala/index.html#org.apache.spark.sql.Dataset`.

Creating and using RDD versus DataFrame versus Dataset from a text file in Spark 2.0

In this recipe, we explore the subtle differences in creating RDD, DataFrame, and Dataset from a text file and their relationship to each other via a short sample code:

```
Dataset: spark.read.textFile()
RDD: spark.sparkContext.textFile()
DataFrame: spark.read.text()
```

Assume `spark` is the session name

How to do it...

1. Start a new project in IntelliJ or in an IDE of your choice. Make sure the necessary JAR files are included.
2. Set up the package location where the program will reside:

   ```
   package spark.ml.cookbook.chapter4
   ```

3. Import the necessary packages for the Spark session to gain access to the cluster and `log4j.Logger` to reduce the amount of output produced by Spark:

```
import org.apache.log4j.{Level, Logger}
import org.apache.spark.sql.SparkSession
```

4. We also define a `case class` to host the data used:

```
case class Beatle(id: Long, name: String)
```

5. Set the output level to ERROR to reduce Spark's logging output:

```
Logger.getLogger("org").setLevel(Level.ERROR)
```

6. Initialize a Spark session specifying configurations with the builder pattern, thus making an entry point available for the Spark cluster:

```
val spark = SparkSession
.builder
.master("local[*]")
.appName("DatasetvsRDD")
.config("spark.sql.warehouse.dir", ".")
.getOrCreate()
```

7. In the following block, we let Spark *create a dataset* object from a text file.

   The text file contains very simple data (each line contains an ID and name separated by a comma):

```
import spark.implicits._

val ds =
spark.read.textFile("../data/sparkml2/chapter4/beatles.txt").map(li
ne => {
val tokens = line.split(",")
Beatle(tokens(0).toLong, tokens(1))
}).as[Beatle]
```

   We read the file in and parse the data in the file. The dataset object is created by Spark. We confirm the type in the console and then display the data:

```
println("Dataset Type: " + ds.getClass)
ds.show()
```

From the console output:

```
Dataset Type: class org.apache.spark.sql.Dataset
```

```
+---+------+
| id|  name|
+---+------+
|  1|  John|
|  2|  Paul|
|  3|George|
|  4| Ringo|
+---+------+
```

8. Now we create an RDD with the same data file, in a very similar way as the preceding step:

```
val rdd =
spark.sparkContext.textFile("../data/sparkml2/chapter4/beatles.txt"
).map(line => {
val tokens = line.split(",")
Beatle(tokens(0).toLong, tokens(1))
  })
```

We then confirm that it is an RDD and display the data in the console:

```
println("RDD Type: " + rdd.getClass)
rdd.collect().foreach(println)
```

Note that the method is very similar but different.

From the console output:

```
RDD Type: class org.apache.spark.rdd.MapPartitionsRDD
Beatle(1,John)
Beatle(2,Paul)
Beatle(3,George)
Beatle(4,Ringo)
```

9. DataFrame is another common data structure utilized by Spark communities. We show a similar way to create a DataFrame using the similar method based on the same data file:

```
val df =
spark.read.text("../data/sparkml2/chapter4/beatles.txt").map(
  row => { // Dataset[Row]
val tokens = row.getString(0).split(",")
  Beatle(tokens(0).toLong, tokens(1))
  }).toDF("bid", "bname")
```

We then confirm that it is a DataFrame.

```
println("DataFrame Type: " + df.getClass)
df.show()
```

 Note that `DataFrame = Dataset[Row]`, so the type is Dataset.

From the console output:

```
DataFrame Type: class org.apache.spark.sql.Dataset
```

```
+---+------+
|bid| bname|
+---+------+
|  1|  John|
|  2|  Paul|
|  3|George|
|  4| Ringo|
+---+------+
```

10. We close the program by stopping the Spark session:

```
spark.stop()
```

How it works...

We create an RDD, DataFrame, and Dataset object using a similar method from the same text file and confirm the type using the `getClass` method:

```
Dataset: spark.read.textFile
RDD: spark.sparkContext.textFile
DataFrame: spark.read.text
```

Please note that they are very similar and sometimes confusing. Spark 2.0 has transformed DataFrame into an alias for `Dataset[Row]`, making it truly a dataset. We showed the preceding methods to let the user pick an example to create their own datatype flavor.

There's more...

Documentation for datatypes is available at `http://spark.apache.org/docs/latest/sql-programming-guide.html`.

If you are unsure as to what kind of data structure you have at hand (sometimes the difference is not obvious), use the `getClass` method to verify.

Spark 2.0 has transformed DataFrame into an alias for `Dataset[Row]`. While RDD and Dataram remain fully viable for near future, it is best to learn and code new projects using the dataset.

See also

Documentation for RDD and Dataset is available at the following websites:

- `http://spark.apache.org/docs/latest/api/scala/index.html#org.apache.spark.rdd.RDD`
- `http://spark.apache.org/docs/latest/api/scala/index.html#org.apache.spark.sql.Dataset`

LabeledPoint data structure for Spark ML

LabeledPoint is a data structure that has been around since the early days for packaging a feature vector along with a label so it can be used in unsupervised learning algorithms. We demonstrate a short recipe that uses LabeledPoint, the **Seq** data structure, and DataFrame to run a logistic regression for binary classification of the data. The emphasis here is on LabeledPoint, and the regression algorithms are covered in more depth in Chapter 5, *Practical Machine Learning with Regression and Classification in Spark 2.0 - Part I* and Chapter 6, *Practical Machine Learning with Regression and Classification in Spark 2.0 - Part II*.

How to do it...

1. Start a new project in IntelliJ or in an IDE of your choice. Make sure that the necessary JAR files are included.

2. Set up the package location where the program will reside:

```
package spark.ml.cookbook.chapter4
```

3. Import the necessary packages for SparkContext to get access to the cluster:

```
import org.apache.spark.ml.feature.LabeledPoint
import org.apache.spark.ml.linalg.Vectors
import org.apache.spark.ml.classification.LogisticRegression
import org.apache.spark.sql._
```

4. Create Spark's configuration and SparkContext so we can have access to the cluster:

```
val spark = SparkSession
.builder
.master("local[*]")
.appName("myLabeledPoint")
.config("spark.sql.warehouse.dir", ".")
.getOrCreate()
```

5. We create the LabeledPoint, using the SparseVector and DenseVector. In the following code blocks, the first four LabeledPoints are created by the DenseVector, the last two LabeledPoints are created by the SparseVector:

```
val myLabeledPoints = spark.createDataFrame(Seq(
LabeledPoint(1.0, Vectors.dense(0.0, 1.1, 0.1)),
LabeledPoint(0.0, Vectors.dense(2.0, 1.0, -1.0)),
LabeledPoint(0.0, Vectors.dense(2.0, 1.3, 1.0)),
LabeledPoint(1.0, Vectors.dense(0.0, 1.2, -0.5)),

LabeledPoint(0.0, Vectors.sparse(3, Array(0,2), Array(1.0,3.0))),
LabeledPoint(1.0, Vectors.sparse(3, Array(1,2), Array(1.2,-0.4)))

))
```

The DataFrame objects are created from the preceding LabeledPoint.

6. We verify the raw data count and process data count.

7. You can operate a `show()` function call to the DataFrame created:

```
myLabeledPoints.show()
```

8. You will see the following in the console:

```
+-----+--------------------+
|label|            features|
+-----+--------------------+
|  1.0|      [0.0,1.1,0.1]|
|  0.0|      [2.0,1.0,-1.0]|
|  0.0|      [2.0,1.3,1.0]|
|  1.0|      [0.0,1.2,-0.5]|
|  0.0| (3,[0,2],[1.0,3.0])|
|  1.0|(3,[1,2],[1.2,-0.4])|
+-----+--------------------+
```

9. We create a simple LogisticRegression model from the data structure we just created:

```
val lr = new LogisticRegression()

lr.setMaxIter(5)
.setRegParam(0.01)
val model = lr.fit(myLabeledPoints)

println("Model was fit using parameters: " +
model.parent.extractParamMap())
```

In the console, it will show the following `model` parameters:

```
Model was fit using parameters: {
 logreg_6aebbb683272-elasticNetParam: 0.0,
 logreg_6aebbb683272-featuresCol: features,
 logreg_6aebbb683272-fitIntercept: true,
 logreg_6aebbb683272-labelCol: label,
 logreg_6aebbb683272-maxIter: 5,
 logreg_6aebbb683272-predictionCol: prediction,
 logreg_6aebbb683272-probabilityCol: probability,
 logreg_6aebbb683272-rawPredictionCol: rawPrediction,
 logreg_6aebbb683272-regParam: 0.01,
 logreg_6aebbb683272-standardization: true,
 logreg_6aebbb683272-threshold: 0.5,
 logreg_6aebbb683272-tol: 1.0E-6
}
```

10. We then close the program by stopping the Spark session:

```
spark.stop()
```

How it works...

We used a LabeledPoint data structure to model features and drive training of a logistics regression model. We began by defining a group of LabeledPoints, which are used to create a DataFrame for further processing. Then, we created a logistic regression object and passed LabeledPoint DataFrame as an argument to it so we could train our model. Spark ML APIs are designed to work well with the LabeledPoint format and require minimal intervention.

There's more...

A LabeledPoint is a popular structure used to package data as a `Vector` + a `Label` which can be purposed for supervised machine learning algorithms. A typical layout of the LabeledPoint is given here:

```
Seq(
LabeledPoint (Label, Vector(data, data, data))
......
LabeledPoint (Label, Vector(data, data, data))
)
```

Please note that not only dense but also sparse vectors can be used with LabeledPoint, which will make a huge difference in efficiency especially if you have a large and sparse dataset housed in the driver during testing and development.

See also

- LabeledPoint API documentation is available
  at `https://spark.apache.org/docs/latest/api/scala/index.html#org.apache.spark.ml.feature.LabeledPoint`
- DenseVector API documentation is available
  at `https://spark.apache.org/docs/latest/api/scala/index.html#org.apache.spark.ml.linalg.DenseVector`
- SparseVector API documentation is available
  at `https://spark.apache.org/docs/latest/api/scala/index.html#org.apache.spark.ml.linalg.SparseVector`

Getting access to Spark cluster in Spark 2.0

In this recipe, we demonstrate how to get access to a Spark cluster using a single point access named `SparkSession`. Spark 2.0 abstracts multiple contexts (such as SQLContext, HiveContext) into a single entry point, `SparkSession`, which allows you to get access to all Spark subsystems in a unified way.

How to do it...

1. Start a new project in IntelliJ or in an IDE of your choice. Make sure that the necessary JAR files are included.
2. Set up the package location where the program will reside:

   ```
   package spark.ml.cookbook.chapter4
   ```

3. Import the necessary packages for SparkContext to get access to the cluster.
4. In Spark 2.x, `SparkSession` is more commonly used instead.

   ```
   import org.apache.spark.sql.SparkSession
   ```

5. Create Spark's configuration and `SparkSession` so we can have access to the cluster:

   ```
   val spark = SparkSession
   .builder
   .master("local[*]") // if use cluster master("spark://master:7077")
   .appName("myAccesSparkCluster20")
   .config("spark.sql.warehouse.dir", ".")
   .getOrCreate()
   ```

The preceding code utilizes the `master()` function to set the cluster type to `local`. A comment is provided to show how to run the local cluster running on a specific port.

The `-D` option value will be overridden by the cluster master parameter set in the code if both exist.
In a `SparkSession` object, we typically use the `master()` function, while pre-Spark 2.0, in the `SparkConf` object, uses the `setMaster()` function.

The following are the three sample ways to connect to a cluster in different modes:

1. Running in `local` mode:

```
master("local")
```

2. Running in cluster mode:

```
master("spark://yourmasterhostIP:port")
```

3. Passing the master value in:

```
-Dspark.master=local
```

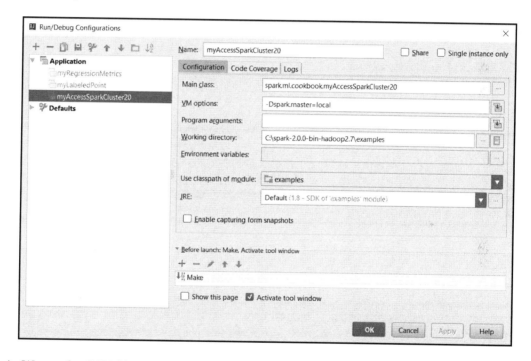

4. We read a CSV file in and parse the CSV file into Spark using the following code:

```
val df = spark.read
    .option("header","True")
    .csv("../data/sparkml2/chapter4/mySampleCSV.csv")
```

5. We show the DataFrame in the console:

```
df.show()
```

6. And you will see the following in the console:

```
+----+----+----+----------+
|col1|col2|col3|      col4|
+----+----+----+----------+
|   1|  16| 4.0|1217897793|
|   1|  24| 1.5|1217895807|
|   1|  32| 4.0|1217896246|
|   1|  47| 4.0|1217896556|
|   1|  50| 4.0|1217896523|
+----+----+----+----------+
```

7. We then close the program by stopping the Spark session:

```
spark.stop()
```

How it works...

In this example, we show how to connect to a Spark cluster using local and remote options for an application. First, we create a `SparkSession` object which will grant us access to a Spark cluster by specifying whether the cluster is local or remote using the `master()` function. You can also specify the master location by passing a JVM argument when starting your client program. In addition, you can configure an application name and a working data directory. Next, you invoked the `getOrCreate()` method to create a new `SparkSession` or hand you a reference to an already existing session. Finally, we execute a small sample program to prove our `SparkSession` object creation is valid.

There's more...

A Spark session has numerous parameters and APIs that can be set and exercised, but it is worth consulting the Spark documentation since some of the methods/parameters are marked with the status **Experimental** or left blank - for non-experimental statuses (15 minimum as of our last examination).

Another change to be aware of is to use `spark.sql.warehouse.dir` for the location of the tables. Spark 2.0 uses `spark.sql.warehouse.dir` to set warehouse locations to store tables rather than `hive.metastore.warehouse.dir`. The default value for `spark.sql.warehouse.dir` is `System.getProperty("user.dir")`.

Also see `spark-defaults.conf` for more details.

Also noteworthy are the following:

- Some of our favorite and interesting APIs from the Spark 2.0 documentation:

  ```
  Def version: String
  ```

The version of Spark on which this application is running:

- Def **sql**(sqlText: String): `DataFrame`

  Executes a SQL query using Spark, returning the result as a `DataFrame` - **Preferred Spark 2.0**

- Val **sqlContext**: `SQLContext`

  A wrapped version of this session in the form of a `SQLContext`, for backward compatibility.

- lazy val **conf**: `RuntimeConfig`

  Runtime configuration interface for Spark.

- lazy val **catalog**: `Catalog`

  Interface through which the user may create, drop, alter, or query underlying databases, tables, functions, and so on.

- **Def newSession(): SparkSession**

  Starts a new session with isolated SQL configurations and temporary tables; registered functions are isolated, but share the underlying `SparkContext` and cached data.

- Def **udf**: `UDFRegistration`

  A collection of methods for registering user-defined functions (UDF).

We can create both DataFrame and Dataset directly via the Spark session. It works, but is marked as experimental in Spark 2.0.0.

If you are going to do any SQL related work, SparkSession is now the entry point to Spark SQL. SparkSession is the first object that you have to create in order to create Spark SQL applications.

See also

Documentation for `SparkSession` API documents is available at `https://spark.apache.org/docs/latest/api/scala/index.html#org.apache.spark.sq l.SparkSession`.

Getting access to Spark cluster pre-Spark 2.0

This is a *pre-Spark 2.0 recipe*, but it will be helpful for developers who want to quickly compare and contrast the cluster access for porting pre-Spark 2.0 programs to Spark 2.0's new paradigm.

How to do it...

1. Start a new project in IntelliJ or in an IDE of your choice. Make sure that the necessary JAR files are included.

2. Set up the package location where the program will reside:

   ```
   package spark.ml.cookbook.chapter4
   ```

3. Import the necessary packages for SparkContext to get access to the cluster:

   ```
   import org.apache.spark.{SparkConf, SparkContext}
   ```

4. Create Spark's configuration and SparkContext so we can have access to the cluster:

   ```
   val conf = new SparkConf()
   .setAppName("MyAccessSparkClusterPre20")
   .setMaster("local[4]") // if cluster
   setMaster("spark://MasterHostIP:7077")
   .set("spark.sql.warehouse.dir", ".")

   val sc = new SparkContext(conf)
   ```

The preceding code utilizes the `setMaster()` function to set the cluster master location. As you can see, we are running the code in `local` mode.

The -D option value will be overridden by the cluster master parameter set in the code if both exist).

The following are the three sample ways to connect to the cluster in different modes:

1. Running in local mode:

```
setMaster("local")
```

2. Running in cluster mode:

```
setMaster("spark://yourmasterhostIP:port")
```

3. Passing the master value in:

```
-Dspark.master=local
```

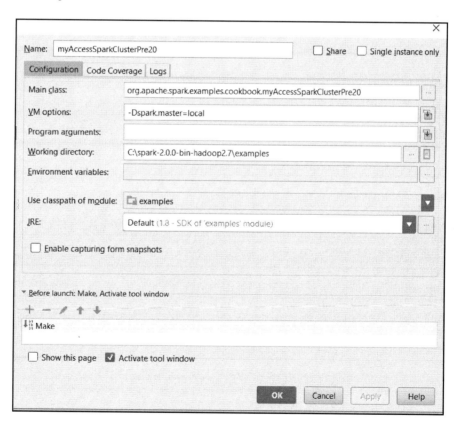

4. We use the preceding SparkContext to read a CSV file in and parse the CSV file into Spark using the following code:

```
val file = sc.textFile("../data/sparkml2/chapter4/mySampleCSV.csv")
val headerAndData = file.map(line => line.split(",").map(_.trim))
val header = headerAndData.first
val data = headerAndData.filter(_(0) != header(0))
val maps = data.map(splits => header.zip(splits).toMap)
```

5. We take the sample result and print them in the console:

```
val result = maps.take(4)
result.foreach(println)
```

6. And you will see the following in the console:

```
Map(col1 -> 1, col2 -> 16, col3 -> 4.0, col4 -> 1217897793)
Map(col1 -> 1, col2 -> 24, col3 -> 1.5, col4 -> 1217895807)
Map(col1 -> 1, col2 -> 32, col3 -> 4.0, col4 -> 1217896246)
Map(col1 -> 1, col2 -> 47, col3 -> 4.0, col4 -> 1217896556)
```

7. We then close the program by stopping the SparkContext:

```
sc.stop()
```

How it works...

In this example, we show how to connect to a Spark cluster using the local and remote modes prior to Spark 2.0. First, we create a `SparkConf` object and configure all the required parameters. We will specify the master location, application name, and working data directory. Next, we create a SparkContext passing the `SparkConf` as an argument to access a Spark cluster. Also, you can specify the master location my passing a JVM argument when starting your client program. Finally, we execute a small sample program to prove our SparkContext is functioning correctly.

There's more...

Prior to Spark 2.0, getting access to a Spark cluster was done via **SparkContext**.

The access to the subsystems such as SQL was per-specific names context (for example, SQLContext**)**.

Spark 2.0 changed how we gain access to a cluster by creating a single unified access point (namely, `SparkSession`).

See also

Documentation for SparkContext is available at https://spark.apache.org/docs/latest/api/scala/index.html#org.apache.spark.Sp arkContext.

Getting access to SparkContext vis-a-vis SparkSession object in Spark 2.0

In this recipe, we demonstrate how to get hold of SparkContext using a SparkSession object in Spark 2.0. This recipe will demonstrate the creation, usage, and back and forth conversion of RDD to Dataset. The reason this is important is that even though we prefer Dataset going forward, we must still be able to use and augment the legacy (pre-Spark 2.0) code mostly utilizing RDD.

How to do it...

1. Start a new project in IntelliJ or in an IDE of your choice. Make sure the necessary JAR files are included.
2. Set up the package location where the program will reside:

   ```
   package spark.ml.cookbook.chapter4
   ```

3. Import the necessary packages for the Spark session to gain access to the cluster and `log4j.Logger` to reduce the amount of output produced by Spark:

```scala
import org.apache.log4j.{Level, Logger}
import org.apache.spark.sql.SparkSession
import scala.util.Random
```

4. Set the output level to ERROR to reduce Spark's logging output:

```scala
Logger.getLogger("org").setLevel(Level.ERROR)
```

5. Initialize a Spark session specifying configurations with the builder pattern, thus making an entry point available for the Spark cluster:

```scala
val session = SparkSession
.builder
.master("local[*]")
.appName("SessionContextRDD")
.config("spark.sql.warehouse.dir", ".")
.getOrCreate()
```

6. We first show how to use `sparkContext` to create RDD. The following code samples were very common in Spark 1.x:

```scala
import session.implicits._

// SparkContext
val context = session.sparkContext
```

We get the `SparkContext` object:

```scala
println("SparkContext")

val rdd1 = context.makeRDD(Random.shuffle(1 to 10).toList)
rdd1.collect().foreach(println)
println("-" * 45)

val rdd2 = context.parallelize(Random.shuffle(20 to 30).toList)
rdd2.collect().foreach(println)
println("\n End of SparkContext> " + ("-" * 45))
```

We first create `rdd1` from the `makeRDD` method and display the RDD in the console:

```
SparkContext
4
6
1
10
5
2
7
3
9
8
```

We then use the `parallelize` method to generate `rdd2`, and display the data in the RDD in the console.

From the console output:

```
25
28
30
29
20
22
27
23
24
26
21
End of SparkContext
```

7. Now we show the way to use the `session` object to create the dataset:

```scala
val dataset1 = session.range(40, 50)
dataset1.show()

val dataset2 = session.createDataset(Random.shuffle(60 to
70).toList)
dataset2.show()
```

We generated `dataset1` and `dataset2` using different methods.

From the console output:

For dataset1:

```
+---+
| id|
+---+
| 40|
| 41|
| 42|
| 43|
| 44|
| 45|
| 46|
| 47|
| 48|
| 49|
+---+
```

For dataset2:

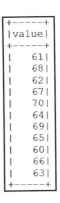

```
+-----+
|value|
+-----+
|   61|
|   68|
|   62|
|   67|
|   70|
|   64|
|   69|
|   65|
|   60|
|   66|
|   63|
+-----+
```

8. We show the way to retrieve the underlying RDD from the dataset:

```
// retrieve underlying RDD from Dataset
val rdd3 = dataset2.rdd
rdd3.collect().foreach(println)
```

From the console output:

```
61
68
62
67
70
64
69
```

```
65
60
66
63
```

9. The following block shows a way to convert RDD to Dataset object:

```
// convert rdd to Dataset
val rdd4 = context.makeRDD(Random.shuffle(80 to 90).toList)
val dataset3 = session.createDataset(rdd4)
dataset3.show()
```

From the console output:

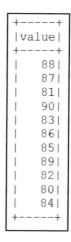

```
+-----+
|value|
+-----+
|   88|
|   87|
|   81|
|   90|
|   83|
|   86|
|   85|
|   89|
|   82|
|   80|
|   84|
+-----+
```

10. We close the program by stopping the Spark session:

```
session.stop()
```

How it works...

We created RDD using the SparkContext; this was widely used in Spark 1.x. We also demonstrated a way to create Dataset in Spark 2.0 using the Session object. The conversion back and forth is necessary to deal with pre-Spark 2.0 code in production today.

The technical message from this recipe is that while DataSet is the preferred method of data wrangling going forward, we can always use the API to go back and forth to RDD and vice versa.

There's more...

More about the datatypes can be found at `http://spark.apache.org/docs/latest/sql-programming-guide.html`.

See also

Documentation for SparkContext and SparkSession is available at the following websites:

- `http://spark.apache.org/docs/latest/api/scala/index.html#org.apache.spark.SparkContext`
- `http://spark.apache.org/docs/latest/api/scala/index.html#org.apache.spark.sql.SparkSession`

New model export and PMML markup in Spark 2.0

In this recipe, we explore the model export facility available in Spark 2.0 to use **Predictive Model Markup Language** (**PMML**). This standard XML-based language allows you to export and run your models on other systems (some limitations apply). You can explore the *There's more...* section for more information.

How to do it...

1. Start a new project in IntelliJ or in an IDE of your choice. Make sure that the necessary JAR files are included.
2. Set up the package location where the program will reside:

   ```
   package spark.ml.cookbook.chapter4
   ```

3. Import the necessary packages for SparkContext to get access to the cluster:

```
import org.apache.spark.mllib.linalg.Vectors
import org.apache.spark.sql.SparkSession
import org.apache.spark.mllib.clustering.KMeans
```

4. Create Spark's configuration and SparkContext:

```
val spark = SparkSession
.builder
.master("local[*]")    // if use cluster
master("spark://master:7077")
.appName("myPMMLExport")
.config("spark.sql.warehouse.dir", ".")
.getOrCreate()
```

5. We read the data from a text file; the data file contains a sample dataset for a KMeans model:

```
val data =
spark.sparkContext.textFile("../data/sparkml2/chapter4/my_kmeans_da
ta_sample.txt")

val parsedData = data.map(s => Vectors.dense(s.split('
').map(_.toDouble))).cache()
```

6. We set up the parameters for the KMeans model, and train the model using the preceding datasets and parameters:

```
val numClusters = 2
val numIterations = 10
val model = KMeans.train(parsedData, numClusters, numIterations)
```

7. We have effectively created a simple KMeans model (by setting the number of clusters to 2) from the data structure we just created.

```
println("MyKMeans PMML Model:\n" + model.toPMML)
```

In the console, it will show the following model:

```
MyKMeans PMML Model:
<?xml version="1.0" encoding="UTF-8" standalone="yes"?>
<PMML version="4.2" xmlns="http://www.dmg.org/PMML-4_2">
    <Header description="k-means clustering">
        <Application name="Apache Spark MLlib" version="2.0.0"/>
        <Timestamp>2016-11-06T13:34:57</Timestamp>
    </Header>
    <DataDictionary numberOfFields="3">
        <DataField name="field_0" optype="continuous"
dataType="double"/>
        <DataField name="field_1" optype="continuous"
dataType="double"/>
        <DataField name="field_2" optype="continuous"
dataType="double"/>
    </DataDictionary>
    <ClusteringModel modelName="k-means" functionName="clustering"
modelClass="centerBased" numberOfClusters="2">
        <MiningSchema>
            <MiningField name="field_0" usageType="active"/>
            <MiningField name="field_1" usageType="active"/>
            <MiningField name="field_2" usageType="active"/>
        </MiningSchema>
        <ComparisonMeasure kind="distance">
            <squaredEuclidean/>
        </ComparisonMeasure>
        <ClusteringField field="field_0"
compareFunction="absDiff"/>
        <ClusteringField field="field_1"
compareFunction="absDiff"/>
        <ClusteringField field="field_2"
compareFunction="absDiff"/>
        <Cluster name="cluster_0">
            <Array n="3" type="real">9.06 9.179999999999998
9.12</Array>
        </Cluster>
        <Cluster name="cluster_1">
            <Array n="3" type="real">0.11666666666666665
0.11666666666666665 0.13333333333333333</Array>
        </Cluster>
    </ClusteringModel>
</PMML>
```

8. We then export the PMML to an XML file in the data directory:

```
model.toPMML("../data/sparkml2/chapter4/myKMeansSamplePMML.xml")
```

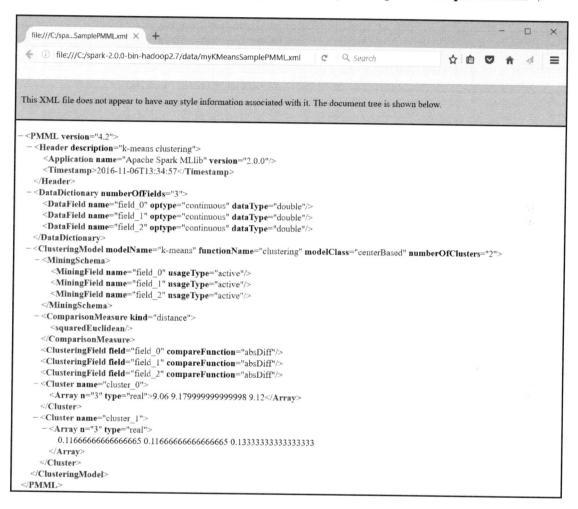

9. We then close the program by stopping the Spark session:

```
spark.stop()
```

How it works...

After you spend time to train a model, the next step will be to persist the model for future use. In this recipe, we began by training a KMeans model to generate model info for persistence in later steps. Once we have the trained model, we invoke the `toPMML()` method on the model converting it into PMML for storage. The invocation of the method generates an XML document, then the XML document text can easily be persisted to a file.

There's more...

PMML is a standard developed by the **Data Mining Group** (**DMG**). The standard enables inter-platform interoperability by letting you build on one system and then deploy to another system in production. The PMML standard has gained momentum and has been adopted by most vendors. At its core, the standard is based on an XML document with the following:

- Header with general information
- Dictionary describing field level definitions used by the third component (the model)
- Model structure and parameters

As of this writing, the Spark 2.0 Machine Library support for PMML exporting is currently limited to:

- Linear Regression
- Logistic Regression
- Ridge Regression
- Lasso
- SVM
- KMeans

You can export the model to the following file types in Spark:

- Local filesystem:

```
Model_a.toPMML("/xyz/model-name.xml")
```

- Distributed filesystem:

```
Model_a.toPMML(SparkContext, "/xyz/model-name")
```

- Output stream--acting as a pipe:

```
Model_a.toPMML(System.out)
```

See also

Documentation for `PMMLExportable` API documents at `http://spark.apache.org/docs/latest/api/scala/index.html#org.apache.spark.mllib.pmml.PMMLExportable`.

Regression model evaluation using Spark 2.0

In this recipe, we explore how to evaluate a regression model (a regression decision tree in this example). Spark provides the **RegressionMetrics** facility which has basic statistical facilities such as **Mean Squared Error** (**MSE**), R-Squared, and so on, right out of the box.

The objective in this recipe is to understand the evaluation metrics provided by Spark out of the box. It is best to concentrate on step 8 since we cover regression in more detail in `Chapter 5`, *Practical Machine Learning with Regression and Classification in Spark 2.0 - Part I* and `Chapter 6`, *Practical Machine Learning with Regression and Classification in Spark 2.0 - Part II* and throughout the book.

How to do it...

1. Start a new project in IntelliJ or in an IDE of your choice. Make sure that the necessary JAR files are included.

2. Set up the package location where the program will reside:

```
package spark.ml.cookbook.chapter4
```

3. Import the necessary packages for SparkContext to get access to the cluster:

```
import org.apache.spark.mllib.evaluation.RegressionMetrics
import org.apache.spark.mllib.linalg.Vectors
import org.apache.spark.mllib.regression.LabeledPoint
import org.apache.spark.mllib.tree.DecisionTree
import org.apache.spark.sql.SparkSession
```

4. Create Spark's configuration and SparkContext:

```
val spark = SparkSession
 .builder
 .master("local[*]")
 .appName("myRegressionMetrics")
 .config("spark.sql.warehouse.dir", ".")
 .getOrCreate()
```

5. We utilize the Wisconsin breast cancer dataset as an example dataset for the regression model.

The **Wisconsin breast cancer** dataset was obtained from the University of Wisconsin Hospital from Dr. William H Wolberg. The dataset was gained periodically as Dr.Wolberg reported his clinical cases.

More details on the dataset can be found in Chapter 9, *Optimization - Going Down the Hill with Gradient Descent*.

```
val rawData =
spark.sparkContext.textFile("../data/sparkml2/chapter4/breast-
cancer-wisconsin.data")
val data = rawData.map(_.trim)
    .filter(text => !(text.isEmpty || text.indexOf("?") > -1))
    .map { line =>
      val values = line.split(',').map(_.toDouble)
      val slicedValues = values.slice(1, values.size)
      val featureVector = Vectors.dense(slicedValues.init)
      val label = values.last / 2 -1
      LabeledPoint(label, featureVector)

    }
```

We load the data into Spark and filter the missing values in the data.

6. We split the dataset in the ratio of 70:30 to create two datasets, one used for training the model, and the other for testing the model:

```
val splits = data.randomSplit(Array(0.7, 0.3))
val (trainingData, testData) = (splits(0), splits(1))
```

7. We set up the parameters and using the `DecisionTree` model, after the training dataset, we use the test dataset to do the prediction:

```scala
val categoricalFeaturesInfo = Map[Int, Int]()
val impurity = "variance"
val maxDepth = 5
val maxBins = 32

val model = DecisionTree.trainRegressor(trainingData,
categoricalFeaturesInfo, impurity,
maxDepth, maxBins)
val predictionsAndLabels = testData.map(example =>
(model.predict(example.features), example.label)
)
```

8. We instantiate the `RegressionMetrics` object and start the evaluation:

```scala
val metrics = new RegressionMetrics(predictionsAndLabels)
```

9. We print out the statistics value in the console:

```scala
// Squared error
println(s"MSE = ${metrics.meanSquaredError}")
 println(s"RMSE = ${metrics.rootMeanSquaredError}")

// R-squared
println(s"R-squared = ${metrics.r2}")

// Mean absolute error
println(s"MAE = ${metrics.meanAbsoluteError}")

// Explained variance
println(s"Explained variance = ${metrics.explainedVariance}")
```

From the console output:

```
MSE = 0.06071332254584681
RMSE = 0.2464007356844675
R-squared = 0.7444017305996473
MAE = 0.0691747572815534
Explained variance = 0.22591111058744653
```

10. We then close the program by stopping the Spark session:

```scala
spark.stop()
```

How it works...

In this recipe, we explored the generation of regression metrics to help us evaluate our regression model. We began to load a breast cancer data file and then split it in a 70/30 ratio to create training and test datasets. Next, we trained a `DecisionTree` regression model and utilized it to make predictions on our test set. Finally, we took the predictions and generated regression metrics which gave us the squared error, R-squared, mean absolute error, and explained variance.

There's more...

We can use `RegressionMetrics()` to produce the following statistical measures:

- MSE
- RMSE
- R-squared
- MAE
- Explained variance

Documentation on regression validation is available at `https://en.wikipedia.org/wiki/Regression_validation`.

R-Squared/coefficient of determination is available at `https://en.wikipedia.org/wiki/Coefficient_of_determination`.

See also

- The Wisconsin breast cancer dataset could be downloaded at `ftp://ftp.cs.wisc.edu/math-prog/cpo-dataset/machine-learn/cancer/cancer1/datacum`
- Regression metrics documents are available at `http://spark.apache.org/docs/latest/api/scala/index.html#org.apache.spark.mllib.evaluation.RegressionMetrics`

Binary classification model evaluation using Spark 2.0

In this recipe, we demonstrate the use of the `BinaryClassificationMetrics` facility in Spark 2.0 and its application to evaluating a model that has a binary outcome (for example, a logistic regression).

The purpose here is not to showcase the regression itself, but to demonstrate how to go about evaluating it using common metrics such as **receiver operating characteristic (ROC)**, Area Under ROC Curve, thresholds, and so on.

We recommend that you concentrate on step 8 since we cover regression in more detail in Chapter 5, *Practical Machine Learning with Regression and Classification in Spark 2.0 - Part I* and Chapter 6, *Practical Machine Learning with Regression and Classification in Spark 2.0 - Part II.*

How to do it...

1. Start a new project in IntelliJ or in an IDE of your choice. Make sure that the necessary JAR files are included.

2. Set up the package location where the program will reside:

   ```
   package spark.ml.cookbook.chapter4
   ```

3. Import the necessary packages for SparkContext to get access to the cluster:

   ```
   import org.apache.spark.sql.SparkSession
   import
   org.apache.spark.mllib.classification.LogisticRegressionWithLBFGS
   import
   org.apache.spark.mllib.evaluation.BinaryClassificationMetrics
   import org.apache.spark.mllib.regression.LabeledPoint
   import org.apache.spark.mllib.util.MLUtils
   ```

4. Create Spark's configuration and SparkContext:

   ```
   val spark = SparkSession
   .builder
   .master("local[*]")
   ```

```
.appName ("myBinaryClassification")
.config ("spark.sql.warehouse.dir", ".")
.getOrCreate ()
```

5. We download the dataset, originally from the UCI, and modify it to fit the need for the code:

```
// Load training data in LIBSVM format
//https://www.csie.ntu.edu.tw/~cjlin/libsvmtools/datasets/binary.ht
ml
val data = MLUtils.loadLibSVMFile(spark.sparkContext,
"../data/sparkml2/chapter4/myBinaryClassificationData.txt")
```

The dataset is a modified dataset. The original adult dataset has 14 features, among which six are continuous and eight are categorical. In this dataset, continuous features are discretized into quantiles, and each quantile is represented by a binary feature. We modified the data to fit the purpose of the code. Details of the dataset feature can be found at the http://archive.ics.uci.edu/ml/index.php UCI site.

6. We split the dataset into training and test parts in a ratio of 60:40 random split, then get the model:

```
val Array(training, test) = data.randomSplit(Array(0.6, 0.4), seed
= 11L)
 training.cache()

 // Run training algorithm to build the model
val model = new LogisticRegressionWithLBFGS ()
 .setNumClasses(2)
 .run(training)
```

7. We create the prediction using the model created by the training dataset:

```
val predictionAndLabels = test.map { case LabeledPoint (label,
features) =>
 val prediction = model.predict(features)
 (prediction, label)
 }
```

8. We create the BinaryClassificationMetrics object from the predication, and start the evaluation on the metrics:

```
val metrics = new BinaryClassificationMetrics(predictionAndLabels)
```

9. We print out the precision by `Threashold` in the console:

```
val precision = metrics.precisionByThreshold
precision.foreach { case (t, p) =>
println(s"Threshold: $t, Precision: $p")
}
```

From the console output:

```
Threshold: 2.9751613212299755E-210, Precision: 0.5405405405405406
Threshold: 1.0, Precision: 0.4838709677419355
Threshold: 1.5283665404870175E-268, Precision: 0.5263157894736842
Threshold: 4.889258814400478E-95, Precision: 0.5
```

10. We print out the `recallByThreshold` in the console:

```
val recall = metrics.recallByThreshold
recall.foreach { case (t, r) =>
println(s"Threshold: $t, Recall: $r")
}
```

From the console output:

```
Threshold: 1.0779893231660571E-300, Recall: 0.6363636363636364
Threshold: 6.830452412352692E-181, Recall: 0.5151515151515151
Threshold: 0.0, Recall: 1.0
Threshold: 1.1547199216963482E-194, Recall: 0.5757575757575758
```

11. We print out the `fmeasureByThreshold` in the console:

```
val f1Score = metrics.fMeasureByThreshold
f1Score.foreach { case (t, f) =>
println(s"Threshold: $t, F-score: $f, Beta = 1")
}
```

From the console output:

```
Threshold: 1.0, F-score: 0.46874999999999994, Beta = 1
Threshold: 4.889258814400478E-95, F-score: 0.49230769230769234,
Beta = 1
Threshold: 2.2097791212639423E-117, F-score: 0.48484848484848486,
Beta = 1

val beta = 0.5
val fScore = metrics.fMeasureByThreshold(beta)
f1Score.foreach { case (t, f) =>
  println(s"Threshold: $t, F-score: $f, Beta = 0.5")
}
```

From the console output:

```
Threshold: 2.9751613212299755E-210, F-score: 0.5714285714285714,
Beta = 0.5
Threshold: 1.0, F-score: 0.46874999999999994, Beta = 0.5
Threshold: 1.5283665404870175E-268, F-score: 0.5633802816901409,
Beta = 0.5
Threshold: 4.889258814400478E-95, F-score: 0.49230769230769234,
Beta = 0.5
```

12. We print out the `Area Under Precision Recall Curve` in the console:

```
val auPRC = metrics.areaUnderPR
println("Area under precision-recall curve = " + auPRC)
```

From the console output:

```
Area under precision-recall curve = 0.5768388996048239
```

13. We print out the Area Under ROC curve in the console:

```
val thresholds = precision.map(_._1)

val roc = metrics.roc

val auROC = metrics.areaUnderROC
println("Area under ROC = " + auROC)
```

From the console output:

```
Area under ROC = 0.6983957219251337
```

14. We then close the program by stopping the Spark session:

```
spark.stop()
```

How it works...

In this recipe, we investigated the evaluation of metrics for binary classification. First, we loaded the data, which is in the `libsvm` format, and split it in the ratio of 60:40, resulting in the creation of a training and a test set of data. Next, we trained a logistic regression model followed by generating predictions from our test set.

Once we had our predictions, we created a binary classification metrics object. Finally, we retrieved the true positive rate, positive predictive value, receiver operating curve, area under receiver operating curve, area under precision recall curve, and F-measure to evaluate our model for fitness.

There's more...

Spark provides the following metrics to facilitate evaluation:

- TPR - True Positive Rate
- PPV - Positive Predictive Value
- F - F-Measure
- ROC - Receiver Operating Curve
- AUROC - Area Under Receiver Operating Curve
- AUORC - Area Under Precision-Recall Curve

The following links should provide a good introductory material for the metrics:

- https://en.wikipedia.org/wiki/Receiver_operating_characteristic
- https://en.wikipedia.org/wiki/Sensitivity_and_specificity
- https://en.wikipedia.org/wiki/F1_score

See also

Documentation for the original dataset information is available at the following links:

- https://www.csie.ntu.edu.tw/~cjlin/libsvmtools/datasets/binary.html
- http://archive.ics.uci.edu/ml/datasets.html

Documentation for binary classification metrics is available at http://spark.apache.org/docs/latest/api/scala/index.html#org.apache.spark.mllib.evaluation.BinaryClassificationMetrics.

Multiclass classification model evaluation using Spark 2.0

In this recipe, we explore `MulticlassMetrics`, which allows you to evaluate a model that classifies the output to more than two labels (for example, red, blue, green, purple, do-not-know). It highlights the use of confusion matrix (`confusionMatrix`) and model accuracy.

How to do it...

1. Start a new project in IntelliJ or in an IDE of your choice. Make sure that the necessary JAR files are included.

2. Set up the package location where the program will reside:

    ```
    package spark.ml.cookbook.chapter4
    ```

3. Import the necessary packages for SparkContext to get access to the cluster:

    ```
    import org.apache.spark.sql.SparkSession
    import
    org.apache.spark.mllib.classification.LogisticRegressionWithLBFGS
    import org.apache.spark.mllib.evaluation.MulticlassMetrics
    import org.apache.spark.mllib.regression.LabeledPoint
    import org.apache.spark.mllib.util.MLUtils
    ```

4. Create Spark's configuration and SparkContext:

    ```
    val spark = SparkSession
    .builder
    .master("local[*]")
    .appName("myMulticlass")
    .config("spark.sql.warehouse.dir", ".")
    .getOrCreate()
    ```

5. We download the dataset, originally from the UCI, and modify it to fit the need of the code:

    ```
    // Load training data in LIBSVM format
    //https://www.csie.ntu.edu.tw/~cjlin/libsvmtools/datasets/multiclas
    s.html
    val data = MLUtils.loadLibSVMFile(spark.sparkContext,
    "../data/sparkml2/chapter4/myMulticlassIrisData.txt")
    ```

The dataset is a modified dataset. The original Iris Plant dataset has four features. We modified the data to fit the purpose of the code. Details of the dataset features can be found at the UCI site.

6. We split the dataset into training and test parts in a ratio of 60% versus 40% random split, then get the model:

```
val Array(training, test) = data.randomSplit(Array(0.6, 0.4), seed
= 11L)
 training.cache()

 // Run training algorithm to build the model
val model = new LogisticRegressionWithLBFGS()
 .setNumClasses(3)
 .run(training)
```

7. We compute the raw score on the test dataset:

```
val predictionAndLabels = test.map { case LabeledPoint(label,
features) =>
 val prediction = model.predict(features)
 (prediction, label)
 }
```

8. We create the `MulticlassMetrics` object from the predication, and start the evaluation on the metrics:

```
val metrics = new MulticlassMetrics(predictionAndLabels)
```

9. We print out the confusion matrix in the console:

```
println("Confusion matrix:")
println(metrics.confusionMatrix)
```

From the console output:

```
Confusion matrix:
18.0 0.0 0.0
0.0 15.0 8.0
0.0 0.0 22.0
```

10. We print out the overall statistics in the console:

```
val accuracy = metrics.accuracy
println("Summary Statistics")
println(s"Accuracy = $accuracy")
```

From the console output:

```
Summary Statistics
Accuracy = 0.873015873015873
```

11. We print out the precision by label value in the console:

```
val labels = metrics.labels
labels.foreach { l =>
  println(s"Precision($l) = " + metrics.precision(l))
  }
```

From the console output:

```
Precision(0.0) = 1.0
Precision(1.0) = 1.0
Precision(2.0) = 0.7333333333333333
```

12. We print out the recall by label in the console:

```
labels.foreach { l =>
  println(s"Recall($l) = " + metrics.recall(l))
  }
```

From the console output:

```
Recall(0.0) = 1.0
Recall(1.0) = 0.6521739130434783
Recall(2.0) = 1.0
```

13. We print out the false positive rate by label in the console:

```
labels.foreach { l =>
  println(s"FPR($l) = " + metrics.falsePositiveRate(l))
  }
```

From the console output:

```
FPR(0.0) = 0.0
FPR(1.0) = 0.0
FPR(2.0) = 0.1951219512195122
```

14. We print out the F-measure by label in the console:

```
labels.foreach { l =>
  println(s"F1-Score($l) = " + metrics.fMeasure(l))
  }
```

From the console output:

```
F1-Score(0.0) = 1.0
F1-Score(1.0) = 0.7894736842105263
F1-Score(2.0) = 0.846153846153846
```

15. We print out the weighted statistics value in the console:

```
println(s"Weighted precision: ${metrics.weightedPrecision}")
 println(s"Weighted recall: ${metrics.weightedRecall}")
 println(s"Weighted F1 score: ${metrics.weightedFMeasure}")
 println(s"Weighted false positive rate:
${metrics.weightedFalsePositiveRate}")
```

From the console output:

```
Weighted precision: 0.9068783068783068
Weighted recall: 0.873015873015873
Weighted F1 score: 0.8694171325750273
Weighted false positive rate: 0.06813782423538521
```

16. We then close the program by stopping the Spark session:

```
spark.stop()
```

How it works...

In this recipe, we explored generating evaluation metrics for a multi-classification model. First, we loaded the Iris data into memory and split it in a ratio 60:40. Second, we trained a logistic regression model with the number of classifications set to three. Third, we made predictions with the test dataset and utilized `MultiClassMetric` to generate evaluation measurements. Finally, we evaluated metrics such as the model accuracy, weighted precision, weighted recall, weighted F1 score, weighted false positive rate, and so on.

There's more...

While the scope of the book does not allow for a complete treatment of the confusion matrix, a short explanation and a link are provided as a quick reference.

The confusion matrix is just a fancy name for an error matrix. It is mostly used in unsupervised learning to visualize the performance. It is a layout that captures actual versus predicted outcomes with an identical set of labels in two dimensions:

Confusion Matrix

	Predicted		
	Label1	*Label2*	*Label3*
Actual	*18.0*	*0.0*	*0.0*
	0.0	*15.0*	*8.0*
	0.0	*0.0*	*22.0*

To get a quick introduction to the confusion matrix in unsupervised and supervised statistical learning systems, see `https://en.wikipedia.org/wiki/Confusion_matrix`.

See also

Documentation for original dataset information is available at the following websites:

- `https://www.csie.ntu.edu.tw/~cjlin/libsvmtools/datasets/multiclass.html`
- `http://archive.ics.uci.edu/ml/datasets/Iris`

Documentation for multiclass classification metrics is available at:

- `http://spark.apache.org/docs/latest/api/scala/index.html#org.apache.spark.mllib.evaluation.MulticlassMetrics`

Multilabel classification model evaluation using Spark 2.0

In this recipe, we explore multilabel classification `MultilabelMetrics` in Spark 2.0 which should not be mixed up with the previous recipe dealing with multiclass classification `MulticlassMetrics`. The key to exploring this recipe is to concentrate on evaluation metrics such as Hamming loss, accuracy, f1-measure, and so on, and what they measure.

How to do it...

1. Start a new project in IntelliJ or in an IDE of your choice. Make sure that the necessary JAR files are included.

2. Set up the package location where the program will reside:

   ```
   package spark.ml.cookbook.chapter4
   ```

3. Import the necessary packages for SparkContext to get access to the cluster:

   ```
   import org.apache.spark.sql.SparkSession
   import org.apache.spark.mllib.evaluation.MultilabelMetrics
   import org.apache.spark.rdd.RDD
   ```

4. Create Spark's configuration and SparkContext:

   ```
   val spark = SparkSession
   .builder
   .master("local[*]")
   .appName("myMultilabel")
   .config("spark.sql.warehouse.dir", ".")
   .getOrCreate()
   ```

5. We create the dataset for the evaluation model:

   ```
   val data: RDD[(Array[Double], Array[Double])] =
   spark.sparkContext.parallelize(
   Seq((Array(0.0, 1.0), Array(0.1, 2.0)),
       (Array(0.0, 2.0), Array(0.1, 1.0)),
       (Array.empty[Double], Array(0.0)),
       (Array(2.0), Array(2.0)),
       (Array(2.0, 0.0), Array(2.0, 0.0)),
       (Array(0.0, 1.0, 2.0), Array(0.0, 1.0)),
       (Array(1.0), Array(1.0, 2.0))), 2)
   ```

6. We create the `MultilabelMetrics` object from the predication, and start the evaluation on the metrics:

   ```
   val metrics = new MultilabelMetrics(data)
   ```

7. We print out the overall statistics summary in the console:

```
println(s"Recall = ${metrics.recall}")
println(s"Precision = ${metrics.precision}")
println(s"F1 measure = ${metrics.f1Measure}")
println(s"Accuracy = ${metrics.accuracy}")
```

From the console output:

```
Recall = 0.5
Precision = 0.5238095238095238
F1 measure = 0.4952380952380952
Accuracy = 0.4523809523809524
```

8. We print out the individual label value in the console:

```
metrics.labels.foreach(label =>
 println(s"Class $label precision = ${metrics.precision(label)}"))
 metrics.labels.foreach(label => println(s"Class $label recall =
 ${metrics.recall(label)}"))
 metrics.labels.foreach(label => println(s"Class $label F1-score =
 ${metrics.f1Measure(label)}"))
```

From the console output:

```
Class 0.0 precision = 0.5
Class 1.0 precision = 0.6666666666666666
Class 2.0 precision = 0.5
Class 0.0 recall = 0.6666666666666666
Class 1.0 recall = 0.6666666666666666
Class 2.0 recall = 0.5
Class 0.0 F1-score = 0.5714285714285715
Class 1.0 F1-score = 0.6666666666666666
Class 2.0 F1-score = 0.5
```

9. We print out the micro statistics value in the console:

```
println(s"Micro recall = ${metrics.microRecall}")
println(s"Micro precision = ${metrics.microPrecision}")
println(s"Micro F1 measure = ${metrics.microF1Measure}")
From the console output:
Micro recall = 0.5
Micro precision = 0.5454545454545454
Micro F1 measure = 0.5217391304347826
```

10. We print out the Hamming loss and subset accuracy from the metrics in the console:

```
println(s"Hamming loss = ${metrics.hammingLoss}")
println(s"Subset accuracy = ${metrics.subsetAccuracy}")
From the console output:
Hamming loss = 0.39285714285714285
Subset accuracy = 0.2857142857142857
```

11. We then close the program by stopping the Spark session.

```
spark.stop()
```

How it works...

In this recipe, we investigated generating evaluation metrics for the multilabel classification model. We began with manually creating a dataset for the model evaluation. Next, we passed our dataset as an argument to the `MultilabelMetrics` and generated evaluation metrics. Finally, we printed out various metrics such as micro recall, micro precision, micro f1-measure, Hamming loss, subset accuracy, and so on.

There's more...

Note that the multilabel and multiclass classifications sound similar, but they are two different things.

All multilabel `MultilabelMetrics()` method is trying to accomplish is to map a number of inputs (x) to a binary vector (y) rather than numerical values in a typical classification system.

The important metrics associated with the multilabel classification are (see the preceding code):

- Accuracy
- Hamming loss
- Precision
- Recall
- F1

A full explanation of each parameter is out of scope, but the following link provides a short treatment for the multilabel metrics:

```
https://en.wikipedia.org/wiki/Multi-label_classification
```

See also

Documentation for multilabel classification metrics:

- `http://spark.apache.org/docs/latest/api/scala/index.html#org.apache.sp ark.mllib.evaluation.MultilabelMetrics`

Using the Scala Breeze library to do graphics in Spark 2.0

In this recipe, we will use the functions `scatter()` and `plot()` from the Scala Breeze linear algebra library (part of) to draw a scatter plot from a two-dimensional data. Once the results are computed on the Spark cluster, either the actionable data can be used in the driver for drawing or a JPEG or GIF can be generated in the backend and pushed forward for efficiency and speed (popular with GPU-based analytical databases such as MapD)

How to do it...

1. First, we need to download the necessary ScalaNLP library. Download the JAR from the Maven repository available
   at `https://repo1.maven.org/maven2/org/scalanlp/breeze-viz_2.11/0.12/bre eze-viz_2.11-0.12.jar`.

2. Place the JAR in the `C:\spark-2.0.0-bin-hadoop2.7\examples\jars` directory on a Windows machine:

3. In macOS, please put the JAR in its correct path. For our setting examples, the path is `/Users/USERNAME/spark/spark-2.0.0-bin-hadoop2.7/examples/jars/`.

4. The following is the sample screenshot showing the JARs:

5. Start a new project in IntelliJ or in an IDE of your choice. Make sure the necessary JAR files are included.

6. Set up the package location where the program will reside:

```
package spark.ml.cookbook.chapter4
```

7. Import the necessary packages for the Spark session to gain access to the cluster and `log4j.Logger` to reduce the amount of output produced by Spark:

```
import org.apache.log4j.{Level, Logger}
import org.apache.spark.sql.SparkSession
import breeze.plot._

import scala.util.Random
```

8. Set the output level to ERROR to reduce Spark's logging output:

```
Logger.getLogger("org").setLevel(Level.ERROR)
```

9. Initialize a Spark session by specifying configurations with the builder pattern, thus making an entry point available for the Spark cluster:

```
val spark = SparkSession
.builder
.master("local[*]")
.appName("myBreezeChart")
.config("spark.sql.warehouse.dir", ".")
.getOrCreate()
```

10. Now we create the figure object, and set the parameter for the figure:

```
import spark.implicits._

val fig = Figure()
val chart = fig.subplot(0)

chart.title = "My Breeze-Viz Chart"
chart.xlim(21,100)
chart.ylim(0,100000)
```

11. We create a dataset from random numbers, and display the dataset.

12. The dataset will be used later.

```
val ages = spark.createDataset(Random.shuffle(21 to
100).toList.take(45)).as[Int]

ages.show(false)
```

From the console output:

```
+-----+
|value|
+-----+
|85   |
|51   |
|82   |
|78   |
|45   |
|42   |
|35   |
|94   |
|72   |
|22   |
|44   |
|33   |
|48   |
|29   |
|47   |
|59   |
|91   |
|21   |
|28   |
|64   |
+-----+
only showing top 20 rows
```

13. We collect the dataset, and set up the *x* and *y* axis.

14. For the photo part, we convert the datatype to double, and derive the value to $y2$.

15. We use the Breeze library's scatter method to put the data into the chart, and plot the diagonal line with the plot method from Breeze:

```
val x = ages.collect()
val y = Random.shuffle(20000 to 100000).toList.take(45)

val x2 = ages.collect().map(xx => xx.toDouble)
val y2 = x2.map(xx => (1000 * xx) + (xx * 2))

chart += scatter(x, y, _ => 0.5)
chart += plot(x2, y2)

chart.xlabel = "Age"
chart.ylabel = "Income"

fig.refresh()
```

16. We set the label for both the x axis and y axis and refresh the figure object.
17. The following is the generated Breeze chart:

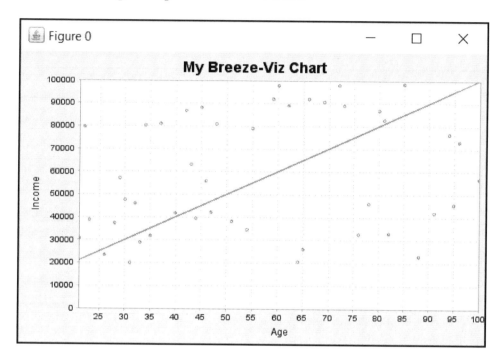

18. We close the program by stopping the Spark session:

```
spark.stop()
```

How it works...

In this recipe, we created a dataset in Spark from random numbers. We then created a Breeze figure and set up the basic parameters. We derived x, y data from the created dataset.

We used Breeze's `scatter()` and `plot()` functions to do graphics using the Breeze library.

There's more...

One can use Breeze as an alternative to more complicated and powerful charting libraries such as JFreeChart, demonstrated in the previous chapter. The ScalaNLP project tends to be optimized with Scala goodies such as implicit conversions that make the coding relatively easier.

The Breeze graphics JAR file can be downloaded at `http://central.maven.org/maven2/org/scalanlp/breeze-viz_2.11/0.12/breeze-viz_2.11-0.12.jar`.

More about Breeze graphics can be found at `https://github.com/scalanlp/breeze/wiki/Quickstart`.

The API document (please note, the API document is not necessarily up-to-date) can be found at `http://www.scalanlp.org/api/breeze/#package`.

 Note that once you are in the root package, you need click on **Breeze** to see the details.

See also

For more information on Breeze, see the original material on GitHub at `https://github.com/scalanlp/breeze`.

 Note that once you are in the root package, you need to click on **Breeze** to see the details.

For more information regarding the Breeze API documentation, please download the `https://repo1.maven.org/maven2/org/scalanlp/breeze-viz_2.11/0.12/breeze-viz_2.11-0.12-javadoc.jar` JAR.

5
Practical Machine Learning with Regression and Classification in Spark 2.0 - Part I

In this chapter, we will cover the following recipes:

- Fitting a linear regression line to data the old-fashioned way
- Generalized linear regression in Spark 2.0
- Linear regression API with Lasso and L-BFGS in Spark 2.0
- Linear regression API with Lasso and auto optimization selection in Spark 2.0
- Linear regression API with ridge regression and auto optimization selection in Spark 2.0
- Isotonic regression in Apache Spark 2.0
- Multilayer perceptron classifier in Apache Spark 2.0
- One versus Rest classifier (One-vs-All) in Apache Spark 2.0
- Survival regression - parametric AFT model in Apache Spark 2.0

Introduction

This chapter, along with the next chapter, covers the fundamental techniques for regression and classification available in Spark 2.0 ML and MLlib library. Spark 2.0 highlights a new direction by moving the RDD-based regressions (see the next chapter) to maintenance mode while emphasizing **Linear Regression** and **Generalized Regression** going forward.

At a high level, the new API design favors parameterization of elastic net to produce the ridge versus Lasso regression and everything in between, as opposed to a named API (for example, `LassoWithSGD`). The new API approach is a much cleaner design and forces you to learn elastic net and its power when it comes to feature engineering that remains an art in data science. We provide adequate examples, variations, and notes to guide you through the complexities in these techniques.

The following figure depicts the regression and classification coverage (part 1) in this chapter:

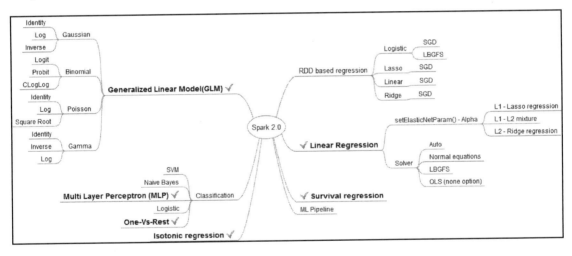

First, you will learn how to implement linear regression using algebraic equations via just Scala code and RDDs from scratch to get an insight for the math and why we need an iterative optimization method to estimate the solution for a large system of regressions. Second, we explore the **generalized linear model (GLM)** and its various statistical distribution families and link functions while stressing its limitation to 4,096 parameters only in the current implementation. Third, we tackle the **linear regression model (LRM)** and how to use the elastic net parameterization to mix and match L1 and L2 penalty functions to achieve logistic, ridge, Lasso, and everything in between. We also explore the solver (that is, optimizer) method and how to set it to use L-BFGS optimization, auto optimizer selection, and so on.

After exploring the GLM and linear regression recipes, we proceed to provide recipes for more exotic regression/classification methods such as isotonic regression, multilayer perceptron (that is, form of neuron net), One-vs-Rest, and survival regression to demonstrate Spark 2.0's power and completeness to deal with cases that are not addressed by linear techniques. With the increased risks in the financial world in the early 21st century and new advancements in genome, Spark 2.0 also pulls together four important methods (isotonic regression, multilayer perceptron, One-vs-Rest, and survival regression or parametric ATF) in an easy to use machine learning library. The parametric ATF method at scale should be of particular interest to financial, data scientist, or actuarial professionals alike.

Even though some of these methods such as `LinearRegression()` API, have theoretically been available since 1.3x+, it is important to note that Spark 2.0 pulls all of them together in an easy-to-use and maintainable API (that is, backward compatibility) in a glmnet R-like manner as they move the RDD-based regression API into maintenance mode. The L-BFGS optimizer and normal equations take a front seat while SGD is available in RDD-based APIs for backward compatibility.

Elastic net is the preferred method that can not only deal with L1 (Lasso regression) and L2 (ridge regression) in absolute terms prefered method for regularization, but also provide a dial-like mechanism that enables the user to fine-tune the penalty function (parameter shrinkage versus selection). While we recall using the elastic net function in 1.4.2, Spark 2.0 pulls it all together without the need to deal with each individual API for parameter tuning (important when selecting a model dynamically based on the latest data). As we start diving into the recipes, we strongly encourage the user to explore various parameter settings `setElasticNetParam()` and `setSolver()` configurations to master these powerful APIs. It is important not to mix the penalty function `setElasticNetParam(value: Double)` (L1 , L2, OLs, elastic net: linearly mixed L1/L2), which are regular or model penalty schemes with optimization (normal, L-BFGS, auto, and so on) techniques that are related to cost function optimization techniques.

It is critical to note that the RDD-based regressions are still very important since there are a lot of current ML implementation systems that rely heavily on the previous API regime and its SGD optimizer. Please see the next chapter for complete treatment with teaching notes covering RDD-based regressions.

Fitting a linear regression line to data the old fashioned way

In this recipe, we use RDDs and a closed form formula to code a simple linear equation from scratch. The reason we use this as the first recipe is to demonstrate that you can always implement any given statistical learning algorithm via the RDDs to achieve computational scale using Apache Spark.

How to do it...

1. Start a new project in IntelliJ or in an IDE of your choice. Make sure the necessary JAR files are included.

2. Set up the package location where the program will reside:

   ```
   package spark.ml.cookbook.chapter5
   ```

3. Import the necessary packages for `SparkSession` to gain access to the cluster and `log4j.Logger` to reduce the amount of output produced by Spark:

   ```
   import org.apache.spark.sql.SparkSession
   import scala.math._
   import org.apache.log4j.Logger
   import org.apache.log4j.Level
   ```

4. Initialize a `SparkSession` specifying configurations with the builder pattern thus making an entry point available for the Spark cluster:

   ```
   val spark = SparkSession
    .builder
    .master("local[4]")
    .appName("myRegress01_20")
    .config("spark.sql.warehouse.dir", ".")
    .getOrCreate()
   ```

5. Set output level to ERROR to reduce Spark's output:

   ```
   Logger.getLogger("org").setLevel(Level.ERROR)
   Logger.getLogger("akka").setLevel(Level.ERROR)
   ```

6. We create two arrays representing the dependent (that is, y) and an independent variable (that is, x):

```
val x =
Array(1.0,5.0,8.0,10.0,15.0,21.0,27.0,30.0,38.0,45.0,50.0,64.0)
val y =
Array(5.0,1.0,4.0,11.0,25.0,18.0,33.0,20.0,30.0,43.0,55.0,57.0)
```

7. We use `sc.parallelize(x)` to transform the two arrays to RDDs:

```
val xRDD = sc.parallelize(x)
val yRDD = sc.parallelize(y)
```

8. In this step, we demonstrate the `zip()` method of an RDD that creates pairs of dependent/independent tuples *(y,x)* from the two RDDs. We introduce this function since you must often learn to work with pairs in machine learning algorithms:

```
val zipedRDD = xRDD.zip(yRDD)
```

9. To make sure we understand the `zip()` functionality, let's take a look at the output, but make sure you include the `collect()` or some other form of action to make sure the data is presented in order. If we do not use an action method, the output from RDDs will be random:

```
zipedRDD.collect().foreach(println)
(5.0,1.0)
(8.0,4.0)
(10.0,11.0)
(15.0,25.0)
(21.0,18.0)
(27.0,33.0)
(30.0,20.0)
(38.0,30.0)
(45.0,43.0)
(50.0,55.0)
(64.0,57.0)
```

10. This is an important step that demonstrates how to iterate, access, and compute on each individual member of the pair. In order to compute the regression line, we need to compute sum, product, and averages (that is, *sum(x)*, *sum(y)*, and *sum (x * y)*). The `map(_._1).sum()` function is a mechanism in which the RDD pairs are iterated upon, but only the first elements are considered:

```
val xSum = zipedRDD.map(_._1).sum()
val ySum = zipedRDD.map(_._2).sum()
val xySum= zipedRDD.map(c => c._1 * c._2).sum()
```

11. In this step we continue with computing the averages of individual RDD's pair member along with their product. These individual computations (that is, *mean(x)*, *mean(y)*, and *mean(x*y)*), along with mean squared, will be used to compute the slope and intercept of the regression line. While we could have computed the mean from the previous statistics in the previous steps manually, we should make sure we are familiar with methods that are available intrinsically via an RDD:

```
val n= zipedRDD.count()
val xMean = zipedRDD.map(_._1).mean()
val yMean = zipedRDD.map(_._2).mean()
val xyMean = zipedRDD.map(c => c._1 * c._2).mean()
```

12. This is the final step, in which we compute the mean of x and y squared:

```
val xSquaredMean = zipedRDD.map(_._1).map(x => x * x).mean()
val ySquaredMean = zipedRDD.map(_._2).map(y => y * y).mean()
```

13. We print the statistic for completeness:

```
println("xMean yMean xyMean", xMean, yMean, xyMean)
xMean yMean xyMean ,26.16,25.16,989.08
```

14. We compute the numerator and denominator for the formula:

```
val numerator = xMean * yMean  - xyMean
val denominator = xMean * xMean - xSquaredMean
```

15. We finally compute the slope of the regression line:

```
val slope = numerator / denominator
println("slope %f5".format(slope))


slope 0.9153145
```

16. We now calculate the intercept and print. If you do not want the intercept (intercept to be set to 0), then the formula for the slope needs to be slightly modified. You can look for more details in other sources such as the internet and find the required equation:

```
val b_intercept = yMean - (slope*xMean)
println("Intercept", b_intercept)

Intercept,1.21
```

17. Using the slope and intercept, we write the regression line equation as follows:

```
Y = 1.21 + .9153145 * X
```

How it works...

We declared two Scala arrays, parallelized them into two RDDs that are separate vectors of `x()` and `y()`. We then used the `zip()` method from the RDD API to produce a paired (that is, zipped) RDD. It results in an RDD in which each member is an *(x , y)* pair. We then proceed to calculate the mean, sum, and so on, and apply the closed form formula as described to find the intercept and slope for the regression line.

In Spark 2.0, the alternative would have been to use the GLM API out of the box. It is worth mentioning that the maximum number of parameters for a closed normal form scheme supported by GLM is limited to 4,096.

We used a closed form formula to demonstrate that a regression line associated with a set of numbers *(Y1, X1), ..., (Yn, Xn)* is simply the line that minimizes the sum of the square errors. In a simple regression equation, the line is as follows:

- Slope of the regression line $\beta = \dfrac{\bar{xy} - \bar{x}\bar{y}}{\bar{x^2} - \bar{x}^2}$

- Offset of the regression line $a = \bar{y} - \beta \bar{x}$

- The equation for the regression line $y = a + \beta x$

A regression line is simply the best fit line that minimizes the sum of the square error. For a set of points (dependent variable, independent variable), there are many lines that can pass through these points and capture the general linear relationship, but only one of those lines is the line that minimizes all the errors from such a fit.

For the example, we presented the line $Y = 1.21 + .9153145 * X$. Shown in the following figure is such a line and we computed the slope and the offset with a closed form formula. The linear model depicted by the linear equation of a line represents our best linear model (*slope=.915345, intercept= 1.21*) for the given data using closed form formulas:

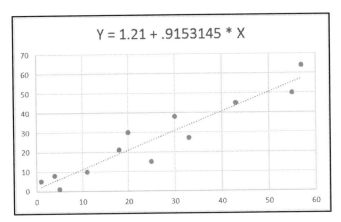

The data points plotted in the preceding figure are as follows:

```
(Y,  X)
(5.0,     1.0)
(8.0,     4.0)
(10.0,   11.0)
(15.0,   25.0)
(21.0,   18.0)
(27.0,   33.0)
(30.0,   20.0)
(38.0,   30.0)
(45.0,   43.0)
(50.0,   55.0)
(64.0,   57.0)
```

There's more...

It should be noted that not all regression forms have a closed form formula or become very inefficient (that is, impractical) with a large number of parameters on large datasets - this is the reason we use optimization techniques such as SGD or L-BFGS.

It is critical to recall from the previous recipes that you should make sure you cache any RDD or data structure associated with machine learning algorithms to avoid lazy instantiation due to the way Spark optimizes and maintains lineage (that is, lazy instantiation).

See also

We recommend a book from Stanford University, which can be downloaded from the following site for free. It is a classic and a must-read whether you are a new or advanced practitioner in the field:

The Elements of Statistical Learning, Data Mining, Inference, and Prediction, Second Edition, by Hastie, Tibshirani, and Friedman (2009). Springer-Verlag (`http://web.stanford.edu/~hastie/ElemStatLearn/`).

Generalized linear regression in Spark 2.0

This recipe covers the **generalized regression model** (**GLM**) implementation in Spark 2.0. There is a great parallel between this `GeneralizedLinearRegression` in Spark 2.0 and `glmnet` implementation in R. This API is a welcome addition that allows you to select and set both distribution family (for example, Gaussian) and link functions (for example, inverse log) with a coherent and well-designed API.

How to do it...

1. We use a housing dataset from the UCI machine library depository.

2. Download the entire dataset from the following URLs:
   - `https://archive.ics.uci.edu/ml/datasets/Housing`
   - `https://archive.ics.uci.edu/ml/machine-learning-databases/housing/`

   The dataset is comprised of 14 columns with the first 13 columns being the independent variables (that is, features) that try to explain the median price (that is, last column) of an owner-occupied house in Boston, USA.

   We have chosen and cleaned the first eight columns as features. We use the first 200 rows to train and predict the median price:

   - **CRIM**: Per capita crime rate by town
   - **ZN**: Proportion of residential land zoned for lots over 25,000 sq.ft
   - **INDUS**: Proportion of non-retail business acres per town
   - **CHAS**: Charles River dummy variable (= 1 if tract bounds river; 0 otherwise)

- **NOX**: Nitric oxide concentration (parts per 10 million)
- **RM**: Average number of rooms per dwelling
- **AGE**: Proportion of owner-occupied units built prior to 1940

3. Please use the `housing8.csv` file and make sure you move it to the following directory:

   `../data/sparkml2/chapter5/housing8.csv`

4. Start a new project in IntelliJ or in an IDE of your choice. Make sure the necessary JAR files are included.

5. Set up the package location where the program will reside:

   ```
   package spark.ml.cookbook.chapter5.
   ```

6. Import the necessary packages for `SparkSession` to gain access to the cluster and `log4j.Logger` to reduce the amount of output produced by Spark:

   ```
   import org.apache.spark.ml.feature.LabeledPoint
   import org.apache.spark.ml.linalg.Vectors
   import org.apache.spark.ml.regression.GeneralizedLinearRegression
   import org.apache.spark.sql.SparkSession
   import org.apache.log4j.{Level, Logger}
   ```

7. Set the output level to ERROR to reduce Spark's logging output:

   ```
   Logger.getLogger("org").setLevel(Level.ERROR)
   Logger.getLogger("akka").setLevel(Level.ERROR)
   ```

8. Initialize a `SparkSession` specifying configurations to gain access to the Spark cluster:

   ```
   val spark = SparkSession
   .builder
   .master("local[*]")
   .appName("GLR")
   .config("spark.sql.warehouse.dir", ".")
   .getOrCreate()
   ```

9. We need to import implicits for data conversion routines:

   ```
   import spark.implicits._
   ```

10. Next, we load housing data into a dataset:

```
val data = spark.read.textFile( "../data/sparkml2/
/chapter5/housing8.csv" ).as[ String ]
```

11. Let's parse the housing data and convert it into label points:

```
val regressionData = data.map { line =>
val columns = line.split(',')
LabeledPoint(columns(13).toDouble ,
Vectors.dense(columns(0).toDouble,columns(1).toDouble,
columns(2).toDouble, columns(3).toDouble,columns(4).toDouble,
columns(5).toDouble,columns(6).toDouble, columns(7).toDouble))
}
```

12. Now display the loaded data using the following code:

```
regressionData.show(false)
```

The output is as shown here:

```
+-----+-----------------------------------------------------+
|label|features                                             |
+-----+-----------------------------------------------------+
|24.0 |[0.00632,18.0,2.31,0.0,0.538,6.575,65.2,4.09]        |
|21.6 |[0.02731,0.0,7.07,0.0,0.469,6.421,78.9,4.9671]       |
|34.7 |[0.02729,0.0,7.07,0.0,0.469,7.185,61.1,4.9671]       |
|33.4 |[0.03237,0.0,2.18,0.0,0.458,6.998,45.8,6.0622]       |
|36.2 |[0.06905,0.0,2.18,0.0,0.458,7.147,54.2,6.0622]       |
|28.7 |[0.02985,0.0,2.18,0.0,0.458,6.43,58.7,6.0622]        |
|22.9 |[0.08829,12.5,7.87,0.0,0.524,6.012,66.6,5.5605]      |
|27.1 |[0.14455,12.5,7.87,0.0,0.524,6.172,96.1,5.9505]      |
|16.5 |[0.21124,12.5,7.87,0.0,0.524,5.631,100.0,6.0821]|
|18.9 |[0.17004,12.5,7.87,0.0,0.524,6.004,85.9,6.5921]      |
|15.0 |[0.22489,12.5,7.87,0.0,0.524,6.377,94.3,6.3467]      |
|18.9 |[0.11747,12.5,7.87,0.0,0.524,6.009,82.9,6.2267]      |
|21.7 |[0.09378,12.5,7.87,0.0,0.524,5.889,39.0,5.4509]      |
|20.4 |[0.62976,0.0,8.14,0.0,0.538,5.949,61.8,4.7075]       |
|18.2 |[0.63796,0.0,8.14,0.0,0.538,6.096,84.5,4.4619]       |
|19.9 |[0.62739,0.0,8.14,0.0,0.538,5.834,56.5,4.4986]       |
|23.1 |[1.05393,0.0,8.14,0.0,0.538,5.935,29.3,4.4986]       |
|17.5 |[0.7842,0.0,8.14,0.0,0.538,5.99,81.7,4.2579]         |
|20.2 |[0.80271,0.0,8.14,0.0,0.538,5.456,36.6,3.7965]       |
|18.2 |[0.7258,0.0,8.14,0.0,0.538,5.727,69.5,3.7965]        |
+-----+-----------------------------------------------------+
only showing top 20 rows
```

13. Next, we configure a generalized linear regression algorithm for generating a new model:

```
val glr = new GeneralizedLinearRegression()
.setMaxIter(1000)
.setRegParam(0.03) //the value ranges from 0.0 to 1.0.
Experimentation required to identify the right value.
.setFamily("gaussian")
.setLink( "identity" )
```

Feel free to experiment with different parameters for better fit.

14. We fit the model to the housing data:

```
val glrModel = glr.fit(regressionData)
```

15. Next, we retrieve the summary data to judge the accuracy of the model:

```
val summary = glrModel.summary
```

16. Finally, we print out the summary statistics:

```
val summary = glrModel.summary
summary.residuals().show()
println("Residual Degree Of Freedom: " +
summary.residualDegreeOfFreedom)
println("Residual Degree Of Freedom Null: " +
summary.residualDegreeOfFreedomNull)
println("AIC: " + summary.aic)
println("Dispersion: " + summary.dispersion)
println("Null Deviance: " + summary.nullDeviance)
println("Deviance: " +summary.deviance)
println("p-values: " + summary.pValues.mkString(","))
println("t-values: " + summary.tValues.mkString(","))
println("Coefficient Standard Error: " +
summary.coefficientStandardErrors.mkString(","))
}
```

17. We close the program by stopping the SparkSession:

```
spark.stop()
```

How it works...

In this recipe, we showed a generalized linear regression algorithm in action. We began by loading and parsing a CSV file into a dataset. Next, we created a generalized linear regression algorithm and generated a new model by passing our dataset to the `fit()` method. Once the fit operation was completed, we retrieved summary statistics from the model and displayed computed values to reconcile accuracy.

In this example, we explored fitting the data with a *Gaussian* distribution and *Identity*, but there are many more configurations that we can use to solve a specific regression fit, which are explained in the next section.

There's more...

The GLM in Spark 2.0 is a general-purpose regression model that can support many configurations. We are impressed with the number of families available as of the initial release of Spark 2.0.0.

It is important to note as of Spark 2.0.2:

- The maximum number of parameters for a regression is currently limited to 4,096 max.
- The only optimization (that is, solver) currently supported is **iteratively reweighted least squares** (**IRLS**), which is also the default solve.
- When you set the solver to *auto*, it defaults to IRLS.
- The `setRegParam()` sets the regularization parameter for L2 regularization. The regularization term is *0.5 * regParam * L2norm(coefficients)^2* per Spark 2.0 documentation - make sure you understand the implications.

If you are not sure how to handle the distribution fitting, we highly recommend one of our favorite books, *Handbook of Fitting Statistical Distributions with R*, that has served us well when modeling agricultural commodities such as CBOT Wheat, which has a reverse volatility smile curve (very different from equities).

Configuration and available options are as follows:

Distribution Family	Link Functions Currently Supported in Spark 2.0.0		
Gaussian	Identity	Log	Inverse
Binomial	Logit	Probit	CLogLog
Poisson	Identity	Log	Square Root
Gamma	Identity	Log	Inverse

Be sure to experiment with different families and link functions to make sure your assumption of the underlying distribution is correct.

See also

Documentation for `GeneralizedLinearRegression()` is available at the following link:

```
http://spark.apache.org/docs/latest/api/scala/index.html#org.apache.spark.ml.r
egression.GeneralizedLinearRegression
```

Some of the important API calls within `GeneralizedLinearRegression`:

- def **setFamily**(value: String): GeneralizedLinearRegression.this.type
- def **setLink**(value: String): GeneralizedLinearRegression.this.type
- def **setMaxIter**(value: Int): GeneralizedLinearRegression.this.type
- def **setRegParam**(value: Double): GeneralizedLinearRegression.this.type
- def **setSolver**(value: String): GeneralizedLinearRegression.this.type
- def **setFitIntercept**(value: Boolean): GeneralizedLinearRegression.this.type

The solver is currently IRLS; a quick reference can be found at the following link:

`https://en.wikipedia.org/wiki/Iteratively_reweighted_least_squares`

For complete understanding of the new approach with GLM and linear regression in Spark 2.0+, please be sure to consult and understand CRAN glmnet implementation in R:

- Main page is available
  at `https://cran.r-project.org/web/packages/glmnet/index.html`
- User guide is available at
  `https://cran.r-project.org/web/packages/glmnet/glmnet.pdf`

Linear regression API with Lasso and L-BFGS in Spark 2.0

In this recipe, we will demonstrate the use of Spark 2.0's `LinearRegression()` API to showcase a unified/parameterized API to tackle the linear regression in a comprehensive way capable of extension without backward-compatibility issues of an RDD-based named API. We show how to use the `setSolver()` to set the optimization method to first-order memory-efficient L-BFGS, which can deal with numerous amount of parameters (that is, especially in sparse configuration) with ease.

In this recipe, the `.setSolver()` is set to `lbgfs`, which makes the L-BFGS (see RDD-based regression for more detail) the selected optimization method. The `.setElasticNetParam()` is not set, so the default of `0` remains in effect, which makes this a Lasso regression.

How to do it...

1. We use a housing dataset from the UCI machine library depository.

2. Download the entire data set from the following URLs:
   - `https://archive.ics.uci.edu/ml/datasets/Housing`
   - `https://archive.ics.uci.edu/ml/machine-learning-databases/housing/`

The dataset is comprised of 14 columns with the first 13 columns being independent variables (that is, features) that try to explain the median price (that is, last column) of an owner-occupied house in Boston, USA.

We have chosen and cleaned the first eight columns as features. We use the first 200 rows to train and predict the median price:

- **CRIM**: Per capita crime rate by town
- **ZN**: Proportion of residential land zoned for lots over 25,000 sq.ft.
- **INDUS**: Proportion of non-retail business acres per town
- **CHAS**: Charles River dummy variable (= 1 if tract bounds river; 0 otherwise)
- **NOX**: Nitric oxide concentration (parts per 10 million)
- **RM**: Average number of rooms per dwelling
- **AGE**: Proportion of owner-occupied units built prior to 1940

3. Please use the `housing8.csv` file and make sure you move it to the following directory:

   ../data/sparkml2/chapter5/housing8.csv

4. Start a new project in IntelliJ or in an IDE of your choice. Make sure the necessary JAR files are included.

5. Set up the package location where the program will reside:

   ```
   package spark.ml.cookbook.chapter5.
   ```

6. Import the necessary packages for the `SparkSession` to gain access to the cluster and `log4j.Logger` to reduce the amount of output produced by Spark:

   ```
   import org.apache.spark.ml.regression.LinearRegression
   import org.apache.spark.ml.feature.LabeledPoint
   import org.apache.spark.sql.SparkSession
   import org.apache.spark.ml.linalg.Vectors
   import org.apache.log4j.{Level, Logger}
   ```

7. Set the output level to ERROR to reduce Spark's logging output:

```
Logger.getLogger("org").setLevel(Level.ERROR)
Logger.getLogger("akka").setLevel(Level.ERROR)
```

8. Initialize a SparkSession specifying configurations to gain access to the Spark cluster:

```
val spark = SparkSession
.builder
.master("local[*]")
.appName("myRegress02")
.config("spark.sql.warehouse.dir", ".")
.getOrCreate()
```

9. We need to import implicits for data conversion routines:

```
import spark.implicits._
```

10. Next, we load the housing data into a dataset:

```
val data = spark.read.text(
  "../data/sparkml2/chapter5/housing8.csv"
).as[
  String
]
```

11. Let's parse the housing data and convert it into label points:

```
val RegressionDataSet = data.map { line =>
val columns = line.split(',')
LabeledPoint(columns(13).toDouble ,
Vectors.dense(columns(0).toDouble,columns(1).toDouble,
columns(2).toDouble,  columns(3).toDouble,columns(4).toDouble,
columns(5).toDouble,columns(6).toDouble,  columns(7).toDouble
))
}
```

12. Now display the loaded data:

```
RegressionDataSet.show(false)
```

The output is as shown here:

```
+-----+-------------------------------------------------+
||label||features                                         |
+-----+-------------------------------------------------+
|24.0 |[0.00632,18.0,2.31,0.0,0.538,6.575,65.2,4.09]     |
|21.6 |[0.02731,0.0,7.07,0.0,0.469,6.421,78.9,4.9671]    |
|34.7 |[0.02729,0.0,7.07,0.0,0.469,7.185,61.1,4.9671]    |
|33.4 |[0.03237,0.0,2.18,0.0,0.458,6.998,45.8,6.0622]    |
|36.2 |[0.06905,0.0,2.18,0.0,0.458,7.147,54.2,6.0622]    |
|28.7 |[0.02985,0.0,2.18,0.0,0.458,6.43,58.7,6.0622]     |
|22.9 |[0.08829,12.5,7.87,0.0,0.524,6.012,66.6,5.5605]   |
|27.1 |[0.14455,12.5,7.87,0.0,0.524,6.172,96.1,5.9505]   |
|16.5 |[0.21124,12.5,7.87,0.0,0.524,5.631,100.0,6.0821]  |
|18.9 |[0.17004,12.5,7.87,0.0,0.524,6.004,85.9,6.5921]   |
|15.0 |[0.22489,12.5,7.87,0.0,0.524,6.377,94.3,6.3467]   |
|18.9 |[0.11747,12.5,7.87,0.0,0.524,6.009,82.9,6.2267]   |
|21.7 |[0.09378,12.5,7.87,0.0,0.524,5.889,39.0,5.4509]   |
|20.4 |[0.62976,0.0,8.14,0.0,0.538,5.949,61.8,4.7075]    |
|18.2 |[0.63796,0.0,8.14,0.0,0.538,6.096,84.5,4.4619]    |
|19.9 |[0.62739,0.0,8.14,0.0,0.538,5.834,56.5,4.4986]    |
|23.1 |[1.05393,0.0,8.14,0.0,0.538,5.935,29.3,4.4986]    |
|17.5 |[0.7842,0.0,8.14,0.0,0.538,5.99,81.7,4.2579]      |
|20.2 |[0.80271,0.0,8.14,0.0,0.538,5.456,36.6,3.7965]    |
|18.2 |[0.7258,0.0,8.14,0.0,0.538,5.727,69.5,3.7965]     |
+-----+-------------------------------------------------+
only showing top 20 rows
```

13. Next, we configure a linear regression algorithm for generating a model:

```
val numIterations = 10
val lr = new LinearRegression()
.setMaxIter(numIterations)
.setSolver("l-bfgs")
```

14. Now we fit the model to the housing data:

```
val myModel = lr.fit(RegressionDataSet)
```

15. Next, we retrieve summary data to reconcile the accuracy of the model:

```
val summary = myModel.summary
```

16. Finally, we print out the summary statistics:

```
println ( "training Mean Squared Error = " + summary.
meanSquaredError )
println("training Root Mean Squared Error = " +
summary.rootMeanSquaredError) }
training Mean Squared Error = 13.608987362865541
training Root Mean Squared Error = 3.689036102136375
```

17. We close the program by stopping the SparkSession:

```
spark.stop()
```

How it works...

In this recipe, we use the housing data again to demonstrate the Spark 2.0 `LinearRegression()` API using the L-BFGS optimization option. We read the file in, parse the data, and select specific columns for the regression. We keep the recipe short by accepting default parameters, but set number of iterations (for convergence to a solution) and optimization method to `lbfgs` before running the `.fit()` method. We then proceed to output a couple of quick metrics (that is, MSE and RMSE) for demonstration only. We show how to implement/compute these metrics yourself with RDD. Using Spark 2.0 native facilities/metrics and RDDs-based regression recipes, we show how Spark can do these metrics out of the box now, which is testimony to how far we have come from Spark 1.0.1!

Using Newton's optimization technique (for example, `lbfgs`) for small number of columns is an overkill, which will be demo later in this book to enable the readers to use these recipes on large datasets in real-world settings (for example, typical cancer/genome data readily available from sources mentioned in Chapter 1, *Practical Machine Learning with Spark Using Scala*).

There's more...

Elastic net (contributed by DB Tsai and others) and evangelized by Alpine Labs showed up in our radar starting with Spark 1.4 and 1.5, which is now the de facto technique in Spark 2.0.

To level set, elastic net is a linear combination of L1 and L2 penalty. It can be modeled conceptually as a dial that can decide how much of L1 and how much of L2 to include in the penalty (Shrinkage versus Selection).

We want to stress that we can now select between the type of regression via the parameter setting rather than named APIs. This is an important departure from RDD-based APIs (that is, now in maintenance mode) that we demonstrate later in this chapter.

The following table provides a quick cheat sheet for setting parameters to select between Lasso, Ridge, OLS, and elastic net.

Please see the following table `setElasticNetParam(value: Double):`

Regression Type	Penalty	Parameter
Lasso	L1	0
Ridge	L2	1
Elastic net	L1 + L2	0.0 < alpha < 1.0
OLS	Ordinary least square	None

It is crucial to understand how regularization is controlled via an elastic net parameter (corresponding to Alpha) described in this following brief treatment:

- Simple: `https://en.wikipedia.org/wiki/Elastic_net_regularization`
- Complete: `http://www.stat.purdue.edu/~tlzhang/mathstat/ElasticNet.pdf`
- Using genome
  data: `https://www.ncbi.nlm.nih.gov/pmc/articles/PMC3232376/`

See also

- Documentation for
  `LinearRegression(): http://spark.apache.org/docs/latest/api/scala/index.html#org.apache.spark.ml.regression.LinearRegression`
- Be sure to consult the actual source code since it extends the
  Regressor itself: `https://github.com/apache/spark/blob/v2.0.2/mllib/src/main/scala/org/apache/spark/ml/regression/LinearRegression.scala`
- Some of the important API calls within `LinearRegression`:
    - `def setElasticNetParam(value: Double): LinearRegression.this.type`
    - `def setRegParam(value: Double): LinearRegression.this.type`
    - `def setSolver(value: String): LinearRegression.this.type`
    - `def setMaxIter(value: Int): LinearRegression.this.type`
    - `def setFitIntercept(value: Boolean): LinearRegression.this.type`

An important aspect of Spark ML is its simple yet exceptionally powerful API set that allows scaling to billions of rows at very little extra effort by the developer on an existing cluster. You will be surprised the scale at which Lasso can be used to discover relevant feature sets while L-BFGS optimization (that does not require a direct hessian matrix presence) can handle a tremendous number of features with ease. The details of the `updater` implementation for LBFGS in Spark 2.0 source code is beyond the scope of this book.

We will cover the optimizations that relate to these ML algorithms in a follow-up chapter due to their complexity.

Linear regression API with Lasso and 'auto' optimization selection in Spark 2.0

In this recipe, we build on the previous recipe `LinearRegression` by selecting LASSO regression explicitly via the `setElasticNetParam(0.0)` while letting Spark 2.0 pick the optimization on its own using `setSolver('auto')`. We remind again that the RDD-based regression API is now in maintenance mode and this is the preferred method going forward.

How to do it...

1. We use a housing data set from the UCI machine library depository..

2. Download the entire data set from the following URLs:

- `https://archive.ics.uci.edu/ml/datasets/Housing`
- `https://archive.ics.uci.edu/ml/machine-learning-databases/housing/`

The dataset is comprised of 14 columns with the first 13 columns being the independent variables (that is, features) that try to explain the median price (that is, last column) of an owner-occupied house in Boston, USA.

We have chosen and cleaned the first eight columns as features. We use the first 200 rows to train and predict the median price:

- **CRIM:** Per capita crime rate by town
- **ZN:** Proportion of residential land zoned for lots over 25,000 sq.ft.
- **INDUS:** Proportion of non-retail business acres per town
- **CHAS:** Charles River dummy variable (= 1 if tract bounds river; 0 otherwise)
- **NOX:** Nitric oxide concentration (parts per 10 million)
- **RM:** Average number of rooms per dwelling
- **AGE:** Proportion of owner-occupied units built prior to 1940

3. Please use the `housing8.csv` file and make sure you move it to the following directory:

```
../data/sparkml2/chapter5/housing8.csv
```

4. Start a new project in IntelliJ or in an IDE of your choice. Make sure the necessary JAR files are included.

5. Set up the package location where the program will reside:

```
package spark.ml.cookbook.chapter5.
```

6. Import the necessary packages for the `SparkSession` to gain access to the cluster and `Log4j.Logger` to reduce the amount of output produced by Spark:

```
import org.apache.spark.ml.regression.LinearRegression
import org.apache.spark.ml.feature.LabeledPoint
import org.apache.spark.sql.SparkSession
import org.apache.spark.ml.linalg.Vectors
import org.apache.log4j.{Level, Logger}
```

7. Set the output level to ERROR to reduce Spark's logging output:

```
Logger.getLogger("org").setLevel(Level.ERROR)
 Logger.getLogger("akka").setLevel(Level.ERROR)
```

8. Initialize a SparkSession specifying configurations to gain access to the Spark cluster:

```
val spark = SparkSession
.builder
.master("local[*]")
.appName("myRegress03")
.config("spark.sql.warehouse.dir", ".")
.getOrCreate()
```

9. We need to import implicits for data conversion routines:

```
import spark.implicits._
```

10. Next, we load the housing data into a dataset:

```
val data = spark.read.text(
"../data/sparkml2/chapter5/housing8.csv" ).as[ String ]
```

11. Let's parse the housing data and convert it into label points:

```
val RegressionDataSet = data.map { line =>
val columns = line.split(',')
LabeledPoint(columns(13).toDouble ,
Vectors.dense(columns(0).toDouble,columns(1).toDouble,
columns(2).toDouble,  columns(3).toDouble,columns(4).toDouble,
columns(5).toDouble,columns(6).toDouble,  columns(7).toDouble
))
}
```

12. Now display the loaded data:

```
                    RegressionDataSet.show(false)

+-----+------------------------------------------------------+
|label|features                                               |
+-----+------------------------------------------------------+
|24.0 |[0.00632,18.0,2.31,0.0,0.538,6.575,65.2,4.09]        |
|21.6 |[0.02731,0.0,7.07,0.0,0.469,6.421,78.9,4.9671]       |
|34.7 |[0.02729,0.0,7.07,0.0,0.469,7.185,61.1,4.9671]       |
|33.4 |[0.03237,0.0,2.18,0.0,0.458,6.998,45.8,6.0622]       |
|36.2 |[0.06905,0.0,2.18,0.0,0.458,7.147,54.2,6.0622]       |
|28.7 |[0.02985,0.0,2.18,0.0,0.458,6.43,58.7,6.0622]        |
|22.9 |[0.08829,12.5,7.87,0.0,0.524,6.012,66.6,5.5605]      |
|27.1 |[0.14455,12.5,7.87,0.0,0.524,6.172,96.1,5.9505]      |
|16.5 |[0.21124,12.5,7.87,0.0,0.524,5.631,100.0,6.0821]     |
|18.9 |[0.17004,12.5,7.87,0.0,0.524,6.004,85.9,6.5921]      |
|15.0 |[0.22489,12.5,7.87,0.0,0.524,6.377,94.3,6.3467]      |
|18.9 |[0.11747,12.5,7.87,0.0,0.524,6.009,82.9,6.2267]      |
|21.7 |[0.09378,12.5,7.87,0.0,0.524,5.889,39.0,5.4509]      |
|20.4 |[0.62976,0.0,8.14,0.0,0.538,5.949,61.8,4.7075]       |
|18.2 |[0.63796,0.0,8.14,0.0,0.538,6.096,84.5,4.4619]       |
|19.9 |[0.62739,0.0,8.14,0.0,0.538,5.834,56.5,4.4986]       |
|23.1 |[1.05393,0.0,8.14,0.0,0.538,5.935,29.3,4.4986]       |
|17.5 |[0.7842,0.0,8.14,0.0,0.538,5.99,81.7,4.2579]         |
|20.2 |[0.80271,0.0,8.14,0.0,0.538,5.456,36.6,3.7965]       |
|18.2 |[0.7258,0.0,8.14,0.0,0.538,5.727,69.5,3.7965]        |
+-----+------------------------------------------------------+
only showing top 20 rows
```

13. Next, we configure a linear regression algorithm for generating a model:

```
val lr = new LinearRegression()
.setMaxIter(1000)
.setElasticNetParam(0.0)
.setRegParam(0.01)
.setSolver( "auto" )
```

14. Now we fit the model to the housing data:

```
val myModel = lr.fit(RegressionDataSet)
```

15. Next, we retrieve summary data to reconcile the accuracy of the model:

```
val summary = myModel.summary
```

16. Finally, we print out the summary statistics:

```
println ( "training Mean Squared Error = " + summary.
meanSquaredError )
println("training Root Mean Squared Error = " +
summary.rootMeanSquaredError) }
training Mean Squared Error = 13.609079490110766
training Root Mean Squared Error = 3.6890485887435482
```

17. We close the program by stopping the SparkSession:

```
spark.stop()
```

How it works...

We read the housing data and load selected columns and use them to predict the price of a housing unit. We use the following code snippet to select the regression as LASSO and let Spark pick up the optimization on its own:

```
val lr = new LinearRegression()
.setMaxIter(1000)
.setElasticNetParam(0.0)
.setRegParam(0.01)
.setSolver( "auto" )
```

We change the `setMaxIter()` to `1000` for demonstration purposes. The default setting is `100` out of the box.

There's more...

While Spark does a very nice implementation of L-BFGS, please see the following links for a quick understanding of BFGS and its inner workings as it relates to this recipe:

- Simple treatment of BFGS: `https://en.wikipedia.org/wiki/Broyden-Fletcher-Goldfarb-Shanno_algorithm`
- From the *Journal of Machine Learning Research* and also nice limited-memory BGFS treatment from a mathematical programming viewpoint: `http://www.jmlr.org/papers/volume14/hennig13a/hennig13a.pdf`

  Also see the RDD-based regression recipes for more details on LBGFS. The following links provide implementation details if you need to understand the BFGS techniques.

  This implementation in C language helps us to develop a solid understanding of the first-order optimization at code level: `http://www.chokkan.org/software/liblbfgs/`

- The *cctbx* also provides good implementation details if you need to see more: `http://cctbx.sourceforge.net`
- Pretty good treatment from Harvard University on L-BFGS in R: `https://cran.r-project.org/web/packages/lbfgs/vignettes/Vignette.pdf`

See also

- Documentation for
  LinearRegression(): `http://spark.apache.org/docs/latest/api/scala/index.html#org.apache.spark.ml.regression.LinearRegression`
- Documentation for BFGS and L-BFGS:
  - `https://en.wikipedia.org/wiki/Broyden-Fletcher-Goldfarb-Shanno_algorithm`
  - `https://en.wikipedia.org/wiki/Limited-memory_BFGS`

Linear regression API with ridge regression and 'auto' optimization selection in Spark 2.0

In this recipe, we implement ridge regression using the `LinearRegression` interface. We use the elastic net parameter to set the appropriate value to a full L2 penalty, which in turn selects the ridge regression accordingly.

How to do it...

1. We use a housing data set from the UCI machine library depository.

2. Download the entire data set from the following URLs:
   - `https://archive.ics.uci.edu/ml/datasets/Housing`
   - `https://archive.ics.uci.edu/ml/machine-learning-databases/housing/`

The dataset is comprised of 14 columns with the first 13 columns being the independent variables (that is, features) that try to explain the median price (that is, last column) of an owner-occupied house in Boston, USA.

We have chosen and cleaned the first eight columns as features. We use the first 200 rows to train and predict the median price:

- **CRIM**: Per capita crime rate by town
- **ZN**: Proportion of residential land zoned for lots over 25,000 sq.ft.
- **INDUS**: Proportion of non-retail business acres per town

- **CHAS**: Charles River dummy variable (= 1 if tract bounds river; 0 otherwise)
- **NOX**: Nitric oxide concentration (parts per 10 million)
- **RM**: Average number of rooms per dwelling
- **AGE**: Proportion of owner-occupied units built prior to 1940

3. Please use the `housing8.csv` file and make sure you move it to the following directory:

```
../data/sparkml2/chapter5/housing8.csv
```

4. Start a new project in IntelliJ or in an IDE of your choice. Make sure the necessary JAR files are included.

5. Set up package location where the program will reside:

```
package spark.ml.cookbook.chapter5.
```

6. Import the necessary packages for `SparkSession` to gain access to the cluster and `Log4j.Logger` to reduce the amount of output produced by Spark:

```
import org.apache.spark.ml.feature.LabeledPoint
import org.apache.spark.ml.linalg.Vectors
import org.apache.spark.ml.regression.LinearRegression
import org.apache.spark.sql.SparkSession
import org.apache.log4j.{Level, Logger}
```

7. Set the output level to ERROR to reduce Spark's logging output:

```
Logger.getLogger("org").setLevel(Level.ERROR)
Logger.getLogger("akka").setLevel(Level.ERROR)
```

8. Initialize a `SparkSession` specifying configurations to gain access to the Spark cluster:

```
val spark = SparkSession
.builder
.master("local[*]")
.appName("myRegress04")
.config("spark.sql.warehouse.dir", ".")
.getOrCreate()
```

9. We need to import implicits for data conversion routines:

```
import spark.implicits._
```

10. Next, we load the housing data into a dataset:

```
val data = spark.read.text(
"../data/sparkml2/chapter5/housing8.csv" ).as[ String ]
```

11. Let's parse the housing data and convert it into label points:

```
val RegressionDataSet = data.map { line =>
val columns = line.split(',')
LabeledPoint(columns(13).toDouble ,
Vectors.dense(columns(0).toDouble,columns(1).toDouble,
columns(2).toDouble, columns(3).toDouble,columns(4).toDouble,
columns(5).toDouble,columns(6).toDouble, columns(7).toDouble
))
}
```

12. Now display the loaded data:

```
                  RegressionDataSet.show(false)
+-----+------------------------------------------------+
|label|features                                        |
+-----+------------------------------------------------+
|24.0 |[0.00632,18.0,2.31,0.0,0.538,6.575,65.2,4.09]   |
|21.6 |[0.02731,0.0,7.07,0.0,0.469,6.421,78.9,4.9671]  |
|34.7 |[0.02729,0.0,7.07,0.0,0.469,7.185,61.1,4.9671]  |
|33.4 |[0.03237,0.0,2.18,0.0,0.458,6.998,45.8,6.0622]  |
|36.2 |[0.06905,0.0,2.18,0.0,0.458,7.147,54.2,6.0622]  |
|28.7 |[0.02985,0.0,2.18,0.0,0.458,6.43,58.7,6.0622]   |
|22.9 |[0.08829,12.5,7.87,0.0,0.524,6.012,66.6,5.5605] |
|27.1 |[0.14455,12.5,7.87,0.0,0.524,6.172,96.1,5.9505] |
|16.5 |[0.21124,12.5,7.87,0.0,0.524,5.631,100.0,6.0821]|
|18.9 |[0.17004,12.5,7.87,0.0,0.524,6.004,85.9,6.5921] |
|15.0 |[0.22489,12.5,7.87,0.0,0.524,6.377,94.3,6.3467] |
|18.9 |[0.11747,12.5,7.87,0.0,0.524,6.009,82.9,6.2267] |
|21.7 |[0.09378,12.5,7.87,0.0,0.524,5.889,39.0,5.4509] |
|20.4 |[0.62976,0.0,8.14,0.0,0.538,5.949,61.8,4.7075]  |
|18.2 |[0.63796,0.0,8.14,0.0,0.538,6.096,84.5,4.4619]  |
|19.9 |[0.62739,0.0,8.14,0.0,0.538,5.834,56.5,4.4986]  |
|23.1 |[1.05393,0.0,8.14,0.0,0.538,5.935,29.3,4.4986]  |
|17.5 |[0.7842,0.0,8.14,0.0,0.538,5.99,81.7,4.2579]    |
|20.2 |[0.80271,0.0,8.14,0.0,0.538,5.456,36.6,3.7965]  |
|18.2 |[0.7258,0.0,8.14,0.0,0.538,5.727,69.5,3.7965]   |
+-----+------------------------------------------------+
```

13. Next, we configure a linear regression algorithm for generating a model:

```
val lr = new LinearRegression()
.setMaxIter(1000)
.setElasticNetParam(1.0)
.setRegParam(0.01)
.setSolver( "auto" )
```

14. Now, we fit the model to the housing data:

```
val myModel = lr.fit(RegressionDataSet)
```

15. Next, we retrieve the summary data to reconcile the accuracy of the model:

```
val summary = myModel.summary
```

16. Finally, we print out the summary statistics:

```
println ( "training Mean Squared Error = " + summary.
meanSquaredError )
println("training Root Mean Squared Error = " +
summary.rootMeanSquaredError) }
training Mean Squared Error = 13.61187856748311
training Root Mean Squared Error = 3.6894279458315906
```

17. We close the program by stopping the `SparkSession`:

```
spark.stop()
```

How it works...

We loaded the data by reading the housing data and loading the appropriate columns. We then proceeded to set the parameters that will force the `LinearRegression()` to perform a Ridge regression while keeping the optimization to 'auto'. The following code shows how the linear regression API can be used to set the desired type of regression to ridge:

```
val lr = new LinearRegression()
.setMaxIter(1000)
.setElasticNetParam(1.0)
.setRegParam(0.01)
.setSolver( "auto" )
```

We then used `.fit()` to fit the model to the data. We finally used `.summary` to extract the model summary and print the MSE and RMSE for the model.

There's more...

To make sure we are clear on the difference between ridge and Lasso regression, we must first highlight the difference between parameter shrinkage (that is, we squash the weight using a square root function, but never set it to zero) and feature engineering or parameter selection (that is, we shrink the parameters all the way to 0, thereby causing some of the parameters to disappear altogether from the model):

- Ridge regression: `https://en.wikipedia.org/wiki/Tikhonov_regularization`
- Lasso regression: `https://en.wikipedia.org/wiki/Lasso_(statistics)`
- Elastic net - Stanford University: `http://web.stanford.edu/~hastie/TALKS/enet_talk.pdf`

See also

Documentation on Linear regression: `http://spark.apache.org/docs/latest/api/scala/index.html#org.apache.spark.ml.regression.LinearRegression`

Isotonic regression in Apache Spark 2.0

In this recipe, we demonstrate the `IsotonicRegression()` function in Spark 2.0. The isotonic or monotonic regression is used when order is expected in the data and we want to fit an increasing ordered line (that is, manifest itself as a step function) to a series of observations. The terms **isotonic regression** (**IR**) and **monotonic regression** (**MR**) are synonymous in literature and can be used interchangeably.

In short, what we are trying to do with the `IsotonicRegression()` recipe is to provide a better fit versus some of the shortcomings of Naive Bayes and SVM. While they are both powerful classifiers, Naive Bayes lacks a good estimate of $P(C \mid X)$ and **Support Vector Machines** (**SVM**) at best provides only a proxy (can use hyperplane distance), which is not an accurate estimator in some cases.

How to do it...

1. Go to the website to download the file and save the file into the data path mentioned in the following code blocks. We use the famous Iris data and fit a step line to the observation. We use the Iris data in LIBSVM format from the library to demonstrate the IR.

   The filename we choose is `iris.scale.txt` https://www.csie.ntu.edu.tw/~cjlin/libsvmtools/datasets/multiclass/iris.scale.

2. Start a new project in IntelliJ or in an IDE of your choice. Make sure the necessary JAR files are included.

3. Set up the package location where the program will reside:

   ```
   package spark.ml.cookbook.chapter5
   ```

4. Import the necessary packages for `SparkSession` to gain access to the cluster and `Log4j.Logger` to reduce the amount of output produced by Spark:

   ```
   import org.apache.spark.sql.SparkSession
   import org.apache.spark.ml.regression.IsotonicRegression
   ```

5. Set the output level to ERROR to reduce Spark's logging output:

   ```
   Logger.getLogger("org").setLevel(Level.ERROR)
   Logger.getLogger("akka").setLevel(Level.ERROR)
   ```

6. Initialize a `SparkSession` specifying configurations with the builder pattern thus making an entry point available for the Spark cluster:

   ```
   val spark = SparkSession
    .builder
    .master("local[4]")
    .appName("myIsoTonicRegress")
    .config("spark.sql.warehouse.dir", ".")
    .getOrCreate()
   ```

7. We then read the data file in, print out the data schema, and display the data in the console:

   ```
   val data = spark.read.format("libsvm")
    .load("../data/sparkml2/chapter5/iris.scale.txt")
   data.printSchema()
   data.show(false)
   ```

We get the following console output:

```
root
 |-- label: double (nullable = true)
 |-- features: vector (nullable = true)

+-----+----------------------------------------------------------+
|label|features                                                  |
+-----+----------------------------------------------------------+
|1.0  |(4,[0,1,2,3],[-0.555556,0.25,-0.864407,-0.916667])        |
|1.0  |(4,[0,1,2,3],[-0.666667,-0.166667,-0.864407,-0.916667])   |
|1.0  |(4,[0,2,3],[-0.777778,-0.898305,-0.916667])               |
|1.0  |(4,[0,1,2,3],[-0.833333,-0.0833334,-0.830508,-0.916667])  |
|1.0  |(4,[0,1,2,3],[-0.611111,0.333333,-0.864407,-0.916667])    |
|1.0  |(4,[0,1,2,3],[-0.388889,0.583333,-0.762712,-0.75])        |
|1.0  |(4,[0,1,2,3],[-0.833333,0.166667,-0.864407,-0.833333])    |
|1.0  |(4,[0,1,2,3],[-0.611111,0.166667,-0.830508,-0.916667])    |
|1.0  |(4,[0,1,2,3],[-0.944444,-0.25,-0.864407,-0.916667])       |
|1.0  |(4,[0,1,2,3],[-0.666667,-0.0833334,-0.830508,-1.0])       |
|1.0  |(4,[0,1,2,3],[-0.388889,0.416667,-0.830508,-0.916667])    |
|1.0  |(4,[0,1,2,3],[-0.722222,0.166667,-0.79661,-0.916667])     |
|1.0  |(4,[0,1,2,3],[-0.722222,-0.166667,-0.864407,-1.0])        |
|1.0  |(4,[0,1,2,3],[-1.0,-0.166667,-0.966102,-1.0])             |
|1.0  |(4,[0,1,2,3],[-0.166667,0.666667,-0.932203,-0.916667])    |
|1.0  |(4,[0,1,2,3],[-0.222222,1.0,-0.830508,-0.75])             |
|1.0  |(4,[0,1,2,3],[-0.388889,0.583333,-0.898305,-0.75])        |
|1.0  |(4,[0,1,2,3],[-0.555556,0.25,-0.864407,-0.833333])        |
|1.0  |(4,[0,1,2,3],[-0.222222,0.5,-0.762712,-0.833333])         |
|1.0  |(4,[0,1,2,3],[-0.555556,0.5,-0.830508,-0.833333])         |
+-----+----------------------------------------------------------+
only showing top 20 rows
```

8. We then split the data set to training and test set in a ratio of *0.7:0.3*:

```
val Array(training, test) = data.randomSplit(Array(0.7, 0.3), seed
= System.currentTimeMillis())
```

9. Next, we create the `IsotonicRegression` object and fit it in the training data:

```
val itr = new IsotonicRegression()

val itrModel = itr.fit(training)
```

10. Now we print out the model boundary and predictions in the console:

```
println(s"Boundaries in increasing order: ${itrModel.boundaries}")
 println(s"Predictions associated with the boundaries:
${itrModel.predictions}")
```

We get the following console output:

```
Boundaries in increasing order:
[-1.0,-0.666667,-0.666667,-0.5,-0.5,-0.388889,-0.388889,-0.333333,-
0.333333,-0.222222,-0.222222,-0.166667,-0.166667,0.111111,0.111111,
0.333333,0.333333,0.5,0.555555,1.0]
Predictions associated with the boundaries:
```

```
[1.0,1.0,1.1176470588235294,1.1176470588235294,1.1666666666666663,1
.1666666666666663,1.3333333333333333,1.3333333333333333,1.9,1.9,2.0
,2.0,2.3571428571428577,2.3571428571428577,2.5333333333333314,2.533
3333333333314,2.7777777777777786,2.7777777777777786,3.0,3.0]
```

11. We let the model transform the test data and display the result:

```
itrModel.transform(test).show()
```

We get the following console output:

```
+-----+--------------------+------------------+
|label|            features|        prediction|
+-----+--------------------+------------------+
|  1.0|(4,[0,1,2,3],[-0....|               1.0|
|  1.0|(4,[0,1,2,3],[-0....|               1.0|
|  1.0|(4,[0,1,2,3],[-0....|               1.0|
|  1.0|(4,[0,1,2,3],[-0....|1.2499999999999998|
|  1.0|(4,[0,1,2,3],[-0....|1.2499999999999998|
|  1.0|(4,[0,1,2,3],[-0....|1.2499999999999998|
|  1.0|(4,[0,1,2,3],[-0....|1.2499999999999998|
|  1.0|(4,[0,1,2,3],[-0....|1.2499999999999998|
|  1.0|(4,[0,1,2,3],[-0....|1.2499999999999998|
|  1.0|(4,[0,1,2,3],[-0....|1.2499999999999998|
|  1.0|(4,[0,1,2,3],[-0....|               1.5|
|  1.0|(4,[0,1,2,3],[-0....|               1.5|
|  1.0|(4,[0,1,2,3],[-0....|               2.0|
|  1.0|(4,[0,1,2,3],[-0....|               2.0|
|  1.0|(4,[0,2,3],[-0.77...|               1.0|
|  2.0|(4,[0,1,2,3],[-0....|1.2499999999999998|
|  2.0|(4,[0,1,2,3],[-0....|1.2499999999999998|
|  2.0|(4,[0,1,2,3],[-0....|               2.0|
|  2.0|(4,[0,1,2,3],[-0....|               2.0|
|  2.0|(4,[0,1,2,3],[-0....|               2.0|
+-----+--------------------+------------------+
only showing top 20 rows
```

12. We close the program by stopping the `SparkSession`:

```
spark.stop()
```

How it works...

In this example, we explored the features of the Isotonic Regress model. We first read the dataset file into Spark in a `libsvm` format. We then split the data (*70/30*) and proceeded. Next, we displayed the DataFrame in the console by calling the `.show()` function. We then created the `IsotonicRegression()` object and let the model run for itself by calling the `fit(data)` function. In this recipe, we kept it simple and did not change any default parameters, but the readers should experiment and use the JChart package to graph the line and see the effect on the increasing and stepped line result in action.

Finally, we displayed the model boundary and predictions in the console and used the model to transform the test dataset and displayed the result DataFrame in the console with the prediction field included. All Spark ML algorithms are sensitive to hyper parameter value. While there are no hard and fast rules for setting these parameters, a good amount of experimentation using the scientific method is required before going to production.

We have covered a good number of model evaluation facilities provided by Spark in previous chapters and have discussed evaluation metrics throughout the book without being redundant. Spark provides the following model evaluation methods. A developer must pick and choose the specific evaluation metric facility based on the type of algorithm being evaluated (for example, discrete, continuous, binary, multiclass, and so on).

We will cover the evaluation metrics individually using recipes, but please see the following link for Spark's model evaluation coverage: http://spark.apache.org/docs/latest/mllib-evaluation-metrics.html.

There's more...

The Spark 2.0 implementation has the following restrictions at the time of writing:

- Only single feature (that is, univariate) algorithms are supported:

```
def setFeaturesCol(value: String): IsotonicRegression.this.type
```

- The implementation is currently set to **parallelized pool adjacent violators algorithm (PAVA)**:
- As of Spark 2.1.0, it is a univariate monotonic implementation
- See CRAN implementation like Spark 2.0: https://cran.r-project.org/web/packages/isotone/vignettes/isotone.pdf
- See UCLA paper (PAVA): http://gifi.stat.ucla.edu/janspubs/2009/reports/deleeuw_hornik_mair_R_09.pdf
- See University of Wisconsin: https://www.biostat.wisc.edu/sites/default/files/tr_116.pdf

- Documentation for Isotonic regression:
    - https://spark.apache.org/docs/latest/ml-classification-regression.html#isotonic-regression
    - https://spark.apache.org/docs/latest/api/scala/index.html#org.apache.spark.ml.regression.IsotonicRegression
    - https://spark.apache.org/docs/latest/api/scala/index.html#org.apache.spark.ml.regression.IsotonicRegressionModel

See also

More information about Isotonic Regression can be found at:

https://en.wikipedia.org/wiki/Isotonic_regression

The isotonic regression line ends up being a step function as opposed to a linear regression, which is a straight line. The following figure (source: Wikipedia) provides a good reference:

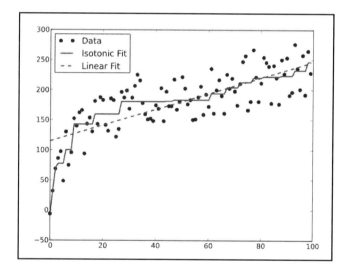

Multilayer perceptron classifier in Apache Spark 2.0

In this recipe, we explore Spark's 2.0 **multilayer perceptron classifier** (**MLPC**), which is another name for feed-forward neural networks. We use the iris data set to predict a binary outcome for the feature vectors that describes the input. The key point to remember is that, even though the name sounds a bit complicated, at its core the MLP is just a non-linear classifier for data that cannot be separated via a simple linear line or hyperplane.

How to do it...

1. Go to the LIBSVM Data: Classification (Multi-class) Repository and download the file from the following
   URL: https://www.csie.ntu.edu.tw/~cjlin/libsvmtools/datasets/multiclas
   s/iris.scale

2. Start a new project in IntelliJ or in an IDE of your choice. Make sure the necessary JAR files are included.

3. Set up the package location where the program will reside:

   ```
   package spark.ml.cookbook.chapter5
   ```

4. Import the necessary packages for `SparkSession` to gain access to the cluster and `Log4j.Logger` to reduce the amount of output produced by Spark:

   ```
   import org.apache.spark.ml.classification
   .MultilayerPerceptronClassifier
   import org.apache.spark.ml.evaluation.
   MulticlassClassificationEvaluator
   import org.apache.spark.sql.SparkSession
   import org.apache.log4j.{ Level, Logger}
   ```

5. Set the output level to ERROR to reduce Spark's logging output:

   ```
   Logger.getLogger("org").setLevel(Level.ERROR)
   Logger.getLogger("akka").setLevel(Level.ERROR)
   ```

6. Initialize a `SparkSession` specifying configurations to gain access to the Spark cluster:

```
val spark = SparkSession
 .builder
 .master("local[*]")
 .appName("MLP")
 .getOrCreate()
```

7. We begin by loading the `libsvm` formatted data file into memory:

```
val data = spark.read.format( "libsvm" )
 .load("../data/sparkml2/chapter5/iris.scale.txt")
```

8. Now display the loaded data:

   From the console, this is the output:

```
data.show(false)
```

```
+-----+--------------------------------------------------------+
|label|features                                                |
+-----+--------------------------------------------------------+
|1.0  |(4,[0,1,2,3],[-0.555556,0.25,-0.864407,-0.916667])      |
|1.0  |(4,[0,1,2,3],[-0.666667,-0.166667,-0.864407,-0.916667]) |
|1.0  |(4,[0,2,3],[-0.777778,-0.898305,-0.916667])             |
|1.0  |(4,[0,1,2,3],[-0.833333,-0.0833334,-0.830508,-0.916667])|
|1.0  |(4,[0,1,2,3],[-0.611111,0.333333,-0.864407,-0.916667])  |
|1.0  |(4,[0,1,2,3],[-0.388889,0.583333,-0.762712,-0.75])      |
|1.0  |(4,[0,1,2,3],[-0.833333,0.166667,-0.864407,-0.833333])  |
|1.0  |(4,[0,1,2,3],[-0.611111,0.166667,-0.830508,-0.916667])  |
|1.0  |(4,[0,1,2,3],[-0.944444,-0.25,-0.864407,-0.916667])     |
|1.0  |(4,[0,1,2,3],[-0.666667,-0.0833334,-0.830508,-1.0])     |
|1.0  |(4,[0,1,2,3],[-0.388889,0.416667,-0.830508,-0.916667])  |
|1.0  |(4,[0,1,2,3],[-0.722222,0.166667,-0.79661,-0.916667])   |
|1.0  |(4,[0,1,2,3],[-0.722222,-0.166667,-0.864407,-1.0])      |
|1.0  |(4,[0,1,2,3],[-1.0,-0.166667,-0.966102,-1.0])           |
|1.0  |(4,[0,1,2,3],[-0.166667,0.666667,-0.932203,-0.916667])  |
|1.0  |(4,[0,1,2,3],[-0.222222,1.0,-0.830508,-0.75])           |
|1.0  |(4,[0,1,2,3],[-0.388889,0.583333,-0.898305,-0.916667])  |
|1.0  |(4,[0,1,2,3],[-0.555556,0.25,-0.864407,-0.833333])      |
|1.0  |(4,[0,1,2,3],[-0.222222,0.5,-0.762712,-0.833333])       |
|1.0  |(4,[0,1,2,3],[-0.555556,0.5,-0.830508,-0.833333])       |
+-----+--------------------------------------------------------+
only showing top 20 rows
```

9. Next, we utilize the Datasets `randomSplit` method to divide data into two buckets with allocations of 80% and 20% for each bucket:

```
val splitData = data.randomSplit(Array( 0.8 , 0.2 ), seed =
System.currentTimeMillis())
```

10. The `randomSplit` method returns an array with two sets of data, the training set being the 80% portion and testing set being the 20% portion:

```
val train = splitData(0)
val test = splitData(1)
```

11. Next, we configure the multilayer perceptron classifier with an input layer of four nodes, a hidden layer of five nodes, and a four-node layer for output:

```
val layers = Array[Int](4, 5, 4)
val mlp = new MultilayerPerceptronClassifier()
.setLayers(layers)
.setBlockSize(110)
.setSeed(System.currentTimeMillis())
.setMaxIter(145)
```

- **Blocksize**: Block size for stacking input data in matrices to speed up the computation. This is more of an efficiency parameter with a recommended size between `10` and `1000`. This parameter concerns the total amount of data that is shoved into a partition for efficiency reasons.
- **MaxIter**: Maximum number of iterations to run the model.
- **Seed**: Set the seed for weight initialization if weights are not set.

The following two lines from the Spark source code on GitHub reveals the default set within the code:

```
setDefault(maxIter->100, tol -> 1e-6, blockSize ->128, solver ->
MultilayerPerceptronClassifier.LBFGS, stepSize ->0.03)
```

To understand the parameters and seeding better, see the MLP source code at `https://github.com/apache/spark/blob/master/mllib/src/main/scala/org/apache/spark/ml/classification/MultilayerPerceptronClassifier.scala`.

12. We generate a model by invoking the fit method:

```
val mlpModel = mlp.fit(train)
```

13. Next, we put the trained model to use transforming the test data and displaying the predicted results:

```
val result = mlpModel.transform(test)
result.show(false)
```

The result will be displayed in console like the following:

```
+-----+------------------------------------------------------------+----------+
|label|features                                                    |prediction|
+-----+------------------------------------------------------------+----------+
|1.0  |(4,[0,1,2,3],[-1.0,-0.166667,-0.966102,-1.0])               |1.0       |
|1.0  |(4,[0,1,2,3],[-0.666667,-0.0833334,-0.830508,-1.0])         |1.0       |
|1.0  |(4,[0,1,2,3],[-0.611111,0.0833333,-0.864407,-0.916667])     |1.0       |
|1.0  |(4,[0,1,2,3],[-0.555556,0.5,-0.694915,-0.75])               |1.0       |
|1.0  |(4,[0,1,2,3],[-0.5,0.75,-0.830508,-1.0])                    |1.0       |
|1.0  |(4,[0,1,2,3],[-0.388889,0.583333,-0.898305,-0.75])          |1.0       |
|1.0  |(4,[0,1,2,3],[-0.166667,0.666667,-0.932203,-0.916667])      |1.0       |
|1.0  |(4,[0,2,3],[-0.777778,-0.79661,-0.916667])                  |1.0       |
|2.0  |(4,[0,1,2,3],[-0.666667,-0.666667,-0.220339,-0.25])         |2.0       |
|2.0  |(4,[0,1,2,3],[-0.555556,-0.583333,-0.322034,-0.166667])     |2.0       |
|2.0  |(4,[0,1,2,3],[-0.5,-0.416667,-0.0169491,0.0833333])         |2.0       |
|2.0  |(4,[0,1,2,3],[-0.333333,-0.5,0.152542,-0.0833333])          |2.0       |
|2.0  |(4,[0,1,2,3],[-0.277778,-0.25,-0.118644,-4.03573E-8])       |2.0       |
|2.0  |(4,[0,1,2,3],[-0.222222,-0.5,-0.152542,-0.25])              |2.0       |
|2.0  |(4,[0,1,2,3],[-0.222222,-0.333333,0.186441,-4.03573E-8])    |2.0       |
|2.0  |(4,[0,1,2,3],[-0.222222,-0.166667,0.0847457,-0.0833333])    |2.0       |
|2.0  |(4,[0,1,2,3],[-0.166667,-0.416667,-0.0169491,-0.0833333])   |2.0       |
|2.0  |(4,[0,1,2,3],[-0.0555556,-0.833333,0.0169491,-0.25])        |2.0       |
|2.0  |(4,[0,1,2,3],[-0.0555556,-0.25,0.186441,0.166667])          |2.0       |
|2.0  |(4,[0,1,2,3],[0.0555554,-0.25,0.118644,-4.03573E-8])        |2.0       |
+-----+------------------------------------------------------------+----------+
only showing top 20 rows
```

14. Finally, we extract predictions and labels from the results and pass them to a Multi Class Classification Evaluator to generate an accuracy value:

```
val predictions = result.select("prediction", "label")
val eval = new
MulticlassClassificationEvaluator().setMetricName("accuracy")
println("Accuracy: " + eval.evaluate(predictions))
Accuracy: 0.967741935483871
```

15. We close the program by stopping the SparkSession:

```
spark.stop()
```

How it works...

In this recipe, we demonstrated usage of a multilayer perceptron classifier. We began by loading the classic Iris dataset in libsvm format. Next, we split the dataset with a ratio of 80% for training set data and 20% for test set data. In our definition phase, we configured the multilayer perceptron classifier with an input layer of four nodes, a hidden layer of five nodes, and a four-node layer for output. We generated a trained model by invoking the fit() method, and then produced predictions utilizing the trained model.

Finally, we retrieved predictions and labels, passing them to the multi-class classification evaluator that computes an accuracy value.

A simple visual inspection of predicted versus actual without much experimentation and fitting seems very impressive and acts a testimony as to why neural networks (much different than the early 1990s version) are back in favor. They do a great job in capturing non-linear surfaces. Here are some examples of non-linear surfaces (source: Graphing Calculator 4 on Mac App Store).

The following figure shows a 2D depiction of a sample non-linear case:

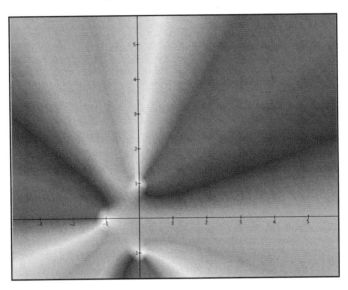

The following figure shows a 3D depiction of a sample non-linear case.

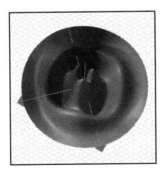

Generally speaking, a neural network is defined first by a code sample as follows:

```
val layers = Array[Int](4, 5, 4)
val mlp = new MultilayerPerceptronClassifier()
.setLayers(layers)
.setBlockSize(110)
.setSeed(System.currentTimeMillis())
.setMaxIter(145)
```

That defines the physical configuration of the network. In this case, we have a *4 x 5 x 4* MLP, meaning four input layers, five hidden layers, and four output layers. The `BlockSize` is set to 110 by using the `setBlockSize(110)` method for demonstration purposes, but 128 is the default out of the box. It is important to have a good random function to initialize the weights, which in this case is the current system time `setSeed(System.`*currentTimeMillis*`()`. The `setMaxIter(145)` is the maximum number of iterations used by the `setSolver()` method, which is `l-bfgs` solver by default.

There's more...

Multilayer Perceptron (MLP) or **Feed Forward Network (FFN)** is usually the first type of neuron network that one comes to understand before graduating to **Restricted Boltzmann Machines (RBM)** and **Recurrent Neural Network (RRN)** that are common in deep learning. While MLP technically can be configured/referred to as deep network, one must investigate a bit and understand as to why it is considered a first step (only) in a journey toward deep learning networks.

In Spark's 2.0 implementation, sigmoid function (non-linear activation) is used in a deep stackable network configuration (more than three layer) to map the output to a `Softmax` function to create a non-trivial mapping surface that can capture extreme non-linear behavior of the data.

Spark uses a sigmoid function to achieve non-linear mapping in a stackable configuration via an easy-to-use API. The following image depicts a Sigmoid function and its graph using a graphing calculator software on Mac

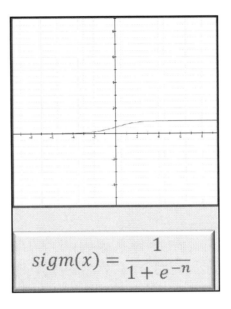

$$sigm(x) = \frac{1}{1 + e^{-n}}$$

See also

- Documentation for Spark's 2.0
  MLP: http://spark.apache.org/docs/latest/api/scala/index.html#org.apache.spark.ml.classification.MultilayerPerceptronClassifier
- For a quick introduction to MLP, see the following:
    - https://en.wikipedia.org/wiki/Multilayer_perceptron
    - https://en.wikipedia.org/wiki/Perceptron
    - http://www.di.ubi.pt/~lfbaa/pubs/NN2008.pdf

- See Spark MLP source code
  at https://github.com/apache/spark/blob/master/mllib/src/main/scala/org/apache/spark/ml/classification/MultilayerPerceptronClassifier.scala

Classic papers needed to understand deep belief networks (absolute minimum) and its contrast to a simple MLP:

- Deep belief networks: `https://www.cs.toronto.edu/~hinton/absps/fastnc.pdf`
- Stacked auto encoders: `http://papers.nips.cc/paper/3048-greedy-layer-wise-training-of-deep-networks.pdf`
- Sparse representation: `http://www.cs.nyu.edu/~ranzato/publications/ranzato-nips06.pdf`

Some of the important API calls within `MultilayerPerceptronClassifier`:

The `BlockSize` by default is set to 128 - you should only start adjusting this parameter when you feel you have mastered the MLP in full:

- def **setLayers**(value: Array[Int]): MultilayerPerceptronClassifier.this.type
- def **setFeaturesCol**(value: String): MultilayerPerceptronClassifier
- def **setLabelCol**(value: String): MultilayerPerceptronClassifier
- def **setSeed**(value: Long): MultilayerPerceptronClassifier.this.type
- def **setBlockSize**(value: Int): MultilayerPerceptronClassifier.this.type
- def **setSolver**(value: String): MultilayerPerceptronClassifier.this.type

One-vs-Rest classifier (One-vs-All) in Apache Spark 2.0

In this recipe, we demonstrate One-vs-Rest in Apache Spark 2.0. What we are trying to achieve with the `OneVsRest()` classifier is to make a binary logistic regression to work for a multi-class / multi-label classification problem. The recipe is a two-step approach in which we first configure a `LogisticRegression()` object and then use it in a `OneVsRest()` classifier to solve a multi-class classification problem using logistic regression.

How to do it...

1. Go to the LIBSVM Data: Classification (Multi-class) Repository and download the file: https://www.csie.ntu.edu.tw/~cjlin/libsvmtools/datasets/multiclass/iris.scale

2. Start a new project in IntelliJ or in an IDE of your choice. Make sure the necessary JAR files are included.

3. Set up the package location where the program will reside:

```
package spark.ml.cookbook.chapter5
```

4. Import the necessary packages for the SparkSession to gain access to the cluster and Log4j.Logger to reduce the amount of output produced by Spark:

```
import org.apache.spark.sql.SparkSession
import org.apache.spark.ml.classification
.{LogisticRegression, OneVsRest}
import org.apache.spark.ml.evaluation
.MulticlassClassificationEvaluator
import org.apache.log4j.{ Level, Logger}
```

5. Set the output level to ERROR to reduce Spark's logging output:

```
Logger.getLogger("org").setLevel(Level.ERROR)
 Logger.getLogger("akka").setLevel(Level.ERROR)
```

6. Initialize a SparkSession specifying configurations constructing an entry point to the Spark cluster:

```
val spark = SparkSession
 .builder
 .master("local[*]")
 .appName("One-vs-Rest")
 .getOrCreate()
```

7. We begin by loading into memory the libsvm formatted data file:

```
val data = spark.read.format("libsvm")
 .load("../data/sparkml2/chapter5/iris.scale.txt")
```

8. Now display the loaded data:

```
data.show(false)
```

```
+-----+----------------------------------------------------------+
|label|features                                                  |
+-----+----------------------------------------------------------+
|1.0  |(4,[0,1,2,3],[-0.555556,0.25,-0.864407,-0.916667])        |
|1.0  |(4,[0,1,2,3],[-0.666667,-0.166667,-0.864407,-0.916667])   |
|1.0  |(4,[0,2,3],[-0.777778,-0.898305,-0.916667])               |
|1.0  |(4,[0,1,2,3],[-0.833333,-0.0833334,-0.830508,-0.916667])  |
|1.0  |(4,[0,1,2,3],[-0.611111,0.333333,-0.864407,-0.916667])    |
|1.0  |(4,[0,1,2,3],[-0.388889,0.583333,-0.762712,-0.75])        |
|1.0  |(4,[0,1,2,3],[-0.833333,0.166667,-0.864407,-0.833333])    |
|1.0  |(4,[0,1,2,3],[-0.611111,0.166667,-0.830508,-0.916667])    |
|1.0  |(4,[0,1,2,3],[-0.944444,-0.25,-0.864407,-0.916667])       |
|1.0  |(4,[0,1,2,3],[-0.666667,-0.0833334,-0.830508,-1.0])       |
|1.0  |(4,[0,1,2,3],[-0.388889,0.416667,-0.830508,-0.916667])    |
|1.0  |(4,[0,1,2,3],[-0.722222,0.166667,-0.79661,-0.916667])     |
|1.0  |(4,[0,1,2,3],[-0.722222,-0.166667,-0.864407,-1.0])        |
|1.0  |(4,[0,1,2,3],[-1.0,-0.166667,-0.966102,-1.0])             |
|1.0  |(4,[0,1,2,3],[-0.166667,0.666667,-0.932203,-0.916667])    |
|1.0  |(4,[0,1,2,3],[-0.222222,1.0,-0.830508,-0.75])             |
|1.0  |(4,[0,1,2,3],[-0.388889,0.583333,-0.898305,-0.75])        |
|1.0  |(4,[0,1,2,3],[-0.555556,0.25,-0.864407,-0.833333])        |
|1.0  |(4,[0,1,2,3],[-0.222222,0.5,-0.762712,-0.833333])         |
|1.0  |(4,[0,1,2,3],[-0.555556,0.5,-0.830508,-0.833333])         |
+-----+----------------------------------------------------------+
only showing top 20 rows
```

9. Next, we utilize the datasets `randomSplit` method splitting the dataset with a ratio of 80% training data and 20% test data:

```
val Array (train, test) = data.randomSplit(Array( 0.8 , 0.2 ), seed
= System.currentTimeMillis())
```

10. Let's configure a logistics regression algorithm to use as a classifier for the One-vs-Rest algorithm:

```
val lrc = new LogisticRegression()
.setMaxIter(15)
.setTol(1E-3)
.setFitIntercept(true)
```

11. Next, we create the one versus rest object passing our newly created logistic regression object as an argument:

```
val ovr = new OneVsRest().setClassifier(lrc)
```

12. We generated the model by invoking the fit method on our one-vs-rest object:

```
val ovrModel = ovr.fit(train)
```

13. Now, we will use the trained model to generate predictions for the test data and display the results:

```
+-----+---------------------------------------------------------------+----------+
|label|features                                                       |prediction|
+-----+---------------------------------------------------------------+----------+
|1.0  |(4,[0,1,2,3],[-0.833333,-0.0833334,-0.830508,-0.916667])       |1.0       |
|1.0  |(4,[0,1,2,3],[-0.833333,0.166667,-0.864407,-0.833333])         |1.0       |
|1.0  |(4,[0,1,2,3],[-0.722222,-0.166667,-0.864407,-0.833333])        |1.0       |
|1.0  |(4,[0,1,2,3],[-0.722222,-0.0833334,-0.79661,-0.916667])        |1.0       |
|1.0  |(4,[0,1,2,3],[-0.555556,0.5,-0.830508,-0.833333])              |1.0       |
|1.0  |(4,[0,1,2,3],[-0.555556,0.5,-0.694915,-0.75])                  |1.0       |
|1.0  |(4,[0,1,2,3],[-0.444444,0.416667,-0.830508,-0.916667])         |1.0       |
|1.0  |(4,[0,1,2,3],[-0.333333,0.833333,-0.864407,-0.916667])         |1.0       |
|1.0  |(4,[0,2,3],[-0.944444,-0.898305,-0.916667])                    |1.0       |
|1.0  |(4,[0,2,3],[-0.777778,-0.898305,-0.916667])                    |1.0       |
|2.0  |(4,[0,1,2,3],[-0.611111,-0.75,-0.220339,-0.25])                |2.0       |
|2.0  |(4,[0,1,2,3],[-0.333333,-0.666667,-0.0508475,-0.166667])       |2.0       |
|2.0  |(4,[0,1,2,3],[-0.333333,-0.583333,0.0169491,-4.03573E-8])      |2.0       |
|2.0  |(4,[0,1,2,3],[-0.166667,-0.5,0.0169491,-0.0833333])            |2.0       |
|2.0  |(4,[0,1,2,3],[-0.0555556,-0.416667,0.38983,0.25])              |3.0       |
|2.0  |(4,[0,1,2,3],[0.277778,-0.25,0.220339,-4.03573E-8])            |2.0       |
|2.0  |(4,[0,2,3],[0.5,0.254237,0.0833333])                           |2.0       |
|3.0  |(4,[0,1,2,3],[-0.166667,-0.416667,0.38983,0.5])                |3.0       |
|3.0  |(4,[0,1,2,3],[0.166667,-0.333333,0.559322,0.75])               |3.0       |
|3.0  |(4,[0,1,2,3],[0.222222,-0.166667,0.423729,0.583333])           |3.0       |
+-----+---------------------------------------------------------------+----------+
only showing top 20 rows
```

14. Finally, we pass predictions to the Multi Class Classification Evaluator to generate an accuracy value:

```
val eval = new MulticlassClassificationEvaluator()
.setMetricName("accuracy")
val accuracy = eval.evaluate(predictions)
println("Accuracy: " + eval.evaluate(predictions))
Accuracy: 0.9583333333333334
```

15. We close the program by stopping the SparkSession:

```
spark.stop()
```

How it works...

In this example, we demonstrated usage of the One-vs-Rest classifier. We began by loading the classic Iris dataset in `libsvm` format. Next, we split the dataset with a ratio of 80% for a training dataset and 20% for a test dataset. We draw the users' attention to how we use system time for randomness in a split as follows:

```
data.randomSplit(Array( 0.8 , 0.2 ), seed = System.currentTimeMillis())
```

The algorithm can be best described as a three-step process:

1. We first configure the regression object without having to have a base logistic model at hand so it can be fed into our classifier:

   ```
   LogisticRegression()
   .setMaxIter(15)
   .setTol(1E-3)
   .setFitIntercept(true)
   ```

2. In the next step, we feed the configured regression model into our classifier and call the `fit()` function to finish the job accordingly:

   ```
   val ovr = new OneVsRest().setClassifier(lrc)
   ```

3. We generate a trained model and transform the test data by way of the model. Finally, we pass predictions to the multi class classification evaluator, generating an accuracy value.

There's more...

The typical usage of this algorithm is for tagging and bagging different news items of interest about a person into various categories (such as friendly versus hostile, lukewarm versus elated, and so on). Another usage in medical billing could be the classification of patient diagnostic into different medical codes used for automated billing and revenue cycle maximization.

One-vs-Rest: As shown in the following figure, this solves an *n*-label classification problem by binary logistic regression:

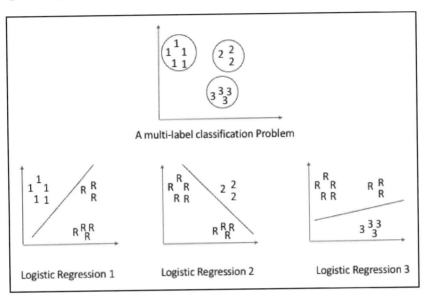

See also
========

Spark's 2.0 documentation for `OneVsRest()` can be found at:

`http://spark.apache.org/docs/latest/api/scala/index.html#org.apache.spark.ml.classification.OneVsRest`

Another way to visualize this is, to assess for a given binary classifier can we break down an n-class input into *N* number of logistic regressions and then pick the one that describes the data the best. There are numerous examples of this classifier using Scikit Learn library in Python as follows:

`http://scikit-learn.org/stable/modules/generated/sklearn.multiclass.OneVsOneClassifier.html#sklearn.multiclass.OneVsOneClassifier`

But we recommend you do a quick scan of the actual Scala source code (less than 400 lines only) at GitHub:

```
https://github.com/apache/spark/blob/v2.0.2/mllib/src/main/scala/org/apache/spark/ml/classification/OneVsRest.scala
```

Survival regression – parametric AFT model in Apache Spark 2.0

In this recipe, we explore Spark 2.0's implementation for Survival regression, which is not the typical proportional hazard model, but the **Accelerated Failure Time** (**AFT**) model instead. This is an important distinction that should be kept in mind while running this recipe otherwise the results would not make sense.

The survival regression analysis considers itself with models of *time to an event* nature, which are common in medicine, insurance, and anytime survivability of the subject is of interest. One of my coauthors happen to be a fully trained medical doctor (in addition to being a computer scientist), so we use a real dataset HMO-HIM+ study from a well-respected book in the field so we can obtain a reasonable output.

Currently, we are using this technique to do drought modeling at scale to predict price impact on agricultural commodities in long-range time frames and forecasts.

How to do it...

1. Go to the UCLA website to download the file:

   ```
   https://stats.idre.ucla.edu/stat/r/examples/asa/hmohiv.csv
   ```

The dataset we used is the actual data that is in the book *Applied Survival Analysis: Regression Modeling of Time to Event Data* by David W Hosmer and Stanley Lemeshow (1999). The data came from a HMO-HIM+ study and the data contains the following fields:

```
LIST OF VARIABLES:

Variable        Description          Codes / Units

ID              Subject ID Code      1-100

ENTDATE         Entry date           ddmmmyr

ENDDATE         End date             ddmmmyr

TIME            Survival Time        survival time (in months)

AGE             Age                  years

DRUG            History of           0 = No
                IV Drug Use          1 = Yes

CENSOR          Follow-Up Status     1 = Death due to AIDS
                                         or AIDS related factors

                                     0 = Alive at study end
                                         or lost to follow-up
```

2. Start a new project in IntelliJ or in an IDE of your choice. Make sure the necessary JAR files are included.

3. Set up the package location where the program will reside:

```
package spark.ml.cookbook.chapter5
```

4. Import the necessary packages for `SparkSession` to gain access to the cluster and `Log4j.Logger` to reduce the amount of output produced by Spark:

```
import org.apache.log4j.{Level, Logger}
import org.apache.spark.ml.linalg.Vectors
import org.apache.spark.ml.regression.AFTSurvivalRegression
import org.apache.spark.sql.SparkSession
```

5. Set the output level to ERROR to reduce Spark's logging output:

```
Logger.getLogger("org").setLevel(Level.ERROR)
Logger.getLogger("akka").setLevel(Level.ERROR)
```

6. Initialize a SparkSession specifying configurations with the builder pattern thus making an entry point available for the Spark Cluster:

```
val spark = SparkSession
 .builder
 .master("local[4]")
 .appName("myAFTSurvivalRegression")
 .config("spark.sql.warehouse.dir", ".")
 .getOrCreate()
```

7. We then read the csv file in, skipping the first line (header).

   Note: there are multiple ways to read in the csv files to a Spark DataFrame:

```
val file =
spark.sparkContext.textFile("../data/sparkml2/chapter5/hmohiv.csv")
 val headerAndData = file.map(line => line.split(",").map(_.trim))
 val header = headerAndData.first
 val rawData = headerAndData.filter(_(0) != header(0))
```

8. We convert the field from string to double. We are only interested in the ID, time, age, and censor fields. The four fields then form a DataFrame:

```
val df = spark.createDataFrame(rawData
 .map { line =>
 val id = line(0).toDouble
 val time =line(1).toDouble
 val age = line(2).toDouble
 val censor = line(4).toDouble
 (id, censor,Vectors.dense(time,age))
 }).toDF("label", "censor", "features")
```

The new features fields is a vector composed of time and age fields.

9. Next, we display the DataFrame in the console:

```
df.show()
```

From the console, this is the output:

```
+-----+------+-----------+
|label|censor|   features|
+-----+------+-----------+
|  1.0|   1.0|  [5.0,46.0]|
|  2.0|   0.0|  [6.0,35.0]|
|  3.0|   1.0|  [8.0,30.0]|
|  4.0|   1.0|  [3.0,30.0]|
|  5.0|   1.0| [22.0,36.0]|
|  6.0|   0.0|  [1.0,32.0]|
|  7.0|   1.0|  [7.0,36.0]|
|  8.0|   1.0|  [9.0,31.0]|
|  9.0|   1.0|  [3.0,48.0]|
| 10.0|   1.0| [12.0,47.0]|
| 11.0|   0.0|  [2.0,28.0]|
| 12.0|   1.0| [12.0,34.0]|
| 13.0|   1.0|  [1.0,44.0]|
| 14.0|   1.0| [15.0,32.0]|
| 15.0|   1.0| [34.0,36.0]|
| 16.0|   1.0|  [1.0,36.0]|
| 17.0|   1.0|  [4.0,54.0]|
| 18.0|   0.0| [19.0,35.0]|
| 19.0|   0.0|  [3.0,44.0]|
| 20.0|   1.0|  [2.0,38.0]|
+-----+------+-----------+
```

10. Now we will create the AFTSurvivalRegression object, and set the parameters.

The quantile probabilities are set to 0.3 and 0.6 for this particular recipe. The values depict the boundaries of quantile, which are numerical vectors of probabilities with values in the range of *0.0* to *1.0* [*0.0,1.0*]. For example, using (0.25, 0.5, 0.75) for quantile probability vector is a common theme.

The quantiles column name is set to *quantiles*.

In the following code, we create the AFTSurvivalRegression() object and set the column name and quantile probability vector.

The following code from Spark's source code on GitHub shows default values:

```
@Since("1.6.0")
def getQuantileProbabilities: Array[Double] =
$(quantileProbabilities)
setDefault(quantileProbabilities -> Array(0.01, 0.05, 0.1, 0.25,
0.5, 0.75, 0.9, 0.95, 0.99))
```

To understand parameterization and seeding, *Spark Source Code for Survival Regression* can be referenced on GitHub at https://github.com/apache/spark/blob/master/mllib/src/main/scala/org/apache/spark/ml/regression/AFTSurvivalRegression.scala.

```
val aft = new AFTSurvivalRegression()
  .setQuantileProbabilities(Array(0.3, 0.6))
  .setQuantilesCol("quantiles")
```

11. We let the model run:

```
val aftmodel = aft.fit(df)
```

12. We print out the model data into the console:

```
println(s"Coefficients: ${aftmodel.coefficients} ")
 println(s"Intercept: ${aftmodel.intercept}" )
 println(s"Scale: ${aftmodel.scale}")
```

The following output will be seen in the console:

```
Coefficients: [6.601321816135838E-4,-0.02053601452465816]
Intercept: 4.887746420937845
Scale: 0.572288831706005
```

13. We use the preceding model to transform the dataset and display the result in the console:

```
aftmodel.transform(df).show(false)
```

The following output will be seen in the console:

```
+-----+------+----------+--------------------+------------------------------------------+
|label|censor|features  |prediction          |quantiles                                 |
+-----+------+----------+--------------------+------------------------------------------+
|1.0  |1.0   |[5.0,46.0]|51.74823957599236   |[28.685748759847954,49.222952282613235]   |
|2.0  |0.0   |[6.0,35.0]|64.90643073742339   |[35.979766273942765,61.739030529362026]   |
|3.0  |1.0   |[8.0,30.0]|72.02022934303396   |[39.92317847889386,68.50567944691363]     |
|4.0  |1.0   |[3.0,30.0]|71.78290686342322   |[39.79162283408433,68.27993818140997]     |
|5.0  |1.0   |[22.0,36.0]|64.2622782089048   |[35.62269137154014,61.12631231065947]     |
|6.0  |0.0   |[1.0,32.0]|68.80346371249446   |[38.14001964193549,65.44589031333595]     |
|7.0  |1.0   |[7.0,36.0]|63.6290943019092    |[35.27169673628918,60.5240274504297]      |
|8.0  |1.0   |[9.0,31.0]|70.60289577548494   |[39.137503933039895,67.15751102349198]    |
|9.0  |1.0   |[3.0,48.0]|49.600361415100075  |[27.49510935269207,47.1798894636895]      |
|10.0 |1.0   |[12.0,47.0]|50.93118075248749  |[28.23282621938822,48.44576550657986]     |
|11.0 |0.0   |[2.0,28.0]|74.74320301794558   |[41.432612217281985,71.09577341658692]    |
|12.0 |1.0   |[12.0,34.0]|66.51606605395698  |[36.872039995008286,63.27011647600164]    |
|13.0 |1.0   |[1.0,44.0]|53.77571192552251   |[29.80964327128835,51.15148503141692]     |
|14.0 |1.0   |[15.0,32.0]|69.44228242760066  |[38.494137836385654,66.05353500595851]    |
|15.0 |1.0   |[34.0,36.0]|64.77335899648169  |[35.90600023747531,61.61245262046681]     |
|16.0 |1.0   |[1.0,36.0]|63.37757106945811   |[35.13226914778617,60.28477842147041]     |
|17.0 |1.0   |[4.0,54.0]|43.87927729909251   |[24.323724530127254,41.737991289868255]   |
|18.0 |0.0   |[19.0,35.0]|65.46583634335191  |[36.289863173818,62.271137431410544]      |
|19.0 |0.0   |[3.0,44.0]|53.84675697038553   |[29.849025872982075,51.21906311488144]    |
|20.0 |1.0   |[2.0,38.0]|60.86742469702023   |[33.74081257302759,57.89712589212319]     |
+-----+------+----------+--------------------+------------------------------------------+
only showing top 20 rows
```

14. We close the program by stopping the `SparkSession`:

```
spark.stop()
```

How it works...

We explored features of the **Accelerated Failure time (AFT)** model. We first read the dataset file into Spark using the `sparkContext.textFile()`. There are multiple ways to read a `csv` format file. We just picked one showing more detailed steps.

Next, we filtered out the head row, and converted the interested fields from string to double, and then converted the double dataset into a new DataFrame with a new `features` field.

We then created the `AFTSurvivalRegression` object and set the quantile parameters, and let the model run for itself by calling the `fit(data)` function.

Finally, we displayed the model summary and used the model to transform the dataset and displayed the resulting DataFrame with prediction and quantiles fields included.

There's more...

Spark implementation of survival regression (`AFTSurvivalRegression`):

- **Model**: Accelerated Failure Time (AFT).
- **Parametric:** Using Weibull distribution.
- **Optimization:** Spark chooses AFT because it is easier to parallelize and views the problem as a convex optimization problem with L-BFGS being the method of choice as optimization method.
- **R/SparkR users:** When fitting `AFTSurvivalRegressionModel` without intercept on dataset with constant nonzero column, Spark MLlib outputs zero coefficients for constant nonzero columns. This behavior is different from R `survival::survreg`. (from Spark 2.0.2 documentation)

You should think of the outcome as the time until the occurrence of an event of interest occurs, such as occurrence of a disease, winning, losing, time to mortgage default, marriage, divorce, landing a job after graduation, and so on. What is unique about these models is that the *time event* is a duration and does not necessarily have an explanatory variable (that is, it is just a duration in days, months, or years).

The reasons you might use survival models as opposed to simple regression (that is, tempting) are as follows:

- Need to model the outcome variable as a time event
- Censoring - not all the data is known or used (common when using long-range commodity data from past centuries)
- Non-normality distributed outcome - often the case with time
- It might or might not be a case of multivariate analysis

While there are two approaches to survival regression as outlined here, at the time of writing, Spark 2.0 only supports the AFT model and not the most-talked-about version, which is the proportional hazard model:

- **Proportional hazard model (PH)**:
    - Proportionality assumed over time
    - Multiplying a constant by covariance over consideration time
    - Example: Cox Proportional Hazard Model
    - $hx(y) = h0(y)*g(X)$

- Accelerated Time Failure (ATF) - Spark 2.0 implementation:
    - Proportionality assumption can be assumed or is violated
    - The constant value multiplied by covariance to get the regression coefficient values may be:
        - Accelerated
        - Decelerated
    - Allows for stages in unfolding of the regression:
        - Stages of disease
        - Stages of survivability
    - $Yx * g(X) = Y0$

        $Sx(y) = S0(yg(X))$

        where,

        Y: survival time,

        X: covariate vector,

        $hx(y)$: the hazard function,

        $Sx(y)$: the survival function of Y given X,

        Yx: Y given X

- Parametric modeling - underlying distribution of time variable:
    - Exponential
    - Weibull - Spark 2.0 implementation
    - Log Logistic
    - Normal
    - Gamma
- See also - very popular in R - we have used these two packages:
    - Library(survival): Standard Survival Analysis
    - Library(eha): For AFT modeling

Documentation for `SurvivalRegression` is available at the following URLs:

- `http://spark.apache.org/docs/latest/api/scala/index.html#org.apache.spark.ml.regression.AFTSurvivalRegressionModel`
- `https://spark.apache.org/docs/latest/ml-classification-regression.html#survival-regression`

The original format of the `HMOHIV` data set can be found at - connect as guest:

`ftp://ftp.wiley.com/public/sci_tech_med/survival`

A deep and complete comparison of Proportional versus AFT (Spark 2.0) hazard models can be found at:

`https://ecommons.usask.ca/bitstream/handle/10388/etd-03302009-140638/JiezhiQiThesis.pdf`

End-to-end real-world medical study with charts:

`https://www.researchgate.net/profile/Richard_Kay2/publication/254087561_On_the_Use_of_the_Accelerated_Failure_Time_Model_as_an_Alternative_to_the_Proportional_Hazards_Model_in_the_Treatment_of_Time_to_Event_Data_A_Case_Study_in_Influenza/links/548ed67e0cf225bf66a710ce.pdf`

See also

- Documentation for AFT survival implementation:
    - `https://spark.apache.org/docs/latest/api/scala/index.html#org.apache.spark.ml.feature.MinMaxScaler`
    - `https://spark.apache.org/docs/latest/api/scala/index.html#org.apache.spark.ml.regression.AFTSurvivalRegression`
    - `https://spark.apache.org/docs/latest/api/scala/index.html#org.apache.spark.ml.regression.AFTSurvivalRegressionModel`
- Spark source code for survival regression can be referenced on GitHub: `https://github.com/apache/spark/blob/master/mllib/src/main/scala/org/apache/spark/ml/regression/AFTSurvivalRegression.scala`

6

Practical Machine Learning with Regression and Classification in Spark 2.0 - Part II

In this chapter, we will cover the following recipes:

- Linear regression with SGD optimization in Spark 2.0
- Logistic regression with SGD optimization in Spark 2.0
- Ridge regression with SGD optimization in Spark 2.0
- Lasso regression with SGD optimization in Spark 2.0
- Logistic regression with L-BFGS optimization in Spark 2.0
- Support Vector Machine (SVM) with Spark 2.0
- Naïve Bayes machine learning with Spark 2.0 MLlib
- Exploring ML pipelines and DataFrames using logistic regression in Spark 2.0

Introduction

In this chapter, the second half of regression and classification in Spark 2.0, we highlight RDD-based regression, which is currently in practice in a lot of existing Spark ML implementations. Any intermediate to advanced practitioner is expected to be able to work with these techniques due to the existing code base.

In this chapter, you will learn how to implement a small application using various regressions (linear, logistic, ridge, and lasso) with **Stochastic Gradient Descent (SGD)** and L-BFGS optimization with linear yet powerful classifiers such as **Support Vector Machines (SVM)** and **Naive Bayes classifiers** using the Apache Spark API. We augment each recipe with sample fit measurement when appropriate (for example, MSE, RMSE, ROC, and binary and multi-class metrics) to demonstrate the power and completeness of Spark MLlib. We introduce RDD-based linear, logistic, ridge, and lasso regression, and then discuss SVM and Naïve Bayes to demonstrate more sophisticated classifiers.

The following diagram depicts the regression and classification coverage in this chapter:

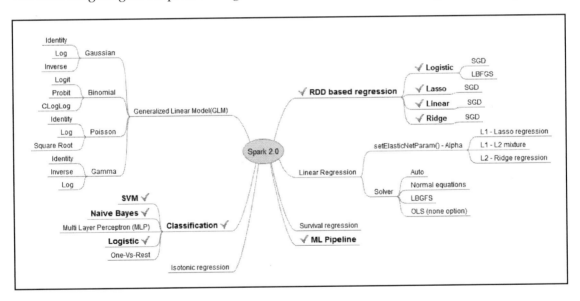

There have been reports of issues with regression using SGD in the field, but the issues are most likely due to poor tuning of SGD or a failure to understand the pros and cons of this technique in large parametric systems.

In this chapter and going forward, we start moving toward more complete (plug and play) regression and classification systems that can be leveraged while building ML applications. While each recipe is a program by itself, a more complicated system can be assembled using Spark's ML pipeline to create an end-to-end ML system (for example, classifying cancer clusters via Naive Bayes then performing parameter selection on each segment using lasso). You will see a good example of ML pipelines in the last recipe in this chapter. While the two regression and classification chapters give you a good sample of what is available in Spark 2.0 classification, we reserve the more complicated methods for later chapters.

It is preferable to use the latest methods in data science, but it is important to master the fundamentals first, starting with GLM, LRM, ridge, lasso, and SVM - make sure you understand when to use each model before graduating to more complex models.

Linear regression with SGD optimization in Spark 2.0

In this recipe, we use Spark RDD-based regression API to demonstrate how to use an iterative optimization technique to minimize the cost function and arrive at a solution for a linear regression.

We examine how Spark uses an iterative method to converge on a solution to the regression problem using a well-known method called **Gradient Descent**. Spark provides a more practical implementation known as SGD, which is used to compute the intercept (in this case set to 0) and the weights for the parameters.

How to do it...

1. We use a housing dataset from the UCI machine library depository. You can download the entire dataset from the following URL:

   ```
   https://archive.ics.uci.edu/ml/machine-learning-databases/housing/
   ```

   The dataset comprises 14 columns with the first 13 columns being the independent variables (features) that try to explain the median price (last column) of an owner-occupied house in Boston, USA.

We have chosen and cleaned the first eight columns as features. We use the first 200 rows to train and predict the median price:

1	CRIM	Per capita crime rate by town
2	ZN	Proportion of residential land zoned for lots over 25,000 sq. ft.
3	INDUS	Proportion of non-retail business acres per town
4	CHAS	Charles River dummy variable (= 1 if tract bounds river; 0 otherwise)
5	NOX	Nitric oxides concentration (parts per 10 million)
6	RM	Average number of rooms per dwelling
7	AGE	Proportion of owner-occupied units built prior to 1940

2. Start a new project in IntelliJ or in an IDE of your choice. Make sure that the necessary JAR files are included.

3. Set up the package location where the program will reside:

```
package spark.ml.cookbook.chapter6
```

4. Import the necessary packages for Spark session to gain access to the cluster and `Log4j.Logger` to reduce the amount of output produced by Spark:

```
import org.apache.spark.mllib.regression.{LabeledPoint,
LinearRegressionWithSGD}
import org.apache.spark.sql.SparkSession
import org.apache.spark.mllib.linalg.{Vector, Vectors}
import org.apache.log4j.Logger
import org.apache.log4j.Level
```

5. Initialize a SparkSession specifying configurations with the builder pattern, thus making an entry point available for the Spark cluster:

```
val spark = SparkSession
 .builder
 .master("local[4]")
 .appName("myRegress02")
 .config("spark.sql.warehouse.dir", ".")
 .getOrCreate()
```

6. Set the output level to ERROR to reduce Spark's output:

```
Logger.getLogger("org").setLevel(Level.ERROR)
Logger.getLogger("akka").setLevel(Level.ERROR)
```

7. We ingest and parallelize the dataset (first 200 rows only):

```
val data = sc.textFile("../data/sparkml2/chapter6/housing8.csv")
```

8. We take the parallelized RDD (that is, the data variable) and split the columns using a map() function. We then proceed to walk through the columns and store them in a structure required by Spark (LabeledPoint). LabeledPoint is a data structure with the first column being the dependent variable (that is, label) followed by a DenseVector (that is, Vectors.Dense). We must present the data in this format for Spark's LinearRegressionWithSGD() algorithm:

```
val RegressionDataSet = data.map { line =>
    val columns = line.split(',')

    LabeledPoint(columns(13).toDouble ,
Vectors.dense(columns(0).toDouble,columns(1).toDouble,
columns(2).toDouble,  columns(3).toDouble,columns(4).toDouble,
    columns(5).toDouble,columns(6).toDouble,  columns(7).toDouble
    ))
 }
```

9. We now examine the regression data via the output to get ourselves familiar with the LabeledPoint data structure:

```
RegressionDataSet.collect().foreach(println(_))

(24.0,[0.00632,18.0,2.31,0.0,0.538,6.575,65.2,4.09])
(21.6,[0.02731,0.0,7.07,0.0,0.469,6.421,78.9,4.9671])
(34.7,[0.02729,0.0,7.07,0.0,0.469,7.185,61.1,4.9671])
(33.4,[0.03237,0.0,2.18,0.0,0.458,6.998,45.8,6.0622])
(36.2,[0.06905,0.0,2.18,0.0,0.458,7.147,54.2,6.0622])
```

10. We set model parameters, which are the number of iterations and SGD steps. Since this is a gradient descent approach, one must experiment with various values to find the optimal values that result in a good fit and avoid wasting resources. We usually use values ranging from 100 to 20000 (rare cases) for iterations and values ranging from .01 to .00001 for SGD steps:

```
val numIterations = 1000
val stepsSGD      = .001
```

11. We make a call to build the model:

```
val myModel = LinearRegressionWithSGD.train(RegressionDataSet,
numIterations,stepsSGD)
```

12. In this step, we use the dataset to predict values using the model that was built in the previous step. We then place the predicted and labelled values in the `predictedLabelValue` data structure. To clarify, the previous step was to build a model (that is, decide on the fit for the data), while this step uses the model to predict:

```
val predictedLabelValue = RegressionDataSet.map { lp => val
predictedValue = myModel.predict(lp.features)
    (lp.label, predictedValue)
  }
```

13. In this step, we examine the intercept (by default, no intercept selected) and the weights for the eight columns (columns 0 to 7):

```
println("Intercept set:",myModel.intercept)
println("Model Weights:",myModel.weights)
```

The output is as follows:

```
Intercept set: 0.0
Model
Weights:,[-0.03734048699612366,0.254990126659302,0.0049174024137692
99,
0.004611027094514264,0.027391067379836438,0.6401657695067162,0.1911
635554630619,0.408578077994874])
```

14. To get a feel for the predicted value, we randomly select twenty values without replacement using the `takesample()` function. In this case, we show the values for only seven of the twenty values:

```
predictedLabelValue.takeSample(false,5).foreach(println(_))
```

The output is as follows:

```
(21.4,21.680880143786645)
(18.4,24.04970929955823)
(15.0,27.93421483734525)
(41.3,23.898190127554827)
(23.6,21.29583657363941)
(33.3,34.58611522445151)
(23.8,19.93920838257026)
```

15. We use Root Mean Squared Error (one of the many) to quantify the fit. The fit can be improved drastically (more data, stepsSGD, the number of iterations, and most importantly, experimentation with feature engineering), but we leave that to a statistics book to explore. Here is the formula for RMSD:

$$RMSD = \sqrt{\frac{\sum_{t=1}^{n}(\hat{y}_t - y)^2}{n}}$$

```
val MSE = predictedLabelValue.map{ case(l, p) => math.pow((l - p),
2)}.reduce(_ + _) / predictedLabelValue.count
 val RMSE = math.sqrt(MSE)println("training Mean Squared Error = "
+ MSE)
 println("training Root Mean Squared Error = " + RMSE)
```

The output is as follows:

```
training Mean Squared Error = 91.45318188628684
training Root Mean Squared Error = 9.563115699722912
```

How it works...

We used selected columns from a housing data (independent variables) file to predict housing prices (dependent variable). We used the RDD-based regression method with an SGD optimizer to iterate toward a solution. We then proceeded to output the intercept and each parameter's weight. In the last step, we predicted with sample data and showed the output. The last step was to output the MSE and RMSE values for the model. Please note that this was for demonstration purposes only and you should use the evaluation metrics demonstrated in Chapter 4, *Common Recipes for Implementing a Robust Machine Learning System*, for model evaluation and the final selection process.

The Signatures for this method constructor are as follows:

```
newLinearRegressionWithSGD()
```

Defaults for parameters:

- `stepSize= 1.0`
- `numIterations= 100`
- `miniBatchFraction= 1.0`

`miniBatchFraction` is an important parameter that can have a significant impact on performance. This is what is referred to as batch gradient versus gradient in academic literature.

There's more...

1. We can also change the default intercept behavior using the constructor to create a new regression model and then using `setIntercept(true)` accordingly:

   The sample code is as follows:

   ```
   val myModel = new LinearRegressionWithSGD().setIntercept(true)
   ```

2. If the weight for the model is computed as NaN, you must change the model parameters (SGD steps or number of iterations) until you get convergence. An example is model weights that are not computed correctly (there is a convergence problem with SGD in general) due to poor parameter selection. The first move should be to use a more fine-grain step parameter for SGD:

   ```
   (Model Weights:, [NaN,NaN,NaN,NaN,NaN,NaN,NaN,NaN])
   ```

See also

We cover both Gradient Descent and SGD in detail in Chapter 9, *Optimization - Going Down the Hill with Gradient Descent*. In this chapter, the reader should abstract the SGD as an optimization technique that minimizes the loss function for fitting a line to a series of points. There are parameters that will affect the behavior of the SGD and we encourage the reader to change these parameters to either extreme to observe poor performance and non-convergence (that is, the result will appear as NaN).

The documentation for the `LinearRegressionWithSGD()` constructor is available at the following URL:

```
http://spark.apache.org/docs/latest/api/scala/index.html#org.apache.spark.packa
ge
```

Logistic regression with SGD optimization in Spark 2.0

In this recipe, we use admission data from the UCI Machine Library Repository to build and then train a model to predict student admissions based on a given set of features (GRE, GPA, and Rank) used during the admission process using the RDD-based `LogisticRegressionWithSGD()` Apache Spark API set.

This recipe demonstrates both optimization (SGD) and regularization (penalizing the model for complexity or over-fitting). We emphasize that they are two different things and often cause confusion to beginners. In the upcoming chapter, we demonstrate both concepts in more detail since understanding both is fundamental to a successful study of ML.

How to do it...

1. We use the admission dataset from the UCLA **Institute for Digital Research and Education (IDRE)**. You can download the entire dataset from the following URLs:
   - For home page, you can refer to `http://www.ats.ucla.edu/stat/`
   - For data file, you can refer to `https://stats.idre.ucla.edu/stat/data/binary.csv`

   The dataset comprises four columns, with the first column being the dependent variable (label - whether the student was admitted or not) and the next three columns being the explanatory variables, that is, the features that will explain the admission of a student.

   We have chosen and cleaned the first three columns as features. We use the first 200 rows to train and predict the median price:

   - Admission - 0, 1 indicating whether the student was admitted or not
   - GRE - The score from Graduate Record Examination
   - GPA - Grade Point Average score
   - RANK - The ranking

Here's sample data from the first 10 rows:

Admit	GRE	GPA	Rank
0	380	3.61	3
1	660	3.67	3
1	800	4	1
1	640	3.19	4
0	520	2.93	4
1	760	3	2
1	560	2.98	1
0	400	3.08	2
1	540	3.39	3

2. Start a new project in IntelliJ or in an IDE of your choice. Make sure that the necessary JAR files are included.

3. Set up the package location where the program will reside:

    ```
    package spark.ml.cookbook.chapter6
    ```

4. Import the necessary packages for the Spark session to gain access to the cluster, and `Log4j.Logger` to reduce the amount of output produced by Spark:

    ```
    import
    org.apache.spark.mllib.classification.LogisticRegressionWithSGD
      import org.apache.spark.mllib.linalg.Vectors
      import org.apache.spark.mllib.regression.{LabeledPoint,
    LassoWithSGD}
      import org.apache.spark.sql.{SQLContext, SparkSession}
      import org.apache.spark.{SparkConf, SparkContext}
      import org.apache.spark.ml.classification.{LogisticRegression,
    LogisticRegressionModel}
    import org.apache.log4j.Logger
    import org.apache.log4j.Level
    ```

5. Initialize a `SparkSession` specifying configurations with the builder pattern, thus making an entry point available for the Spark cluster:

    ```
    val spark = SparkSession
     .builder
     .master("local[4]")
    ```

```
.appName("myRegress05")
.config("spark.sql.warehouse.dir", ".")
.getOrCreate()
```

6. Set the output level to ERROR to reduce Spark's output:

```
Logger.getLogger("org").setLevel(Level.ERROR)
 Logger.getLogger("akka").setLevel(Level.ERROR)
```

7. Load the data file and turn it into RDDs:

```
val data = sc.textFile("../data/sparkml2/chapter6/admission1.csv")
```

8. Ingest the data by splitting it and then converting to double while building a LabeledPoint (a data structure required by Spark) dataset. Column 1 (position 0) is the dependent variable in the regression, while columns 2 through 4 (GRE, GPA, Rank) are features:

```
val RegressionDataSet = data.map { line =>
   val columns = line.split(',')

   LabeledPoint(columns(0).toDouble ,
Vectors.dense(columns(1).toDouble,columns(2).toDouble,
columns(3).toDouble ))

 }
```

9. We examine the dataset after loading, which is always recommended, and also demonstrate the label point internals, which is a single value (for example, label or dependent variable), followed by a DenseVector of features we are trying to use to explain the dependent variable:

```
RegressionDataSet.collect().foreach(println(_))

(0.0,[380.0,3.61,3.0])
(1.0,[660.0,3.67,3.0])
(1.0,[800.0,4.0,1.0])
(1.0,[640.0,3.19,4.0])
   . . . . .
 . . . . .
 . . . . .
 . . . . .
```

10. We set up the model parameter for `LogisticRegressionWithSGD()`.

These parameters ultimately control the fit, and hence, some level of experimentation is required to achieve a good fit. We saw the first two parameters in the previous recipe. The third parameter's value will affect the selection of the weights. You must experiment and use model selection techniques to decide the final value. In the *There's more...* section of this recipe, we show the weight selection of the features (that is, which weights are set to 0) based on two extreme values:

```
// Logistic Regression with SGD r Model parameters

val numIterations = 100
val stepsSGD = .00001
val regularizationParam = .05 // 1 is the default
```

11. Create and train the logistic regression model with a call to `LogisticRegressionWithSGD()` using the LabeledPoint and the preceding parameters:

```
val myLogisticSGDModel =
LogisticRegressionWithSGD.train(RegressionDataSet,
numIterations,stepsSGD, regularizationParam)
```

12. Predict the values using our model and the dataset (similar to all Spark regression methods):

```
val predictedLabelValue = RegressionDataSet.map { lp => val
predictedValue =  myLogisticSGDModel.predict(lp.features)
    (lp.label, predictedValue)
}
```

13. We print our model intercept and weights. If you compare values with linear or ridge regression, you will see the selection effect. The effect will be more dramatic at extreme values or when choosing a dataset with more collinearity.

In this example, lasso eliminated three parameters by setting the weights to 0.0 using a regularization parameter (for example, 4.13):

```
println("Intercept set:",myRidgeModel.intercept)
println("Model Weights:",myRidgeModel.weights)

(Intercept set:,0.0)
(Model
Weights:,[-0.0012241832336285247,-7.351033538710254E-6,-8.625514722
380274E-6])
```

The principles of model parameter selection from statistics still applies whether we use Spark MLlib or not. For example, a parameter weight of -8.625514722380274E-6 might be too small to include in the model. We need to look at t-statistic and p value for each parameter and decide on the final model.

14. We randomly choose 20 predicted values and visually inspect the predicted result (only the first five values are shown here):

```
(0.0,0.0)
(1.0,0.0)
(1.0,0.0)
(0.0,0.0)
(1.0,0.0)
 .  .  .  .  .
 .  .  .  .  .
```

15. We calculate the RMSE and show the result:

```
val MSE = predictedLabelValue.map{ case(l, p) => math.pow((l - p),
2)}.reduce(_ + _) / predictedLabelValue.count

val RMSE = math.sqrt(MSE)



println("training Mean Squared Error = " + MSE)
println("training Root Mean Squared Error = " + RMSE)
```

The output is as follows:

```
training Mean Squared Error = 0.3175

training Root Mean Squared Error = 0.5634713834792322
```

How it works...

We used the admission data and tried to use the logistic regression with some of the features in order to predict whether a student with a given feature set (vector) will be admitted or not (the label). We fitted the regression, set SGD parameters (you should experiment), and ran the API. We then output intercept and model weights for the regression coefficients. Using the model, we predicted and output some predicted values for visual inspection. The last step was to output MSE and RMSE values for the model. Please note that this was for demonstration purposes only and you should use evaluation metrics demonstrated in the previous chapter for model evaluation and the final selection process. Looking at SME and RMSE, we probably need a different model, parameter settings, parameters, or more data points to do a better job.

The Signatures for this method constructor are as follows:

```
newLogisticRegressionWithSGD()
```

Defaults for Parameters:

- `stepSize`= 1.0
- `numIterations`= 100
- `regParm`= 0.01
- `miniBatchFraction`= 1.0

There's more...

While non-logistic regression attempts to discover a linear or non-linear relationship that relates the explanatory factors (features) to a numeric variable on the left-hand side of the equation, logistic regression attempts to classify a feature set to a set of discrete classes (for example, pass/fail, good/bad, or multi-class).

The best way to understand logistic regression is to think of the domain on the left-side as a discrete set of outcomes (that is, the classification class) that is used to label a new prediction. Using a discrete label (for example, 0 or 1) we are able to predict whether a set of features belong to a specific class (for example, the presence or absence of disease).

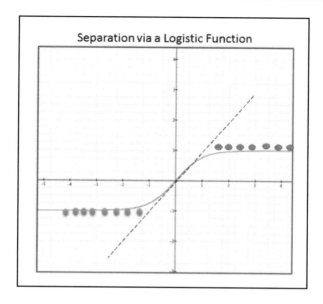

In short, the main difference between regular regression and logistic regression is the type of variable that can be used on the left-hand side. In regular regression, the predicted outcome (that is, the label) will be a numeric value, while in logistic regression, prediction is a selection from a discrete class of possible outcomes (that is, labels).

In the interest of time and space, we do not cover breaking a dataset to train and test in every recipe since we have demonstrated this in the previous recipes. We also do not use any caching, but emphasize that a real-life application must cache the data due to the way lazy instantiation, staging, and optimization is used in Spark. See Chapter 4, *Common Recipes for Implementing a Robust Machine Learning System*, to refer to recipes regarding caching and training/test data split during ML development.

If the weight for the model is computed as NaN, you must change the model parameters (that is, SGD steps or number of iterations) until you get convergence.

See also

Here's the documentation for the constructor:

```
http://spark.apache.org/docs/latest/api/scala/index.html#org.apache.spark.mllib
.classification.LogisticRegressionWithSGD
```

Ridge regression with SGD optimization in Spark 2.0

In this recipe, we use admission data from the UCI Machine Library Repository to build and then train a model to predict student admission using the RDD-based `LogisticRegressionWithSGD()` Apache Spark API set. We use a given set of features (GRE, GPA, and Rank) used during the admission to predict model weights using ridge regression. We demonstrate the input feature standardization in a different recipe, but it should be noted that parameter standardization has an important effect on the results, especially in a ridge regression setting.

Spark's ridge regression API (`LogisticRegressionWithSGD`) is meant to deal with multicollinearity (the explanatory variable or features are correlated and the assumption of intendent and randomly distributed feature variables are somewhat flawed). Ridge is about shrinking (penalizing via L2 regularization or a quadratic function) some of the parameters, therefore reducing their effect and in turn reducing complexity. It is critical to remember that `LogisticRegressionWithSGD()` does not have a lasso effect in which some of the parameters are actually reduced to zero (that is, eliminated). Ridge regression only shrinks the parameter and does not set them to zero (a small effect will still remain after shrinkage).

How to do it...

1. We use a housing dataset from UCI Machine Library Repository. You can download the entire dataset from the following URL:

   ```
   https://archive.ics.uci.edu/ml/machine-learning-databases/housing/
   ```

   The dataset comprises 14 columns, with the first 13 columns being the independent variables (that is, features) that try to explain the median price (the last column) of an owner-occupied house in Boston, USA.

   We have chosen and cleaned the first eight columns as features. We use the first 200 rows to train and predict the median price.

1	CRIM	Per capita crime rate by town
2	ZN	Proportion of residential land zoned for lots over 25,000 sq. ft.
3	INDUS	Proportion of non-retail business acres per town
4	CHAS	Charles River dummy variable (= 1 if tract bounds river; 0 otherwise)
5	NOX	Nitric oxides concentration (parts per 10 million)
6	RM	Average number of rooms per dwelling
7	AGE	Proportion of owner-occupied units built prior to 1940

2. Start a new project in IntelliJ or in an IDE of your choice. Make sure that the necessary JAR files are included.

3. Set up the package location where the program will reside:

```
package spark.ml.cookbook.chapter6
```

4. Import the necessary packages for SparkSession to gain access to the cluster and `Log4j.Logger` to reduce the amount of output produced by Spark:

```
import org.apache.spark.mllib.regression.{LabeledPoint,
LinearRegressionWithSGD, RidgeRegressionWithSGD}
 import org.apache.spark.sql.{SQLContext, SparkSession}

 import org.apache.spark.ml.tuning.{ParamGridBuilder,
TrainValidationSplit}
 import org.apache.spark.mllib.linalg.{Vector, Vectors}
import org.apache.log4j.Logger
import org.apache.log4j.Level
```

5. Initialize a SparkSession specifying configurations with the builder pattern, thus making an entry point available for the Spark cluster:

```
val spark = SparkSession
 .builder
 .master("local[4]")
 .appName("myRegress03")
 .config("spark.sql.warehouse.dir", ".")
 .getOrCreate()
```

6. To effectively demonstrate the shrinkage of the model parameter (it will shrink to a small value, but never get eliminated) in ridge regression, we use the same housing data file, and clean and use the first eight columns to predict the value of last column (median housing price):

```
val data = sc.textFile("../data/sparkml2/chapter6/housing8.csv")
```

7. Ingest the data by splitting it and then converting to double while building a LabeledPoint (a data structure required by Spark) dataset:

```
val RegressionDataSet = data.map { line =>
    val columns = line.split(',')

    LabeledPoint(columns(13).toDouble ,
Vectors.dense(columns(0).toDouble,columns(1).toDouble,
columns(2).toDouble,  columns(3).toDouble,columns(4).toDouble,
        columns(5).toDouble,columns(6).toDouble,  columns(7).toDouble
    ))

}
```

8. Examine the dataset after loading, which is always recommended, and also demonstrate the LabeledPoint internals, which is a single value (label/ dependent variable), followed by a DenseVector of the features we are trying to use to explain the dependent variable:

```
RegressionDataSet.collect().foreach(println(_))

(24.0,[0.00632,18.0,2.31,0.0,0.538,6.575,65.2,4.09])
(21.6,[0.02731,0.0,7.07,0.0,0.469,6.421,78.9,4.9671])
(34.7,[0.02729,0.0,7.07,0.0,0.469,7.185,61.1,4.9671])


  .  .  .  .  .
  .  .  .  .  .
  .  .  .  .  .
  .  .  .  .  .


(33.3,[0.04011,80.0,1.52,0.0,0.404,7.287,34.1,7.309])
(30.3,[0.04666,80.0,1.52,0.0,0.404,7.107,36.6,7.309])
(34.6,[0.03768,80.0,1.52,0.0,0.404,7.274,38.3,7.309])
(34.9,[0.0315,95.0,1.47,0.0,0.403,6.975,15.3,7.6534])
```

We set up the model parameter for `RidgeRegressionWithSGD()`.

In the *There's more...* section of this recipe, we show the shrinkage effect based on two extreme values.

```
// Ridge regression Model parameters
val numIterations = 1000
val stepsSGD = .001
val regularizationParam = 1.13
```

9. Create and train the ridge regression model with a call to `RidgeRegressionWithSGD()` and LabeledPoint using the preceding parameters:

```
val myRidgeModel = RidgeRegressionWithSGD.train(RegressionDataSet,
numIterations,stepsSGD, regularizationParam)
```

10. Predict values using our model and the dataset (similar to all Spark regression methods):

```
val predictedLabelValue = RegressionDataSet.map { lp => val
predictedValue = myRidgeModel.predict(lp.features)
   (lp.label, predictedValue)
 }
```

11. Print the model intercept and weights. If you compare values with linear regression, you will see the shrinkage effect. The effect will be more dramatic at extreme values or when choosing a dataset with more collinearity:

```
println("Intercept set:",myRidgeModel.intercept)
 println("Model Weights:",myRidgeModel.weights)


(Intercept set:,0.0)
(Model
Weights:,[-0.03570346878210774,0.2577081687536239,0.005415957423129
407,0.004368409890400891,
0.026279497009143078,0.6130086051124276,0.19363086562068213,0.39265
5338663542])
```

12. Randomly choose 20 predicted values and visually inspect the predicted result (only the first five values are shown):

```
(23.9,15.121761357965845)
(17.0,23.11542703857021)
(20.5,24.075526274194395)
(28.0,19.209708926376237)
(13.3,23.386162089812697)



. . . . .
. . . . .
```

13. Calculate the RMSE and show the result:

```
val MSE = predictedLabelValue.map{ case(l, p) => math.pow((l - p),
2)}.reduce(_ + _) / predictedLabelValue.count
val RMSE = math.sqrt(MSE)

println("training Mean Squared Error = " + MSE)
println("training Root Mean Squared Error = " + RMSE)
```

The output is as follows:

```
training Mean Squared Error = 92.60723710764655
training Root Mean Squared Error = 9.623265407731752
```

How it works...

To be able to compare with other regression methods and see the shrinkage effect, we used the housing data again and trained a model using `RidgeRegressionWithSGD.train`. After fitting the model, we output intercept and parameter weights for the model that we just trained. We then proceeded to predict the values using the `.predict()` API. We printed the predicted values and visually inspected the first 20 numbers before outputting the MSE and RMSE.

The Signature for this method constructor is as follows:

```
new RidgeRegressionWithSGD()
```

These parameters ultimately control the fit, and hence, some level of experimentation is required to achieve a good fit. We saw the first two parameters in the previous recipe. The third parameter will affect the shrinkage of the weights based on the value selected. You must experiment and use model selection techniques to decide the final value.

Defaults for Parameters:

- `stepSize`= 1.0
- `numIterations`= 100
- `regParm`= 0.01
- `miniBatchFraction`= 1.0

We cover optimization and L1 (absolute value) versus L2 (quadratic) in detail in `Chapter 9`, *Optimization - Going Down the Hill with Gradient Descent*, but for the purposes of this recipe the reader should understand that ridge regression uses L2 to penalize (that is, shrink some of the parameters) while the upcoming recipe, *Lasso regression with SGD optimization in Spark 2.0*, uses L1 to penalize (that is, eliminate some of the parameters based on the threshold used). We encourage the user to compare the weights of this recipe with the linear and lasso regression recipes to see the effect first-hand. We use the same housing dataset to demonstrate the effect.

The following diagram shows ridge regression with a regularization function:

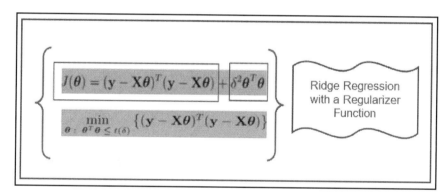

In short, it is a remedy to deal with feature dependency by adding a small bias factor (ridge regression) that reduces the variables using a regularization penalty. Ridge regression shrinks the explanatory variable but never sets it to 0, unlike lasso regression, which will eliminate variables.

The scope of this recipe is limited to a demonstration of the API call for ridge regression in Spark. The math and a deep explanation for ridge regression is a topic of multiple chapters in statistical books. For better understanding, we strongly recommend that the reader familiarizes himself/herself with the concept while taking into account the topics of L1, L2, ... L4 regularization along with the relationship between ridge and linear PCA.

There's more...

The amount of shrinkage for parameters varies by parameter selection, but the presence of collinearity is required for the weights to shrink. You can demonstrate this to yourself by using truly random (IID explanatory variables generated by a random generator) versus features that are highly dependent on one another (for example, waist line and weight).

Here are two examples of extreme regularization values and their effect on model weights and shrinkage:

```
val regularizationParam = .00001
(Model Weights:,
[-0.0373404807799996, 0.25499013376755847, 0.0049174051853082094,
0.0046110262713086455, 0.027391063252456684, 0.6401656691002464,
0.1911635644638509, 0.4085780172461439 ])

val regularizationParam = 50
(Model Weights:,[-0.012912409941749588, 0.2792184353165915,
0.016208621185873275, 0.0014162706383970278, 0.011205887829385417,
0.2466274224421205, 0.2261797091664634, 0.1696120633704305])
```

If the weight for the model is computed as NaN, you must change the model parameters (SGD steps or number of iterations) until you get convergence.

Here is an example of model weights that are not computed correctly due to poor parameter selection. The first move should be to use a more fine-grained step parameter for SGD:

```
(Model Weights:,[NaN,NaN,NaN,NaN,NaN,NaN,NaN,NaN])
```

See also

Here's the documentation for the constructor:

```
http://spark.apache.org/docs/latest/api/scala/index.html#org.apache.spark.mllib
.regression.RidgeRegressionWithSGD
```

Lasso regression with SGD optimization in Spark 2.0

In this recipe, we will use the housing dataset from the previous recipes to demonstrate shrinkage with Spark's RDD-based lasso regression `LassoWithSGD()`, which can select a subset of parameters by setting the other weights to zero (hence eliminating some parameters based on the threshold) while reducing the effect of others (regularization). We emphasize again that ridge regression reduces the parameter weight, but never sets it to zero.

`LassoWithSGD()`, which is Spark's RDD-based lasso (Least Absolute Shrinkage and Selection Operator) API, a regression method that performs both variable selection and regularization at the same time in order to eliminate non-contributing explanatory variables (that is, features), therefore enhancing the prediction's accuracy. Lasso, which is based on **Ordinary Least Squares (OLS)**, can be easily extended to other methods, such as **General Liner Methods (GLM)**.

How to do it...

1. Start a new project in IntelliJ or in an IDE of your choice. Make sure that the necessary JAR files are included.

2. Set up the package location where the program will reside:

   ```
   package spark.ml.cookbook.chapter6
   ```

3. Import the necessary packages for SparkSession to gain access to the cluster and `Log4j.Logger` to reduce the amount of output produced by Spark:

   ```
   import org.apache.spark.mllib.regression.{LabeledPoint,
   LassoWithSGD, LinearRegressionWithSGD, RidgeRegressionWithSGD}
    import org.apache.spark.sql.{SQLContext, SparkSession}
    import org.apache.spark.ml.classification.LogisticRegression
    import org.apache.spark.ml.tuning.{ParamGridBuilder,
   TrainValidationSplit}
    import org.apache.spark.mllib.linalg.{Vector, Vectors}
   import org.apache.log4j.Logger
   import org.apache.log4j.Level
   ```

4. Initialize a SparkSession specifying configurations with the builder pattern, thus making an entry point available for the Spark cluster:

```
val spark = SparkSession
 .builder
 .master("local[4]")
 .appName("myRegress04")
 .config("spark.sql.warehouse.dir", ".")
 .getOrCreate()
```

5. To effectively demonstrate the shrinkage of the model parameter (it will shrink to a small value but never get eliminated) in ridge regression, we use the same housing data file and clean and use the first eight columns to predict the value of the last column (median housing price):

```
val data = sc.textFile("../data/sparkml2/chapter6/housing8.csv")
```

6. We ingest the data by splitting it and then converting it to double while building a LabeledPoint (a data structure required by Spark) dataset:

```
val RegressionDataSet = data.map { line =>
val columns = line.split(',')

  LabeledPoint(columns(13).toDouble ,
Vectors.dense(columns(0).toDouble,columns(1).toDouble,
columns(2).toDouble,  columns(3).toDouble,columns(4).toDouble,

    columns(5).toDouble,columns(6).toDouble,  columns(7).toDouble

  ))


}
```

7. We examine the dataset after loading, which is always recommended, and also demonstrate the Label point internals, which is a single value (that is, the label/dependent variable), followed by a DenseVector of the features we are trying to use to explain the dependent variable:

```
RegressionDataSet.collect().foreach(println(_))

(24.0,[0.00632,18.0,2.31,0.0,0.538,6.575,65.2,4.09])
. . . . .
. . . . .
. . . . .
. . . . .
```

```
(34.6,[0.03768,80.0,1.52,0.0,0.404,7.274,38.3,7.309])
(34.9,[0.0315,95.0,1.47,0.0,0.403,6.975,15.3,7.6534])
```

8. We set up the model parameter for `lassoWithSGD()`. These parameters ultimately control the fit, so some level of experimentation is required to achieve a good fit. We saw the first two parameters in the previous recipe. The third parameter's value will affect the selection of the weights. You must experiment and use model selection techniques to decide the final value. In the *There's more...* section of this recipe, we show the weight selection of the features (that is, which weights are set to 0) based on two extreme values:

```
// Lasso regression Model parameters


val numIterations = 1000
val stepsSGD = .001
val regularizationParam = 1.13
```

9. We create and train the ridge regression model with a call to `RidgeRegressionWithSGD()` and our LabeledPoint using the preceding parameters:

```
val myRidgeModel = LassoWithSGD.train(RegressionDataSet,
numIterations,stepsSGD, regularizationParam)
```

10. We predict values using our model and the dataset (similar to all Spark regression methods):

```
val predictedLabelValue = RegressionDataSet.map { lp => val
predictedValue = myRidgeModel.predict(lp.features)
  (lp.label, predictedValue)


}
```

11. We print our model intercept and weights. If you compare values with linear or ridge regression, you will see the selection effect. The effect will be more dramatic at extreme values or when choosing a dataset with more collinearity.

In this example, lasso eliminated three parameters by setting the weights to 0.0 using a regularization parameter (for example, 4.13):

```
println("Intercept set:",myRidgeModel.intercept)
println("Model Weights:",myRidgeModel.weights)
```

```
(Intercept set:,0.0)
(Model
Weights:,[-0.0,0.2714890393052161,0.0,0.0,0.0,0.4659131582283458
,0.2090072656520274,0.2753771238137026])
```

12. We randomly choose 20 predicted values and visually inspect the predicted result (only the first five values shown here):

```
(18.0,24.145326403899134)
(29.1,25.00830500878278)
(23.1,10.127919006877956)
(18.5,21.133621139346403)
(22.2,15.755470439755092)
. . . . .
. . . . .
```

13. We calculate the RMSE and show the result:

```
val MSE = predictedLabelValue.map{ case(l, p) => math.pow((l - p),
2)}.reduce(_ + _) / predictedLabelValue.count

val RMSE = math.sqrt(MSE)
```

```
println("training Mean Squared Error = " + MSE)
println("training Root Mean Squared Error = " + RMSE)
```

The output is as follows:

```
training Mean Squared Error = 99.84312606110213
 training Root Mean Squared Error = 9.992153224460788
```

How it works...

Again, we used the housing data so we can compare this method with ridge regression and show how lasso not only shrinks the parameters, like ridge regression, but it goes all the way and sets the parameters that are not significantly contributing to zero.

The Signatures for this method constructor are as follows:

```
new LassoWithSGD()
```

Defaults for Parameters:

- `stepSize`= 1.0
- `numIterations`= 100
- `regParm`= 0.01
- `miniBatchFraction`= 1.0

As a reminder, ridge regression reduces the parameter's weight but does not eliminate them. When dealing with a huge number of parameters without a deep learning system in data mining/machine learning, lasso is usually preferred to reduce the number of inputs in the early stages of a ML pipeline, at least in the exploration phase.

Lasso plays a substantial role in advanced data mining and machine learning due to its ability to select a subset of the weights (that is, parameters) based on the threshold. In short, lasso regression decides which parameters to include or exclude (that is, set weight to 0) based on the threshold.

While ridge regression can substantially reduce a parameter's contribution to the overall result, it will never reduce the weight to zero. Lasso regression differs from ridge regression by being able to reduce the weight of a feature's contribution to zero (hence selecting a subset of features that contribute the most).

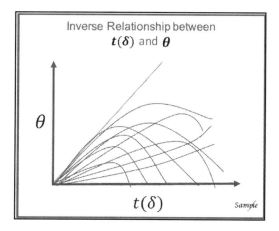

There's more...

The parameter selection (that is, setting some weights to zero) varies by regularization parameter value.

Here's two examples of extreme regularization values and their effect on model weights and shrinkage:

```
val regularizationParam = .30
```

In this case, we eliminated one of the parameters using lasso:

```
    (Model
Weights:,[-0.02870908693284211,0.25634834423693936,1.707233741603369E-4,
0.0,0.01866468882602282,0.6259954005818621,0.19327180817037548,0.3974126613
6942227])

val regularizationParam = 4.13
```

In this case, we eliminated four of the parameters using lasso:

```
(Model Weights:,[-0.0,0.2714890393052161,0.0,0.0,0.0,
0.4659131582283458,0.2090072656520274,0.2753771238137026])
```

If the weight for the model is computed as NaN, you must change the model parameters (that is, SGD steps or number of iterations) until you get convergence.

Here is an example of model weights that are not computed correctly (that is, convergence problem with SGD in general) due to poor parameter selection. The first move should be to use a more fine-grained step parameter for SGD:

```
(Model Weights:,[NaN,NaN,NaN,NaN,NaN,NaN,NaN,NaN])
```

See also

Here is the documentation for the constructor:

```
http://spark.apache.org/docs/latest/api/scala/index.html#org.apache.spark.mllib
.regression.LassoWithSGD
```

Logistic regression with L-BFGS optimization in Spark 2.0

In this recipe, we will use the UCI admission dataset again so we can demonstrate Spark's RDD-based logistic regression solution, `LogisticRegressionWithLBFGS()`, for an extremely large number of parameters that are present in certain types of ML problem.

We recommend L-BFGS for very large variable space since the Hessian matrix of second derivatives can be approximated using updates. If you have an ML problem with millions or billions of parameters, we recommend deep learning techniques.

How to do it...

1. We use the admission dataset from UCLA IDRE. You can download the entire dataset from the following URLs:
    - For home page go through the `http://www.ats.ucla.edu/stat/` link.
    - For the data file go through the `https://stats.idre.ucla.edu/stat/data/binary.csv` link.

   The dataset comprises four columns, with the first column being the dependent variable (that is, the label - whether the student was admitted or not) and the next three columns being the explanatory variables (features that will explain the admission of a student).

   We have chosen and cleaned the first eight columns as features. We use the first 200 rows to train and predict the median price.

1	Admission	0, 1 indicating whether the student was admitted or not
2	GRE	The score from Graduate Record Examination
3	GPA	Grade Point Average score
4	RANK	The ranking

Here is some sample data from the first three rows:

Admit	GRE	GPA	Rank
0	380	3.61	3
1	660	3.67	3
1	800	4	1

2. Start a new project in IntelliJ or in an IDE of your choice. Make sure that the necessary JAR files are included.

3. Set up the package location where the program will reside:

```
package spark.ml.cookbook.chapter6
```

4. Import the necessary packages for SparkSession to gain access to the cluster and `Log4j.Logger` to reduce the amount of output produced by Spark:

```
import org.apache.spark.mllib.linalg.Vectors
import org.apache.spark.mllib.regression.LabeledPoint
import
org.apache.spark.mllib.classification.LogisticRegressionWithLBFGS
import org.apache.spark.sql.{SQLContext, SparkSession}
import org.apache.log4j.Logger
import org.apache.log4j.Level
```

5. Initialize a SparkSession specifying configurations with the builder pattern, thus making an entry point available for the Spark cluster:

```
val spark = SparkSession
 .builder
.master("local[4]")
 .appName("myRegress06")
 .config("spark.sql.warehouse.dir", ".")
 .getOrCreate()
```

6. Load the data file and turn it into RDDs:

```
val data = sc.textFile("../data/sparkml2/chapter6/admission1.csv")
```

7. Ingest the data by splitting it and then converting to double while building a LabeledPoint (that is, data structure required by Spark) dataset. Column 1 (that is, position 0) is the dependent variable in the regression, while columns 2 through 4 (that is, GRE, GPA, Rank) are the features:

```
val RegressionDataSet = data.map { line =>
   val columns = line.split(',')

   LabeledPoint(columns(0).toDouble ,
Vectors.dense(columns(1).toDouble, columns(2).toDouble,
columns(3).toDouble ))

}
```

8. Examine the dataset after loading, which is always recommended, and also demonstrate the Label point internals, which is a single value (that is, the label/dependent variable), followed by a DenseVector of the features we are trying to use to explain the dependent variable:

```
RegressionDataSet.collect().foreach(println(_))

(0.0,[380.0,3.61,3.0])
(1.0,[660.0,3.67,3.0])
(1.0,[800.0,4.0,1.0])
(1.0,[640.0,3.19,4.0])
    .  .  .  .  .
 .  .  .  .  .
 .  .  .  .  .
 .  .  .  .  .
```

9. Create a LBFGS regression object with new operator and set the intercept to false so we can compare the result equally with the `logisticregressionWithSGD()` recipe:

```
val myLBFGSestimator = new
LogisticRegressionWithLBFGS().setIntercept(false)
```

10. Use the `run()` method to create the trained model using the dataset (that is, structured as LabeledPoint):

```
val model1 = myLBFGSestimator.run(RegressionDataSet)
```

11. The model is trained. Use the `predict()` method to have it predict and classify the groups accordingly. In the next lines, simply use a dense vector to define two students' data (the GRE, GPA, and Rank features) and have it predict whether the student will be admitted or not (0 means denied admission and 1 means the student will be admitted):

```
// predict a single applicant on the go
val singlePredict1 = model1.predict(Vectors.dense(700,3.4, 1))
println(singlePredict1)

val singlePredict2 = model1.predict(Vectors.dense(150,3.4, 1))
println(singlePredict2)
```

The output will be as follows:

```
1.0
0.0
```

12. To show a slightly complicated process, define a SEQ data structure for five students and attempt to use `map()` and `predict()` in the next step to predict in bulk. It should be obvious that any data file can be read at this point and converted so we can predict in larger chunks:

```
val newApplicants=Seq(
(Vectors.dense(380.0, 3.61, 3.0)),
(Vectors.dense(660.0, 3.67, 3.0)),
(Vectors.dense(800.0, 1.3, 1.0)),
(Vectors.dense(640.0, 3.19, 4.0)),
(Vectors.dense(520.0, 2.93, 1.0))
)
```

13. Now use `map()` and `predict()` to run through the SEQ data structure and produce predictions in bulk with the trained model:

```
val predictedLabelValue = newApplicants.map {lp => val
predictedValue =  model1.predict(lp)
  ( predictedValue)
}
```

14. Look at the output and the resulting predictions for the students. The presence of 0 or 1 indicates denial or acceptance of the student based on the model:

```
predictedLabelValue.foreach(println(_))

Output:
0.0
```

```
0.0
1.0
0.0
1.0
```

How it works...

We used the UCI admission data with `LogisticRegressionWithLBFGS()` to predict whether a student will be admitted or not. The intercept was set to false and the `.run()` and `.predict()` API is used to predict with the fitted model. The point here was that L-BFGS is suitable for an extremely large number of parameters, particularly when there is a lot of sparsity. Regardless of what optimization technique was used, we emphasized again that ridge regression reduces the parameter weight, but never sets it to zero.

The Signature for this method constructor is as follows:

```
LogisticRegressionWithLBFGS ()
```

L-BFGS optimization in Spark, `L-BFGS()`, is based on Newton's optimization algorithm (uses curvature in addition to 2nd derivative of the curve at point), which can be thought of as a maximizing likelihood function that seeks a stationary point on a differentiable function. The convergence for this algorithm should be given special attention (that is, require optimal or gradient of zero).

Please note that this recipe is for demonstration purposes only and you should use the evaluation metrics demonstrated in Chapter 4, *Common Recipes for Implementing a Robust Machine Learning System,*for model evaluation and the final selection process.

There's more...

The `LogisticRegressionWithLBFGS()` object has a method called `setNumClasses()` that allows it to deal with multinomials (that is, more than two groups). By default, it is set to two, which is a binary logistic regression.

L-BFGS is a limited memory adaptation of the original BFGS (Broyden-Fletcher-Goldfarb-Shanno) method. L-BFGS is well suited for regression models that deal with a large number of variables. It is a form of BFGS approximation with limited memory in which it tries to estimate the Hessian matrix while searching through the large search space.

We encourage the reader to step back and look at the problem as regression plus an optimization technique (regression with SGD versus regression with L-BFGS). In this recipe, we used logistic regression, which itself is a form of linear regression except with discrete labels, plus an optimization algorithm (that is, we choose L-BFGS rather than SGD) to solve the problem.

In order to appreciate the details of L-BFGS, one must understand the Hessian matrix and its role, along with the concomitant difficulties with large numbers of parameters (Hessian or Jacobian techniques), especially when using a sparse matrix configuration in optimization.

See also

Here is the documentation for the constructor:

```
http://spark.apache.org/docs/latest/api/scala/index.html#org.apache.spark.mllib
.classification.LogisticRegressionWithLBFGS
```

Support Vector Machine (SVM) with Spark 2.0

In this recipe, we use Spark's RDD-based SVM API `SVMWithSGD` with SGD to classify the population into two binary classes, and then use count and `BinaryClassificationMetrics` to look at model performance.

In the interest of time and space, we use the sample `LIBSVM` format already supplied with Spark, but provide links to additional data files offered by National Taiwan University so the reader can experiment on their own. **Support Vector Machine (SVM)** as a concept is fundamentally very simple, unless you want to get into the details of its implementation in Spark or any other package.

While the mathematics behind SVM is beyond the scope of this book, readers are encouraged to read the following tutorials and the original SVM paper for a deeper understanding.

The original papers are by *Vapnik* and *Chervonenkis* (1974, 1979 - in Russian) and there's also *Vapnik's* 1982 translation of his 1979 book:

```
https://www.amazon.com/Statistical-Learning-Theory-Vladimir-Vapnik/dp/047103003
1
```

For a more modern write up, we recommend the following three books from our library:

- *The Nature of Statistical Learning Theory* by V. Vapnik:

  ```
  https://www.amazon.com/Statistical-Learning-Information-Science-Statis
  tics/dp/0387987800
  ```

- *Learning with Kernels: Support Vector Machines, Regularization, Optimization, and Beyond* by B. Scholkopf and A. Smola:

  ```
  https://mitpress.mit.edu/books/learning-kernels
  ```

- *Machine Learning: A Probabilistic Perspective* by K. Murphy:

  ```
  https://mitpress.mit.edu/books/machine-learning-0
  ```

How to do it...

1. Start a new project in IntelliJ or in an IDE of your choice. Make sure that the necessary JAR files are included.

2. Set up the package location where the program will reside:

   ```
   package spark.ml.cookbook.chapter6
   ```

3. Import the necessary packages for SparkSession to gain access to the cluster and `Log4j.Logger` to reduce the amount of output produced by Spark:

   ```
   import org.apache.spark.mllib.util.MLUtils
   import org.apache.spark.mllib.classification.{SVMModel,
   SVMWithSGD}
   import
   org.apache.spark.mllib.evaluation.{BinaryClassificationMetrics,
   MultilabelMetrics, binary}
   import org.apache.spark.sql.{SQLContext, SparkSession}
   import org.apache.log4j.Logger
   import org.apache.log4j.Level
   ```

4. Initialize a SparkSession specifying configurations with the builder pattern thus making an entry point available for the Spark cluster:

   ```
   val spark = SparkSession
   .builder
   .master("local[4]")
   .appName("mySVM07")
   ```

```
.config("spark.sql.warehouse.dir", ".")
.getOrCreate()
```

5. Spark provides the MLUtils package, which enables us to read any file that is properly formatted as `libsvm`. We use `LoadLibSVMFile()` to load one of the short sample files (100 rows) that is included with Spark for easy experimentation. The `sample_libsvm_data` file can be found in the `.../data/mlib/` directory of Spark home. We simply copy the file into our own directory on a Windows machine as is:

```
val dataSetSVM = MLUtils.loadLibSVMFile(sc,"
../data/sparkml2/chapter6/sample_libsvm_data.txt")
```

6. Print and examine the content of the sample file via output. A short version of the output is included for reference:

```
println("Top 10 rows of LibSVM data")
dataSetSVM.collect().take(10).foreach(println(_))

Output:
(0.0,(692,[127,128,129,130,131,154, .... ]))
(1.0,(692,[158,159,160,161,185,186, .... ]))
```

7. Check to make sure all the data is loaded and there are no duplicates of the file:

```
println(" Total number of data vectors =", dataSetSVM.count())
val distinctData = dataSetSVM.distinct().count()
println("Distinct number of data vectors = ", distinctData)

Output:
( Total number of data vectors =,100)
(Distinct number of data vectors = ,100)
```

8. In this step, split the data into two sets (80/20) and get ready to train the model accordingly. The `allDataSVM` variable will have two randomly selected sections based on the split ratios. The sections can be referenced by an index, 0 and 1 to refer to the training and test datasets respectively. You can also use a second parameter in `randomSplit()` to define the initial seed for random split:

```
val trainingSetRatio = .20
val populationTestSetRatio = .80


val splitRatio = Array(trainingSetRatio, populationTestSetRatio)

val allDataSVM = dataSetSVM.randomSplit(splitRatio)
```

9. Set the number of iterations to 100. The next two parameters are SGD steps and the regularization parameter - we use the defaults here, but you must experiment to make sure the algorithms converge:

```
val numIterations = 100

 val myModelSVM = SVMWithSGD.train(allDataSVM(0),
numIterations,1,1)
```

10. After training the model in the previous step, now use the `map()` and `predict()` functions to predict the outcome for the test data (that is, index 1 of the split data):

```
val predictedClassification = allDataSVM(1).map( x =>
(myModelSVM.predict(x.features), x.label))
```

11. Visually examine the predictions via output (shortened for convenience). The next steps attempt to quantify how well we did with our predictions:

```
predictedClassification.collect().foreach(println(_))
```

```
(1.0,1.0)
(1.0,1.0)
(1.0,1.0)
(1.0,1.0)
(0.0,0.0)
(0.0,1.0)
(0.0,0.0)
.......
.......
```

12. First, use a quick count/ratio method to get a feel for the accuracy. Since we did not set the seed, the numbers will vary from run to run (but remain stable):

```
val falsePredictions = predictedClassification.filter(p => p._1 !=
p._2)

println(allDataSVM(0).count())
 println(allDataSVM(1).count())

println(predictedClassification.count())
 println(falsePredictions.count())

Output:
13
```

```
87
87
2
```

13. Now use a more formal way to quantify the ROC (that is, the area under the curve). This is one of the most basic standard measures of accuracy. Readers can find many tutorials on this subject. We use a combination of standard and proprietary methods (that is, hand-coded) to quantify the measurement.

14. Spark comes with a binary classification quantification measurement out of the box. Use this to collect the measurement:

```
val metrics = new
BinaryClassificationMetrics(predictedClassification)
```

15. Access the `areaUnderROC()` method to obtain the ROC measurement:

```
val areaUnderROCValue = metrics.areaUnderROC()
   println("The area under ROC curve = ", areaUnderROCValue)

Output:
(The area under ROC curve = ,0.9743589743589743)
```

How it works...

We used the sample data provided with Spark, which is in `LIBSVM` format, to run the SVM classification recipe. After reading the file, we used `SVMWithSGD.train` to train the model and then proceeded to predict the data into two sets of labeled output, 0 and 1. We used the `BinaryClassificationMetrics` metric to measure the performance. We focused on a popular metric, the area under the ROC curve, using `metrics.areaUnderROC()` to measure performance.

The Signature for this method constructor is as follows:

```
new SVMWithSGD()
```

Defaults for Parameters:

- `stepSize`= 1.0
- `numIterations`= 100
- `regParm`= 0.01
- `miniBatchFraction`= 1.0

It is suggested that the readers should experiment with various parameters in order to get the best settings.

What makes SVM great is the fact that it is OK for some of the points to fall on the wrong side, but the model penalizes the models to pick the best fit.

The SVM implementation in Spark uses SGD optimization to classify the labels for the feature sets. When we use SVM in Spark, we need to prepare the data into a format called `libsvm`. The user can use the following links to understand the format and also obtain ready-to-use datasets in `libsvm` format from National Taiwan University:

https://www.csie.ntu.edu.tw/~cjlin/libsvm/

https://www.csie.ntu.edu.tw/~cjlin/libsvmtools/datasets/

In short, the `libsvm` format is as follows:

```
<label> <index1>:<value1> <index2>:<value2> ...
```

You can simply create pipelines with Python or Scala programs to transform text files into `libsvm` format as needed.

Spark has a good number of sample files for various algorithms in the `/data/mlib` directory. We encourage the readers to use these files while getting familiar with the Spark MLlib algorithms:

```
SVMWithSGD()
```

Receiver Operating Characteristic (ROC) is a graphical plot that illustrates the diagnostic ability of a binary classifier system, as its discrimination threshold is varied.

A tutorial for ROC can be found at the following link:

https://en.wikipedia.org/wiki/Receiver_operating_characteristic

There's more...

You can either use publically available data sources in `libsvm` format or a Spark API call, `SVMDataGenerator()`, which generates sample data for SVM (that is, Gaussian distribution):

```
object SVMDataGenerator()
```

The idea behind SVM can be summarized as follows: rather than using a linear discriminant (for example, selecting a line among many lines) and an objective function (for example, least square minimization) to separate and label the left-hand variable, use the largest separating margin (as shown in the following graph) first and then draw the solid line in between the largest margin. Another way to think about it is how you can use two lines (the dashed lines in the following graph) to separate the classes the most (that is, the best and most discriminate separators). In short, the wider we can separate the classes, the better the discrimination, and hence, more accuracy in labeling the classes.

Perform the following steps to find out more about SVM:

1. Pick the widest margin that can best separate the two groups.
2. Second, draw a line that divides the widest margin. This will serve as a linear discriminant.
3. The objective function: maximize the two separating lines.

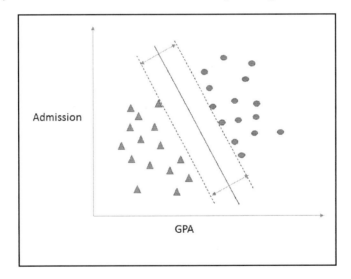

See also

Here is the documentation for the constructor:

http://spark.apache.org/docs/latest/api/scala/index.html#org.apache.spark.mllib
.classification.SVMWithSGD

Naive Bayes machine learning with Spark 2.0 MLlib

In this recipe, we use the famous Iris dataset and use Apache Spark API `NaiveBayes()` to classify/predict which of the three classes of flower a given set of observations belongs to. This is an example of a multi-class classifier and requires multi-class metrics for measurements of fit. The previous recipe used a binary classification and metric to measure the fit.

How to do it...

1. For the Naive Bayes exercise, we use a famous dataset called `iris.data`, which can be obtained from UCI. The dataset was originally introduced in the 1930s by R. Fisher. The set is a multivariate dataset with flower attribute measurements classified into three groups.

   In short, by measuring four columns, we attempt to classify a species into one of the three classes of Iris flower (that is, Iris Setosa, Iris Versicolor, Iris Virginica).

   We can download the data from here:

   `https://archive.ics.uci.edu/ml/datasets/Iris/`

   The column definition is as follows:

   - Sepal length in cm
   - Sepal width in cm
   - Petal length in cm
   - Petal width in cm
   - Class:

       - -- Iris Setosa => Replace it with 0
       - -- Iris Versicolour => Replace it with 1
       - -- Iris Virginica => Replace it with 2

The steps/actions we need to perform on the data are as follows:

- Download and then replace column five (that is, the label or classification classes) with a numerical value, thus producing the iris.data.prepared data file. The Naïve Bayes call requires numerical labels and not text, which is very common with most tools.
- Remove the extra lines at the end of the file.
- Remove duplicates within the program by using the `distinct()` call.

2. Start a new project in IntelliJ or in an IDE of your choice. Make sure that the necessary JAR files are included.

3. Set up the package location where the program will reside:

```
package spark.ml.cookbook.chapter6
```

4. Import the necessary packages for SparkSession to gain access to the cluster and `Log4j.Logger` to reduce the amount of output produced by Spark:

```
import org.apache.spark.mllib.linalg.{Vector, Vectors}
import org.apache.spark.mllib.regression.LabeledPoint
import org.apache.spark.mllib.classification.{NaiveBayes,
NaiveBayesModel}
import
org.apache.spark.mllib.evaluation.{BinaryClassificationMetrics,
MulticlassMetrics, MultilabelMetrics, binary}
import org.apache.spark.sql.{SQLContext, SparkSession}

import org.apache.log4j.Logger
import org.apache.log4j.Level
```

5. Initialize a SparkSession specifying configurations with the builder pattern, thus making an entry point available for the Spark cluster:

```
val spark = SparkSession
 .builder
 .master("local[4]")
 .appName("myNaiveBayes08")
 .config("spark.sql.warehouse.dir", ".")
 .getOrCreate()
```

6. Load the `iris.data` file and turn the data file into RDDs:

```
val data =
sc.textFile("../data/sparkml2/chapter6/iris.data.prepared.txt")
```

7. Parse the data using `map()` and then build a LabeledPoint data structure. In this case, the last column is the Label and the first four columns are the features. Again, we replace the text in the last column (that is, the class of Iris) with numeric values (that is, 0, 1, 2) accordingly:

```
val NaiveBayesDataSet = data.map { line =>
    val columns = line.split(',')

    LabeledPoint(columns(4).toDouble ,
Vectors.dense(columns(0).toDouble,columns(1).toDouble,columns(2).to
Double,columns(3).toDouble ))

    }
```

8. Then make sure that the file does not contain any redundant rows. In this case, it has three redundant rows. We will use the distinct dataset going forward:

```
println(" Total number of data vectors =",
NaiveBayesDataSet.count())
 val distinctNaiveBayesData = NaiveBayesDataSet.distinct()
 println("Distinct number of data vectors = ",
distinctNaiveBayesData.count())

Output:

(Total number of data vectors =,150)
(Distinct number of data vectors = ,147)
```

9. We inspect the data by examining the output:

```
distinctNaiveBayesData.collect().take(10).foreach(println(_))

Output:
(2.0,[6.3,2.9,5.6,1.8])
(2.0,[7.6,3.0,6.6,2.1])
(1.0,[4.9,2.4,3.3,1.0])
(0.0,[5.1,3.7,1.5,0.4])
(0.0,[5.5,3.5,1.3,0.2])
(0.0,[4.8,3.1,1.6,0.2])
(0.0,[5.0,3.6,1.4,0.2])
```

```
(2.0,[7.2,3.6,6.1,2.5])
. . . . . . . . . . . . . .
. . . . . . . . . . . . . . .
. . . . . . . . . . . .
```

10. Split the data into training and test sets using a 30% and 70% ratio. The 13L in this case is simply a seeding number (L stands for long data type) to make sure the result does not change from run to run when using a `randomSplit()` method:

```
val allDistinctData =
distinctNaiveBayesData.randomSplit(Array(.30,.70),13L)
  val trainingDataSet = allDistinctData(0)
  val testingDataSet = allDistinctData(1)
```

11. Print the count for each set:

```
println("number of training data =",trainingDataSet.count())
  println("number of test data =",testingDataSet.count())

Output:
(number of training data =,44)
(number of test data =,103)
```

12. Build the model using `train()` and the training dataset:

```
val myNaiveBayesModel = NaiveBayes.train(trainingDataSet)
```

13. Use the training dataset plus the `map()` and `predict()` methods to classify the flowers based on their features:

```
val predictedClassification = testingDataSet.map( x =>
(myNaiveBayesModel.predict(x.features), x.label))
```

14. Examine the predictions via the output:

```
predictedClassification.collect().foreach(println(_))

(2.0,2.0)
(1.0,1.0)
(0.0,0.0)
(0.0,0.0)
(0.0,0.0)
(2.0,2.0)
. . . . . . .
. . . . . . .
. . . . . . .
```

15. Use `MulticlassMetrics()` to create metrics for the multi-class classifier. As a reminder, this is different from the previous recipe, in which we used `BinaryClassificationMetrics()`:

```
val metrics = new MulticlassMetrics(predictedClassification)
```

16. Use the commonly used confusion matrix to evaluate the model:

```
val confusionMatrix = metrics.confusionMatrix
 println("Confusion Matrix= \n",confusionMatrix)
```

```
Output:
   (Confusion Matrix=
   ,35.0   0.0    0.0
    0.0    34.0   0.0
    0.0    14.0   20.0   )
```

17. We examine other properties to evaluate the model:

```
val
myModelStat=Seq(metrics.precision,metrics.fMeasure,metrics.recall)
 myModelStat.foreach(println(_))
```

```
Output:
0.8640776699029126
0.8640776699029126
0.8640776699029126
```

How it works...

We used the IRIS dataset for this recipe, but we prepared the data ahead of time and then selected the distinct number of rows by using the `NaiveBayesDataSet.distinct()` API. We then proceeded to train the model using the `NaiveBayes.train()` API. In the last step, we predicted using `.predict()` and then evaluated the model performance via `MulticlassMetrics()` by outputting the confusion matrix, precision, and F-Measure metrics.

The idea here was to classify the observations based on a selected feature set (that is, feature engineering) into classes that correspond to the left-hand label. The difference here was that we are applying joint probability given conditional probability to the classification. This concept is known as **Bayes' theorem**, which was originally proposed by Thomas Bayes in the 18th century. There is a strong assumption of independence that must hold true for the underlying features to make Bayes' classifier work properly.

At a high level, the way we achieved this method of classification was to simply apply Bayes' rule to our dataset. As a refresher from basic statistics, Bayes' rule can be written as follows:

$$P(A|B) = \frac{P(B|A)\,P(A)}{P(B)}$$

The formula states that the probability of A given B is true is equal to probability of B given A is true times probability of A being true divided by probability of B being true. It is a complicated sentence, but if we step back and think about it, it will make sense.

The Bayes' classifier is a simple yet powerful one that allows the user to take the entire probability feature space into consideration. To appreciate its simplicity, one must remember that probability and frequency are two sides of the same coin. The Bayes' classifier belongs to the incremental learner class in which it updates itself upon encountering a new sample. This allows the model to update itself on-the-fly as the new observation arrives rather than only operating in batch mode.

There's more...

We evaluated a model with different metrics. Since this is a multi-class classifier, we have to use `MulticlassMetrics()` to examine model accuracy.

For more information, see the following link:

`http://spark.apache.org/docs/latest/api/scala/index.html#org.apache.spark.mllib.evaluation.MulticlassMetrics`

See also

Here is the documentation for the constructor:

`http://spark.apache.org/docs/latest/api/scala/index.html#org.apache.spark.ml.classification.NaiveBayes`

Exploring ML pipelines and DataFrames using logistic regression in Spark 2.0

We have gone out of our way to present the code in detail and as simply as possible so you can get started without the additional syntactic sugar that Scala uses.

Getting ready

In this recipe, we combine the ML pipelines and logistic regression to demonstrate how you can combine various steps in a single pipeline that operates on DataFrames as they get transformed and travel through the pipe. We skip some of the steps, such as splitting the data and model evaluation, and reserve them for later chapters to make the program shorter, but provide a full treatment of pipeline, DataFrame, estimators, and transformers in a single recipe.

This recipe explores the details of the pipeline and DataFrames as they travel through the pipeline and get operated on.

How to do it...

1. Start a new project in IntelliJ or in an IDE of your choice. Make sure that the necessary JAR files are included.

2. Set up the package location where the program will reside:

   ```
   package spark.ml.cookbook.chapter6
   ```

3. Import the `LogisticRegression` package required to build and train the model. There are others forms of `LogisticRegression` in Spark MLlib, but for now we just concentrate on the basic logistic regression method:

   ```
   import org.apache.spark.ml.classification.LogisticRegression
   ```

4. Import SparkSession so we can gain access to the cluster, and Spark SQL, and hence the DataFrame and Dataset abstractions as needed via SparkSession:

   ```
   org.apache.spark.sql.SparkSession
   ```

5. Import the Vector Package from `ml.linlang`. This will allow us to import and use vectors, both dense and sparse, from the Spark ecosystem:

   ```
   import org.apache.spark.ml.linalg.Vector
   ```

6. Import the necessary packages from `log4j` so we can set the output level to ERROR and make the output less verbose for the program:

   ```
   import org.apache.log4j.Logger
    import org.apache.log4j.Level
   ```

7. Use the imported SparkSession to set various parameters needed to successfully initiate and gain a handle to the Spark cluster. The style for instantiating and getting access to Spark has changed in Spark 2.0. See the *There's more...* section in this recipe for more detail.

8. Set the parameters as follows:

```
val spark = SparkSession
 .builder
 .master("local[*]")
 .appName("myfirstlogistic")
 .config("spark.sql.warehouse.dir", ".")
 .getOrCreate()
```

9. Set the type of Spark cluster that you need and define the additional parameters needed to get access to Spark.

10. Here, set it to a local cluster and let it grab as many threads/cores as are available. You can use a number rather than * to tell Spark exactly how many cores/threads to

```
master("local[*]")
```

11. You have the option of specifying the exact number of cores you want to allocate by using a number rather than *:

```
master("local[2]")
```

This will allocate two cores. This might come handy on smaller laptops with limited resources.

12. Set the application name so it is easy to trace if more than one app is running on the cluster:

```
appName("myfirstlogistic")
```

13. Configure the working directory relative to Spark home:

```
config("spark.sql.warehouse.dir", ".")
```

14. We now progress toward building the data structure needed to house the first 20 rows of the downloaded student admission data (see the previous recipe):

```
val trainingdata=Seq(
 (0.0, Vectors.dense(380.0, 3.61, 3.0)),
 (1.0, Vectors.dense(660.0, 3.67, 3.0)),
 (1.0, Vectors.dense(800.0, 1.3, 1.0)),
```

```
(1.0, Vectors.dense(640.0, 3.19, 4.0)),
(0.0, Vectors.dense(520.0, 2.93, 4.0)),
(1.0, Vectors.dense(760.0, 3.00, 2.0)),
(1.0, Vectors.dense(560.0, 2.98, 1.0)),
(0.0, Vectors.dense(400.0, 3.08, 2.0)),
(1.0, Vectors.dense(540.0, 3.39, 3.0)),
(0.0, Vectors.dense(700.0, 3.92, 2.0)),
(0.0, Vectors.dense(800.0, 4.0, 4.0)),
(0.0, Vectors.dense(440.0, 3.22, 1.0)),
(1.0, Vectors.dense(760.0, 4.0, 1.0)),
(0.0, Vectors.dense(700.0, 3.08, 2.0)),
(1.0, Vectors.dense(700.0, 4.0, 1.0)),
(0.0, Vectors.dense(480.0, 3.44, 3.0)),
(0.0, Vectors.dense(780.0, 3.87, 4.0)),
(0.0, Vectors.dense(360.0, 2.56, 3.0)),
(0.0, Vectors.dense(800.0, 3.75, 2.0)),
(1.0, Vectors.dense(540.0, 3.81, 1.0))
)
```

15. The best way to understand a given row is to look at it as two parts:
    - The label - 0.0, meaning the student was not admitted.
    - The feature vector - `Vectors.dense(380.0, 3.61, 3.0)`, which shows the student's GRE, GPA, and RANK. We will cover the details of a dense vector in upcoming chapters.

16. SEQ is a Scala collection with special properties. Sequences can be thought of as iterable data structures with defined orders. For more information on SEQ see the following URL:

    `http://www.scala-lang.org/api/current/index.html#scala.collection.Seq`

17. The next step takes the SEQ structure and converts it into a DataFrame. We highly recommend that you use DataFrame and Dataset rather than the low-level RDDs for any new programming, in order to stay aligned with the new Spark programming paradigm:

    ```
    val trainingDF = spark.createDataFrame(trainingdata).toDF("label",
    "features")
    ```

    `label` and `feature` will be the column headings in the DataFrame.

18. An Estimator is an API abstraction that accepts its data as a DataFrame and produces an actual model by calling the `Fit` function. Here, we create an Estimator from the `LogisticRegression` class in Spark MLlib and then set the maximum iteration to 80; it is 100 by default. We set the regularization parameter to 0.01 and tell the model we want to also fit an intercept:

```
val lr_Estimator = new
LogisticRegression().setMaxIter(80).setRegParam(0.01).setFitInterce
pt(true)
```

19. To get a better feeling for what the program does, see the following output and examine the parameters:

```
println("LogisticRegression parameters:\n" +
lr_Estimator.explainParams() + "\n")
```

Output is as follows:

```
Admission_lr_Model parameters:
{
logreg_34d0e7f2a3f9-elasticNetParam: 0.0,
logreg_34d0e7f2a3f9-featuresCol: features,
logreg_34d0e7f2a3f9-fitIntercept: true,
logreg_34d0e7f2a3f9-labelCol: label,
logreg_34d0e7f2a3f9-maxIter: 80,
logreg_34d0e7f2a3f9-predictionCol: prediction,
logreg_34d0e7f2a3f9-probabilityCol: probability,
logreg_34d0e7f2a3f9-rawPredictionCol: rawPrediction,
logreg_34d0e7f2a3f9-regParam: 0.01,
logreg_34d0e7f2a3f9-standardization: true,
logreg_34d0e7f2a3f9-threshold: 0.5,
logreg_34d0e7f2a3f9-tol: 1.0E-6
}
```

20. Here is how to interpret and understand the `Admission_lr_Model` parameters listed in the previous step:
    - `elasticNetParam`: The ElasticNet mixing parameter, in the range [0, 1]. For alpha = 0, the penalty is an L2 penalty. For alpha = 1, it is an L1 penalty (default: 0.0).
    - `featuresCol`: Features column name (default: features).
    - `fitIntercept`: Whether to fit an intercept term (default: true, current: true).

- `labelCol`: Label column name (default: label).
- `maxIter`: Maximum number of iterations (>= 0) (default: 100, current: 80).
- `predictionCol`: Prediction column name (default: prediction).
- `probabilityCol`: Column name for predicted class conditional probabilities. Note that not all models output well-calibrated probability estimates! These probabilities should be treated as confidences, not precise probabilities (default: probability).
- `rawPredictionCol`: Raw prediction, otherwise known as confidence, column name (default: rawPrediction).
- `regParam`: Regularization parameter (>= 0) (default: 0.0, current: 0.01).
- `standardization`: Whether to standardize the training features before fitting the model (default: true).
- `threshold`: Threshold in binary classification prediction, in range [0, 1] (default: 0.5).
- `thresholds`: Thresholds in multi-class classification to adjust the probability of predicting each class. The array must have a length equal to the number of classes, with values >= 0. The class with the largest value p/t is predicted, where p is the original probability of that class and t is the class' threshold (undefined).
- `tol`: The convergence tolerance for iterative algorithms (default: 1.0E-6).

21. Now make the call to fit the prepared DataFrame and produce our logistic regression model:

```
val Admission_lr_Model=lr_Estimator.fit(trainingDF)
```

22. Now explore the model summary to understand what we get after fitting. We need to understand the components so we know what to extract for next steps:

```
println(Admission_lr_Model.summary.predictions)
```

Here is the output:

```
Admission_lr_Model Summary:
[label: double, features: vector ... 3 more fields]
```

23. Now build the actual and final model from our training DataFrame. Take the Estimator we created and have it run the model by executing the transform function. We will now have a new DataFrame with all the parts populated (for example, predictions). Print the schema for our DataFrame to get a feel for the newly populated DataFrame:

```
// Build the model and predict
 val predict=Admission_lr_Model.transform(trainingDF)
```

This is the actual transformation step.

24. Print the schema to understand the newly populated DataFrame:

```
// print a schema as a guideline
predict.printSchema()
```

The output is as follows:

```
root
|-- label: double (nullable = false)
|-- features: vector (nullable = true)
|-- rawPrediction: vector (nullable = true)
|-- probability: vector (nullable = true)
|-- prediction: double (nullable = true)
```

The first two columns are our label and features vector as we set in our API call when converting to DataFrames. The `rawPredictions` column is referred to as confidence. The probability column will contain our probability pair. The last column, prediction, will be the outcome predicted by our model. This shows us the structure for the fitted model and what information is available for each parameter.

25. We now proceed with extracting the model parameter for the regression. To make the code clear and simple, we extract each parameter's property separately into a collection:

```
// Extract pieces that you need looking at schema and parameter
// explanation output earlier in the program
// Code made verbose for clarity
val label1=predict.select("label").collect()
val features1=predict.select("features").collect()
val probability=predict.select("probability").collect()
val prediction=predict.select("prediction").collect()
val rawPrediction=predict.select("rawPrediction").collect()
```

26. For information only purposes, we print the number of the original training set:

```
println("Training Set Size=", label1.size )
```

The output is as follows:

(Training Set Size=,20)

27. We now proceed to extract the model predictions (outcome, confidence, and probability) for each row:

```
println("No. Original Feature Vector Predicted Outcome confidence
probability")
println("--- ------------------------- ----------------------
------------------------ -------------------")
for( i <- 0 to label1.size-1) {
print(i, " ", label1(i), features1(i), " ", prediction(i), " ",
rawPrediction(i), " ", probability(i))
println()
}
```

The output is as follows:

```
No. Original Feature Vector Predicted Outcome confidence
probability
--- ------------------------- ---------------------- -------------
------------- --------------------
(0, ,[0.0],[[380.0,3.61,3.0]], ,[0.0],
,[[1.8601472910617978,-1.8601472910617978]],
,[[0.8653141150964327,0.13468588490356728]])
(1, ,[1.0],[[660.0,3.67,3.0]], ,[0.0],
,[[0.6331801846053525,-0.6331801846053525]],
,[[0.6532102092668394,0.34678979073316063]])
(2, ,[1.0],[[800.0,1.3,1.0]], ,[1.0],
,[[-2.6503754234982932,2.6503754234982932]],
,[[0.06596587423646814,0.9340341257635318]])
(3, ,[1.0],[[640.0,3.19,4.0]], ,[0.0],
,[[1.1347022244505625,-1.1347022244505625]],
,[[0.7567056336714486,0.2432943663285514]])
(4, ,[0.0],[[520.0,2.93,4.0]], ,[0.0],
,[[1.5317564062962097,-1.5317564062962097]],
,[[0.8222631520883197,0.17773684791168035]])
(5, ,[1.0],[[760.0,3.0,2.0]], ,[1.0],
,[[-0.8604923106990942,0.8604923106990942]],
,[[0.2972364981043905,0.7027635018956094]])
(6, ,[1.0],[[560.0,2.98,1.0]], ,[1.0],
,[[-0.6469082170084807,0.6469082170084807]],
,[[0.3436866013868022,0.6563133986131978]])
```

```
(7, ,[0.0],[[400.0,3.08,2.0]], ,[0.0],
,[[0.803419600659086,-0.803419600659086]],
,[[0.6907054912633392,0.30929450873666076]])
(8, ,[1.0],[[540.0,3.39,3.0]], ,[0.0],
,[[1.0192401951528316,-1.0192401951528316]],
,[[0.7348245722723596,0.26517542772764036]])
(9, ,[0.0],[[700.0,3.92,2.0]], ,[1.0],
,[[-0.08477122662243242,0.08477122662243242]],
,[[0.4788198754740347,0.5211801245259653]])
(10, ,[0.0],[[800.0,4.0,4.0]], ,[0.0],
,[[0.8599949503972665,-0.8599949503972665]],
,[[0.7026595993369233,0.29734040066307665]])
(11, ,[0.0],[[440.0,3.22,1.0]], ,[0.0],
,[[0.025000247291374955,-0.025000247291374955]],
,[[0.5062497363126953,0.49375026368730474]])
(12, ,[1.0],[[760.0,4.0,1.0]], ,[1.0],
,[[-0.9861694953382877,0.9861694953382877]],
,[[0.27166933762974904,0.728330662370251]])
(13, ,[0.0],[[700.0,3.08,2.0]], ,[1.0],
,[[-0.5465264211455029,0.5465264211455029]],
,[[0.3666706806887138,0.6333293193112862]])
```

28. Looking at the output from the previous step, we can examine how the model performed and what it predicted versus the actual via the output. In the subsequent chapters, we will use models to predict outcomes.

    Here's some examples from a couple of rows:

    - **Row 10**: Model predicted correctly
    - **Row 13**: Model predicted incorrectly

29. In the last step, we stop the cluster and signal resource de-allocation:

    ```
    spark.stop()
    ```

How it works...

We started by defining a `Seq` data structure to house a series of vectors, each being a label and a feature vector. We then proceeded to convert the data structure to a DataFrame and ran it through `Estimator.fit()` to produce a model that fits the data. We examined the model's parameters and DataFrame schemas to understand the resulting model. We then proceeded to combine `.select()` and `.predict()` to decompose the DataFrame before looping to display the predictions and result.

While we don't have to use pipelines (a workflow concept in Spark borrowed from scikit-learn, `http://scikit-learn.org/stable/index.html`) to run a regression, we decided to expose you to the power of Spark ML pipelines and logistic regression algorithms in an all-in-one recipe.

In our experience, all the production ML code uses a form of pipeline to combine multiple steps (for example, wrangle data, cluster, and regress). The upcoming chapters show you how to use these algorithms without a pipeline to reduce coding during the development process.

There's more...

Since we have just seen how to code pipeline concepts in Scala and Spark, let's revisit and define some of the concepts at a high level for a solid conceptual understanding.

PipeLine

Spark makes it easy to combine steps in the machine learning pipelines (MLlib) by standardizing APIs that can be combined into a workflow (that is, referred to as pipeline in Spark). While a regression can be invoked without these pipelines, the reality of a working system (that is, end-to-end) requires us to take a multi-step pipeline approach.

The pipeline concept comes from another popular library called **scikit-learn**:

- **Transformer**: A Transformer is a method that can transform one DataFrame into another DataFrame.
- **Estimator**: An Estimator operates on a DataFrame to produce a Transformer.

Vectors

A base class of vectors supports both dense and sparse vectors. The fundamental difference is the efficiency of presentation for data structures with sparsity. The dense vector is the choice here, since the training data is all meaningful per row and very little sparsity is present. In the cases where we deal with sparse vectors, matrices, and so on, the sparse tuple will contain the index and corresponding values at the same time.

See also

While using the Spark documentation and Scala references is optional and perhaps too early for this chapter, they are included for completeness:

- SEQ documentation in Scala is available
  at `http://www.scala-lang.org/api/current/index.html#scala.collection.Seq`

- Spark DataFrame documentation is available
  at `http://spark.apache.org/docs/latest/sql-programming-guide.html`

- Spark vectors documentation is available
  at `http://spark.apache.org/docs/latest/api/scala/index.html#org.apache.spark.ml.linalg.Vectors$`

- Spark pipeline documentation is available at the following URLs:
    - `http://spark.apache.org/docs/latest/api/scala/index.html#org.apache.spark.ml.Pipeline`
    - `http://spark.apache.org/docs/latest/api/scala/index.html#org.apache.spark.ml.PipelineModel`
    - `http://spark.apache.org/docs/latest/api/scala/index.html#org.apache.spark.ml.PipelineStage`

- You should also familiarize yourself with the basic linear algebra package in Spark, you can do this by referring
  to `http://spark.apache.org/docs/latest/mllib-statistics.html`

- Familiarity with basic data types, especially vectors, is highly recommended, for that, you can refer
  to `http://spark.apache.org/docs/latest/mllib-data-types.html` link

7
Recommendation Engine that Scales with Spark

In this chapter, we will cover:

- Setting up the required data for a scalable recommendation engine in Spark 2.0
- Exploring the movies data details for the recommendation system in Spark 2.0
- Exploring the ratings data details for the recommendation system in Spark 2.0
- Building a scalable recommendation engine using collaborative filtering in Spark 2.0

Introduction

In the previous chapters, we used short recipes and extremely simplified code to demonstrate basic building blocks and concepts governing the Spark machine library. In this chapter, we present a more developed application that addresses specific machine learning library domains using Spark's API and facilities. The number of recipes are less in this chapter; however, we get into a more ML application setting.

In this chapter, we explore the recommendation system and its implementation using a matrix factorization technique that draws on latent factor models called **alternating least square** (**ALS**). In a nutshell, when we try to factorize a large matrix of user-item ratings into two lower ranked, skinnier matrices, we often face a non-linear or non-convex optimization problem that is very difficult to solve. It happens that we are very good at solving convex optimization problems by fixing one leg and partially solving the other and then going back and forth (hence alternating); we can solve this factorization (hence discovering a set of latent factors) much better using known optimization techniques in parallel.

We use a popular dataset (movie lens dataset) to implement the recommendation engine, but unlike in other chapters, we use two recipes to explore the data, and also show how you can introduce graphical elements such as the JFreeChart popular library to your Spark machine learning toolkit.

The following figure shows the flow of the concepts and recipes in this chapter to demonstrate an ALS recommendation application:

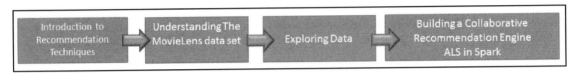

Recommendation engines have been around for a long time and were used in early e-commerce systems of the 1990s, using techniques ranging from hardcoded product association to content-based recommendations driven by profiling. The modern systems use **collaboration filtering** (**CF**) to address the shortcomings of the early systems and also to address the scale and latency (for example, 100 ms max and less) that is necessary to compete in modern commerce systems (for example, Amazon, Netflix, eBay, News, and so on).

The modern systems use CF based on historical interactions and records (page view, purchases, rating, and so on). These systems address two major issues, mainly scalability and sparseness (that is, we do not have all the ratings for all movies or songs). Most systems use a variation of Alternating Least Square with Weighted Lambda Regularization that can be parallelized on most major platforms (for example, Spark). Having said that, a practical system implemented for commercial purposes uses many augmentations to deal with bias (that is, not all movies and users are equal) and temporal issues (that is, users' choice will change and the inventory of items will change) that are present in today's ecosystem. Having worked on a smart and leading edge e-commerce system, building a competitive recommender is not a purist approach, but a practical one that uses multiple techniques, arriving at the affinity matrix/heat map as the context utilizing all three techniques (collaborative filtering, content-based filtering, and similarity) at the minimum.

The reader is encouraged to look up white papers and material that refer to the problem of cold start in recommendation systems.

To set the context, the following figure provides a high-level taxonomy of methods that are available to build recommendation systems. We briefly cover some of the pros and cons of each system, but concentrate on matrix factorization (latent factor model) that is available in Spark. While both **single value decomposition (SVD)** and **alternative least squares (ALS)** are available, we concentrate on ALS implementation with MovieLens data due to the shortcomings of SVD in handling missing data among other things. We will explore SVD in detail in `Chapter 11`, *Curse of High-Dimensionality in Big Data*.

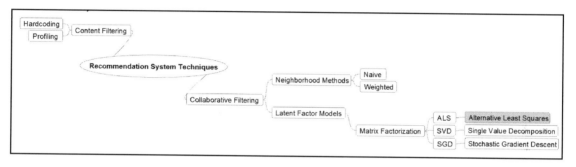

The recommendation engine techniques in use are explained in the following section.

Content filtering

Content filtering is one of the original techniques for recommendation engines. It relies on user profiles to make recommendations. This approach relies mostly on pre-existing profiles for users (type, demographics, income, geo-location, ZIP code) and inventory (characteristics of a product, movie, or a song) to infer attribution which then can be filtered and acted upon. The main issue is that the pre-existing knowledge is often incomplete and expensive to source. This technique is more than a decade old and is still being practiced.

Collaborative filtering

Collaborative filtering is the workhorse of modern recommendation systems and relies on user interaction in the ecosystem rather than profiles to make recommendations.

This technique relies on past user behavior and product ratings and does not assume any pre-existing knowledge. In short, users rate the inventory items and the assumption is that customer taste will remain relatively constant over time, which can be exploited to provide recommendations. Having said that, an intelligent system will augment and reorder recommendations with any available context (for example, the user is a female who has logged in from China).

The main issue with this class of techniques is cold start, but its advantages of being domain free, with more accuracy and easy scalability, has made it a winner in the age of big data.

Neighborhood method

This technique is mostly implemented as **weighted local neighborhood**. In its core, it is a similarity technique and relies heavily on assumptions about items and users. While it is easy to understand and implement the technique, the algorithm suffers from a lack of scalability and accuracy.

Latent factor models techniques

This technique attempts to explain users' ratings of inventory items (for example, products on Amazon) by inferring a secondary set of latent factors which are inferred from ratings. The power comes from the fact that you do not need to know the factors ahead of time (similar to PCA techniques), but they are simply inferred from the ratings themselves. We derive the latent factors using matrix factorization techniques which are popular due to the extreme scalability, accuracy of predictions, and flexibility (they allow for bias and the temporal nature of the user and inventory).

- **Singular Value Decomposition (SVD)**: SVD has been available in Spark from the early days, but we recommend not to use it as a core technique due to the problem of its ability to deal with sparseness of data in real life (for example, a user will not usually rate everything), overfitting, and order (do we really need to produce the bottom 1,000 recommendations?).
- **Stochastic Gradient Decent (SGD)**: SGD is easy to implement and has faster running times due to its approach of looking at one movie and one user/item vector at a time (pick a movie and update the profile a little bit for that user versus a batch approach). We can implement this using the matrix facility and SGD in Spark as needed.
- **Alternating Least Square (ALS)**: Please see ALS before you take on this journey. Available in Spark, ALS can take advantage of parallelization from the start. Spark implements full matrix factorization under the hood, contrary to the common belief that Spark uses half factorization. We encourage the reader to refer to the source code to verify this for themselves. Spark provides API for both **explicit** (rating available) and **implicit** (an indirect inference needed--for example, the length of time a track is played rather than a rating). We discuss the bias and temporal issues in the recipe itself, by introducing mathematics and intuition to make our point.

Setting up the required data for a scalable recommendation engine in Spark 2.0

In this recipe, we examine downloading the MovieLens public dataset and take a first exploratory view of the data. We will use the explicit data based on customer ratings from the MovieLens dataset. The MovieLens dataset contains 1,000,000 ratings of 4,000 movies from 6,000 users.

You will need one of the following command line tools to retrieve the specified data: `curl` (recommended for Mac) or `wget` (recommended for Windows or Linux).

How to do it...

1. You can start with downloading the dataset using either of the following commands:

   ```
   wget http://files.grouplens.org/datasets/movielens/ml-1m.zip
   ```

   You can also use the following command:

   ```
   curl http://files.grouplens.org/datasets/movielens/ml-1m.zip -o
   ml-1m.zip
   ```

2. Now you need to decompress the ZIP:

   ```
   unzip ml-1m.zip
   creating: ml-1m/
   inflating: ml-1m/movies.dat
   inflating: ml-1m/ratings.dat
   inflating: ml-1m/README
   inflating: ml-1m/users.dat
   ```

   The command will create a directory named `ml-1m` with data files decompressed inside.

3. Change into the directory `m1-1m`:

   ```
   cd m1-1m
   ```

4. Now we begin our first steps of data exploration by verifying how the data in `movies.dat` is formatted:

```
head -5 movies.dat
1::Toy Story (1995)::Animation|Children's|Comedy
2::Jumanji (1995)::Adventure|Children's|Fantasy
3::Grumpier Old Men (1995)::Comedy|Romance
4::Waiting to Exhale (1995)::Comedy|Drama
5::Father of the Bride Part II (1995)::Comedy
```

5. Now we take a look at the ratings data to know how it is formatted:

```
head -5 ratings.dat
1::1193::5::978300760
1::661::3::978302109
1::914::3::978301968
1::3408::4::978300275
1::2355::5::978824291
```

How it works...

The MovieLens dataset is an excellent alternative to the original Netflix KDD cup dataset. This dataset comes in multiple sets ranging from small (100 K set) to large (1 M and 20 M set). For those users interested in tweaking the source code to add their own augmentation (for example, the change regularization technique), the range of the dataset makes it easy to study the scaling effect and look at the performance curve versus Spark utilization per executive, as the data scales from 100 K to 20 M.

The URL to download is `http://grouplens.org/datasets/movielens/`.

There's more...

Take a closer look at where we downloaded the data from, because more datasets are available for use at `http://files.grouplens.org/datasets/`.

The following figure depicts the size and extent of the data. For this chapter, we use the small set so it can easily run on a small laptop with limited resources.

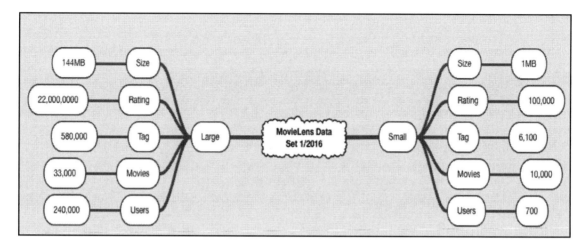

Source: MovieLens

See also

Please read through the README file contained within the directory that you unzipped the data to. The README file contains information about data file formats and data descriptions.

There is also a MovieLens genome tag set that can be used for reference.

- Computed tag-movie 11 million
- Relevance scores from a pool of 1,100 tags
- Applied to 10,000 movies

For those interested in exploring the original Netflix dataset, please see the `http://academictorrents.com/details/9b13183dc4d60676b773c9e2cd6de5e5542cee9a` URL.

Exploring the movies data details for the recommendation system in Spark 2.0

In this recipe, we will begin to explore the movie data file by parsing data into a Scala `case` class and generating a simple metric. The key here is to acquire an understanding of our data, so in the later stages, if nebulous results arise, we will have some insight to make an informed conclusion about the correctness of our results.

This is the first of the two recipes which explore the movie dataset. Data exploration is an important first step in statistical analysis and machine learning.

One of the best ways to understand the data quickly is to generate a data visualization of it, and we will use JFreeChart to do that. It is very important to make sure you feel comfortable with the data and understand firsthand what is in each file, and the story it tries to tell.

We must always explore, understand, and visualize the data before we do anything else. Most performances and misses with ML and others systems can be traced to a lack of understanding of how the data is laid out and how it changes over time. If we look at the chart given in step 14 in this recipe, one immediately realizes that the distribution of movies over the years is not uniform, but skewed with high kurtosis. While we are not going to explore this property for optimization and sampling in this book, it makes an important point about the nature of the movie data.

How to do it...

1. Start a new project in IntelliJ or in an IDE of your choice. Make sure the necessary JAR files are included.

2. JFreeChart JAR can be downloaded from the `https://sourceforge.net/projects/jfreechart/files/` site.

3. Please make sure that the JFreeChart library and its dependencies (JCommon) are on the classpath for the chapter.

4. We define the package information for the Scala program:

   ```
   package spark.ml.cookbook.chapter7
   ```

5. Import the necessary packages:

   ```
   import java.text.DecimalFormat
   import org.apache.log4j.{Level, Logger}
   import org.apache.spark.sql.SparkSession
   import org.jfree.chart.{ChartFactory, ChartFrame, JFreeChart}
   import org.jfree.chart.axis.NumberAxis
   import org.jfree.chart.plot.PlotOrientation
   import org.jfree.data.xy.{XYSeries, XYSeriesCollection}
   ```

6. We now define a Scala `case class` to model movie data:

```
case class MovieData(movieId: Int, title: String, year: Int, genre:
Seq[String])
```

7. Let's define a function to display a JFreeChart within a window that will be invoked later. There are many options for charts and plots in this package that can be explored:

```
def show(chart: JFreeChart) {
 val frame = new ChartFrame("plot", chart)
 frame.pack()
 frame.setVisible(true)
 }
```

8. In this step, we define a function for parsing a single line of data from the `movie.dat` file into our movie `case class`:

```
def parseMovie(str: String): MovieData = {
 val columns = str.split("::")
 assert(columns.size == 3)

 val titleYearStriped = """\(|\)""".r.replaceAllIn(columns(1), " ")
 val titleYearData = titleYearStriped.split(" ")

 MovieData(columns(0).toInt,
 titleYearData.take(titleYearData.size - 1).mkString(" "),
 titleYearData.last.toInt,
 columns(2).split("|"))
 }
```

9. We are ready to start building our `main` function, so let's start with defining the location of our `movie.dat` file:

```
val movieFile = "../data/sparkml2/chapter7/movies.dat"
```

10. Create Spark's session object and setup configuration:

```
val spark = SparkSession
 .builder
.master("local[*]")
 .appName("MovieData App")
 .config("spark.sql.warehouse.dir", ".")
 .config("spark.executor.memory", "2g")
 .getOrCreate()
```

11. The interleaving of log messages leads to hard-to-read output; therefore, set the logging level to ERROR:

```
Logger.getLogger("org").setLevel(Level.ERROR)
```

12. Create a dataset of all the movies from the data file:

```
import spark.implicits._
val movies = spark.read.textFile(movieFile).map(parseMovie)
```

13. Group all the movies by year, released using Spark SQL:

```
movies.createOrReplaceTempView("movies")
val moviesByYear = spark.sql("select year, count(year) as count
from movies group by year order by year")
```

14. We now display a histogram chart with the movies grouped by the year of release:

```
val histogramDataset = new XYSeriesCollection()
 val xy = new XYSeries("")
 moviesByYear.collect().foreach({
 row => xy.add(row.getAs[Int]("year"), row.getAs[Long]("count"))
 })

 histogramDataset.addSeries(xy)

 val chart = ChartFactory.createHistogram(
 "", "Year", "Movies Per Year", histogramDataset,
PlotOrientation.VERTICAL, false, false, false)
 val chartPlot = chart.getXYPlot()

 val xAxis = chartPlot.getDomainAxis().asInstanceOf[NumberAxis]
 xAxis.setNumberFormatOverride(new DecimalFormat("####"))

 show(chart)
```

15. See the chart produced to get a good feel for the movie dataset. There are at least two to four other ways that data can be visualized, which can be explored by the reader.

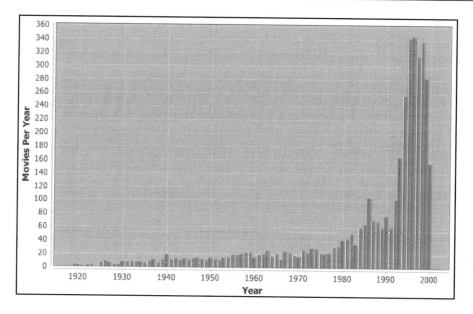

16. We close the program by stopping the Spark session:

```
spark.stop()
```

How it works...

When the program started to execute, we initialized a SparkContext in our driver program to start the task of processing the data. This implies that the data must fit in the driver's memory (user's station), which is not a server requirement in this case. Alternative methods of divide and conquer must be devised to deal with extreme datasets (partial retrieval and the assembly at destination).

We continued by loading and parsing the data file into a dataset with the data type of the movies. The movie dataset was then grouped by year, yielding a map of movies keyed by year, with buckets of associated movies attached.

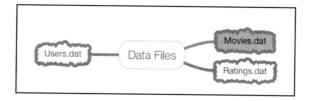

Next, we extracted the year with the count of the number of movies associated with the specific year to generate our histogram. We then collected the data, causing the entire resulting data collection to materialize on the driver, and passed it to JFreeChart to build the data visualization.

There's more...

You need to be cognizant of our use of Spark SQL because of its flexibility. More information is available
at `http://spark.apache.org/docs/latest/sql-programming-guide.html#running-sql-queries-programmatically`.

See also

For more on using JFreechart, refer to the JFreeChart API documentation
at `http://www.jfree.org/jfreechart/api.html`.

You can find a good tutorial on JFreeChart at the `http://www.tutorialspoint.com/jfreechart/` link.

The link for the JFreeChart itself is `http://www.jfree.org/index.html`.

Exploring the ratings data details for the recommendation system in Spark 2.0

In this recipe, we explore the data from the user/rating perspective to understand the nature and property of our data file. We will start to explore the ratings data file by parsing data into a Scala case class and generating visualization for insight. The ratings data will be used a little later to generate features for our recommendation engine. Again, we stress that the first step in any data science/machine learning exercise should be visualization and exploration of the data.

Once again, the best way of understanding data quickly is to generate a data visualization of it, and we will use a JFreeChart scatterplot to do this. A quick look at the chart of *users by ratings* produced by the JFreeChart plot shows a resemblance to a multinomial distribution with outliers, and an increasing sparsity when ratings are increased in magnitude.

How to do it...

1. Start a new project in IntelliJ or in an IDE of your choice. Make sure the necessary JAR files are included.

2. We define the package information for the Scala program:

```
package spark.ml.cookbook.chapter7
```

3. Import the necessary packages:

```
import java.text.DecimalFormat
import org.apache.log4j.{Level, Logger}
import org.apache.spark.sql.SparkSession
import org.jfree.chart.{ChartFactory, ChartFrame, JFreeChart}
import org.jfree.chart.axis.NumberAxis
import org.jfree.chart.plot.PlotOrientation
import org.jfree.data.xy.{XYSeries, XYSeriesCollection}
```

4. We now define a Scala `case class` to model the ratings data:

```
case class Rating(userId: Int, movieId: Int, rating: Float,
timestamp: Long)
```

5. Let's define a function to display a JFreeChart within a window:

```
def show(chart: JFreeChart) {
val frame = new ChartFrame("plot", chart)
frame.pack()
frame.setVisible(true)
}
```

6. In this step, we define a function for parsing a single line of data from the `ratings.dat` file into the rating `case class`:

```
def parseRating(str: String): Rating = {
val columns = str.split("::")
assert(columns.size == 4)
Rating(columns(0).toInt, columns(1).toInt, columns(2).toFloat,
columns(3).toLong)
}
```

7. We are ready to begin building our `main` function, so let's start with the location of our `ratings.dat` file:

```
val ratingsFile = "../data/sparkml2/chapter7/ratings.dat"
```

8. Create Spark's configuration, SparkSession. In this example, we show for the first time how to set the Spark executor memory (for example, 2 gig) on a small laptop. You must increase this allocation if you want to use the large dataset (the 144 MB set):

```
val spark = SparkSession
 .builder
.master("local[*]")
 .appName("MovieRating App")
 .config("spark.sql.warehouse.dir", ".")
 .config("spark.executor.memory", "2g")
 .getOrCreate()
```

9. The interleaving of log messages leads to hard to-read output; therefore, set the logging level to ERROR:

```
Logger.getLogger("org").setLevel(Level.ERROR)
```

10. Create a dataset of all the ratings from the data file:

```
import spark.implicits._
 val ratings = spark.read.textFile(ratingsFile).map(parseRating)
```

11. Now we convert the ratings dataset into a memory table view, where we can execute the Spark SQL query:

```
ratings.createOrReplaceTempView("ratings")
```

12. We now produce a list of all user ratings grouped by user, with their totals:

```
val resultDF = spark.sql("select ratings.userId, count(*) as count
from ratings group by ratings.userId")
resultDF.show(25, false);
```

From the console output:

```
From the Console output;
+------+-----+
|userId|count|
+------+-----+
|148   |624  |
|463   |123  |
|471   |105  |
|496   |119  |
|833   |21   |
|1088  |1176 |
|1238  |45   |
|1342  |92   |
|1580  |37   |
|1591  |314  |
|1645  |522  |
|1829  |30   |
|1959  |61   |
|2122  |208  |
|2142  |77   |
|2366  |41   |
|2659  |161  |
|2866  |205  |
|3175  |87   |
|3749  |118  |
|3794  |44   |
|3918  |26   |
|3997  |315  |
|4101  |95   |
|4519  |42   |
+------+-----+
only showing top 25 rows
```

13. Display a scatterplot chart with ratings per user. We choose a scatterplot to demonstrate a different way to look at the data from the previous recipe. We encourage readers to explore standardization techniques (for example, remove mean) or a volatility varying regime (for example, GARCH) to explore the autoregressive conditional heteroscedasticity property of this dataset (which is beyond the scope of this book). The reader is advised to consult any advanced time series book to develop an understanding of time varying volatility of the time series and how to correct this before usage.

```
val scatterPlotDataset = new XYSeriesCollection()
 val xy = new XYSeries("")

 resultDF.collect().foreach({r => xy.add(
r.getAs[Integer]("userId"), r.getAs[Integer]("count")) })

 scatterPlotDataset.addSeries(xy)

 val chart = ChartFactory.createScatterPlot(
 "", "User", "Ratings Per User", scatterPlotDataset,
```

```
PlotOrientation.VERTICAL, false, false, false)
val chartPlot = chart.getXYPlot()

val xAxis = chartPlot.getDomainAxis().asInstanceOf[NumberAxis]
xAxis.setNumberFormatOverride(new DecimalFormat("####"))
```

14. Display the chart:

```
show(chart)
```

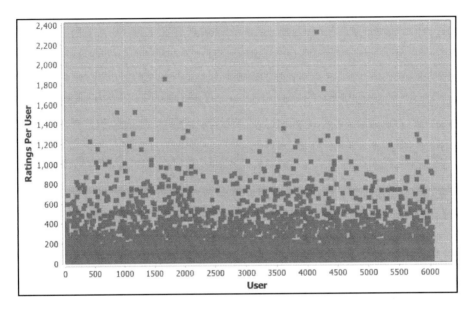

15. We close the program by stopping the Spark session:

```
spark.stop()
```

How it works...

We began by loading and parsing the data file into a dataset with the data type ratings, and finally converted it to a DataFrame. The DataFrame was then used to execute a Spark SQL query that grouped all the ratings by user with their totals.

We explored Dataset/DataFrame in Chapter 3, *Spark's Three Data Musketeers for Machine Learning - Perfect Together*, but we encourage the user to refresh and dig deeper into the Dataset/DataFrame API. A full understanding of the API and its concepts (lazy instantiation, staging, pipelining, and caching) is critical for every Spark developer.

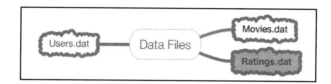

Finally, we passed the result set of data to the JFreeChart scatterplot component to display our chart.

There's more...

A Spark DataFrame is a distributed collection of data organized into named columns. All DataFrame operations are also automatically parallelized and distributed on clusters. Also, DataFrames are lazily evaluated like RDDs.

See also

Documentation on DataFrames can be found at `http://spark.apache.org/docs/latest/sql-programming-guide.html`.

A good tutorial on JFreeChart can be found at the `http://www.tutorialspoint.com/jfreechart/` linking.

JFreeChart can be downloaded from the `http://www.jfree.org/index.html` URL.

Building a scalable recommendation engine using collaborative filtering in Spark 2.0

In this recipe, we will be demonstrating a recommendation system that utilizes a technique known as collaborative filtering. At the core, collaborative filtering analyzes the relationship between users themselves and the dependencies between the inventory (for example, movies, books, news articles, or songs) to identify user-to-item relationships based on a set of secondary factors called **latent factors** (for example, female/male, happy/sad, active/passive). The key here is that you do not need to know the latent factors in advance.

The recommendation will be produced via the ALS algorithm which is a collaborative filtering technique. At a high level, collaborative filtering entails making predictions of what a user may be interested in based on collecting previously known preferences, combined with the preferences of many other users. We will be using the ratings data from the MovieLens dataset and will convert it into input features for the recommendation algorithm.

How to do it...

1. Start a new project in IntelliJ or in an IDE of your choice. Make sure the necessary JAR files are included.

2. We define the package information for the Scala program:

```
package spark.ml.cookbook.chapter7
```

3. Import the necessary packages:

```
import org.apache.log4j.{Level, Logger}
import org.apache.spark.sql.SparkSession
import org.apache.spark.ml.recommendation.ALS
```

4. We now define two Scala case classes, to model movie and ratings data:

```
case class Movie(movieId: Int, title: String, year: Int, genre:
Seq[String])
 case class FullRating(userId: Int, movieId: Int, rating: Float,
timestamp: Long)
```

5. In this step, we define functions for parsing a single line of data from the ratings.dat file into the ratings case class, and for parsing a single line of data from the movies.dat file into the movie case class:

```
def parseMovie(str: String): Movie = {
val columns = str.split("::")
assert(columns.size == 3)

val titleYearStriped = """\(|\)""".r.replaceAllIn(columns(1), " ")
val titleYearData = titleYearStriped.split(" ")

Movie(columns(0).toInt,
      titleYearData.take(titleYearData.size - 1).mkString(" "),
      titleYearData.last.toInt,
      columns(2).split("|"))
```

```
  }

  def parseFullRating(str: String): FullRating = {
  val columns = str.split("::")
  assert(columns.size == 4)
  FullRating(columns(0).toInt, columns(1).toInt, columns(2).toFloat,
  columns(3).toLong)
  }
```

6. We are ready to begin building our `main` function, so let's start with the locations of the `movie.dat` and `ratings.dat` file:

```
val movieFile = "../data/sparkml2/chapter7/movies.dat"
val ratingsFile = "../data/sparkml2/chapter7/ratings.dat"
```

7. Create a SparkSession object and its related configuration:

```
val spark = SparkSession
 .builder
.master("local[*]")
 .appName("MovieLens App")
 .config("spark.sql.warehouse.dir", ".")
 .config("spark.executor.memory", "2g")
 .getOrCreate()
```

8. The interleaving of log messages leads to hard-to-read output; therefore, set the logging level to ERROR:

```
Logger.getLogger("org").setLevel(Level.ERROR)
```

9. Create a dataset of all the ratings and register it as a temporary view in memory so it can be queried with SQL:

```
val ratings = spark.read.textFile(ratingsFile).map(parseFullRating)

val movies =
spark.read.textFile(movieFile).map(parseMovie).cache()
movies.createOrReplaceTempView("movies")
```

10. Execute the SQL query against the view:

```
val rs = spark.sql("select movies.title from movies")
rs.show(25)
```

From the console output:

```
From the Console output:
+--------------------+
|               title|
+--------------------+
|          Toy Story |
|            Jumanji |
|   Grumpier Old Men |
|  Waiting to Exhale |
|Father of the Bri...|
|               Heat |
|            Sabrina |
|       Tom and Huck |
|       Sudden Death |
|          GoldenEye |
|American Presiden...|
|Dracula: Dead and...|
|              Balto |
|              Nixon |
|   Cutthroat Island |
|             Casino |
|Sense and Sensibi...|
|         Four Rooms |
|Ace Ventura: When...|
|        Money Train |
|        Get Shorty  |
|            Copycat |
|           Assassins |
|             Powder |
|   Leaving Las Vegas |
+--------------------+
only showing top 25 rows
```

11. We categorize the ratings data into training and test datasets. The training data will be used to train the alternate least squares recommendation machine learning algorithm, and the test data will be used later to evaluate the accuracy between the predictions and the test data:

```scala
val splits = ratings.randomSplit(Array(0.8, 0.2), 0L)
val training = splits(0).cache()
val test = splits(1).cache()

val numTraining = training.count()
val numTest = test.count()
println(s"Training: $numTraining, test: $numTest.")
```

12. Now create a fictitious user with a user ID of zero, generating a dataset of several ratings. This user will allow us later to better understand the predictions computed by the ALS algorithm:

```
val testWithOurUser = spark.createDataset(Seq(
  FullRating(0, 260, 0f, 0), // Star Wars: Episode IV - A New Hope
  FullRating(0, 261, 0f, 0), // Little Women
  FullRating(0, 924, 0f, 0), // 2001: A Space Odyssey
  FullRating(0, 1200, 0f, 0), // Aliens
  FullRating(0, 1307, 0f, 0) // When Harry Met Sally...
)).as[FullRating]

val trainWithOurUser = spark.createDataset(Seq(
  FullRating(0, 76, 3f, 0), // Screamers
  FullRating(0, 165, 4f, 0), // Die Hard: With a Vengeance
  FullRating(0, 145, 2f, 0), // Bad Boys
  FullRating(0, 316, 5f, 0), // Stargate
  FullRating(0, 1371, 5f, 0), // Star Trek: The Motion Picture
  FullRating(0, 3578, 4f, 0), // Gladiator
  FullRating(0, 3528, 1f, 0) // Prince of Tides
)).as[FullRating]
```

13. Append `testWithOurUser` to the original training set utilizing the dataset union method. Also, use the `unpersist` method on the original training set and the test set of free resources:

```
val testSet = test.union(testWithOurUser)
test.unpersist()
val trainSet = training.union(trainWithOurUser)
training.unpersist()
```

14. Create the ALS object and set up the parameters.

Use the train dataset to get the model.

```
val als = new ALS()
 .setUserCol("userId")
 .setItemCol("movieId")
 .setRank(10)
 .setMaxIter(10)
 .setRegParam(0.1)
 .setNumBlocks(10)
val model = als.fit(trainSet.toDF)
```

15. We let the model work on the test dataset:

```
val predictions = model.transform(testSet.toDF())
predictions.cache()
predictions.show(10, false)
```

From the console output:

```
From the console output:

+------+-------+------+---------+----------+
|userId|movieId|rating|timestamp|prediction|
+------+-------+------+---------+----------+
|53    |148    |5.0   |977987826|3.360202  |
|3184  |148    |4.0   |968708953|3.1396782 |
|1242  |148    |3.0   |974909976|2.4897025 |

|3829  |148    |2.0   |965940170|2.3191774 |
|2456  |148    |2.0   |974178993|2.7297301 |
|4858  |463    |3.0   |963746396|2.4874766 |
|3032  |463    |4.0   |970356224|4.275539  |
|2210  |463    |3.0   |974601869|2.8614724 |
|4510  |463    |2.0   |966800044|2.205242  |
|3562  |463    |2.0   |966790403|2.9360452 |
+------+-------+------+---------+----------+
only showing top 10 rows
```

16. Build an in-memory table which has all the predictions for the Spark SQL query:

```
val allPredictions = predictions.join(movies, movies("movieId") ===
predictions("movieId"), "left")
```

17. Retrieve the ratings and predictions from the table and display the first 20 rows in the console:

```
allPredictions.select("userId", "rating", "prediction",
"title") show(false)
```

From the console output:

```
From the Console output:

+------+------+----------+------------------------+
|userId|rating|prediction|title                   |
+------+------+----------+------------------------+
|53    |5.0   |3.360202  |Awfully Big Adventure, An |
|3184  |4.0   |3.1396782 |Awfully Big Adventure, An |
|1242  |3.0   |2.4897025 |Awfully Big Adventure, An |
|3829  |2.0   |2.3191774 |Awfully Big Adventure, An |
|2456  |2.0   |2.7297301 |Awfully Big Adventure, An |
|4858  |3.0   |2.4874766 |Guilty as Sin           |
|3032  |4.0   |4.275539  |Guilty as Sin           |
|2210  |3.0   |2.8614724 |Guilty as Sin           |
|4510  |2.0   |2.205242  |Guilty as Sin           |
|3562  |2.0   |2.9360452 |Guilty as Sin           |
|746   |1.0   |2.1229248 |Guilty as Sin           |
|5511  |2.0   |3.4050038 |Guilty as Sin           |
|331   |4.0   |2.572236  |Guilty as Sin           |
|3829  |2.0   |2.0906088 |Guilty as Sin           |
|5831  |4.0   |2.9544487 |Guilty as Sin           |
|392   |4.0   |3.579655  |Hudsucker Proxy, The    |
|1265  |4.0   |3.574471  |Hudsucker Proxy, The    |
|4957  |3.0   |3.473529  |Hudsucker Proxy, The    |
|78    |4.0   |3.5066679 |Hudsucker Proxy, The    |
|1199  |3.0   |2.7609487 |Hudsucker Proxy, The    |
+------+------+----------+------------------------+
only showing top 20 rows
```

18. Now get a specific user's movie prediction:

```
allPredictions.select("userId", "rating", "prediction",
"title").where("userId=0").show(false)
```

From the console output:

```
From the Console output:
+------+------+----------+--------------------------------+
|userId|rating|prediction|title                           |
+------+------+----------+--------------------------------+
|0     |0.0   |2.624456  |When Harry Met Sally...         |
|0     |0.0   |4.1649804 |2001: A Space Odyssey           |
|0     |0.0   |3.994494  |Aliens                          |
|0     |0.0   |2.2429814 |Little Women                    |
|0     |0.0   |4.5856667 |Star Wars: Episode IV - A New Hope |
+------+------+----------+--------------------------------+
```

19. We close the program by stopping the Spark session:

```
spark.stop()
```

How it works...

Due to the complex nature of the program, we provide a conceptual explanation and then proceed to explain the details of the program.

The following figure depicts a conceptual view of ALS and how it factorizes the user/movie/rating matrix, which is a high-ranking order matrix to a lower order tall and skinny matrix, and a vector of latent factors: f(users) and f(movies).

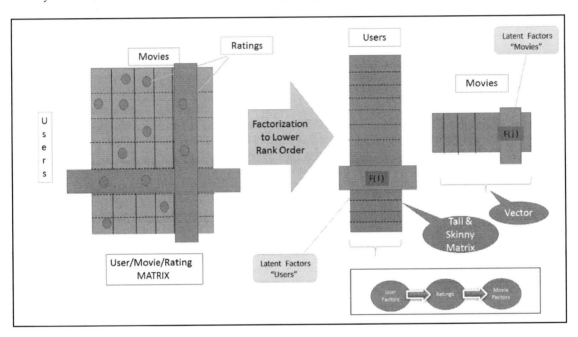

Another way to think about it is that these factors can be used to place the movie in an *n* dimensional space that will be matched to a given recommendation for a given user. It is always desirable to view machine learning as a search query in a dimensional variable space. The point to remember is that the latent factor (learned geometry space) is not pre-defined and can be as low as 10 to 100 or 1,000 depending on what is being searched or factorized. Our recommendation, then, can be viewed as placing a probability mass within the n-dimensional space. The following figure provides an extremely simplified view of a possible two-factor model (two-dimensional) to demonstrate the point:

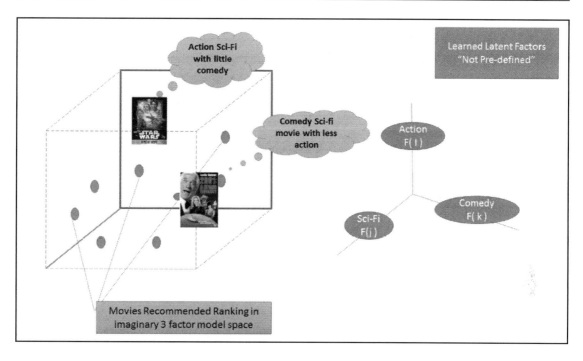

While the implementation of ALS can vary a bit from system to system, at its core it is an iterative full-factorization method (in Spark) with weighed regularization. Spark's documentation and tutorials provide an insight into the actual math and the nature of the algorithm. It depicts the algorithm as follows:

Iterate:

$$f[i] = \arg\min_{w \in \mathbb{R}^d} \sum_{j \in \text{Nbrs}(i)} \left(r_{ij} - w^T f[j] \right)^2 + \lambda \|w\|_2^2$$

Source: Apache Spark Documentation 1.6.1

The best way to understand this formula/algorithm is to think of it as an iterating apparatus which is trying to discover the latent factors by alternating between inputs (that is, fix one of the inputs and then approximate/optimize the other--and then back and forth), while trying to minimize the least square error (MSE) with respect to a regularization penalty of weighted lambda. A more detailed explanation is provided in the next section.

The program flow is as follows:

- The example started by loading the ratings and movie data from the MovieLens dataset. The loaded data was then transformed into Scala case classes for further processing. The next step was to partition the ratings data into a training set and test set. The training set data was used to train the machine learning algorithm. Training is the process in machine learning used to build a model so it can provide the appropriate results needed. The test data will be used to validate the results in the final step.

- The fictitious users, or user ID zero, step configured a single user not included in the original dataset to help lend insight to the results by creating a dataset on the fly with random information, and finally appending it to the training set. The ALS algorithm was invoked by passing the training set data to it, comprised of the user ID, movie ID, and rating, subsequently yielding a matrix factorization model from Spark. The prediction generation was performed for the user ID zero and test dataset.

- The final results were displayed by combining rating information with the movie data so the results could be understood and displayed in the original rating next to the estimated rating. The final step was to compute the root mean squared error of the generated rating, with the existing rating contained within the test dataset. The RMSE will tell us how accurate the train model is.

There's more...

People often struggle with ALS even though at its core it is a simple linear algebra operation with an added regularization penalty. What makes ALS powerful is its ability to be parallelized and to deal with scale (for example, Spotify).

ALS in layman's language involves the following:

- With ALS, you basically want to factorize a large matrix of ratings X (100 million plus users is not a stretch at all) and user product ratings into two matrices of A and B, with lower ranks (see any introductory linear algebra book). The problem is that it often becomes a very hard non-linear optimization problem to solve. To remedy with ALS, you introduce a simple solution (**A** for **Alternating**) in which you fix one of the matrices and partially solve the other leg (the other matrix) using the least square methods for optimization (**LS** stands for **Least Square**). Once this step is complete, you then alternate, but this time you fix the second leg (matrix) and solve the first.

- To control overfitting, we introduce a regularization leg to the original equation. This step is usually a weighted regularization and is controlled by a parameter lambda that controls the amount of penalty or flattening.
- In short, what makes this interesting is the fact that this method matrix factorization lends itself very well to parallel operations, which is Spark's speciality at its core.

For a deep understanding of the ALS algorithm, we cite two original papers that are considered to be classics in this area:

From the ACM Digital Library using `http://dl.acm.org/citation.cfm?id=1608614` link.

From the IEEE Digital Library `http://ieeexplore.ieee.org/xpl/login.jsp?tp=&arnumber=5197422&url=http%3A%2F%2Fieeexplore.ieee.org%2Fxpls%2Fabs_all.jsp%3Farnumber%3D5197422`.

The following figure shows ALS from a more mathematical view, from the original paper cited previously:

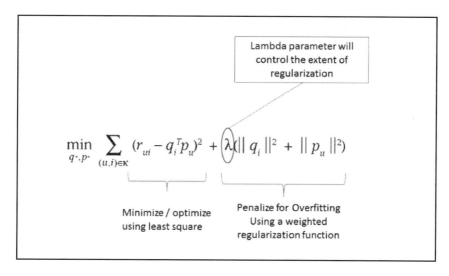

Use the RankingMetrics metrics class to evaluate the model performance. Parameters are similar to classes used for evaluation (binary and multinomial) of the regression models:

- Recall
- Precision
- fMeasure

The RankingMetrics class provided by MLlib can be used for evaluating models and quantifying model effectiveness.

The RankingMetrics API documentation can be found at `http://spark.apache.org/docs/latest/api/scala/index.html#org.apache.spark.mllib.evaluation.RankingMetrics`.

See also

Spark 2.0 ML documentation to explore the ALS API:

- `https://spark.apache.org/docs/latest/mllib-collaborative-filtering.html`
- `https://spark.apache.org/docs/latest/api/scala/index.html#org.apache.spark.ml.recommendation.ALS`
- `https://spark.apache.org/docs/latest/api/scala/index.html#org.apache.spark.ml.recommendation.ALSModel`

Spark 2.0 MLlib documentation is available
at `https://spark.apache.org/docs/latest/api/scala/index.html#org.apache.spark.mllib.recommendation.ALS`.

ALS parameters and their default constructs an ALS instance with default parameters as follows:

```
{numBlocks: -1, rank: 10, iterations: 10, lambda: 0.
numBlocks: -1,
rank: 10,
iterations: 10,
lambda: 0.01,
implicitPrefs: false,
alpha: 1.0
```

Dealing with implicit input for training

There are times when the actual observations (ratings) are not available and one must deal with implied feedback parameters. This can be as simple as which audio track was listened to during an engagement to how long a movie was watched, or the context (indexed in advance) or what caused a switch (a Netflix movie abandoned in the beginning, middle, or near a specific scene). The example provided in the third recipe deals with explicit feedback via the use of `ALS.train()`.

The Spark ML library provides an alternative method, `ALS.trainImplicit()`, with four hyper parameters to control the algorithm and address the implicit data. If you are interested in testing this (it is very similar to the explicit method), you can use the 1,000,000 song dataset for easy training and prediction purposes. You can download the dataset for experimentation from the `http://labrosa.ee.columbia.edu/millionsong/` URL.

The collaborative filtering pros and cons are as follows:

Pros	Cons
Scalable	Cold start problem • New items added to the inventory • New users added to the ecosystem
Discovers hard to find and often illusive data properties without profiles	Requires a decent amount of data
More accurate	
Portable	

8

Unsupervised Clustering with Apache Spark 2.0

In this chapter, we will cover:

- Building a KMeans classification system in Spark 2.0
- Bisecting KMeans, the new kid on the block in Spark 2.0
- Using Gaussian Mixture and Expectation Maximization (EM) in Spark 2.0 to classify data
- Classifying the vertices of a graph using Power Iteration Clustering (PIC) in Spark 2.0
- Using Latent Dirichlet Allocation (LDA) to classify documents and text into topics
- Streaming KMeans to classify data in near real time

Introduction

Unsupervised machine learning is a type of learning technique in which we try to draw inferences either directly or indirectly (through latent factors) from a set of unlabeled observations. In simple terms, we are trying to find the hidden knowledge or structures in a set of data without initially labeling the training data.

While most machine learning library implementation break down when applied to large datasets (iterative, multi-pass, a lot of intermediate writes), the Apache Spark Machine Library succeeds by providing machine library algorithms designed for parallelism and extremely large datasets using memory for intermediate writes out of the box.

At the most abstract level, we can think of unsupervised learning as:

- **Clustering systems**: Classify the inputs into categories either using hard (only belonging to a single cluster) or soft (probabilistic membership and overlaps) categorization.
- **Dimensionality reduction systems**: Find hidden factors using a condensed representation of the original data.

The following figure shows the landscape of machine learning techniques. In the previous chapters, we focused on supervised machine learning techniques. In this chapter, we concentrate on unsupervised machine learning techniques ranging from clustering to latent factor models using Spark's ML/MLIB library API:

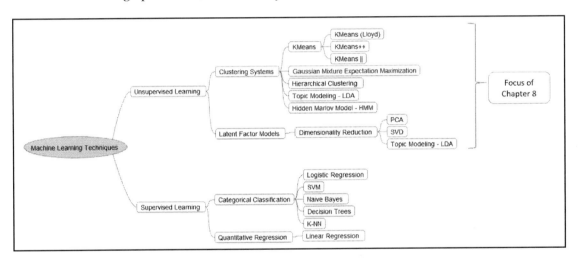

The clusters are often modeled using intra-cluster similarity measurement, such as Euclidian or probabilistic techniques. Spark provides a complete and high-performing set of algorithms which lend themselves to parallel implementation at scale. They not only provide APIs, but also provide full source code which is very helpful for understanding bottlenecks and resolving them (forking to GPU) to fit your needs.

The applications of machine learning are vast and as limitless as you can imagine. Some of the most widely known examples and use cases are:

- Fraud detection (finance, law enforcement)
- Network security (intrusion detection, traffic analysis)
- Pattern recognition (marketing, intelligence community, banking)
- Recommendation systems (retail, entertainment)
- Affinity marketing (e-commerce, recommenders, deep personalization)
- Medical informatics (disease detection, patient care, asset management)
- Image processing (object/sub-object detection, radiology)

A word of caution on ML versus MLIB usage and future direction in Spark:

While the MLIB is and will remain viable for the time being, there is a gradual movement towards Spark's ML library for future development rather than MLIB in Spark. The `org.apache.spark.ml.clustering` is a high-level machine learning package and the API is more focused on the DataFrame. The `org.apache.spark.mllib.clustering` is a lower-level machine learning package and the API is directly on RDD. While both packages will get the benefit of Spark's high performance and scalability, the main difference is the DataFrame. The `org.apache.spark.ml` will be the preferred method going forward.

For example, we encourage the developer to look at why the introduction of KMeans classifying system exists in both ML and MLLIB: `org.apache.spark.ml.clustering` and `org.apache.spark.mllib.clustering`

Building a KMeans classifying system in Spark 2.0

In this recipe, we will load a set of features (for example, x, y, z coordinates) using a LIBSVM file and then proceed to use `KMeans()` to instantiate an object. We will then set the number of desired clusters to three and then use `kmeans.fit()` to action the algorithm. Finally, we will print the centers for the three clusters that we found.

It is really important to note that Spark *does not* implement KMeans++, contrary to popular literature, instead it implements KMeans ‖ (pronounced as KMeans Parallel). See the following recipe and the sections following the code for a complete explanation of the algorithm as it is implemented in Spark.

How to do it...

1. Start a new project in IntelliJ or in an IDE of your choice. Make sure the necessary JAR files are included.

2. Set up the package location where the program will reside:

    ```
    package spark.ml.cookbook.chapter8
    ```

3. Import the necessary packages for Spark context to get access to the cluster and `Log4j.Logger` to reduce the amount of output produced by Spark:

    ```
    import org.apache.log4j.{Level, Logger}
    import org.apache.spark.ml.clustering.KMeans
    import org.apache.spark.sql.SparkSession
    ```

4. Set the output level to ERROR to reduce Spark's logging output:

    ```
    Logger.getLogger("org").setLevel(Level.ERROR)
    ```

5. Create Spark's Session object:

    ```
    val spark = SparkSession
     .builder
    .master("local[*]")
     .appName("myKMeansCluster")
     .config("spark.sql.warehouse.dir", ".")
     .getOrCreate()
    ```

6. We create a training dataset from a file in the `libsvm` format and display the file on the console:

```
val trainingData =
spark.read.format("libsvm").load("../data/sparkml2/chapter8/my_kmea
ns_data.txt")

trainingData.show()
```

From the console, you will see:

```
+-----+--------------------+
|label|            features|
+-----+--------------------+
|  1.0|(3,[0,1,2],[1.0,1...|
|  2.0|(3,[0,1,2],[1.1,1...|
|  3.0|(3,[0,1,2],[1.0,1...|
|  4.0|(3,[0,1,2],[1.0,1...|
|  5.0|(3,[0,1,2],[3.1,3...|
|  6.0|(3,[0,1,2],[3.3,3...|
|  7.0|(3,[0,1,2],[4.0,4...|
|  8.0|(3,[0,1,2],[3.4,3...|
|  9.0|(3,[0,1,2],[8.3,8...|
| 10.0|(3,[0,1,2],[9.3,9...|
| 11.0|(3,[0,1,2],[9.2,9...|
| 12.0|(3,[0,1,2],[9.5,9...|
+-----+--------------------+
```

The following formula visualizes the data via contour maps that depict each feature vector (each row) versus the three unique features in both a 3D and flat contour map:

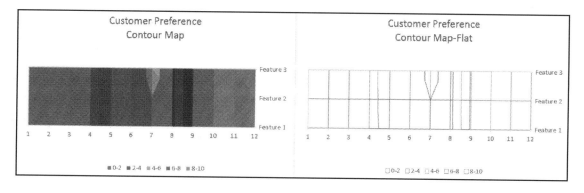

7. We then create a KMeans object and set some key parameters to the KMeans model and set parameters.

   In this case, we set the K value to 3 and set the *feature* column as column "features", which was defined in the previous step. This step is subjective and the optimal value would vary based on specific datasets. We recommend that you experiment with values from 2 to 50 and examine the cluster centers for a final value.

   We also set the maximum iteration count to 10. Most of the values have a default setting as the comments as shown in the following code:

```
// Trains a k-means model
val kmeans = new KMeans()
.setK(3) // default value is 2
.setFeaturesCol("features")
.setMaxIter(10) // default Max Iteration is 20
.setPredictionCol("prediction")
.setSeed(1L)
```

8. We then train the dataset. The `fit()` function will then run the algorithm and perform the calculations. It is based on the dataset created in the previous steps. These steps are common among Spark's ML and do not usually vary from algorithm to algorithm:

```
val model = kmeans.fit(trainingData)
```

   We also display the model's prediction on the console:

```
model.summary.predictions.show()
```

   From the console:

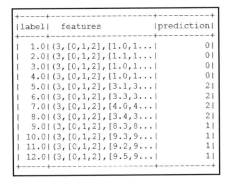

9. We then calculate the cost, using the included `computeCost(x)` function.

10. The KMeans Cost is calculated **Within Set Sum of Squared Errors** (**WSSSE**). The value will be printed out in the program's console:

```
println("KMeans Cost:" +model.computeCost(trainingData))
```

The console output will show the following information:

```
KMeans Cost:4.137499999999979
```

11. We then print out the cluster's center based on the calculation of the model:

```
println("KMeans Cluster Centers: ")
 model.clusterCenters.foreach(println)
```

12. The console output will show the following information:

```
The centers for the 3 cluster (i.e. K= 3)
KMeans Cluster Centers:
[1.025,1.075,1.15]
[9.075,9.05,9.025]
[3.45,3.475,3.55]
```

Based on the setting of the KMeans clustering, we set the K value to 3; the model will calculate three centers based on the training dataset that we fit in.

13. We then close the program by stopping the Spark context:

```
spark.stop()
```

How it works...

We read a LIBSVM file with a set of coordinates (can be interpreted as a tuple of three numbers) and then created a `KMean()` object, but changed the default number of clusters from 2 (out of the box) to 3 for demonstration purposes. We used the `.fit()` to create the model and then used `model.summary.predictions.show()` to display which tuple belongs to which cluster. In the last step, we printed the cost and the center of the three clusters. Conceptually, it can be thought of as having a set of 3D coordinates as data and then assigning each individual coordinate to one of the three clusters using KMeans algorithms.

KMeans is a form of unsupervised machine learning algorithm, with its root in signal processing (vector quantization) and compression (grouping similar vectors of items together to achieve a higher compression rate). Generally speaking, the KMeans algorithm attempts to group a series of observations $\{X_1, X_2, \ldots, X_n\}$ into a series of clusters $\{C_1, C_2 \ldots C_n\}$ using a form of distance measure (local optimization) that is optimized in an iterative manner.

There are three main types of KMeans algorithm that are in use. In a simple survey, we found 12 specialized variations of the KMeans algorithm. It is important to note that Spark implements a version called KMeans || (KMeans Parallel) and *not* KMeans++ or standard KMeans as referenced in some literature or videos.

The following figure depicts KMeans in a nutshell:

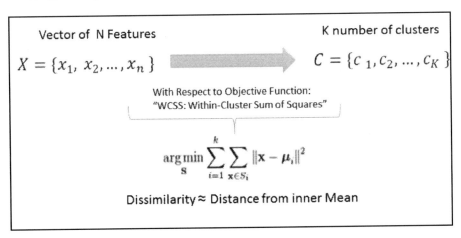

Source: Spark documentation

KMeans (Lloyd Algorithm)

The steps for basic KMeans implementation (Lloyd algorithm) are:

1. Randomly select K datacenters from observations as the initial centroids.
2. Keep iterating till the convergence criteria is met:
   - Measure the distance from a point to each centroid
   - Include each data point in a cluster which is the closest centroid
   - Calculate new cluster centroids based on a distance formula (proxy for dissimilarity)
   - Update the algorithm with new center points

The three generations are depicted in the following figure:

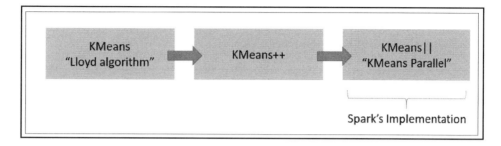

KMeans++ (Arthur's algorithm)

The next improvement over standard KMeans is the KMeans++ proposed by David Arthur and Sergei Vassilvitskii in 2007. Arthur's algorithm improves the initial Lloyd's KMeans by being more selective during the seeding process (the initial step).

KMeans++, rather than picking random centres (random centroids) as starting points, picks the first centroid randomly and then picks the data points one by one and calculates $D(x)$. Then it chooses one more data point at random and, using proportional probability distribution $D(x)2$, it then keeps repeating the last two steps until all K numbers are picked. After the initial seeding, we finally run the KMeans or a variation with the newly seeded centroid. The KMeans++ algorithm is guaranteed to find a solution in an *Omega= O(log k)* complexity. Even though the initial seeding takes extra steps, the accuracy improvements are substantial.

KMeans|| (pronounced as KMeans Parallel)

KMeans || is optimized to run in parallel and can result in one-two orders of magnitude improvement over Lloyd's original algorithm. The limitation of KMeans++ is that it requires K-passes over the dataset, which can severely limit the performance and practicality of running KMeans with large or extreme datasets. Spark's KMeans|| parallel implementation runs faster because it takes fewer passes (a lot less) over the data by sampling m points and oversampling in the process.

The core of the algorithm and the math is depicted in the following figure:

Algorithm 2 k-means$\|$ (k, ℓ) initialization.

1: $C \leftarrow$ sample a point uniformly at random from X
2: $\psi \leftarrow \phi_X(C)$
3: **for** $O(\log \psi)$ times **do**
4:      $C' \leftarrow$ sample each point $x \in X$ independently with probability $p_x = \frac{\ell \cdot d^2(x, C)}{\phi_X(C)}$
5:      $C \leftarrow C \cup C'$
6: **end for**
7: For $x \in C$, set w_x to be the number of points in X closer to x than any other point in C
8: Recluster the weighted points in C into k clusters

Source: http://theory.stanford.edu/~sergei/papers/vldb12-kmpar.pdf
Stanford University : Bahman Bahmani plus others

In a nutshell, the highlight of the KMeans || (Parallel KMeans) is the course-grain sampling which repeats in *log(n)* rounds and at the end we are left with *k * log(n)* remaining points that are a C (constant) distance away from the optimal solution! This implementation is also less sensitive to outlier data points that can skew the clustering results in KMeans and KMeans++.

For a deeper understanding of the algorithm, the reader can access the paper by Bahman Bahmani at `http://theory.stanford.edu/~sergei/papers/vldb12-kmpar.pdf`.

There's more...

There is also a streaming version of KMeans implementation in Spark that allows you to classify the features on the fly. The streaming version of KMeans is covered in more detail in `Chapter 13`, *Spark Streaming and Machine Learning Library*.

There is also a class that helps you to generate RDD data for KMeans. We found this to be very useful during our application development process:

```
def generateKMeansRDD(sc: SparkContext, numPoints: Int, k: Int, d: Int, r:
Double, numPartitions: Int = 2): RDD[Array[Double]]
```

This call uses Spark context to create RDDs while allowing you to specify the number of points, clusters, dimensions, and partitions.

A useful related API is: `generateKMeansRDD()`. Documentation for `generateKMeansRDD` can be found at
`http://spark.apache.org/docs/latest/api/scala/index.html#org.apache.spark.mllib.util.KMeansDataGenerator$` for generate an RDD containing test data for KMeans.

See also

We need two pieces of objects to be able to write, measure, and manipulate the parameters of the KMeans || algorithm in Spark. The details of these two pieces of objects can be found at the following websites:

- `KMeans()`:
  `http://spark.apache.org/docs/latest/api/scala/index.html#org.apache.spark.ml.clustering.KMeans`
- `KMeansModel()`: `http://spark.apache.org/docs/latest/api/scala/index.html#org.apache.spark.ml.clustering.KMeansModel`

Bisecting KMeans, the new kid on the block in Spark 2.0

In this recipe, we will download the glass dataset and try to identify and label each glass using a bisecting KMeans algorithm. The Bisecting KMeans is a hierarchical version of the K-Mean algorithm implemented in Spark using the `BisectingKMeans()` API. While this algorithm is conceptually like KMeans, it can offer considerable speed for some use cases where the hierarchical path is present.

The dataset we used for this recipe is the Glass Identification Database. The study of the classification of types of glass was motivated by criminological research. Glass could be considered as evidence if it is correctly identified. The data can be found at NTU (Taiwan), already in LIBSVM format.

How to do it...

1. We downloaded the prepared data file in LIBSVM
   from: `https://www.csie.ntu.edu.tw/~cjlin/libsvmtools/datasets/multiclass/glass.scale`

   The dataset contains 11 features and 214 rows.

2. The original dataset and data dictionary is also available at the UCI
   website: `http://archive.ics.uci.edu/ml/datasets/Glass+Identification`
   - ID number: 1 to 214
   - RI: Refractive index
   - Na: Sodium (unit measurement: weight percent in corresponding oxide, as are attributes 4-10)
   - Mg: Magnesium
   - Al: Aluminum
   - Si: Silicon
   - K: Potassium
   - Ca: Calcium
   - Ba: Barium
   - Fe: Iron

   Type of glass: Will find our class attributes or clusters using
   `BisectingKMeans()`:

   - `building_windows_float_processed`
   - `building_windows_non-_float_processed`
   - `vehicle_windows_float_processed`
   - `vehicle_windows_non-_float_processed` (none in this database)
   - `Containers`
   - `Tableware`
   - `Headlamps`

3. Start a new project in IntelliJ or in an IDE of your choice. Make sure the necessary JAR files are included.

4. Set up the package location where the program will reside:

   ```
   package spark.ml.cookbook.chapter8
   ```

5. Import the necessary packages:

```
import org.apache.spark.ml.clustering.BisectingKMeans
import org.apache.spark.sql.SparkSession
import org.apache.log4j.{Level, Logger}
```

6. Set the output level to ERROR to reduce Spark's logging output:

```
Logger.getLogger("org").setLevel(Level.ERROR)
```

7. Create Spark's Session object:

```
val spark = SparkSession
 .builder
.master("local[*]")
 .appName("MyBisectingKMeans")
 .config("spark.sql.warehouse.dir", ".")
 .getOrCreate()
```

8. We create a dataset from a file in the libsvm format and display the dataset on the console:

```
val dataset =
spark.read.format("libsvm").load("../data/sparkml2/chapter8/glass.s
cale")
 dataset.show(false)
```

From the console, you will see:

```
+-----+------------------------------------------------------------------------------------------------------+
|label|features                                                                                              |
+-----+------------------------------------------------------------------------------------------------------+
|1.0  |(9,[0,1,2,3,4,5,6,7,8],[-0.134323,-0.124812,1.0,-0.495327,-0.296429,-0.980676,-0.3829,-1.0,-1.0])     |
|1.0  |(9,[0,1,2,3,4,5,6,7,8],[-0.432839,-0.0496238,0.603564,-0.333333,0.0428581,-0.845411,-0.553903,-1.0,-1.0]) |
|1.0  |(9,[0,1,2,3,4,5,6,7,8],[-0.55838,-0.157895,0.581292,-0.221184,0.135713,-0.874396,-0.563197,-1.0,-1.0]) |
|1.0  |(9,[0,1,2,3,5,6,7,8],[-0.428443,-0.254135,0.643653,-0.376947,-0.816425,-0.481413,-1.0,-1.0])           |
|1.0  |(9,[0,1,2,3,4,5,6,7,8],[-0.449511,-0.23609,0.612472,-0.4081,0.167857,-0.822866,-0.509294,-1.0,-1.0])   |
|1.0  |(9,[0,1,2,3,4,5,6,7,8],[-0.577701,-0.380451,0.608018,-0.17134,0.128572,-0.793881,-0.509294,-1.0,0.0196078]) |
|1.0  |(9,[0,1,2,3,4,5,6,7,8],[-0.448643,-0.227067,0.603564,-0.470405,0.171427,-0.813205,-0.490706,-1.0,-1.0]) |
|1.0  |(9,[0,1,2,3,4,5,6,7,8],[-0.437224,-0.27218,0.608018,-0.52648,0.224999,-0.816425,-0.477695,-1.0,-1.0])  |
|1.0  |(9,[0,1,2,3,4,5,6,7,8],[-0.294989,-0.00451109,0.594655,-0.327103,-0.189285,-0.819646,-0.466543,-1.0,-1.0]) |
|1.0  |(9,[0,1,2,3,4,5,6,7,8],[-0.438103,-0.317293,0.603564,-0.333333,0.135713,-0.816425,-0.447955,-1.0,-0.568627]) |
|1.0  |(9,[0,1,2,3,4,5,6,7,8],[-0.599648,-0.401504,0.541203,-0.209723,0.210713,-0.784219,-0.505576,-1.0,-0.0588235]) |
|1.0  |(9,[0,1,2,3,4,5,6,7,8],[-0.43108,-0.377443,0.63029,-0.389408,0.142858,-0.806763,-0.418216,-1.0,-1.0]) |
|1.0  |(9,[0,1,2,3,4,5,6,7,8],[-0.583844,-0.353383,0.52784,-0.308411,0.239285,-0.777778,-0.513011,-1.0,-0.0588235]) |
|1.0  |(9,[0,1,2,3,4,5,6,7,8],[-0.444247,-0.359398,0.585746,-0.389408,0.214285,-0.826087,-0.451673,-1.0,-0.333333]) |
|1.0  |(9,[0,1,2,3,4,5,6,7,8],[-0.43108,-0.434586,0.599109,-0.364486,0.242857,-0.813205,-0.429368,-1.0,-1.0]) |
|1.0  |(9,[0,1,2,3,4,5,6,7,8],[-0.432839,-0.374436,0.576837,-0.41433,0.224999,-0.813205,-0.449814,-1.0,-1.0]) |
|1.0  |(9,[0,1,2,3,4,5,6,7,8],[-0.412639,-0.413534,0.634744,-0.457944,0.178571,-0.803543,-0.392193,-1.0,-1.0]) |
|1.0  |(9,[0,1,2,3,4,5,6,7,8],[-0.0509179,0.0917294,0.714922,-0.626168,-0.446428,-0.951691,-0.30855,-1.0,-1.0]) |
|1.0  |(9,[0,1,2,3,4,5,6,7,8],[-0.301143,-0.0466165,0.66147,-0.445483,-0.174999,-0.980676,-0.356877,-1.0,-1.0]) |
|1.0  |(9,[0,1,2,3,4,5,6,7,8],[-0.455665,-0.311278,0.576837,-0.127726,0.0428581,-0.826087,-0.440521,-1.0,-0.72549]) |
+-----+------------------------------------------------------------------------------------------------------+
only showing top 20 rows
```

9. We then split the dataset randomly into two parts in the ratio of 80% and 20%:

```
val splitData = dataset.randomSplit(Array(80.0, 20.0))
 val training = splitData(0)
 val testing = splitData(1)

println(training.count())
println(testing.count())
```

From the console output (total count is 214):

```
180
34
```

10. We then create a `BisectingKMeans` object and set some key parameters to the model.

   In this case, we set the K value to 6 and set the `Feature` column as column "features", which was defined in the previous step. This step is subjective and the optimal value will vary based on specific datasets. We recommend you experiment with values from 2 to 50 and examine the cluster centers for a final value.

11. We also set the maximum iteration count to 65. Most of the values have a default setting, as shown in the following code:

```
// Trains a k-means model
val bkmeans = new BisectingKMeans()
    .setK(6)
    .setMaxIter(65)
    .setSeed(1)
```

12. We then train the dataset. The `fit()` function will then run the algorithm and do the calculations. It is based on the dataset created in the previous steps. We also print out the model parameters:

```
val bisectingModel = bkmeans.fit(training)
 println("Parameters:")
 println(bisectingModel.explainParams())
```

From the console output:

```
Parameters:
featuresCol: features column name (default: features)
k: The desired number of leaf clusters. Must be > 1. (default:
4, current: 6)
```

```
maxIter: maximum number of iterations (>= 0) (default: 20,
current: 65)
minDivisibleClusterSize: The minimum number of points (if >=
1.0) or the minimum proportion of points (if < 1.0) of a
divisible cluster. (default: 1.0)
predictionCol: prediction column name (default: prediction)
seed: random seed (default: 566573821, current: 1)
```

13. We then calculate the cost, using the included computeCost(x) function:

```
val cost = bisectingModel.computeCost(training)
  println("Sum of Squared Errors = " + cost)
```

The console output will show the following information:

```
Sum of Squared Errors = 70.38842983516193
```

14. Then, we print out the cluster's center based on the calculation of the model:

```
println("Cluster Centers:")
val centers = bisectingModel.clusterCenters
centers.foreach(println)
```

The console output will show the following information:

```
The centers for the 6 cluster (i.e. K= 6)
KMeans Cluster Centers:
```

```
Cluster Centers:
[-0.46260928765432086,-0.26111557395061724,0.5348786182716052,-
0.30964194814814805,0.05978796913580248,-0.817260111111111,-
0.4476571234567898,-0.9895747530864197,-0.9544904320987653]
[-0.04337657000000001,-0.041694967272727264,0.6138895227272727,-
0.6060604999999999,-0.3409090454545454,-0.9455423181818183,-
0.23056775045454544,-0.976912,-0.9447415000000001]
[-0.5077198235294117,-0.3592215294117648,0.5011136470588234,-
0.3384643647058823,0.15168052352941175,-0.8168040588235292,-
0.42444800000000005,-0.9902894705882354,-0.028835047058823532]
[-0.2522087266666667,-0.21162887333333336,0.5634743933333334,-
0.4600208666666667,-0.11619064000000001,-0.8570048666666668,-
0.3346964,-0.9784126666666667,-0.2575163]
[-0.5328278250000001,0.1389904357142857,-
0.8722557857142856,0.14753011428571428,0.16109662499999997,-
0.8543823571428572,-0.43892724642857156,-0.3585034142857142,-
0.964986]
[0.07246095882352938,-0.38911972941176465,-0.8026987647058825,-
0.33076779941176465,-0.07563012941176467,-
0.8959931764705884,0.2749834882352941,-0.8733893529411765,-
0.6009227823529412]
```

15. We then use the trained model to make a prediction on the testing dataset:

```
val predictions = bisectingModel.transform(testing)
predictions.show(false)
```

From the console output:

```
+-----+--------------------------------------------------------------------------------------------------------------------+----------+
|label|features                                                                                                            |prediction|
+-----+--------------------------------------------------------------------------------------------------------------------+----------+
|1.0  |(9,[0,1,2,3,4,5,6,7,8],[-0.599648,-0.401504,0.541203,-0.208723,0.210713,-0.784219,-0.505576,-1.0,-0.0588235])      |2         |
|1.0  |(9,[0,1,2,3,4,5,6,7,8],[-0.468832,-0.203007,0.55902,-0.464174,0.0857134,-0.838969,-0.442379,-1.0,-1.0])            |0         |
|1.0  |(9,[0,1,2,3,4,5,6,7,8],[-0.445126,-0.365413,0.55902,-0.470405,0.235713,-0.819646,-0.420074,-1.0,-1.0])             |0         |
|1.0  |(9,[0,1,2,3,4,5,6,7,8],[-0.444247,-0.359398,0.585746,-0.389408,0.214285,-0.826087,-0.451673,-1.0,-0.333333])       |2         |
|1.0  |(9,[0,1,2,3,4,5,6,7,8],[-0.442488,-0.371428,0.581292,-0.252336,0.0499997,-0.826087,-0.42565,-1.0,-0.254902])       |2         |
|1.0  |(9,[0,1,2,3,4,5,6,7,8],[-0.438103,-0.317293,0.603564,-0.333333,0.135713,-0.816425,-0.447955,-1.0,-0.568627])       |0         |
|1.0  |(9,[0,1,2,3,4,5,6,7,8],[-0.426685,-0.422556,0.585746,-0.370717,0.167857,-0.803543,-0.394052,-1.0,-0.45098])        |2         |
|1.0  |(9,[0,1,2,3,4,5,6,7,8],[-0.417035,-0.254135,0.510022,-0.352025,0.0535719,-0.809984,-0.412639,-1.0,-1.0])           |0         |
|1.0  |(9,[0,1,2,3,4,5,6,7,8],[-0.404737,-0.254135,0.550111,-0.302181,0.0107138,-0.809984,-0.442379,-1.0,-1.0])           |0         |
|1.0  |(9,[0,1,2,3,4,5,6,7,8],[-0.391571,-0.18797,0.278396,-0.439252,0.0821412,-0.822866,-0.330855,-1.0,-1.0])            |0         |
|1.0  |(9,[0,1,2,3,4,5,6,7,8],[-0.338015,-0.26015,0.501114,-0.445483,0.0392859,-0.816425,-0.36803,-1.0,-0.372549])        |3         |
|1.0  |(9,[0,1,2,3,4,5,6,7,8],[-0.100752,0.657016,-0.862928,-0.307143,-0.971014,-0.139405,-1.0,-0.372549])                |3         |
|2.0  |(9,[0,1,2,3,4,5,6,7,8],[-0.582965,-0.371428,0.567929,0.00311525,0.0892856,-0.777778,-0.527881,-1.0,-1.0])          |0         |
|2.0  |(9,[0,1,2,3,4,5,6,7,8],[-0.562776,-0.0406013,0.567929,-0.401869,0.0964273,-0.880837,-0.533457,-1.0,-0.45098])      |3         |
|2.0  |(9,[0,1,2,3,4,5,6,7,8],[-0.546972,-0.215037,0.5902,-0.202492,0.0928578,-0.803543,-0.542751,-1.0,-1.0])             |0         |
|2.0  |(9,[0,1,2,3,4,5,6,7,8],[-0.53907,-0.452631,0.550111,-0.0155763,0.221429,-0.797101,-0.507435,-1.0,-0.647059])       |0         |
|2.0  |(9,[0,1,2,3,4,5,6,7,8],[-0.509221,-0.380451,0.567929,-0.221184,0.267857,-0.78744,-0.540892,-1.0,-1.0])             |0         |
|2.0  |(9,[0,1,2,3,4,5,6,7,8],[-0.495175,-0.218045,0.576837,-0.17757,-0.0249999,-0.780998,-0.501859,-1.0,-1.0])           |0         |
|2.0  |(9,[0,1,2,3,4,5,6,7,8],[-0.48024,-0.172932,0.550111,-0.115265,-0.0321442,-0.800322,-0.524164,-1.0,-1.0])           |0         |
|2.0  |(9,[0,1,2,3,4,5,6,7,8],[-0.476734,-0.350376,0.612472,-0.202492,0.124999,-0.803543,-0.501859,-1.0,-1.0])            |0         |
+-----+--------------------------------------------------------------------------------------------------------------------+----------+
only showing top 20 rows
```

16. We then close the program by stopping the Spark context:

```
spark.stop()
```

How it works...

In this session, we explored the Bisecting KMeans model, which is new in Spark 2.0. We utilized the glass dataset in this session and tried to assign a glass type using `BisectingKMeans()`, but changed k to 6 so we have sufficient clusters. As usual, we loaded the data into a dataset with Spark's libsvm loading mechanism. We split the dataset randomly into 80% and 20%, with 80% used to train the model and 20% used for testing the model.

We created the `BiSectingKmeans()` object and used the `fit(x)` function to create the model. We then used the `transform(x)` function for the testing dataset to explore the model prediction and printed out the result in the console output. We also output the cost of computing the clusters (sum of error squared) and then displayed the cluster centers. Finally, we printed the features with their assigned cluster number and stop operation.

Approaches to hierarchical clustering include:

- **Divisive**: Top down approach (Apache Spark implementation)
- **Agglomerative**: Bottom up approach

There's more...

More about the Bisecting KMeans can be found at:

- `http://spark.apache.org/docs/latest/api/scala/index.html#org.apache.spark.ml.clustering.BisectingKMeans`
- `http://spark.apache.org/docs/latest/api/scala/index.html#org.apache.spark.ml.clustering.BisectingKMeansModel`

We use clustering to explore the data and get a feel for what the outcome looks like as clusters. The bisecting KMeans is an interesting case of hierarchical analysis versus KMeans clustering.

The best way to conceptualize it is to think of bisecting KMeans as a recursive hierarchical KMeans. The bisecting KMeans algorithm divides the data using similarity measurement techniques like KMeans, but uses a hierarchical scheme to increase accuracy. It is particularly prevalent in text mining where a hierarchical approach will minimize the intra-cluster dependencies of the corpus body among documents.

The Bisecting KMeans algorithm starts by placing all observations in a single cluster first, but then breaks up the cluster into n partition (K=n) using the KMeans method. It then proceeds to select the most similar cluster (the highest inner cluster score) as the parent (the root cluster) while recursively splitting the other clusters untill the target number of clusters is derived in a hierarchical manner.

The Bisecting KMeans is a powerful tool used in text analytics to reduce the dimensionality of feature vectors for intelligent text/subject classification. By using this clustering technique, we end up grouping similar words/text/document/evidence into similar groups. Ultimately, if you start exploring text analytics, topic propagation, and scoring (for example, what article would go viral?), you are bound to encounter this technique in the early stages of your journey.

A white paper describing the use of Bisecting KMeans for text clustering is available at: `http://www.ijarcsse.com/docs/papers/Volume_5/2_February2015/V5I2-0229.pdf`

See also

There are two approaches to implementing hierarchical clustering--Spark uses a recursive top-down approach in which a cluster is chosen and then splits are performed in the algorithm as it moves down the hierarchy:

- Details about the hierarchical clustering approach can be found
  at `https://en.wikipedia.org/wiki/Hierarchical_clustering`
- Spark 2.0 documentation for Bisecting K-Mean can be found
  at `http://spark.apache.org/docs/latest/ml-clustering.html#bisecting-k-m eans`
- A paper describing how to use Bisecting KMeans to classify web logs can be found
  at `http://research.ijcaonline.org/volume116/number19/pxc3902799.pdf`

Using Gaussian Mixture and Expectation Maximization (EM) in Spark to classify data

In this recipe, we will explore Spark's implementation of **expectation maximization** (EM) `GaussianMixture()`, which calculates the maximum likelihood given a set of features as input. It assumes a Gaussian mixture in which each point can be sampled from K number of sub-distributions (cluster memberships).

How to do it...

1. Start a new project in IntelliJ or in an IDE of your choice. Make sure the necessary JAR files are included.

2. Set up the package location where the program will reside:

   ```
   package spark.ml.cookbook.chapter8.
   ```

3. Import the necessary packages for vector and matrix manipulation:

   ```
   import org.apache.log4j.{Level, Logger}
   import org.apache.spark.mllib.clustering.GaussianMixture
   import org.apache.spark.mllib.linalg.Vectors
   import org.apache.spark.sql.SparkSession
   ```

4. Create Spark's session object:

```
val spark = SparkSession
 .builder
.master("local[*]")
 .appName("myGaussianMixture")
 .config("spark.sql.warehouse.dir", ".")
 .getOrCreate()
```

5. Let us take a look at the dataset and examine the input file. The Simulated SOCR Knee Pain Centroid Location Data represents the centroid location for the hypothetical knee-pain locations for 1,000 subjects. The data includes the X and Y coordinates of the centroids.

This dataset can be used to illustrate the Gaussian Mixture and Expectation Maximization. The data is available
at: http://wiki.stat.ucla.edu/socr/index.php/SOCR_Data_KneePainData_041409

The sample data looks like the following:

- **X**: The *x* coordinate of the centroid location for one subject and one view.
- **Y**: The *y* coordinate of the centroid location for one subject and one view.

X, Y

11 73

20 88

19 73

15 65

21 57

26 101

24 117

35 106

37 96

35 147

41 151

42 137

43 127

41 206

47 213

49 238

40 229

The following figure depicts a knee-pain map based on the SOCR dataset from `wiki.stat.ucla`:

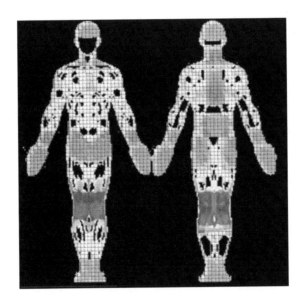

6. We place the data file in a data directory (you can copy the data file to any location you prefer).

The data file contains 8,666 entries:

```
val dataFile ="../data/sparkml2/chapter8/socr_data.txt"
```

7. We then load the data file into RDD:

```
val trainingData = spark.sparkContext.textFile(dataFile).map { line
=>
 Vectors.dense(line.trim.split(' ').map(_.toDouble))
 }.cache()
```

8. We now create a GaussianMixture model, and set the parameters for the model. We set the K value to 4, since the data was collected by four views: **Left Front (LF)**, **Left Back (LB)**, **Right Front (RF)**, and **Right Back (RB)**. We set the convergence to the default value of 0.01, and the maximum iteration count to 100:

```
val myGM = new GaussianMixture()
 .setK(4 ) // default value is 2, LF, LB, RF, RB
 .setConvergenceTol(0.01) // using the default value
 .setMaxIterations(100) // max 100 iteration
```

9. We run the model algorithm:

```
val model = myGM.run(trainingData)
```

10. We print out the key values for the GaussianMixture model after the training:

```
println("Model ConvergenceTol: "+ myGM.getConvergenceTol)
 println("Model k:"+myGM.getK)
 println("maxIteration:"+myGM.getMaxIterations)

 for (i <- 0 until model.k) {
 println("weight=%f\nmu=%s\nsigma=\n%s\n" format
 (model.weights(i), model.gaussians(i).mu,
model.gaussians(i).sigma))
 }
```

11. Since we set the K value to 4, we will have four sets of values printed out in the console logger:

```
Model ConvergenceTol: 0.01
Model k:4
maxIteration:100
weight=0.540515
mu=[147.30681254850833,208.6939884522598]
sigma=
4006.19815647266    -57.93614932156636
-57.93614932156636  662.9821920805127

weight=0.069784
mu=[351.3373566850737,231.83105600780897]
sigma=
33107.731896750345  57.84808144351749
57.84808144351749   4970.810900358368

weight=0.169685
mu=[507.34834190901864,194.47534268192427]
sigma=
4718.979203758771   13.290847642742316
13.290847642742316  178.16831733002988

weight=0.220017
mu=[155.24241473988965,218.9842905595943]
sigma=
3919.96712946773    37.75178487899691
37.75178487899691   149.10605322136172
```

12. We also print out the first 50 cluster-labels based on the GaussianMixture model predictions:

```
println("Cluster labels (first <= 50):")
 val clusterLabels = model.predict(trainingData)
 clusterLabels.take(50).foreach { x =>
 print(" " + x)
 }
```

13. The sample output in the console will show the following:

```
Cluster labels (first <= 50):
 1 1 1 1 1 1 1 1 0 0 0 0 0 0 0 0 0 0 0 0 0 0 0 0 0 0 0 0 0 0 0 0 0
 0 0 0 0 0 0 0 0 0 0 0 0 0 0 0 0 0
```

14. We then close the program by stopping the Spark context:

```
spark.stop()
```

How it works...

In the previous recipe, we observed that KMeans can discover and allocate membership to one and only one cluster based on an iterative method using similarity (Euclidian, and so on). One can think of KMeans as a specialized version of a Gaussian mixture model with EM models in which a discrete (hard) membership is enforced.

But there are cases that have overlap, which is often the case in medicine or signal processing, as depicted in the following figure:

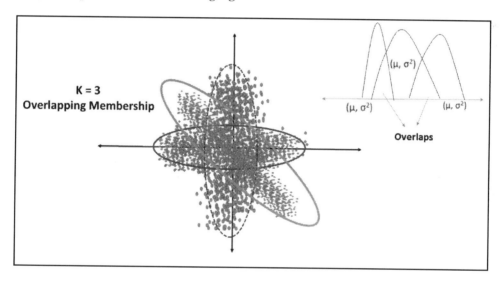

In such cases, we need a probability density function that can express the membership in each sub-distribution. The Gaussian Mixture models with **Expectation Maximization (EM)** is the algorithm `GaussianMixture()` available in Spark that can deal with this use case.

Here is Spark's API for implementing Gaussian Mixture with Expectation Maximization (the maximization of log likelihood).

New GaussianMixture()

This constructs a default instance. The default parameters that control the behavior of the model are:

> K: number of desired clusters, default value 2
>
> convergenceTol: Tolerance value for convergence, default 0.01
>
> maxIterations: Maximum number of Iterations, default 100
>
> seed: seeding at the initialization, default 'random'

The Gaussian Mixture models with Expectation Maximization are a form of soft clustering in which a membership can be inferred using a log maximum likelihood function. In this scenario, a probability density function with mean and covariance is used to define the membership or likelihood of a membership to K number of clusters. It is flexible in the sense that the membership is not quantified which allows for overlapping membership based on probability (indexed to multiple sub-distributions).

The following figure is a snapshot of the EM algorithm:

$$X \sim N(\mu, \sigma^2) \ldots \ldots X \sim N(\mu, \sigma^2)$$

Here are the steps to the EM algorithm:

1. Assume N number of Gaussian distribution.
2. Iterate until we have convergence:
    1. For each point Z drawn with conditional probability of being drawn from distribution Xi written as $P\ (Z\ |\ Xi)$
    2. Adjust the parameter's mean and variance so that they fit the points that are assigned to the sub-distribution

For a more mathematical explanation, including detailed work on maximum likelihood, see the following link:
http://www.ee.iisc.ernet.in/new/people/faculty/prasantg/downloads/GMM_Tutorial_Reynolds.pdf

There's more...

The following figure provides a quick reference point to highlight some of the differences between hard versus soft clustering:

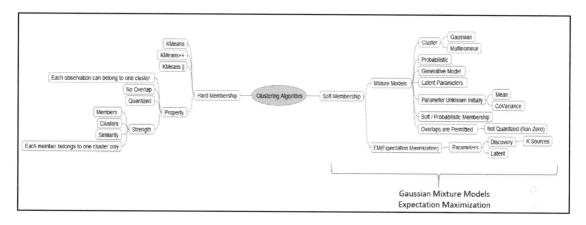

See also

- Documentation for constructor GaussianMixture can be found at `http://spark.apache.org/docs/latest/api/scala/index.html#org.apache.spark.mllib.clustering.GaussianMixture`

- Documentation for constructor GaussianMixtureModel can be found at `http://spark.apache.org/docs/latest/api/scala/index.html#org.apache.spark.mllib.clustering.GaussianMixtureModel`

Classifying the vertices of a graph using Power Iteration Clustering (PIC) in Spark 2.0

This is a classification method for the vertices of a graph given their similarities as defined by their edges. It uses the GraphX library which is ships out of the box with Spark to implement the algorithm. Power Iteration Clustering is similar to other Eigen Vector/Eigen Value decomposition algorithms, but without the overhead of matrix decomposition. It is suitable when you have a large sparse matrix (for example, graphs depicted as a sparse matrix).

GraphFrames will be the replacement/interface proper for the GraphX library going forward (`https://databricks.com/blog/2016/03/03/introducing-graphframes.html`).

How to do it...

1. Start a new project in IntelliJ or in an IDE of your choice. Make sure the necessary JAR files are included.

2. Set up the package location where the program will reside:

   ```
   package spark.ml.cookbook.chapter8
   ```

3. Import the necessary packages for Spark context to get access to the cluster and `Log4j.Logger` to reduce the amount of output produced by Spark:

   ```
   import org.apache.log4j.{Level, Logger}
   import org.apache.spark.mllib.clustering.PowerIterationClustering
   import org.apache.spark.sql.SparkSession
   ```

4. Set up the logger level to ERROR only to reduce the output:

   ```
   Logger.getLogger("org").setLevel(Level.ERROR)
   ```

5. Create Spark's configuration and SQL context so we can have access to the cluster and be able to create and use a DataFrame as needed:

   ```
   // setup SparkSession to use for interactions with Spark
   val spark = SparkSession
    .builder
   .master("local[*]")
    .appName("myPowerIterationClustering")
    .config("spark.sql.warehouse.dir", ".")
    .getOrCreate()
   ```

6. We create a training dataset with a list of datasets and use the Spark `sparkContext.parallelize()` function to create Spark RDD:

   ```
   val trainingData =spark.sparkContext.parallelize(List(
    (0L, 1L, 1.0),
    (0L, 2L, 1.0),
    (0L, 3L, 1.0),
   ```

```
(1L,  2L,  1.0),
(1L,  3L,  1.0),
(2L,  3L,  1.0),
(3L,  4L,  0.1),
(4L,  5L,  1.0),
(4L,  15L, 1.0),
(5L,  6L,  1.0),
(6L,  7L,  1.0),
(7L,  8L,  1.0),
(8L,  9L,  1.0),
(9L,  10L,  1.0),
(10L, 11L,  1.0),
(11L,  12L,  1.0),
(12L,  13L,  1.0),
(13L, 14L,  1.0),
(14L, 15L,  1.0)
))
```

7. We create a `PowerIterationClustering` object and set the parameters. We set the K value to 3 and max iteration count to 15:

```
val pic = new PowerIterationClustering()
.setK(3)
.setMaxIterations(15)
```

8. We then let the model run:

```
val model = pic.run(trainingData)
```

9. We print out the cluster assignment based on the model for the training data:

```
model.assignments.foreach { a =>
 println(s"${a.id} -> ${a.cluster}")
 }
```

10. The console output will show the following information:

```
14 -> 1
4 -> 2
8 -> 2
0 -> 0
13 -> 0
11 -> 0
15 -> 0
5 -> 0
1 -> 0
7 -> 0
6 -> 2
12 -> 1
2 -> 0
10 -> 2
3 -> 0
9 -> 0
```

11. We also print out the model assignment data in a collection for each cluster:

```
val clusters =
model.assignments.collect().groupBy(_.cluster).mapValues(_.map(_.id
))
  val assignments = clusters.toList.sortBy { case (k, v) => v.length
}
  val assignmentsStr = assignments
  .map { case (k, v) =>
  s"$k -> ${v.sorted.mkString("[", ",", "]")}"
}.mkString(", ")
  val sizesStr = assignments.map {
  _._2.length
  }.sorted.mkString("(", ",", ")")
  println(s"Cluster assignments: $assignmentsStr\ncluster sizes:
$sizesStr")
```

12. The console output will display the following information (in total, we have three clusters which were set in the preceding parameters):

```
Cluster assignments: 1 -> [12,14], 2 -> [4,6,8,10], 0 ->
[0,1,2,3,5,7,9,11,13,15]
  cluster sizes: (2,4,10)
```

13. We then close the program by stopping the Spark context:

```
spark.stop()
```

How it works...

We created a list of edges and vertices for a graph and then proceeded to create the object and set the parameters:

```
new PowerIterationClustering().setK(3).setMaxIterations(15)
```

The next step was the model of training data:

```
val model = pic.run(trainingData)
```

The clusters were then outputted for inspection. The code near the end prints out the model assignment data in a collection for each cluster using Spark transformation operators.

At the core **PIC** (**Power Iteration Clustering**) is an eigenvalue class algorithm which avoids matrix decomposition by producing an Eigen Value plus an Eigen Vector to satisfy $Av = \lambda v$. Because PIC avoids the decomposition of the matrix A, it is suitable when the input matrix A (describing a graph in the case of Spark's PIC) is a large sparse matrix.

An example of PIC in image processing (post enhanced for paper) is depicted in the following figure:

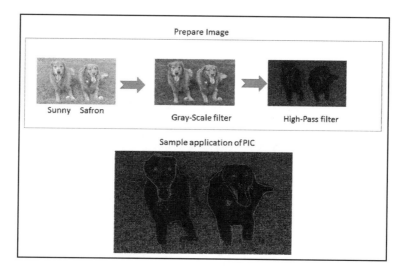

The Spark implementation of the PIC algorithm is an improvement over the previous common implementation (NCut) by computing a pseudo Eigen Vector of the similarities defined as edges given N number of vertices (like an affinity matrix).

The input as depicted in the following figure is a trinary tuple of RDDs describing the graph. The output is a model with a cluster assignment for each node. The algorithm similarities (edges) are assumed to be positive and symmetrical (not shown):

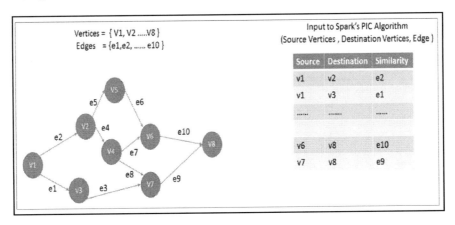

There's more...

For a more detailed mathematical treatment of the subject (power iteration), see the following white paper from Carnegie Mellon University: http://www.cs.cmu.edu/~wcohen/postscript/icml2010-pic-final.pdf

See also

- Documentation for the constructor PowerIterationClustering() can be found
  at http://spark.apache.org/docs/latest/api/scala/index.html#org.apache.spark.mllib.clustering.PowerIterationClustering

- Documentation for the constructor PowerIterationClusteringModel() can be found
  at http://spark.apache.org/docs/latest/api/scala/index.html#org.apache.spark.mllib.clustering.PowerIterationClusteringModel

Latent Dirichlet Allocation (LDA) to classify documents and text into topics

In this recipe, we will explore the **Latent Dirichlet Allocation** (**LDA**) algorithm in Spark 2.0. The LDA we use in this recipe is completely different from linear discrimination analysis. Both Latent Dirichlet Allocation and linear discrimination analysis are referred to as LDA, but they are extremely different techniques. In this recipe, when we use the LDA, we refer to Latent Dirichlet Allocation. The chapter on text analytics is also relevant to understanding the LDA.

LDA is often used in natural language processing which tries to classify a large body of document (for example, emails from the Enron fraud case) into a discrete number of topics or themes so it can be understood. LDA is also a good candidate for selecting articles based on one's interest (for example, as you turn a page and spend time on a specific topic) in a given magazine article or page.

How to do it...

1. Start a new project in IntelliJ or in an IDE of your choice. Make sure the necessary JAR files are included.

2. Set up the package location where the program will reside:

   ```
   package spark.ml.cookbook.chapter8
   ```

3. Import the necessary packages:

   ```
   import org.apache.log4j.{Level, Logger}
   import org.apache.spark.sql.SparkSession
   import org.apache.spark.ml.clustering.LDA
   ```

4. We set up the necessary Spark Session to gain access to the cluster:

   ```
   val spark = SparkSession
    .builder
   .master("local[*]")
    .appName("MyLDA")
    .config("spark.sql.warehouse.dir", ".")
    .getOrCreate()
   ```

5. We have a sample LDA dataset, which is located at the following relative path (you can use an absolute path). The sample file is provided with any Spark distribution and can be found under the home directory of Spark inside the data directory (see the following). Assume the input is a set of features for input to the LDA method:

```
val input = "../data/sparkml2/chapter8/my_lda_data.txt"
```

```
Here is a sample of first 5 line of the file (file is in the libsvm format):

0 1:1 2:2 3:6 4:0 5:2 6:3 7:1 8:1 9:1 10:0 11:3
1 1:0 2:3 3:0 4:1 5:3 6:0 7:0 8:2 9:1 10:0 11:1
2 1:2 2:4 3:1 4:0 5:0 6:4 7:9 8:0 9:2 10:2 11:0
3 1:2 2:1 3:0 4:3 5:0 6:0 7:5 8:0 9:2 10:3 11:9
4 1:3 2:1 3:1 4:9 5:3 6:0 7:2 8:0 9:0 10:1 11:3
5 1:4 2:2 3:0 4:2 5:4 6:5 7:1 8:1 9:1 10:4 11:0
```

6. In this step, we read the file and create the necessary dataset from the input file and show the top five rows in the console:

```
val dataset = spark.read.format("libsvm").load(input)
dataset.show(5)
```

From the console output:

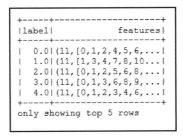

7. We create the LDA object and set the parameters for the object:

```
val lda = new LDA()
 .setK(5)
 .setMaxIter(10)
 .setFeaturesCol("features")
 .setOptimizer("online")
 .setOptimizeDocConcentration(true)
```

8. We then run the model using the high-level API from the package:

```
val ldaModel = lda.fit(dataset)


val ll = ldaModel.logLikelihood(dataset)
val lp = ldaModel.logPerplexity(dataset)

println(s"\t Training data log likelihood: $ll")
println(s"\t Training data log Perplexity: $lp")
```

From the console output:

```
Training data log likelihood: -762.2149142231476
Training data log Perplexity: 2.8869048032045974
```

9. We get the topics distribution from the LDA model for each set of features, and show the topics.

10. We set the `maxTermsPerTopic` value as 3:

```
val topics = ldaModel.describeTopics(3)
 topics.show(false) // false is Boolean value for truncation for
the dataset
```

11. On the console, the output will show the following information:

```
+-----+-----------+-----------------------------------------------------------------+
|topic|termIndices|termWeights                                                      |
+-----+-----------+-----------------------------------------------------------------+
|0    |[2, 5, 7]  |[0.10590438713925907, 0.10552706453241487, 0.10414306358198831]|
|1    |[1, 6, 2]  |[0.10176875268567338, 0.09813701067499785, 0.09625065927903562]|
|2    |[10, 6, 9] |[0.224415590345134, 0.14259821198481398, 0.13437833678670488]  |
|3    |[0, 4, 8]  |[0.10259611161709382, 0.09834614889684987, 0.09809818559264627]|
|4    |[9, 6, 4]  |[0.10443008806658334, 0.10406661341365932, 0.10092788028015136]|
+-----+-----------+-----------------------------------------------------------------+
```

12. We also transform the training dataset from the LDA model, and show the result:

```
val transformed = ldaModel.transform(dataset)
 transformed.show(false)
```

The output will display the following:

```
+-----+----------------------------------------------------------------+-------------------------------------------------------+
|label|features                                                        |topicDistribution                                      |
+-----+----------------------------------------------------------------+-------------------------------------------------------+
|0.0  |(11,[0,1,2,4,5,6,7,8,10],[1.0,2.0,6.0,2.0,3.0,1.0,1.0,1.0,3.0]) |[0.665287570133743,0.009021752920617748,...]           |
|1.0  |(11,[1,3,4,7,8,10],[3.0,1.0,3.0,2.0,1.0,1.0])                   |[0.01584997975758763,0.01581565024938826,...]          |
|2.0  |(11,[0,1,2,5,6,8,9],[2.0,4.0,1.0,4.0,9.0,2.0,2.0])             |[0.007622470464432214,0.007627013290202738,...]        |
|3.0  |(11,[0,1,3,6,8,9,10],[2.0,1.0,3.0,5.0,2.0,3.0,9.0])           |[0.007203235692928609,0.0072124840651476155,...]       |
|4.0  |(11,[0,1,2,3,4,6,9,10],[3.0,1.0,1.0,9.0,3.0,2.0,1.0,3.0])     |[0.007851742406435247,0.00786228763852816,...]         |
|5.0  |(11,[0,1,3,4,5,6,7,8,9],[4.0,2.0,2.0,4.0,5.0,1.0,1.0,1.0,4.0]) |[0.007578630665190091,0.00757561161586504,...]         |
|6.0  |(11,[0,1,3,6,8,9,10],[1.0,1.0,3.0,5.0,2.0,2.0,9.0])           |[0.007800362084464072,0.007809853027526702,...]        |
|7.0  |(11,[0,1,2,3,4,5,6,9,10],[2.0,2.0,2.0,9.0,2.0,1.0,2.0,1.0,3.0])|[0.007564655969980252,0.007567856115057907,...]        |
|8.0  |(11,[0,1,3,4,5,6,7],[4.0,4.0,3.0,4.0,2.0,1.0,3.0])           |[0.008607307662614899,0.008618046211724592,...]        |
|9.0  |(11,[0,1,2,4,6,8,9,10],[1.0,8.0,2.0,3.0,2.0,2.0,7.0,2.0])     |[0.0067234954853242134,0.00672227305280794,...]        |
|10.0 |(11,[0,1,2,3,5,6,9,10],[2.0,1.0,1.0,9.0,2.0,2.0,3.0,3.0])     |[0.007892050842839225,0.007895033920912157,...]        |
|11.0 |(11,[0,1,4,5,6,7,9],[3.0,2.0,4.0,5.0,1.0,3.0,1.0])           |[0.009491103339631072,0.00947274250255502,...]         |
+-----+----------------------------------------------------------------+-------------------------------------------------------+
```

If the preceding method is changed to:

```
transformed.show(true)
```

13. The result will be displayed as truncated:

```
+-----+-------------------+-------------------+
|label|           features|  topicDistribution|
+-----+-------------------+-------------------+
|  0.0|(11,[0,1,2,4,5,6,...|[0.66525666771208...|
|  1.0|(11,[1,3,4,7,8,10...|[0.01584989652565...|
|  2.0|(11,[0,1,2,5,6,8,...|[0.00762242653921...|
|  3.0|(11,[0,1,3,6,8,9,...|[0.00720319194955...|
|  4.0|(11,[0,1,2,3,4,6,...|[0.00785171521188...|
|  5.0|(11,[0,1,3,4,5,6,...|[0.00757858435810...|
|  6.0|(11,[0,1,3,6,8,9,...|[0.00779999202859...|
|  7.0|(11,[0,1,2,3,4,5,...|[0.00756460520509...|
|  8.0|(11,[0,1,3,4,5,6,...|[0.00860724611808...|
|  9.0|(11,[0,1,2,4,6,8,...|[0.00672030365907...|
| 10.0|(11,[0,1,2,3,5,6,...|[0.00789214021488...|
| 11.0|(11,[0,1,4,5,6,7,...|[0.00948779706633...|
+-----+-------------------+-------------------+
```

14. We close the Spark context to end the program:

```
spark.stop()
```

How it works...

LDA assumes that the document is a mixture of different topics with Dirichlet prior distribution. The words in the document are assumed to have an affinity towards a specific topic which allows LDA to classify the overall document (compose and assign a distribution) that best matches a topic.

A topic model is a generative latent model for discovering abstract themes (topics) that occur in the body of documents (often too large for humans to handle). The models are a pre-curser to summarize, search, and browse a large set of unlabeled documents and their contents. Generally speaking, we are trying to find a cluster of features (words, sub-images, and so on) that occur together.

The following figure depicts the overall LDA scheme:

Please be sure to refer to the white paper cited here for completeness `http://ai.stanford.edu/~ang/papers/nips01-lda.pdf`

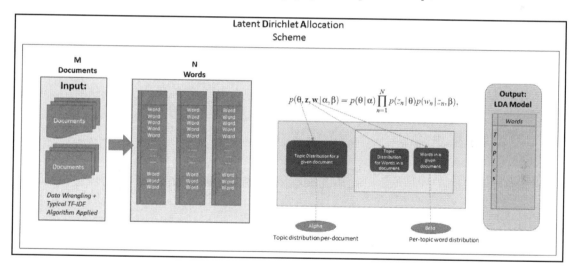

The steps for the LDA algorithm are as follows:

1. Initialize the following parameters (controls concentration and smoothing):

   1. Alpha parameter (high alpha makes documents more similar to each other and contain similar topics)

   2. Beta parameter (high beta means each topic is most likely to contain a mix of most of the words)

2. Randomly initialize the topic assignment.

3. Iterate:

   1. For each document.

      1. For each word in the document.

      2. Resample the topic for each word.

         1. With respect to all other words and their current assignment (for the current iteration).

4. Get the result.

5. Model evaluation

In statistics, Dirichlet distribution Dir(alpha) is a family of continuous multivariate probability distributions parameterized by a vector α of positive real numbers. For a more in-depth treatment of LDA, see the original paper in the

Journal of Machine Learning
at: http://www.jmlr.org/papers/volume3/blei03a/blei03a.pdf

The LDA does not assign any semantics to a topic and does not care what the topics are called. It is only a generative model that uses distribution of fine-grained items (for example, words about cats, dogs, fish, cars) to assign an overall topic that scores the best. It does not know, care, or understand about topics called dogs or cats.

We often have to tokenize and vectorize the document via TF-IDF prior to input to an LDA algorithm.

There's more...

The following figure depicts the LDA in a nutshell:

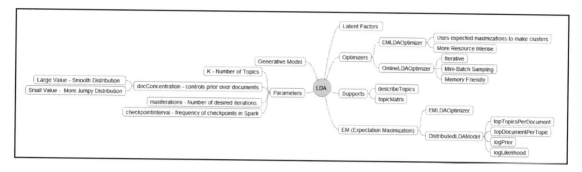

There are two approaches to document analysis. We can simply use matrix factorization to decompose a large matrix of datasets to a smaller matrix (topic assignments) times a vector (topics themselves):

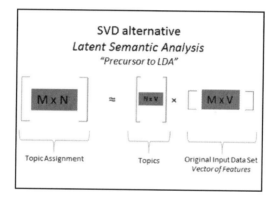

See also

- **LDA**: documentation for a constructor can be found at: http://spark.apache.org/docs/latest/api/scala/index.html#org.apache.spark.ml.clustering.LDA
- **LDAModel**: documentation for a constructor can be found at: http://spark.apache.org/docs/latest/api/scala/index.html#org.apache.e.spark.ml.clustering.LDAModel

See also, via Spark's Scala API, documentation links for the following:

- DistributedLDAModel
- EMLDAOptimizer
- LDAOptimizer
- LocalLDAModel
- OnlineLDAOptimizer

Streaming KMeans to classify data in near real-time

Spark streaming is a powerful facility which lets you combine near real time and batch in the same paradigm. The streaming KMeans interface lives at the intersection of ML clustering and Spark streaming, and takes full advantage of the core facilities provided by Spark streaming itself (for example, fault tolerance, exactly once delivery semantics, and so on).

How to do it...

1. Start a new project in IntelliJ or in an IDE of your choice. Make sure the necessary JAR files are included.

2. Import the necessary packages for streaming KMeans:

   ```
   package spark.ml.cookbook.chapter8.
   ```

3. Import the necessary packages for streaming KMeans:

   ```
   import org.apache.log4j.{Level, Logger}
   import org.apache.spark.mllib.clustering.StreamingKMeans
   import org.apache.spark.mllib.linalg.Vectors
   import org.apache.spark.mllib.regression.LabeledPoint
   import org.apache.spark.sql.SparkSession
   import org.apache.spark.streaming.{Seconds, StreamingContext}
   ```

4. We set up the following parameters for the streaming KMeans program. The training directory will be the directory to send the training data file. The KMeans clustering model utilizes the training data to run algorithms and calculations. The testDirectory will be the test data for predictions. The batchDuration is a number in seconds for a batch run. In the following case, the program will check every 10 seconds to see if there is any new data files for recalculations.

5. The cluster is set to 2, and the data dimensions will be 3:

```
val trainingDir = "../data/sparkml2/chapter8/trainingDir"
val testDir = "../data/sparkml2/chapter8/testDir"
val batchDuration = 10
val numClusters = 2
val numDimensions = 3
```

6. With the preceding settings, the sample training data will contain data like the following (in the format of $[X_1, X_2, ...X_n]$, where n is numDimensions:

[0.0,0.0,0.0]

[0.1,0.1,0.1]

[0.2,0.2,0.2]

[9.0,9.0,9.0]

[9.1,9.1,9.1]

[9.2,9.2,9.2]

[0.1,0.0,0.0]

[0.2,0.1,0.1]

....

The test data file will contain data like the following (in the format of $(y, [X1,X2, .. Xn])$, where n is numDimensions and y is an identifier):

(7,[0.4,0.4,0.4])

(8,[0.1,0.1,0.1])

(9,[0.2,0.2,0.2])

(10,[1.1,1.0,1.0])

(11,[9.2,9.1,9.2])

(12,[9.3,9.2,9.3])

7. We set up the necessary Spark context to gain access to the cluster:

```
val spark = SparkSession
 .builder
.master("local[*]")
 .appName("myStreamingKMeans")
 .config("spark.sql.warehouse.dir", ".")
 .getOrCreate()
```

8. Define the streaming context and micro-batch window:

```
val ssc = new StreamingContext(spark.sparkContext,
Seconds(batchDuration.toLong))
```

9. The following code will create data by parsing the data file in the preceding two directories into `trainingData` and `testData` RDDs:

```
val trainingData =
ssc.textFileStream(trainingDir).map(Vectors.parse)
 val testData = ssc.textFileStream(testDir).map(LabeledPoint.parse)
```

10. We create the `StreamingKMeans` model and set the parameters:

```
val model = new StreamingKMeans()
 .setK(numClusters)
 .setDecayFactor(1.0)
 .setRandomCenters(numDimensions, 0.0)
```

11. The program will train the model using the training dataset and predict using the test dataset:

```
model.trainOn(trainingData)
 model.predictOnValues(testData.map(lp => (lp.label,
lp.features))).print()
```

12. We start the streaming context, and the program will run the batch every 10 seconds to see if a new dataset is available for training, and if there is any new test dataset for prediction. The program will exit if a termination signal is received (exit the batch running):

```
ssc.start()
  ssc.awaitTermination()
```

13. We copy the `testKStreaming1.txt` data file into the preceding `testDir` set and see the following printed out in the console logs:

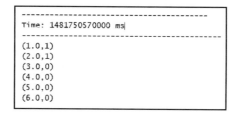

```
-------------------------------------------
Time: 1481750570000 ms|
-------------------------------------------
(1.0,1)
(2.0,1)
(3.0,0)
(4.0,0)
(5.0,0)
(6.0,0)
```

14. For a Windows machine, we copied the `testKStreaming1.txt` file into the directory: `C:\spark-2.0.0-bin-hadoop2.7\data\sparkml2\chapter8\testDir\`.

15. We can also check the SparkUI for more information: `http://localhost:4040/`.

The job panel will display the streaming jobs, as shown in the following figure:

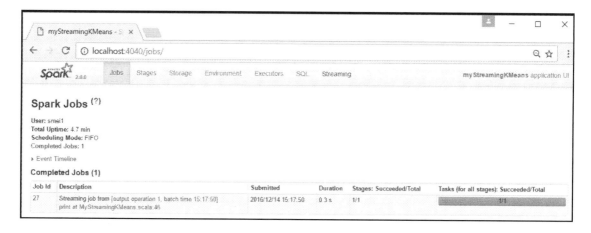

As shown in the following figure, the streaming panel will show the preceding Streaming KMeans matrix as the matrix displayed, the batch job running every 10 seconds in this case:

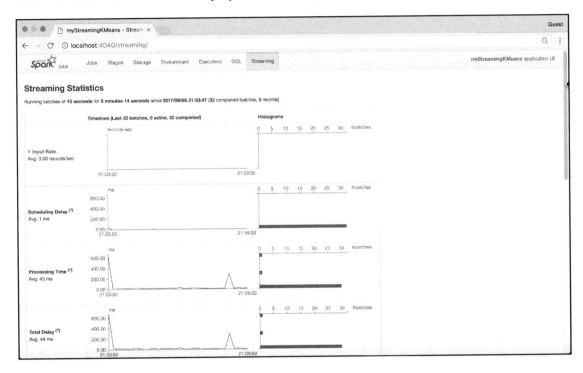

You can get more details on the streaming batch by clicking on any of the batches, as shown in following figure:

How it works...

In certain situations, we cannot use batch methods to load and capture the events and then react to them. We can use creative methods of capturing events in the memory or a landing DB and then rapidly marshal that over to another system for processing, but most of these systems fail to act as streaming systems and often are very expensive to build.

Spark provides a near real time (also referred to as subjective real time) that can receive incoming sources, such as Twitter feeds, signals, and so, on via connectors (for example, a Kafka connector) and then process and present them as an RDD interface.

These are the elements needed to build and construct streaming KMeans in Spark:

1. Use the streaming context as opposed to the regular Spark context used so far:

   ```
   val ssc = new StreamingContext(conf, Seconds(batchDuration.toLong))
   ```

2. Select your connector to connect to a data source and receive events:

   - Twitter
   - Kafka
   - Third party
   - ZeroMQ
   - TCP
   - ....

3. Create your streaming KMeans model; set the parameters as needed:

   ```
   model = new StreamingKMeans()
   ```

4. Train and predict as usual:

   - Have in mind that K cannot be changed on the fly

5. Start the context and await for the termination signal to exit:

   - `ssc.start()`

   - `ssc.awaitTermination()`

There's more...

Streaming KMeans are special cases of KMeans implementation in which the data can arrive at near real time and be classified into a cluster (hard classification) as needed. The applications are vast and can vary from near real-time anomaly detection (fraud, crime, intelligence, monitoring, and surveillance) to fine-grain micro-sector rotation visualization with Voronoi diagrams in finance. Chapter 13, *Spark Streaming and Machine Learning Library* provides a more detailed coverage for streaming.

For a reference to Voronoi diagrams, see the following URL: https://en.wikipedia.org/wiki/Voronoi_diagram

Currently there are other algorithms besides streaming KMeans in the Spark Machine Library, as shown in the following figure:

See also

- Documentation for Streaming KMeans can be found
  at: http://spark.apache.org/docs/latest/api/scala/index.html#org.apache.spark.mllib.clustering.StreamingKMeans

- Documentation for Streaming KMeans Model can be found
  at: http://spark.apache.org/docs/latest/api/scala/index.html#org.apache.spark.mllib.stat.test.StreamingTest

- Documentation for Streaming Test--very useful for data generation--can be found
  at: http://spark.apache.org/docs/latest/api/scala/index.html#org.apache.spark.mllib.clustering.StreamingKMeansModel

9
Optimization - Going Down the Hill with Gradient Descent

In this chapter, we will cover:

- Optimizing a quadratic cost function and finding the minima using just math to gain insight
- Coding a quadratic cost function optimization using Gradient Descent (GD) from scratch
- Coding Gradient Descent optimization to solve Linear regression from scratch
- Normal equations as an alternative to solve Linear regression in Spark 2.0

Introduction

Understanding how optimization works is fundamental for a successful career in machine learning. We picked the **Gradient Descent** (**GD**) method for an end-to-end deep dive to demonstrate the inner workings of an optimization technique. We will develop the concept using three recipes that walk the developer from scratch to a fully developed code to solve an actual problem with real-world data. The fourth recipe explores an alternative to GD using Spark and normal equations (limited scaling for big data problems) to solve a regression problem.

Let's get started. How does a machine learn anyway? Does it really learn from its mistakes? What does it mean when the machine finds a solution using optimization?

At a high level, machines learn based on one of the following five techniques:

- **Error based learning**: In this technique, we search the domain space for a combination of parameter values (weights) that minimize the total error (predicted versus actual) over the training data.

- **Information theory learning**: This method uses concepts such as entropy and information gain that are found in classical Shannon Information theory. The tree-based ML system, rooted classically in the ID3 algorithm, fits well in this category. The ensemble tree models will be the crowning achievement of this category. We will discuss tree models in `Chapter 10`, *Building Machine Learning Systems with Decision Tree and Ensemble Models*.

- **Probability Space Learning**: This branch of machine learning is based on Bayes theorem (`https://en.wikipedia.org/wiki/Bayes'_theorem`). The most well-known method in machine learning is Naïve Bayes (multiple variations). Naïve Bayes culminates with an introduction of the Bayes Network which allows for more control over the model.

- **Similarity measure learning**: This method works by attempting to define a measure of similarity and then fitting an observation's grouping based on that measure. The best known method is KNN (nearest neighbor), which is the standard in any ML toolkit. Spark ML implements K-means++ with parallelism referred to as K-Means|| (K Means Parallel).

- **Genetic algorithms (GA) and evolutionary learning**: This can be viewed as Darwin's theory (Origin of the Species) applied to optimization and machine learning. The idea behind GA is to use a recursive generative algorithm to create a set of initial candidates and then use feedback (fitness landscape) to eliminate distant candidates, fold similar ones while randomly introducing mutations (numerical or symbolic jitter) to unlikely candidates, and then repeat until the solution is found.

Some of the data scientist and ML engineers prefer to think of optimization as maximizing the log likelihood rather than minimizing the cost function - they are really the two sides of the same coin! In this chapter, we will focus on error-based learning, especially **Gradient Descent**.

To provide a solid understanding, we will deep dive into Gradient Descent (GD) by going through three GD recipes as they apply to optimization. We will then provide Spark's Normal Equation recipe as an alternative to numerical optimization methods, such as Gradient Descent (GD) or the **Limited-memory Broyden-Fletcher- Goldfarb-Shanno (LBFGS)** algorithm.

Apache Spark provides an excellent coverage for all categories. The following figure depicts a taxonomy that will guide you through your journey in the field of numerical optimization, which is fundamental to achieving excellence in ML.

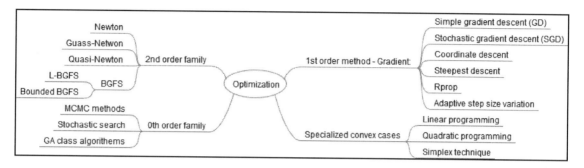

How do machines learn using an error-based system?

Machines learn pretty much the same way we do--they learn from their mistakes. They first start by making an initial guess (random weights for parameters). Second, they use their model (for example, GLM, RRN, isotonic regression) to make a prediction (for example, a number). Third, they look at what the answer should have been (training set). Fourth, they measure the difference between actual versus predicted answers using a variety of techniques (such as least squares, similarity, and so on).

Once all these mechanics are in place, they keep repeating the process over the entire training dataset, while trying to come up with a combination of parameters that has the minimal error when they consider the entire training dataset. What makes this interesting is that each branch of machine learning uses math or domain known facts to avoid a brute-force combinatorics approach which will not terminate in real-world settings.

The error-based ML optimization is a branch of mathematical programming (MP) which is implemented algorithmically, but with limited accuracy (varying accuracy of 10^{-2} to 10^{-6}). Most, if not all, the methods in this category take advantage of simple calculus facts like first derivative (slope), such as the GD technique, and second derivative (curvature), such as the BFGS technique, to minimize a cost function. In the case of BFGS, the invisible hands are the updater function (L1 updater), rank (second rank update), approximating the final answer/solution using a Hessian free technique (https://en.wikipedia.org/wiki/Hessian_matrix) without the actual second derivative matrix.

The following figure depicts some of the facilities that touch on optimization in Spark:

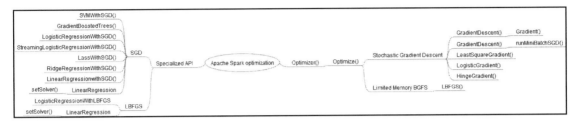

The functions to do SGD and LBFGS optimization are available by themselves in Spark. To utilize them, you should be able to write and supply your own cost function. The functions, such as `runMiniBatchSGD()`, are not only marked private, but also require good understanding of the implementation of both algorithms.

Since this is a cookbook and we cannot go deep into optimization theory, for background and reference we recommend the following books from our library:

- **Optimization**
  (2013): https://www.amazon.com/Optimization-Springer-Texts-Statistics-Ke
  nneth/dp/1461458374/ref=sr_1_8?ie=UTF8&qid=1485744639&sr=8-8&keywords=
  optimization

- **Optimization for Machine Learning**
  (2011): https://www.amazon.com/Optimization-Machine-Learning-Information
  -
  Processing/dp/026201646X/ref=sr_1_1?ie=UTF8&qid=1485744817&sr=8-1&keyw
  ords=optimization+for+machine+learning

- **Convex Optimization**
  (2004): https://www.amazon.com/Convex-Optimization-Stephen-Boyd/dp/05218
  33787/ref=pd_sim_14_2?_encoding=UTF8&psc=1&refRID=7T88DJY5ZWBEREGJ4WT4

- **Genetic Algorithm in Search, Optimization and Machine Learning (1989) - a
  classic!**: https://www.amazon.com/Genetic-Algorithms-Optimization-Machine-
  Learning/dp/0201157675/ref=sr_1_5?s=books&ie=UTF8&qid=1485745151&sr=1-
  5&keywords=genetic+programming

- **Swarm Intelligence from Natural to Artificial Systems**
  (1999): https://www.amazon.com/Swarm-Intelligence-Artificial-Institute-C
  omplexity/dp/0195131592/ref=sr_1_3?s=books&ie=UTF8&qid=1485745559&sr=1
  -3&keywords=swarm+intelligence

Optimizing a quadratic cost function and finding the minima using just math to gain insight

In this recipe, we will explore the fundamental concept behind mathematical optimization using simple derivatives before introducing Gradient Descent (first order derivative) and L-BFGS, which is a Hessian free quasi-Newton method.

We will examine a sample quadratic cost/error function and show how to find the minimum or maximum with just math.

$$f(x) = ax^2 + bx + c$$

We will use both the closed form (vertex formula) and derivative method (slope) to find the minima, but we will defer to later recipes in this chapter to introduce numerical optimization techniques, such Gradient Descent and its application to regression.

How to do it...

1. Let's assume we have a quadratic cost function and we find its minima:

$$f(x) = 2x^2 - 8x + 9$$

2. The cost function in statistical machine learning algorithms acts as a proxy for the level of difficulty, energy spent, or total error as we move around in our search space.

3. The first thing we do is to graph the function and inspect it visually.

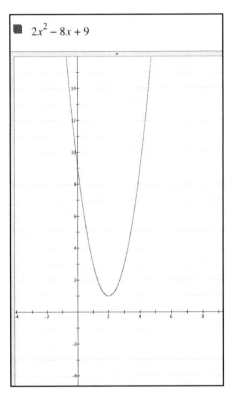

$2x^2 - 8x + 9$

4. Upon visual inspection, we see that $f(x) = 2x^2 - 8x + 9$ is a concave function with its minima at (2,1).

5. Our next step would be to find the minima by optimizing the function. Some examples of presenting the cost or error function in machine learning could be squared error, Euclidian distance, MSSE, or any other similarity measure that can capture how far we are from an optimal numeric answer.

6. The next step is to search for best parameter values that minimize errors (for example, cost) in our ML technique. For example, by optimizing a linear regression cost function (sum of squared errors), we arrive at best values for its parameter.
   - Derivative method: Set the first derivative to zero and solve
   - Vertex method: Use closed algebraic form

7. First, we solve for minima using the derivative method by computing the first derivative, setting it to zero, and solving for x and y.

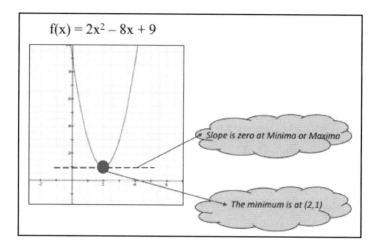

$f(x) = 2x^2 - 8x + 9$

Slope is zero at Minima or Maxima

The minimum is at (2,1)

Given $f(x) = 2x^2 - 8x + 9$ as our cost/error function, the derivative can be computed as:

$$f'(x) = \frac{d}{dx}(2x^2 - 8x + 9)$$

$$f'(x) = 4x - 8$$

[Power rule: $f(x) = x^n$ then $f'(x) = nx^{n-1}$]

$f'(x) = 0$ [We set the derivative equal to 0 and solve for x]

$$4x - 8 = 0$$
$$x = \frac{8}{4}$$
$$= 2$$
$$y = f(2)$$
$$= 2(2^2) + (-8)(2) + 9$$
$$= 1$$

We now verify the minima using the vertex formula method. To compute the minima using the algebraic method please see the following steps.

8. Given the function, $f(x) = ax^2 + bx + c$, the vertex can be found at:

$$\left(-\frac{b}{2a}, f\left(-\frac{b}{2a} \right) \right)$$

9. Let's compute the minima using the vertex algebraic formula:

$$f(x) = 2x^2 - 8x + 9$$

$$x = \frac{-b}{(2a)}$$

$$x = 8/(2 * 2)$$

$$= 2$$

$$y = f(x)$$

$$= 2(2)2 + (-8) (2) +9$$

$$= 1$$

10. As the last step, we check the result of steps 4 and 5 to make sure that our answer using a closed algebraic form yielding the minimum of (2, 1), is consistent with the derivative method which also yields (2, 1).

11. In the last step, we show a pictorial view of $f(x)$ in the left panel along with its derivative on the right panel, so you can visually inspect the answer for yourself.

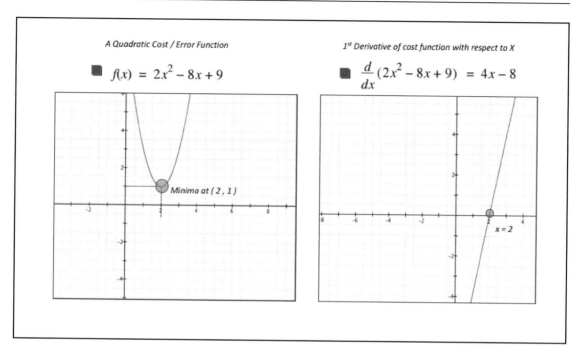

A Quadratic Cost / Error Function

$$f(x) = 2x^2 - 8x + 9$$

Minima at (2 , 1)

1st Derivative of cost function with respect to X

$$\frac{d}{dx}(2x^2 - 8x + 9) = 4x - 8$$

x = 2

12. As you can see, a casual inspection depicts that the minima vertex is at (2,1) on the left hand side { x=2, f(x)=1 } while the right hand side chart shows the derivative of the function with respect to X (only the parameter) with its minima at $X=2$. As seen in the previous steps, we set the derivative of the function to zero and solve for X which results in number 2. You can also visually inspect the two panels and equations to make sure $X=2$ is true and makes sense in both cases.

How it works...

We have two techniques at our disposal for finding the minima of a quadratic function without using a numerical method. In real-life statistical machine learning optimization, we use the derivatives to find the minima of a convex function. If the function is convex (or the optimization is bonded), there is only one local minima, so the work is much simpler than non-linear/non-convex problems that are present in deep learning.

Using the derivative method in the preceding recipe:

- First, we found the derivative by applying the derivative rules (for example, exponent).
- Second, we took advantage of the fact that, for a given simple quadratic function (convex optimization), the minima occurs when the slope of the first derivative is zero.
- Third, we simply found the derivative by following and applying mechanical calculus rules.
- Fourth, we set the derivative of the function to zero $f'(x) = 0$ and solved for x
- Fifth, we used the x value and plugged it into the original equation to find y. Using steps 1 through 5, we ended up with the minima at point (2, 1).

There's more...

Most statistical machine learning algorithms define and search a domain space while using a cost or error function to arrive at a best numerically approximated solution (for example, parameters of a regression). The point at which the function has its minima (minimizing cost/error) or its maxima (maximizing log likelihood) is where the best solution with minimal error (the best approximation) exists.

A quick refresher for differentiation rules can be found
at: https://en.wikipedia.org/wiki/Differentiation_rules and https://www.math.ucda
vis.edu/~kouba/Math17BHWDIRECTORY/Derivatives.pdf

A more mathematical write up for minimizing quadratic functions can be found
at: http://www.cis.upenn.edu/~cis515/cis515-11-sl12.pdf

A scientific write up for quadratic function optimization and forms from MIT can be found
at: https://ocw.mit.edu/courses/sloan-school-of-management/15-084j-nonlinear-pro
gramming-spring-2004/lecture-notes/lec4_quad_form.pdf

See also

- A lengthy write up for quadratic equation from UCSC can be found
  at: `https://people.ucsc.edu/~miglior/chapter%20pdf/Ch08_SE.pdf`
- Quadratic functions can be expressed as one of the following forms:

Quadratic function ax² + bx + c form	Standard form of quadratic function
$f(x) = ax^2 + bx + c$	$f(x) = a(x - h)^2 + k$

Where a, b and c are real numbers.

The following figure provides a quick reference to minima/maxima and the parameters regulating the convex/concave look and feel of the function:

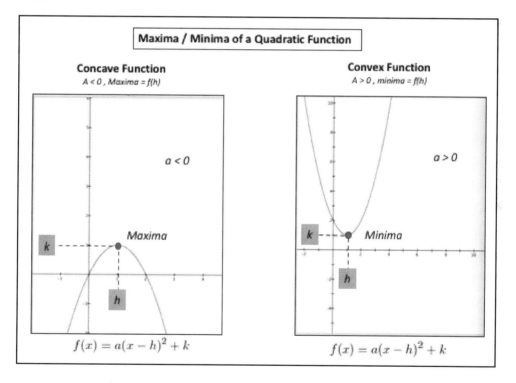

Coding a quadratic cost function optimization using Gradient Descent (GD) from scratch

In this recipe, we will code an iterative numerical optimization technique called gradient descent (GD) to find the minimum of a quadratic function $f(x) = 2x^2 - 8x + 9$.

The focus here shifts from using math to solve for the minima (setting the first derivative to zero) to an iterative numerical method called Gradient Descent (GD) which starts with a guess and then gets closer to the solution in each iteration using a cost/error function as the guideline.

How to do it...

1. Start a new project in IntelliJ or in an IDE of your choice. Make sure the necessary JAR files are included.

2. Set up the path using the package directive: `package spark.ml.cookbook.chapter9`.

3. Import the necessary packages.

    The `scala.util.control.Breaks` will allow us to break out of the program. We use this during the debugging phase only when the program fails to converge or gets stuck in a never ending process (for example, when the step size is too large).

    ```
    import scala.collection.mutable.ArrayBuffer
    import scala.util.control.Breaks._
    ```

4. This step defines the actual quadratic function that we are trying to minimize:

    ```
    def quadratic_function_itself(x:Double):Double = {
    // the function being differentiated
    // f(x) = 2x^2 - 8x + 9
    return 2 * math.pow(x,2) - (8*x) + 9
    }
    ```

5. This step defines the derivative of the function. It is what is referred to as the gradient at point x. It is the first order derivative of function $f(x) = 2x^2 - 8x + 9$.

```
def derivative_of_function(x:Double):Double = {
// The derivative of f(x)
return 4 * x - 8
}
```

6. In this step, we setup a random starting point (set to 13 here). This would become our initial starting point on the *x* axis.

```
var currentMinimumValue = 13.0 // just pick up a random value
```

7. We proceed to set up the actual minima calculated from the previous recipe, *Optimizing a quadratic cost function and finding the minima using just math to gain insight,* so we can compute our estimate with each iteration versus actual.

```
val actualMinima = 2.0 // proxy for a label in training phase
```

This point is trying to act as the labels that you would provide during the training phase of an ML algorithm. In a real-life setting, we would have a training dataset with labels and would let the algorithm train and adjust its parameters accordingly.

8. Set up bookkeeping variables and declare ArrayBuffer data structures to store the cost (error) plus the estimated minima for inspection and graphing:

```
var oldMinimumValue = 0.0
var iteration = 0;
var minimumVector = ArrayBuffer[Double]()
var costVector = ArrayBuffer[Double]()
```

9. The internal control variables for the gradient descent algorithm get set in this step:

```
val stepSize = .01
val tolerance = 0.0001
```

The stepSize, also referred to as the learning rate, guides the program in how much to move each time, while tolerance helps the algorithm to stop when we get sufficiently close to the minima.

10. We first set up a loop to iterate and stop when we are close enough to the minima, based on the desired tolerance:

```
while (math.abs(currentMinimumValue - oldMinimumValue) > tolerance)
{
iteration +=1 //= iteration + 1 for debugging when non-convergence
```

11. We update the minima each time and call on the function to calculate and return the derivative value at the current updated point:

```
oldMinimumValue = currentMinimumValue
val gradient_value_at_point =
derivative_of_function(oldMinimumValue)
```

12. We decide how much to move by first taking the derivative value returned by the last step and multiplying that by the step size (that is, we scale it). We then proceed to update the current minima and decrease it by the movement (derivative value x step size):

```
val move_by_amount = gradient_value_at_point * stepSize
currentMinimumValue = oldMinimumValue - move_by_amount
```

13. We compute our cost function value (error) by using a very simple square distance formula. In real life, the actual minima will be derived from training, but here we use the value from the previous recipe, *Optimizing a quadratic cost function and finding the minima using just math to gain insight*.

```
costVector += math.pow(actualMinima - currentMinimumValue, 2)
minimumVector += currentMinimumValue
```

14. We produce some intermediate output results so you can observe the behavior of currentMinimum at each iteration:

```
print("Iteration= ",iteration," currentMinimumValue= ",
currentMinimumValue)
print("\n")
```

The output will be as follows:

```
(Iteration= ,1, currentMinimumValue= ,12.56)
(Iteration= ,2, currentMinimumValue= ,12.1376)
(Iteration= ,3, currentMinimumValue= ,11.732096)
(Iteration= ,4, currentMinimumValue= ,11.342812160000001)
(Iteration= ,5, currentMinimumValue= ,10.9690996736)
(Iteration= ,6, currentMinimumValue= ,10.610335686656)
(Iteration= ,7, currentMinimumValue= ,10.265922259189761)
```

```
(Iteration= ,8, currentMinimumValue= ,9.935285368822171)
..........
..........
..........
(Iteration= ,203, currentMinimumValue= ,2.0027698292180602)
(Iteration= ,204, currentMinimumValue= ,2.0026590360493377)
(Iteration= ,205, currentMinimumValue= ,2.0025526746073643)
(Iteration= ,206, currentMinimumValue= ,2.00245056762307)
(Iteration= ,207, currentMinimumValue= ,2.002352544918147)
```

15. The following statement is included as a reminder that, regardless of how an optimization algorithm is implemented, it should always provide means for exiting from a non-converging algorithm (that is, it should guard against user input and edge cases):

```
if (iteration == 1000000) break //break if non-convergence -
debugging
}
```

16. The output cost and minima vectors that we collected in each iteration for later analysis and graphing are:

```
print("\n Cost Vector: "+ costVector)
print("\n Minimum Vactor" + minimumVector)
```

The output is:

```
Cost vector: ArrayBuffer(111.51360000000001, 102.77093376000002,
94.713692553216, 87.28813905704389, ........7.0704727116774655E-6,
6.516147651082496E-6, 6.005281675238673E-6, 5.534467591900128E-6)

Minimum VactorArrayBuffer(12.56, 12.1376, 11.732096,
11.342812160000001, 10.9690996736, 10.610335686656,
10.265922259189761, 9.935285368822171, ........2.0026590360493377,
2.0025526746073643, 2.00245056762307, 2.002352544918147)
```

17. We define and set the variables that are the final minima and the actual function value *f(minima)*. They act as (X,Y) for where the minima is located:

```
var minimaXvalue= currentMinimumValue
var minimaYvalue= quadratic_function_itself(currentMinimumValue)
```

18. We print our final results that match our computation in the recipe, *Optimizing a quadratic cost function and finding the minima using just math to gain insight*, using the iterative method. The final output should read as our minimum is located as (2,1), which can be either visually or computationally checked via the recipe, *Optimizing a quadratic cost function and finding the minima using just math to gain insight*.

```
print("\n\nGD Algo: Local minimum found at
X="+f"$minimaXvalue%1.2f")
print("\nGD Algo: Y=f(x)= : "+f"$minimaYvalue%1.2f")
}
```

The output is:

```
GD Algo: Local minimum found at X = : 2.00
GD Algo: Y=f(x)= : 1.00
```

The process finished with the exit code 0

How it works...

The Gradient Descent technique takes advantage of the fact that the gradient of the function (first derivative in this case) points to the direction of the descent. Conceptually, Gradient Descent (GD) optimizes a cost or error function to search for the best parameter for the model. The following figure demonstrates the iterative nature of the gradient descent:

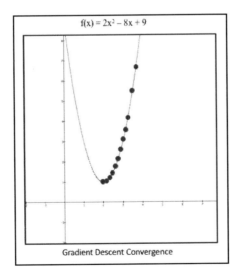

Gradient Descent Convergence

We started the recipe by defining the step size (the learning rate), tolerance, the function to be differentiated, and the function's first derivative, and then proceeded to iterate and get closer to the target minima of zero from the initial guess (13 in this case).

At each iteration, we calculated the gradient of the point (the first derivative at that point) and then scaled it using the step size to regulate the amount of each move. Since we are descending, we subtracted the scaled gradient from the old point to find the next point closer to the solution (to minimize the error).

There is some confusion as to whether the gradient value should be added or subtracted to arrive at the new point, which we try to clarify next. The guiding principle should be whether the slope is negative or positive. To move in the right direction, you must move in the direction of the first derivative (gradient).

The following table and figure provide a guideline for the GD update step:

$\nabla f(p1) < 0$	$\nabla f(p1) > 0$
Negative Gradient	*Positive Gradient*
$P_2 = P_1 - \alpha (\nabla f(x))$	$P_2 = P_1 + \alpha (\nabla f(x))$

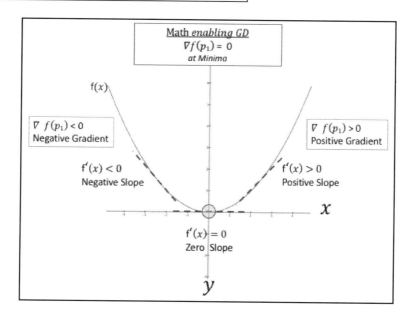

The following figure depicts the inner workings of a single step (the negative slope depicted) in which we either subtract or add the gradient from the starting point to arrive at the next point that will put us one step closer to the minimum of the quadratic function. For example, in this recipe, we start from 13 and after 200+ iterations (depends on the learning rate), we end up at the minima of (2,1), which matches the solution found in the recipe, *Optimizing a quadratic cost function and finding the minima using just math to gain insight* of this chapter.

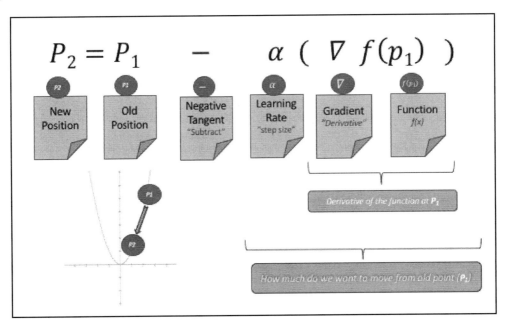

To understand the steps better, let's try to follow a step from the left-hand side of the preceding graph for a simple $f(x) = x^2$ function. In this case, we are on the left-hand side of the curve (the original guess was a negative number) and we are trying to climb down and increase X with each iteration in the direction of the gradient (the first derivative)

The following steps will walk you through the next figure to demonstrate the core concept and the steps in the recipe:

1. Calculate the derivative at the given point--the gradient.
2. Use the gradient from step 1 and scale it by step size--the amount of the move.

3. Find the new position by subtracting the amount of movement:
    - **Negative gradient case**: In the following figure, we subtract the negative gradient (effectively adding the gradient) to the original point so end up climbing down toward the minima of $f(x) = x^2$ at zero. The graph depicted in the figure matches this case.
    - **Positive gradient case**: If we were on the other side of the curve with the positive gradient, we then subtract the positive gradient number from the previous position (effectively subtracting the gradient) to climb down toward the minima. The code in this recipe matches this case, in which we are trying to start from a positive number 13 (the initial guess) and move toward the minima at 0 in an iterative fashion.

4. Update the parameters and move to the new point.
5. We keep repeating these steps untill we converge to a solution and, hence, minimize the function.

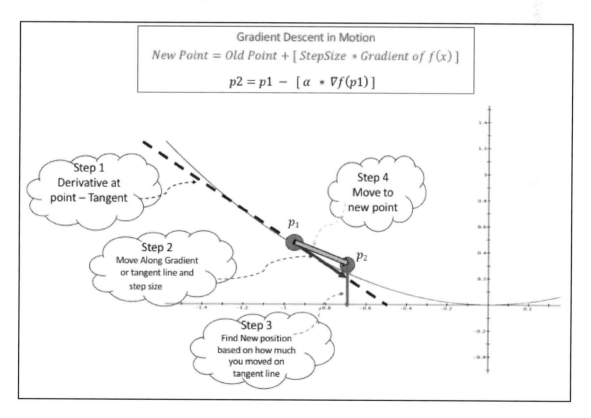

6. It is important to note that Gradient Descent (GD) and its variations use the first order derivative, which means that they are curvature ignorant, while the second order derivative algorithms such as Newton or quasi-Newton (BFGS, LBFGS) methods use both gradient and curvature with or without a Hessian matrix (a partial directives matrix with respect to each variable).

The alternative to GD would be to search the entire domain space for the optimal setting, which is neither practical, nor will it ever terminate in a practical sense, due to the size and scale of real-life big data ML problems.

There's more...

The step size or learning rate is very important to master when you first start with GD. If the step size is too small, it results in computational wastage and gives the appearance that the gradient descent is not converging to a solution. While setting the step size is trivial for demos and small projects, setting it to a wrong value can lead to a high computational loss on large ML projects. On the other hand, if the step size is too large, we end up with a ping-pong situation or moving away from convergences that usually shows up as a blown up error curve, meaning that the error increases rather than decreasing with each iteration.

In our experience, it is best to look at the error versus iteration chart and use the knee to pinpoint the right value. The alternative is to try .01, .001,......0001 and see how the convergence proceeds with each iteration (steps too small or too large). It is helpful to remember that the step size is just a scaling factor, since the actual gradient at the point might be too large for the movement (it will jump over the minimum).

To summarize:

- If the step size is too small, then you have slow convergence.
- If the step size is too large, you will end up skipping the minima (over-shooting), resulting in either slow computation or a ping-pong effect (getting stuck).

The following figure depicts variations based on different step sizes to demonstrate the points mentioned previously.

- **Scenario 1**: Step size = .01 - The step size is appropriate - just a bit too small but it gets the job done in around 200 iterations. We don't like to see anything under 200 because it must be general purpose enough to survive in real life.

- **Scenario 2**: Step size = .001 - The step size is too small and results in slow convergence. While it does not seem to be that bad (1,500+ iterations), it might be considered too fine grained.
- **Scenario 3**: Step size = .05 - The step size is too large. In this case, the algorithm gets stuck and keeps going back and forth without ever converging. It can't be emphasized enough that you must think of an exit policy in case this occurs in real life (the nature and distribution of data changes a lot, so be prepared).
- **Scenario 4**: Step size = .06 - The step size is too large resulting in non-convergence and blow up. The error curve blows up (it increases in a non-linear way) meaning that errors get larger with each iteration rather than getting smaller. In practice, we see more of this case (scenario 4) than the previous scenario, but both can happen so you should be ready for both. As you can see, a small .01 difference in step size between scenarios 3 and 4 made a difference in how the GD behaved. This is the same problem (optimization) that makes algorithmic trading difficult.

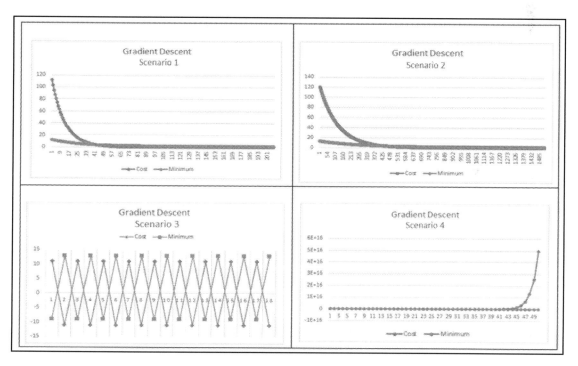

It is worth mentioning that, for this type of smooth convex optimization problem, the local minima are often the same as the global minima. You can think of local minima/maxima as extreme values within a given range. For the same function, the global minima/maxima refers to the global or the most absolute value in the entire range of the function.

See also

Stochastic Gradient Descent: There are multiple variations of Gradient Descent (GD), with Stochastic Gradient Descent (SGD) being the most talked about. Apache Spark supports the Stochastic Gradient Descent (SGD) variation, in which we update the parameters with a subset of training data - which is a bit challenging since we need to update the parameters simultaneously. There are two main differences between SGD and GD. The first difference is that SGD is an online learning/optimization technique while GD is more of an offline learning/optimization technique. The second difference between SGD versus GD is the speed of convergence due to not needing to examine the entire dataset before updating any parameter. This difference is depicted in the following figure:

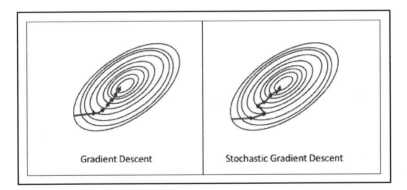

Gradient Descent   Stochastic Gradient Descent

We can set the batch-window size in Apache Spark to make the algorithm more responsive to massive datasets (there is no need to traverse the whole dataset at once). There will be some randomness associated with SGD, but overall it is the "de facto" method used these days. It is a lot faster and can converge much faster.

In both GD and SGD cases, you search for the best parameter for the model by updating the original parameters. The difference is that, in the core GD, you have to run through all your data points to do a single update for a parameter in a given iteration as opposed to SGD, in which you look at each single (or mini-batch) sample from the training dataset to update the parameters.

For a short general purpose write up, a good place to start is with the following:

- GD :https://en.wikipedia.org/wiki/Gradient_descent
- SGD:https://en.wikipedia.org/wiki/Stochastic_gradient_descent

A more mathematical treatment from CMU, Microsoft, and the Journal of Statistical software can be found at:

- CMU:
  https://www.cs.cmu.edu/~ggordon/10725-F12/slides/05-gd-revisited.pdf
- MS : http://cilvr.cs.nyu.edu/diglib/lsml/bottou-sgd-tricks-2012.pdf
- Jstat:https://arxiv.org/pdf/1509.06459v1.pdf

Coding Gradient Descent optimization to solve Linear Regression from scratch

In this recipe, we will explore how to code Gradient Descent to solve a Linear Regression problem. In the previous recipe, we demonstrated how to code GD to find the minimum of a quadratic function.

This recipe demonstrates a more realistic optimization problem in which we optimize (minimize) the least square cost function to solve the linear regression problem in Scala on Apache Spark 2.0+. We will use real data and run our algorithm and compare the result to a tier-1 commercially available statistic software to demonstrate accuracy and speed.

How to do it...

1. We start by downloading the file from Princeton University which contains the following data:

Discrimination in Salaries

These are the salary data used in Weisberg's book, consisting of observations on six variables for 52 tenure-track professors in a small college. The variables are:

- sx = Sex, coded 1 for female and 0 for male
- rk = Rank, coded
  - 1 for assistant professor,
  - 2 for associate professor, and
  - 3 for full professor
- yr = Number of years in current rank
- dg = Highest degree, coded 1 if doctorate, 0 if masters
- yd = Number of years since highest degree was earned
- sl = Academic year salary, in dollars.

Source: Princeton University

2. Download source: http://data.princeton.edu/wws509/datasets/#salary.

3. To keep things simple, we then select the yr and sl to study how the number of years in rank influences the salary. To cut down on data wrangling code, we save those two columns in a file (Year_Salary.csv), as depicted in the following table, to study their linear relationship:

Year	Salary
25.00	36350.00
13.00	35350.00
10.00	28200.00
7.00	26775.00
19.00	33696.00
....	....
....	....

4. We visually inspect the data by using a scatter plot from the IBM SPSS package. It cannot be emphasized enough that a visual inspection should be the first step in any data science project.

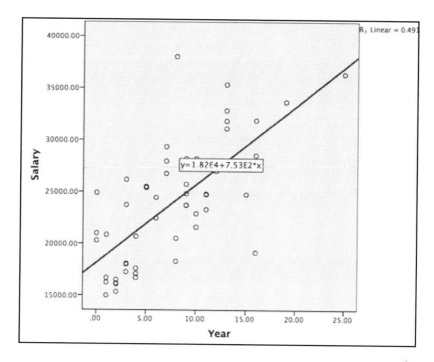

5. Start a new project in IntelliJ or in an IDE of your choice. Make sure the necessary JAR files are included.

6. We use the import package to place the code in the desired place:

```
package spark.ml.cookbook.chapter9.
```

The first four statements import the necessary packages for the JFree chart package so we can graph the GD error and convergence in the same code base. The fifth import takes care of ArrayBuffer, which we use to store intermediate results:

```
import java.awt.Color
import org.jfree.chart.plot.{XYPlot, PlotOrientation}
import org.jfree.chart.{ChartFactory, ChartFrame, JFreeChart}
import org.jfree.data.xy.{XYSeries, XYSeriesCollection}
import scala.collection.mutable.ArrayBuffer
```

7. Define the data structure to hold intermediate results as we minimize errors and converge to a solution for the slope (mStep) and intercept (bStep):

```
val gradientStepError = ArrayBuffer[(Int, Double)]()
val bStep = ArrayBuffer[(Int, Double)]()
val mStep = ArrayBuffer[(Int, Double)]()
```

8. Define the functions for graphing via the JFree chart. The first one just displays the chart and the second one sets the chart properties. This is a boiler-plate code that you can customize based on your preference:

```
def show(chart: JFreeChart) {
val frame = new ChartFrame("plot", chart)
frame.pack()
frame.setVisible(true)
}
def configurePlot(plot: XYPlot): Unit = {
plot.setBackgroundPaint(Color.WHITE)
plot.setDomainGridlinePaint(Color.BLACK)
plot.setRangeGridlinePaint(Color.BLACK)
plot.setOutlineVisible(false)
}
```

8. This function computes the error based on the least square principle which we minimize to find the best fitting solution. The function finds the difference between what we predict and what the actual value (the salary) is available via the training data. After finding the difference, it squares them to compute the total error. The pow() function is a Scala math function to compute the square.

$$\text{Find } \min_{\alpha, \beta} Q(\alpha, \beta), \quad \text{for } Q(\alpha, \beta) = \sum_{i=1}^{n} \varepsilon_i^2 = \sum_{i=1}^{n} (y_i - \alpha - \beta x_i)^2$$

Source: Wikipedia

```
Beta : Slope (m variable)
Alpha : Intercept b variable)
```

```
def compute_error_for_line_given_points(b:Double, m:Double, points:
Array[Array[Double]]):Double = {
var totalError = 0.0
for( point <- points ) {
var x = point(0)
var y = point(1)
totalError += math.pow(y - (m * x + b), 2)
```

```
}
return totalError / points.length
}
```

9. The next function computes two gradients (the first derivative) of the $f(x)= b + mx$ and averages them over the domain (all points). It is the same process as in the second recipe, except that we need partial derivatives (gradient) because we are minimizing two parameters m and b (slope and intercept) and not just one.

> In the last two lines, we scale the gradient by multiplying it by the learning rate (step size). The reason we do that is to make sure we don't end up with large step sizes and overshoot the minimum, resulting in either a ping-pong scenario or error blow up, as discussed in the previous recipe.

```
def step_gradient(b_current:Double, m_current:Double,
points:Array[Array[Double]], learningRate:Double): Array[Double]= {
var b_gradient= 0.0
var m_gradient= 0.0
var N = points.length.toDouble
for (point <- points) {
var x = point(0)
var y = point(1)
b_gradient += -(2 / N) * (y - ((m_current * x) + b_current))
m_gradient += -(2 / N) * x * (y - ((m_current * x) + b_current))
}
var result = new Array[Double](2)
result(0) = b_current - (learningRate * b_gradient)
result(1) = m_current - (learningRate * m_gradient)
return result
}
```

10. This function reads and parses the CSV file:

```
def readCSV(inputFile: String) : Array[Array[Double]] =
{scala.io.Source.fromFile(inputFile)
.getLines()
.map(_.split(",").map(_.trim.toDouble))
.toArray
}
```

11. The following is a wrapper function that loops for N number of iterations and calls on the `step_gradient()` function to compute the gradient at a given point. We then proceed to store the results from every step one by one for processing later (for example, graphing).

> Noteworthy is the use of `Tuple2()` to hold the return value from the `step_gradient()` function.

> In the last steps of the function we call on the `compute_error_for_line_given_points()` function to compute the error for a given combination of the slope and intercept and store it in `gradientStepError`.

```
def gradient_descent_runner(points:Array[Array[Double]],
starting_b:Double, starting_m:Double, learning_rate:Double,
num_iterations:Int):Array[Double]= {
var b = starting_b
var m = starting_m
var result = new Array[Double](2)
var error = 0.0
result(0) =b
result(1) =m
for (i <-0 to num_iterations) {
result = step_gradient(result(0), result(1), points, learning_rate)
bStep += Tuple2(i, result(0))
mStep += Tuple2(i, result(1))
error = compute_error_for_line_given_points(result(0), result(1),
points)
gradientStepError += Tuple2(i, error)
}
```

12. The last and final step is the main program, which sets up the initial starting point for the slope, intercept, number of iterations, and learning rate. We purposely choose a smaller learning rate and larger number of iterations to demonstrate accuracy and speed.
    1. First, we start by the initialization of the key controlling variables for GD (learning rate, number of iterations, and starting point).
    2. Second, we proceed to show the starting point (0,0) and call on `compute_error_for_line_given_points()` to show the starting error. It should be noted that the error should be lower after we are done running through the GD and display the result in the final step.

3. Third, we set up necessary calls and structures for the JFree chart to display two charts that depict the slope, intercept, and error behavior as we merge toward an optimized solution (the best combination of the slope and intercept to minimize the error).

```scala
def main(args: Array[String]): Unit = {
val input = "../data/sparkml2/chapter9/Year_Salary.csv"
val points = readCSV(input)
val learning_rate = 0.001
val initial_b = 0
val initial_m = 0
val num_iterations = 30000
println(s"Starting gradient descent at b = $initial_b, m
=$initial_m, error = "+
compute_error_for_line_given_points(initial_b, initial_m,
points))
println("Running...")
val result= gradient_descent_runner(points, initial_b,
initial_m, learning_rate, num_iterations)
var b= result(0)
var m = result(1)
println( s"After $num_iterations iterations b = $b, m = $m,
error = "+ compute_error_for_line_given_points(b, m,
points))
val xy = new XYSeries("")
gradientStepError.foreach{ case (x: Int,y: Double) =>
xy.add(x,y) }
val dataset = new XYSeriesCollection(xy)
val chart = ChartFactory.createXYLineChart(
"Gradient Descent", // chart title
"Iteration", // x axis label
"Error", // y axis label
dataset, // data
PlotOrientation.VERTICAL,
false, // include legend
true, // tooltips
false // urls)
val plot = chart.getXYPlot()
configurePlot(plot)
show(chart)
val bxy = new XYSeries("b")
bStep.foreach{ case (x: Int,y: Double) => bxy.add(x,y) }
val mxy = new XYSeries("m")
mStep.foreach{ case (x: Int,y: Double) => mxy.add(x,y) }
val stepDataset = new XYSeriesCollection()
stepDataset.addSeries(bxy)
stepDataset.addSeries(mxy)
```

```
val stepChart = ChartFactory.createXYLineChart(
"Gradient Descent Steps", // chart title
"Iteration", // x axis label
"Steps", // y axis label
stepDataset, // data
PlotOrientation.VERTICAL,
true, // include legend
true, // tooltips
false // urls
)
val stepPlot = stepChart.getXYPlot()
configurePlot(stepPlot)
show(stepChart)
}
```

13. The following is the output for this recipe.

First we display the starting point of 0,0 with the error of 6.006 and then allow the algorithm to run and display the result after completing the number of iterations:

```
C:\Java\jdk1.8.0_101\bin\java ...
Starting gradient descent at b = 0, m =0, error = 6.006692873846154E8
Running...
After 30000 iterations b = 18166.147526619356, m = 752.7977590699244, error = 1.748171059198056E7

Process finished with exit code 0
```

Noteworthy is the starting and ending error number and how it reduced over time due to optimization.

14. We used IBM SPSS as a control point to show that the GD algorithm that we put together matches the result (almost 1:1) produced by the SPSS package - it is almost exact!

The following figure shows the output from IBM SPSS for comparing the results:

		Coefficients[a]				
		Unstandardized Coefficients		Standardized Coefficients		
Model		B	Std. Error	Beta	t	Sig.
1	(Constant)	18166.148	1003.658		18.100	.000
	Year	752.798	108.409	.701	6.944	.000
a. Dependent Variable: Salary						

15. In the last step, two charts are produced by the program side by side.

The following figure shows how slope *(m)* and intercept *(b)* converge toward the best combination that minimizes the error as we run through the iterations:

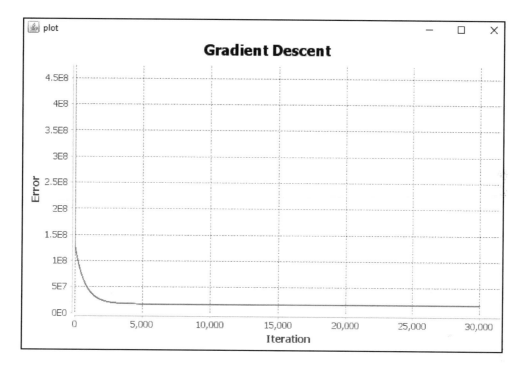

The following figure shows how slope (*m*) and intercept (*b*) converge toward the best combination that minimizes the error as we run through the iterations.

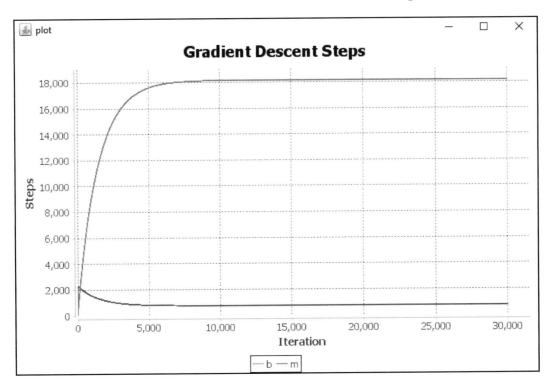

How it works...

Gradient Descent is an iterative numerical method that starts from an initial guess and then asks itself how badly am I doing by looking at an error function that is the squared distance of predicted versus actual data in the training file.

In this program, we selected a simple linear line $f(x) = b + mx$ equation as our model. To optimize and come up with the best combination of slope m, intercept b for our model, we had 52 actual pairs of data (age, salary) that we can plug into our linear model (*Predicted Salary = Slope x Age + Intercept*). In short, we wanted to find the best combination of the slope and intercept that helped us fit a linear line that minimizes the squared distance. The squared function gives us all positive values and lets us concentrate on the magnitude of the error only.

- `ReadCSV()`: Reads and parses the data file in to our datasets:

$$(x_1, y_1), (x_2, y_2), (x_3, y_4), \dots (x_{52}, y_{52})$$

- `Compute_error_for_line_given_points()`: This function implements the cost or error function. We use a linear model (equation of a line) to predict, and then measure, the squared distance from the actual number. After adding up the errors, we average and return the total error:

$$y = mx + b$$

$y_i = mx_i + b$: for all data pair (x, y)

$$\sum_{p=1}^{P} \left(b + x_p w - y_p \right)^2$$

Noteworthy code within the function: the first line of code calculates the squared distance between predicted ($m * x + b$) and the actual (y). The second line of code averages it and returns it:

$$\frac{1}{N} \sum_{i=1}^{N} \left(y_i - \left(mx_i + b \right) \right)^2$$

*totalError += math.pow(y - (m * x + b), 2)*

....

return totalError / points.length

The following figure shows the basic concept of least squares. In short, we take the distance between what the actual training data was for a point versus what our model predicts, and square them and then add them up. The reason we square them is to avoid using the absolute value function `abs()` which is not computationally desirable. The squared difference has better mathematical properties by providing a continuously differentiable property which is preferred when you want to minimize it.

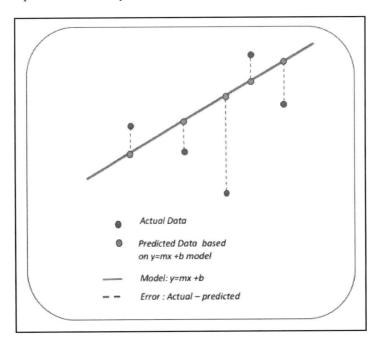

- `step_gradient()`: This function is where the gradient (the first derivative) is calculated using the current point we are iterating over (x_i, y_i). It should be noted that, unlike the previous recipe, we have two parameters so we need to calculate partial derivatives for the intercept (`b_gradient`) and then the slope (`m_gradient`). We then need to divide by the number of points to average.

$$\frac{\partial}{\partial m} = \frac{2}{N} \sum_{i=1}^{N} - x_i (y_i - (mx_i + b))$$

$$\frac{\partial}{\partial b} = \frac{2}{N} \sum_{i=1}^{N} - (y_i - (mx_i + b))$$

- Using a partial derivative with respect to Intercept(*b*):

$$b\_gradient \mathrel{+}= -(2/N) * (y - ((m\_current * x) + b\_current))$$

- Using a partial derivative with respect to Slope(*m*):

$$m\_gradient \mathrel{+}= -(2/N) * x * (y - ((m\_current * x) + b\_current))$$

- The last step is to scale the calculated gradient by the learning-rate (step size) and then move to a newly estimated position for the slope (m_current) and intercept (b_current):

$$result(0) = b\_current - (learningRate * b\_gradient)$$

$$result(1) = m\_current - (learningRate * m\_gradient)$$

- `gradient_descent_runner()`: This is the driver that executes the `step_gradient()` and `compute_error_for_line_given_points()` for the number of iterations defined:

```
r (i <-0 to num_iterations) {
step_gradient()
...
compute_error_for_line_given_points()
...
}
```

There's more...

While this recipe was able to handle real-life data and match the estimation from a commercial package, in practice you need to implement Stochastic Gradient Descent.

Spark 2.0 offers Stochastic Gradient Descent (SGD) with a mini-batch window (for efficiency control).

Spark provides two approaches toward utilizing SGD. The first alternative is to use a standalone optimization technique in which you pass in your optimization function. See the following links: https://spark.apache.org/docs/latest/api/scala/index.html#org.apache.spark.mllib.optimization.Optimizer and https://spark.apache.org/docs/latest/api/scala/index.html#org.apache.spark.mllib.optimization.GradientDescent

The second alternative would be to use specialized APIs that have SGD built-in already as their optimization technique:

- `LogisticRegressionWithSGD()`
- `StreamingLogisticRegressionWithSGD()`
- `LassoWithSGD()`
- `LinearRegressionWithSGD()`
- `RidgeRegressionWithSGD()`
- `SVMWithSGD()`

As of Spark 2.0, all RDD-based regression is in maintenance mode only.

See also

- Optimization with Spark
  2.0: `https://spark.apache.org/docs/latest/mllib-optimization.html#stochastic-gradient-descent-sgd`

Normal equations as an alternative for solving Linear Regression in Spark 2.0

In this recipe, we present an alternative to Gradient Descent (GD) and LBFGS by using Normal Equations to solve linear regression. In the case of normal equations, you are setting up your regression as a matrix of features and vector of labels (dependent variables) while trying to solve it by using matrix operations such as inverse, transpose, and so on.

The emphasis here is to highlight Spark's facility for using Normal Equations to solve Linear Regression and not the details of the model or generated coefficients.

How to do it...

1. We use the same housing dataset which we extensively covered in Chapter 5, *Practical Machine Learning with Regression and Classification in Spark 2.0 - Part I* and Chapter 6, *Practical Machine Learning with Regression and Classification in Spark 2.0 - Part II*, which relate various attributes (for example number of rooms, and so on) to the price of the house.

   The data is available as housing8.csv under the Chapter 9 data directory.

2. We use the package directive to take care of the placement:

   ```
   package spark.ml.cookbook.chapter9
   ```

3. We then import the necessary libraries:

   ```
   import org.apache.spark.ml.feature.LabeledPoint
   import org.apache.spark.ml.linalg.Vectors
   import org.apache.spark.ml.regression.LinearRegression
   import org.apache.spark.sql.SparkSession
   import org.apache.log4j.{Level, Logger}
   import spark.implicits._
   ```

4. Reduce the extra output generated by Spark by setting the Logger information level to Level.ERROR:

   ```
   Logger.getLogger("org").setLevel(Level.ERROR)
   Logger.getLogger("akka").setLevel(Level.ERROR)
   ```

5. Set up SparkSession with the appropriate attributes:

   ```
   val spark = SparkSession
   .builder
   .master("local[*]")
   .appName("myRegressNormal")
   .config("spark.sql.warehouse.dir", ".")
   .getOrCreate()
   ```

6. Read the input file and parse it into a dataset:

   ```
   val data =
   spark.read.text("../data/sparkml2/housing8.csv").as[String]
   val RegressionDataSet = data.map { line => val columns =
   line.split(',')
   LabeledPoint(columns(13).toDouble ,
   Vectors.dense(columns(0).toDouble,columns(1).toDouble,
   ```

```
columns(2).toDouble, columns(3).toDouble, columns(4).toDouble,
columns(5).toDouble, columns(6).toDouble, columns(7).toDouble
))
}
```

7. Display the following dataset contents, but limit them to first three rows for inspection:

```
+-----+----------------------------------------------------+
| label|              features                            |
+-----+----------------------------------------------------+
|24.0 |[0.00632,18.0,2.31,0.0,0.538,6.575,65.2,4.09]  |
|21.6 |[0.02731,0.0,7.07,0.0,0.469,6.421,78.9,4.9671] |
|34.7 |[0.02729,0.0,7.07,0.0,0.469,7.185,61.1,4.9671] |
........
........
```

8. We create a LinearRegression object and set the number of iterations, ElasticNet, and Regularization parameters. The last step is to set the right solver methods by choosing setSolver("normal"):

```
val lr = new LinearRegression()
  .setMaxIter(1000)
  .setElasticNetParam(0.0)
  .setRegParam(0.01)
  .setSolver("normal")
```

Please be sure to set the ElasticNet parameter to 0.0 for the "normal" solver to work.

9. Fit the LinearRegressionModel to the data using:

```
val myModel = lr.fit(RegressionDataSet)
Extract the model summary:
val summary = myModel.summary
```

The following output is generated when you run the program:

```
training Mean Squared Error = 13.609079490110766
training Root Mean Squared Error = 3.6890485887435482
```

Readers can output more information, but the model summary was covered in Chapter 5, *Practical Machine Learning with Regression and Classification in Spark 2.0 - Part I* and Chapter 6, *Practical Machine Learning with Regression and Classification in Spark 2.0 - Part II* via other techniques.

How it works...

We are ultimately trying to solve the following equation for linear regression using the closed form formula:

$$b = (X'X)^{-1}(X')Y$$

Spark provides an out-of-the box fully parallel method for solving this equation by allowing you to set the setSolver("normal").

There's more...

If you fail to set the ElasticNet parameter to 0.0, you will get an error because L2 regularization is used when solving through normal equations in Spark (as of this writing).

Documentation for Spark 2.0 related to isotonic regression can be found at: http://spark.apache.org/docs/latest/api/scala/index.html#org.apache.spark.ml.regression.LinearRegression and http://spark.apache.org/docs/latest/api/scala/index.html#org.apache.spark.ml.regression.LinearRegressionModel

The model summary can be found at: http://spark.apache.org/docs/latest/api/scala/index.html#org.apache.spark.ml.regression.LinearRegressionSummary

See also

Also refer to the following table:

Iterative methods (SGD, LBFGS)	Closed form Normal Equation
Choosing learning Rate	No parameter
Iterations can be large	Does not iterate
Good performance on large feature sets	Slow and impractical on large feature sets
Error prone: getting stuck due to poor parameter selection	$(x^Tx)^{-1}$ is computationally expensive - in the order of n^3

Here is a quick reference on configuration of the LinearRegression object, but be sure to see Chapter 5, *Practical Machine Learning with Regression and Classification in Spark 2.0 - Part I* and Chapter 6, *Practical Machine Learning with Regression and Classification in Spark 2.0 - Part II* for more details.

- L1: Lasso regression
- L2: Ridge regression
- L1 - L2: Elastic net in which you can adjust the dial

The following link is a write-up from Columbia University that explains normal equations as they relate to solving Linear Regression problems:

- http://www.stat.columbia.edu/~fwood/Teaching/w4315/Fall2009/lecture_11

- Octave (https://www.gnu.org/software/octave/) from GNU is a popular matrix manipulation software and you should have it in your toolkit.

- The following link contains a quick tutorial to get you started: http://www.lauradhamilton.com/tutorial-linear-regression-with-octave

10
Building Machine Learning Systems with Decision Tree and Ensemble Models

In this chapter, we will cover:

- Getting and preparing real-world medical data for exploring Decision Trees and Ensemble models in Spark 2.0
- Building a classification system with Decision Trees in Spark 2.0
- Solving regression problems with Decision Trees in Spark 2.0
- Building a classification system with Random Forest Trees in Spark 2.0
- Solving regression problems with Random Forest Trees in Spark 2.0
- Building a classification system with Gradient Boosted Trees (GBT) in Spark 2.0
- Solving regression problems with Gradient Boosted Trees (GBT) in Spark 2.0

Introduction

Decision trees are one of the oldest and more widely used methods of machine learning in commerce. What makes them popular is not only their ability to deal with more complex partitioning and segmentation (they are more flexible than linear models) but also their ability to explain how we arrived at a solution and as to "why" the outcome is predicated or classified as a class/label.

Apache Spark provides a good mix of decision tree based algorithms fully capable of taking advantage of parallelism in Spark. The implementation ranges from the straight forward Single Decision Tree (the CART type algorithm) to Ensemble Trees, such as Random Forest Trees and **GBT** (**Gradient Boosted Tree**). They all have both the variant flavors to facilitate classification (for example, categorical, such as height = short/tall) or regression (for example, continuous, such as height = 2.5 meters).

The following figure depicts a mind map that shows Spark ML library coverage of decision tree algorithms, as at the time of writing:

A quick way to think about the decision tree algorithm is as a smart partitioning algorithm that tries to minimize a loss function (for example, L2 or least square) as it partitions the ranges to come up with a segmented space which are best fitted decision boundaries to the data. The algorithm gets more sophisticated through the application of sampling the data and trying a combination of features to assemble a more complex ensemble model in which each learner (partial sample or feature combination) gets to vote toward the final outcome.

The following figure depicts a simplified version in which a simple binary tree (stumping) is trained to classify the data into segments belonging to two different colors (for example, healthy patient/sick patient). The figure depicts a simple algorithm that just breaks the x/y feature space to one-half every time it establishes a decision boundary (hence classifying) while minimizing the number of errors (for example, a L2 least square measure):

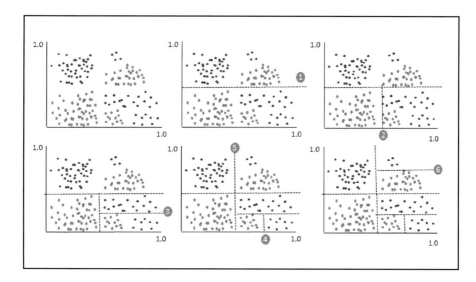

The following figure provides a corresponding tree so we can visualize the algorithm (in this case, a simple divide and conquer) against the proposed segmentation space. What makes decision tree algorithms popular is their ability to show their classification result in a language that can easily be communicated to a business user without much math:

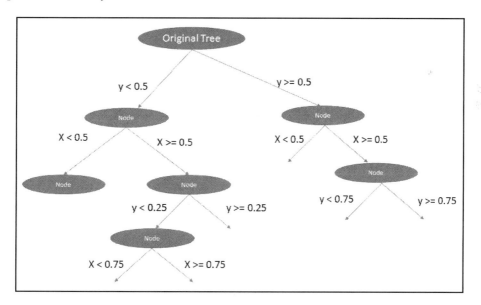

A decision tree in Spark is a parallel algorithm designed to fit and grow a single tree into a dataset that can be categorical (classification) or continuous (regression). It is a greedy algorithm based on stumping (binary split, and so on) that partitions the solution space recursively while attempting to select the best split among all possible splits using Information Gain Maximization (entropy based).

Ensemble models

The other way to look at Spark's offering for decision trees is to think of the algorithm as belonging to two camps. The first camp, which we saw earlier in the introduction, concerns itself with single trees that attempt to find various techniques to find the best single tree for the dataset. While this is OK for a lot of datasets, the greedy nature of the algorithm can lead to unintended consequences, such as overfitting and going too deep to be able to capture all the boundaries within the training data (that is, it is over optimized).

To overcome the overfitting problem and to increase accuracy and the quality of predictions, Spark has implemented two classes of ensemble decision tree models that attempt to create many imperfect learners that either see a subset of data (sampling with or without substitution) and/or a subset of features. While each individual tree is less accurate, the collection of the trees' assembled votes (or the average probability in the case of continuous variables) and the resultant averaging is much more accurate than any individual tree:

- **Random Forest**: This method creates many trees in parallel and then votes/averages the outcome to minimize the overfitting problem prone in single tree algorithms. They are capable of capturing non-linearity and feature interaction without any scaling. They should be seriously considered at least as one of the first toolsets used to dissect the data and understand its makeup. The following figure provides a visual guideline for this implementation in Spark:

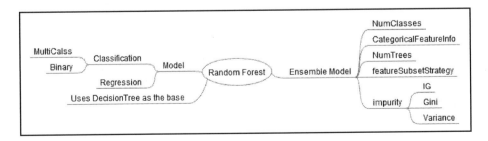

- **Gradient Boosted Trees**: This method is another ensemble model in which an average of many trees (even though they are less perfect) improves the accuracy and quality of the prediction. They differ from Random Forest in that they build one tree at a time and each tree tries to learn from the shortcomings of the previous tree by minimizing the loss function. They are similar to the concept of gradient descent, but they use the minimization (similar to gradient) to select and improve the next tree (they walk in the direction of the tree which creates the best accuracy).

The three options for the loss function are:

- **Log loss**: Negative likelihood for classification
- **L2**: Least square for regression
- **L1**: Absolute error for regression

The following figure provides an easy-to-use visualization reference:

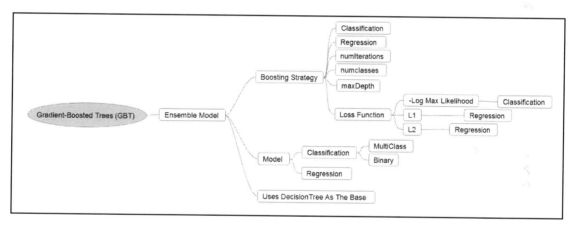

The main packages for Decision Trees in Spark are in ML and are as follows:

```
org.apache.spark.mllib.tree
org.apache.spark.mllib.tree.configuration
org.apache.spark.mllib.tree.impurity
org.apache.spark.mllib.tree.model
```

Measures of impurity

With all machine learning algorithms, we are trying to minimize a set of cost functions which help us to select the best move. Spark uses three possible selections for maximization functions. The following figure depicts the alternatives:

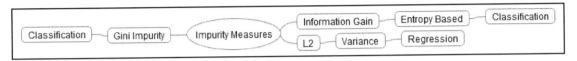

In this section, we will discuss each of the three possible alternatives:

- **Information gain**: Loosely speaking, this measures the level of impurity in a group based on the concept of entropy--see the Shannon information theory and then as later suggested by Quinlan in his ID3 algorithm.

The calculation of entropy is shown in the following equation:

$$\text{Entropy} = \sum_i - p_i \log_2 p_i$$

Information gain helps us to select an attribute in each feature vector space that can best help to separate the classes from each other. We use this attribute to decide how to order the attributes (thus, affecting the decision boundaries) in the nodes of a given tree.

The following figure depicts the calculation visually for easy understanding. In the first step, we want to select an attribute so that we maximize the IG (information gain) in the root or parent node, then build our child nodes for each value of the selected attribute (their associated vectors). We keep repeating the algorithm recursively untill we can no longer see any gains:

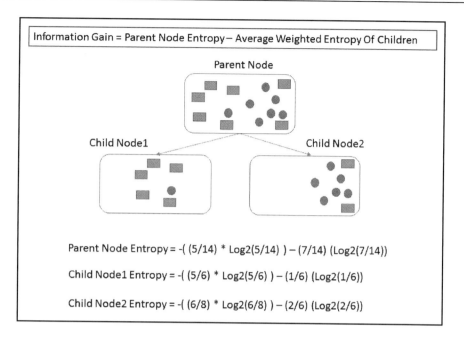

Information Gain = Parent Node Entropy – Average Weighted Entropy Of Children

Parent Node

Child Node1   Child Node2

Parent Node Entropy = -((5/14) * Log2(5/14)) – (7/14) (Log2(7/14))

Child Node1 Entropy = -((5/6) * Log2(5/6)) – (1/6) (Log2(1/6))

Child Node2 Entropy = -((6/8) * Log2(6/8)) – (2/6) (Log2(2/6))

- **Gini Index:** This attempts to improve the IG (information gain) by isolating the classes so that the largest class is separated from the population. The Gini Index is a bit different to entropy, in that you try to have a 50/50 split and then apply further splits to infer the solution. It is meant to reflect the effect of one variable and it does not extend its reach to multi-attribute states. It uses a simple frequency count against the population. Use Gini for higher-dimensional and more noisy data.

  Use Gini Impurity where you have complex multi-dimensional data and you are trying to dissect a simple signal from the set.

On the other hand, use information gain (or any entropy-based system) where you have a cleaner and low dimensional dataset, but you are looking for a more complex (in terms of accuracy and quality) dataset:

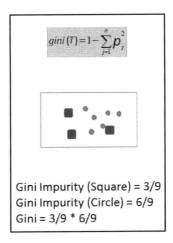

$$gini\,(T) = 1 - \sum_{j=1}^{n} p_j^2$$

Gini Impurity (Square) = 3/9
Gini Impurity (Circle) = 6/9
Gini = 3/9 * 6/9

- **Variance**: The variance is used to signal the regression model for the tree algorithm. In short, we still try to minimize an L2 function, but the difference is that here we seek to minimize the distance-squared of the observation and mean of the node (segment) being considered.

The following figure depicts a simplified version for visualization:

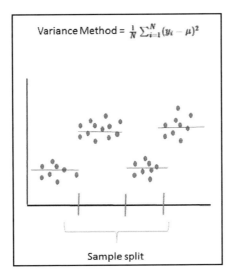

Variance Method = $\frac{1}{N} \sum_{i=1}^{N} (y_i - \mu)^2$

Sample split

The Spark Model Evaluation Tools for evaluation classification and regression with tree models are as listed here:

The confusion matrix is a table that is used to describe the performance of a classification model, out of the test dataset that the true values are known. The confusion matrix itself is relatively simple; it is a 2 x 2 matrix:

		Prediction	Value
		Yes	No
Actual	Yes	True Positive (TP)	False Negative (FN)
Value	No	False Positive (FP)	True Negative (TN)

For our cancer dataset:

- **True Positives (TP):** Those are cases we predicted yes, and they did have breast cancer
- **True Negative (TN):** Those are cases we predicted no, and they didn't have breast cancer
- **False Positives (FP):** We predicted yes, but they didn't have breast cancer
- **False Negatives (FN):** We predicted no, but they did have breast cancer

A good classification system should match the reality closely with good TP and TN values, while having fewer FP and FN values.

Overall, the following terms are also used as markers for a classification model:

1. **Accuracy**: The correctness ratio of the model:
    - *(TP + TN)/Total*

2. **Error**: Overall, the percentage that the model is wrong:
    - *(FP+FN)/Total*
    - Also equals to 1 - Accuracy

In the Spark Machine Learning Library, there is a utility class to handle the calculation for the aforementioned common matrix:

```
org.apache.spark.mllib.evaluation.MulticlassMetrics
```

We will use the utility class in the following sample code.

Similarly, for the regression algorithm, **Mean Squared Error (MSE),** or average of the squares of the errors, is well utilized as a key parameter for the measurement of a model. In the Spark Machine Learning Library, there is also a utility class for it and it will provide the key indicator of a regression model:

```
org.apache.spark.mllib.evaluation.RegressionMetrics
```

Documentation for the Spark Matrix Evaluator can be found

at `http://spark.apache.org/docs/latest/api/scala/index.html#org.apache.spark.mllib.evaluation.MulticlassMetrics`

and `http://spark.apache.org/docs/latest/api/scala/index.html#org.apache.spark.mllib.evaluation.RegressionMetrics`.

Getting and preparing real-world medical data for exploring Decision Trees and Ensemble models in Spark 2.0

The dataset used depicts a real-life application of Decision Trees in machine learning. We used a cancer dataset to predict what makes a patient's case malignant or not. To explore the real power of decision trees, we use a medical dataset that exhibits real life non-linearity with a complex error surface.

How to do it...

The **Wisconsin Breast Cancer** dataset was obtained from the University of Wisconsin Hospital from Dr. William H Wolberg. The dataset was gained periodically as Dr. Wolberg reported his clinical cases.

The dataset can be retrieved from multiple sources, and is available directly from the University of California Irvine's web

server `http://archive.ics.uci.edu/ml/machine-learning-databases/breast-cancer-wisconsin/breast-cancer-wisconsin.data`

The data is also available from the University of Wisconsin's web

server `ftp://ftp.cs.wisc.edu/math-prog/cpo-dataset/machine-learn/cancer/cancer1/datacum`

The dataset currently contains clinical cases from 1989 to 1991. It has 699 instances, with 458 classified as benign tumors and 241 as malignant cases. Each instance is described by nine attributes with an integer value in the range of 1 to 10 and a binary class label. Out of the 699 instances, there are 16 instances that are missing some attributes.

We will remove these 16 instances from the memory and process the rest (in total, 683 instances) for the model calculations.

The sample raw data looks like the following:

```
1000025,5,1,1,1,2,1,3,1,1,2
1002945,5,4,4,5,7,10,3,2,1,2
1015425,3,1,1,1,2,2,3,1,1,2
1016277,6,8,8,1,3,4,3,7,1,2
1017023,4,1,1,3,2,1,3,1,1,2
1017122,8,10,10,8,7,10,9,7,1,4
...
```

The attribute information is as follows:

#	Attribute	Domain
1	Sample code number	ID number
2	Clump Thickness	1 - 10
3	Uniformity of Cell Size	1 - 10
4	Uniformity of Cell Shape	1 - 10
5	Marginal Adhesion	1 - 10
6	Single Epithelial Cell Size	1 - 10
7	Bare Nuclei	1 - 10
8	Bland Chromatin	1 - 10
9	Normal Nucleoli	1 - 10
10	Mitoses	1 - 10
11	Class	(2 for benign, 4 for Malignant)

If presented in the correct columns, it will look like the following:

ID Number	Clump Thickness	Uniformity of Cell Size	Uniformity of Cell Shape	Marginal Adhesion	Single Epithelial Cell Size	Bare Nucleoli	Bland Chromatin	Normal Nucleoli	Mitoses	Class
1000025	5	1	1	1	2	1	3	1	1	2
1002945	5	4	4	5	7	10	3	2	1	2
1015425	3	1	1	1	2	2	3	1	1	2
1016277	6	8	8	1	3	4	3	7	1	2
1017023	4	1	1	3	2	1	3	1	1	2
1017122	8	10	10	8	7	10	9	7	1	4
1018099	1	1	1	1	2	10	3	1	1	2
1018561	2	1	2	1	2	1	3	1	1	2
1033078	2	1	1	1	2	1	1	1	5	2
1033078	4	2	1	1	2	1	2	1	1	2
1035283	1	1	1	1	1	1	3	1	1	2
1036172	2	1	1	1	2	1	2	1	1	2
1041801	5	3	3	3	2	3	4	4	1	4
1043999	1	1	1	1	2	3	3	1	1	2
1044572	8	7	5	10	7	9	5	5	4	4
...	...	...	...	...	...	...	...	...	...	...

There's more...

The Wisconsin Breast Cancer dataset is widely used in the machine learning community. The dataset contains limited attributes and most of them are discrete numbers. It's very easy to apply a classification algorithm and regression model to the dataset.

More than 20 research papers and publications already cite this dataset, and it is available publicly and very easy to use.

The dataset has the multivariate datatype, where attributes are integers, and the number of attributes are only 10. This makes it one of the typical datasets for classification and regression analysis for this chapter.

Building a classification system with Decision Trees in Spark 2.0

In this recipe, we will use the breast cancer data and use classifications to demonstrate the Decision Tree implantation in Spark. We will use the IG and Gini to show how to use the facilities already provided by Spark to avoid redundant coding. This recipe attempts to fit a single tree using a binary classification to train and predict the label (benign (0.0) and malignant (1.0)) for the dataset.

How to do it

1. Start a new project in IntelliJ or in an IDE of your choice. Make sure the necessary JAR files are included.

2. Set up the package location where the program will reside:

```
package spark.ml.cookbook.chapter10
```

3. Import the necessary packages for the Spark context to get access to the cluster and `Log4j.Logger` to reduce the amount of output produced by Spark:

```
import org.apache.spark.mllib.evaluation.MulticlassMetrics
import org.apache.spark.mllib.tree.DecisionTree
import org.apache.spark.mllib.linalg.Vectors
import org.apache.spark.mllib.regression.LabeledPoint
import org.apache.spark.mllib.tree.model.DecisionTreeModel
import org.apache.spark.rdd.RDD
import org.apache.spark.sql.SparkSession
import org.apache.log4j.{Level, Logger}
```

4. Create Spark's configuration and the Spark session so we can have access to the cluster:

```
Logger.getLogger("org").setLevel(Level.ERROR)

val spark = SparkSession
.builder
.master("local[*]")
.appName("MyDecisionTreeClassification")
.config("spark.sql.warehouse.dir", ".")
.getOrCreate()
```

5. We read in the original raw data file:

```
val rawData =
spark.sparkContext.textFile("../data/sparkml2/chapter10/breast-
cancer-wisconsin.data")
```

6. We pre-process the dataset:

```
val data = rawData.map(_.trim)
 .filter(text => !(text.isEmpty || text.startsWith("#") ||
text.indexOf("?") > -1))
 .map { line =>
val values = line.split(',').map(_.toDouble)
val slicedValues = values.slice(1, values.size)
val featureVector = Vectors.dense(slicedValues.init)
val label = values.last / 2 -1
LabeledPoint(label, featureVector)
 }
```

First, we trim the line and remove any empty spaces. Once the line is ready for the next step, we remove the line if it's empty, or if it contains missing values ("?"). After this step, the 16 rows with missing data will be removed from the dataset in the memory.

We then read the comma separated values into RDD. Since the first column in the dataset only contains the instance's ID number, it is better to remove this column from the real calculation. We slice it out with the following command, which will remove the first column from the RDD:

```
val slicedValues = values.slice(1, values.size)
```

We then put the rest of the numbers into a dense vector.

Since the Wisconsin Breast Cancer dataset's classifier is either benign cases (last column value = 2) or malignant cases (last column value = 4), we convert the preceding value using the following command:

```
val label = values.last / 2 -1
```

So the benign case 2 is converted to 0, and the malignant case value 4 is converted to 1, which will make the later calculations much easier. We then put the preceding row into a Labeled Points:

```
Raw data: 1000025,5,1,1,1,2,1,3,1,1,2
Processed Data: 5,1,1,1,2,1,3,1,1,0
Labeled Points: (0.0, [5.0,1.0,1.0,1.0,2.0,1.0,3.0,1.0,1.0])
```

7. We verify the raw data count and process the data count:

```
println(rawData.count())
println(data.count())
```

And you will see the following on the console:

```
699
683
```

8. We split the whole dataset into training data (70%) and test data (30%) randomly. Please note that the random split will generate around 211 test datasets. It is approximately but NOT exactly 30% of the dataset:

```
val splits = data.randomSplit(Array(0.7, 0.3))
val (trainingData, testData) = (splits(0), splits(1))
```

9. We define a metrics calculation function, which utilizes the Spark MulticlassMetrics:

```
def getMetrics(model: DecisionTreeModel, data: RDD[LabeledPoint]):
MulticlassMetrics = {
val predictionsAndLabels = data.map(example =>
(model.predict(example.features), example.label)
)
new MulticlassMetrics(predictionsAndLabels)
}
```

This function will read in the model and test dataset, and create a metric which contains the confusion matrix mentioned earlier. It will contain the model accuracy, which is one of the indicators for the classification model.

10. We define an evaluate function, which can take some tunable parameters for the Decision Tree model, and do the training for the dataset:

```
def evaluate(
trainingData: RDD[LabeledPoint],
testData: RDD[LabeledPoint],
numClasses: Int,
categoricalFeaturesInfo: Map[Int,Int],

impurity: String,
maxDepth: Int,
maxBins:Int
) :Unit = {
```

```
val model = DecisionTree.trainClassifier(trainingData, numClasses,
categoricalFeaturesInfo,
impurity, maxDepth, maxBins)
val metrics = getMetrics(model, testData)
println("Using Impurity :"+ impurity)
println("Confusion Matrix :")
println(metrics.confusionMatrix)
println("Decision Tree Accuracy: "+metrics.precision)
println("Decision Tree Error: "+ (1-metrics.precision))

}
```

The evaluate function will read in several parameters, including the impurity type (Gini or Entropy for the model) and generate the metrics for evaluations.

11. We set the following parameters:

```
val numClasses = 2
val categoricalFeaturesInfo = Map[Int, Int]()
val maxDepth = 5
val maxBins = 32
```

Since we only have benign (0.0) and malignant (1.0), we put numClasses as 2. The other parameters are tunable, and some of them are algorithm stop criteria.

12. We evaluate the Gini impurity first:

```
evaluate(trainingData, testData, numClasses,
categoricalFeaturesInfo,
"gini", maxDepth, maxBins)
```

From the console output:

```
Using Impurity :gini
Confusion Matrix :
115.0 5.0
0 88.0
Decision Tree Accuracy: 0.9620853080568721
Decision Tree Error: 0.03791469194312791
To interpret the above Confusion metrics, Accuracy is equal to
(115+ 88)/ 211 all test cases, and error is equal to 1 -
accuracy
```

13. We evaluate the Entropy impurity:

```
evaluate(trainingData, testData, numClasses,
categoricalFeaturesInfo,
"entropy", maxDepth, maxBins)
```

From the console output:

```
Using Impurity:entropy
Confusion Matrix:
116.0 4.0
9.0 82.0
Decision Tree Accuracy: 0.9383886255924171
Decision Tree Error: 0.06161137440758291
To interpret the preceding confusion metrics, accuracy is equal
to (116+ 82)/ 211 for all test cases, and error is equal to 1 -
accuracy
```

14. We then close the program by stopping the session:

```
spark.stop()
```

How it works...

The dataset is a bit more complex than usual, but apart from some extra steps, parsing it remains the same as other recipes presented in previous chapters. The parsing takes the data in its raw form and turns it into an intermediate format which will end up as a LabelPoint data structure which is common in Spark ML schemes:

```
Raw data: 1000025,5,1,1,1,2,1,3,1,1,2
Processed Data: 5,1,1,1,2,1,3,1,1,0
Labeled Points: (0.0, [5.0,1.0,1.0,1.0,2.0,1.0,3.0,1.0,1.0])
```

We use `DecisionTree.trainClassifier()` to train the classifier tree on the training set. We follow that by examining the various impurity and confusion matrix measurements to demonstrate how to measure the effectiveness of a tree model.

The reader is encouraged to look at the output and consult additional machine learning books to understand the concept of the confusion matrix and impurity measurement to master Decision Trees and variations in Spark.

There's more...

To visualize it better, we included a sample decision tree work flow in Spark which will read the data into Spark first. In our case, we create the RDD from the file. We then split the dataset into training data and test data using a random sampling function.

After the dataset is split, we use the training dataset to train the model, followed by test data to test the accuracy of the model. A good model should have a meaningful accuracy value (close to 1). The following figure depicts the workflow:

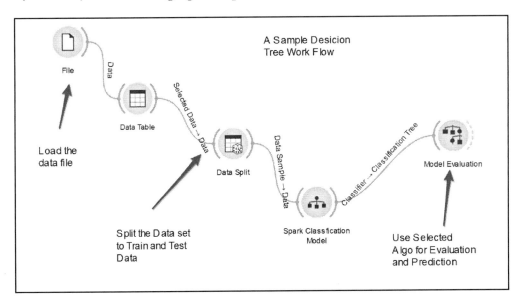

A sample tree was generated based on the Wisconsin Breast Cancer dataset. The red spot represents malignant cases, and the blue ones the benign cases. We can examine the tree visually in the following figure:

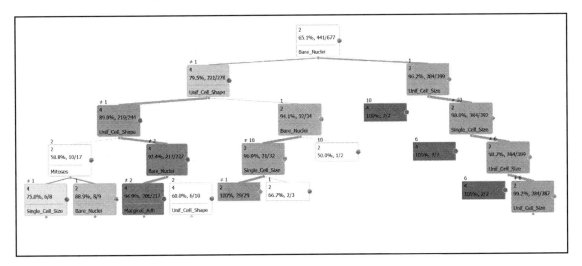

See also

- Documentation for the constructor can be found at: `http://spark.apache.org/docs/latest/api/scala/index.html#org.apache.spark.mllib.tree.DecisionTree` and `http://spark.apache.org/docs/latest/api/scala/index.html#org.apache.spark.mllib.tree.model.DecisionTreeModel`
- Documentation for the Spark Matrix Evaluator can be found at `http://spark.apache.org/docs/latest/api/scala/index.html#org.apache.spark.mllib.evaluation.MulticlassMetrics`

Solving Regression problems with Decision Trees in Spark 2.0

Similar to the previous recipe, we will use the `DecisionTree()` class to train and predict an outcome using a regression tree model. To refresh all these models is a variation on **CART (Classification and Regression Tree)**, which comes in two modes. In this recipe, we explore the regression API for the decision tree implementation in Spark.

How to do it...

1. Start a new project in IntelliJ or in an IDE of your choice. Make sure the necessary JAR files are included.

2. Set up the package location where the program will reside:

   ```
   package spark.ml.cookbook.chapter10
   ```

3. Import the necessary packages for the Spark context to get access to the cluster and `Log4j.Logger` to reduce the amount of output produced by Spark:

   ```
   import org.apache.spark.mllib.evaluation.RegressionMetrics
   import org.apache.spark.mllib.linalg.Vectors
   import org.apache.spark.mllib.regression.LabeledPoint
   import org.apache.spark.mllib.tree.DecisionTree
   import org.apache.spark.mllib.tree.model.DecisionTreeModel
   import org.apache.spark.rdd.RDD

   import org.apache.spark.sql.SparkSession
   import org.apache.log4j.{Level, Logger}
   ```

4. Create Spark's configuration and Spark session so we can have access to the cluster:

```
Logger.getLogger("org").setLevel(Level.ERROR)

val spark = SparkSession
 .builder
.master("local[*]")
 .appName("MyDecisionTreeRegression")
 .config("spark.sql.warehouse.dir", ".")
 .getOrCreate()
```

5. We read in the original raw data file:

```
val rawData =
spark.sparkContext.textFile("../data/sparkml2/chapter10/breast-
cancer-wisconsin.data")
```

6. We pre-process the dataset (see the preceding code for details):

```
val data = rawData.map(_.trim)
 .filter(text => !(text.isEmpty || text.startsWith("#") ||
text.indexOf("?") > -1))
 .map { line =>
val values = line.split(',').map(_.toDouble)
val slicedValues = values.slice(1, values.size)
val featureVector = Vectors.dense(slicedValues.init)
val label = values.last / 2 -1
LabeledPoint(label, featureVector)
 }
```

7. We verify the raw data count and process the data count:

```
println(rawData.count())
println(data.count())
```

And you will see the following on the console:

```
699
683
```

8. We split the whole dataset into training data (70%) and test data (30%) sets:

```
val splits = data.randomSplit(Array(0.7, 0.3))
val (trainingData, testData) = (splits(0), splits(1))
```

9. We define a metrics calculation function, which utilizes the Spark `RegressionMetrics`:

```
def getMetrics(model: DecisionTreeModel, data: RDD[LabeledPoint]):
RegressionMetrics = {
 val predictionsAndLabels = data.map(example =>
 (model.predict(example.features), example.label)
 )
 new RegressionMetrics(predictionsAndLabels)
 }
```

10. We set the following parameters:

```
val categoricalFeaturesInfo = Map[Int, Int]()
val impurity = "variance"
val maxDepth = 5
val maxBins = 32
```

11. We evaluate the Gini impurity first:

```
val model = DecisionTree.trainRegressor(trainingData,
categoricalFeaturesInfo, impurity, maxDepth, maxBins)
val metrics = getMetrics(model, testData)
println("Test Mean Squared Error = " + metrics.meanSquaredError)
println("My regression tree model:\n" + model.toDebugString)
```

From the console output:

```
Test Mean Squared Error = 0.037363769271664016
My regression tree model:
DecisionTreeModel regressor of depth 5 with 37 nodes
If (feature 1 <= 3.0)
   If (feature 5 <= 3.0)
    If (feature 0 <= 6.0)
     If (feature 7 <= 3.0)
      Predict: 0.0
     Else (feature 7 > 3.0)
      If (feature 0 <= 4.0)
       Predict: 0.0
      Else (feature 0 > 4.0)
       Predict: 1.0
    Else (feature 0 > 6.0)
     If (feature 2 <= 2.0)
      Predict: 0.0
     Else (feature 2 > 2.0)
      If (feature 4 <= 2.0)
       Predict: 0.0
      Else (feature 4 > 2.0)
```

```
       Predict: 1.0
  Else (feature 5 > 3.0)
   If (feature 1 <= 1.0)
    If (feature 0 <= 5.0)
     Predict: 0.0
    Else (feature 0 > 5.0)
     Predict: 1.0
   Else (feature 1 > 1.0)
    If (feature 0 <= 6.0)
     If (feature 7 <= 4.0)
      Predict: 0.875
     Else (feature 7 > 4.0)
      Predict: 0.3333333333333333
    Else (feature 0 > 6.0)
     Predict: 1.0
 Else (feature 1 > 3.0)
  If (feature 1 <= 4.0)
   If (feature 4 <= 6.0)
    If (feature 5 <= 7.0)
     If (feature 0 <= 8.0)
      Predict: 0.3333333333333333
     Else (feature 0 > 8.0)
      Predict: 1.0
    Else (feature 5 > 7.0)
     Predict: 1.0
   Else (feature 4 > 6.0)
    Predict: 0.0
  Else (feature 1 > 4.0)
   If (feature 3 <= 1.0)
    If (feature 0 <= 6.0)
     If (feature 0 <= 5.0)
      Predict: 1.0
     Else (feature 0 > 5.0)
      Predict: 0.0
    Else (feature 0 > 6.0)
     Predict: 1.0
   Else (feature 3 > 1.0)
    Predict: 1.0
```

12. We then close the program by stopping the Spark session:

```
spark.stop()
```

How it works...

We use the same dataset, but this time we use a Decision Tree to solve the regression problem with the data. Noteworthy is the creation of a metrics calculation function, which utilizes the Spark `RegressionMetrics()`:

```
def getMetrics(model: DecisionTreeModel, data: RDD[LabeledPoint]):
RegressionMetrics = {
 val predictionsAndLabels = data.map(example =>
 (model.predict(example.features), example.label)
 )
 new RegressionMetrics(predictionsAndLabels)
 }
```

We then proceed to perform the actual regression using `DecisionTree.trainRegressor()` and obtain the impurity measurement (GINI). We then proceed to output the actual regression, which is a series of decision nodes/branches and the value used to make a decision at the given branch:

```
If (feature 0 <= 4.0)
      Predict: 0.0
     Else (feature 0 > 4.0)
      Predict: 1.0
   Else (feature 0 > 6.0)
    If (feature 2 <= 2.0)
     Predict: 0.0
    Else (feature 2 > 2.0)
     If (feature 4 <= 2.0)
. . . . . . . .
. . . . . . . .
. . . . . . .
```

See also

- Documentation for the constructor can be found in the following URLs http://spark.apache.org/docs/latest/api/scala/index.html#org.apache.spark.mllib.tree.

  DecisionTree and http://spark.apache.org/docs/latest/api/scala/index.html#org.apache.spark.mllib.tree.model.DecisionTreeModel

- Documentation for the Spark Matrix Evaluator can be found

  at http://spark.apache.org/docs/latest/api/scala/index.html#org.apache.spark.mllib.evaluation.RegressionMetrics

Building a classification system with Random Forest Trees in Spark 2.0

In this recipe, we will explore Random Forest implementation in Spark. We will use the Random Forest technique to solve a discrete classification problem. We found random forest implementation very fast due to Spark's exploitation of parallelism (growing many trees at once). We also do not need to worry too much about the hyper-parameters and technically we can get away with just setting the number of trees.

How to do it...

1. Start a new project in IntelliJ or in an IDE of your choice. Make sure the necessary JAR files are included.

2. Set up the package location where the program will reside:

```
package spark.ml.cookbook.chapter10
```

3. Import the necessary packages for the Spark context to get access to the cluster and `Log4j.Logger` to reduce the amount of output produced by Spark:

```
import org.apache.spark.mllib.evaluation.MulticlassMetrics
import org.apache.spark.mllib.linalg.Vectors
import org.apache.spark.mllib.regression.LabeledPoint
import org.apache.spark.mllib.tree.model.RandomForestModel
import org.apache.spark.rdd.RDD
import org.apache.spark.mllib.tree.RandomForest

import org.apache.spark.sql.SparkSession
import org.apache.log4j.{Level, Logger}
```

4. Create Spark's configuration and Spark session so we can have access to the cluster:

```
Logger.getLogger("org").setLevel(Level.ERROR)

val spark = SparkSession
 .builder
.master("local[*]")
 .appName("MyRandomForestClassification")
 .config("spark.sql.warehouse.dir", ".")
 .getOrCreate()
```

5. We read in the original raw data file:

```
val rawData =
spark.sparkContext.textFile("../data/sparkml2/chapter10/breast-
cancer-wisconsin.data")
```

6. We pre-process the dataset (see the preceding session for details):

```
val data = rawData.map(_.trim)
 .filter(text => !(text.isEmpty || text.startsWith("#") ||
text.indexOf("?") > -1))
 .map { line =>
 val values = line.split(',').map(_.toDouble)
 val slicedValues = values.slice(1, values.size)
 val featureVector = Vectors.dense(slicedValues.init)
 val label = values.last / 2 -1
 LabeledPoint(label, featureVector)
 }
```

7. We verify the raw data count and process the data count:

```
println("Training Data count:"+trainingData.count())
println("Test Data Count:"+testData.count())
```

And you will see the following in the console:

```
Training Data count: 501
Test Data Count: 182
```

8. We split the whole dataset into training data (70%) and test data (30%) randomly:

```
val splits = data.randomSplit(Array(0.7, 0.3))
val (trainingData, testData) = (splits(0), splits(1))
```

9. We define a metrics calculation function, which utilizes the Spark
   MulticlassMetrics:

```
def getMetrics(model: RandomForestModel, data: RDD[LabeledPoint]):
MulticlassMetrics = {
 val predictionsAndLabels = data.map(example =>
 (model.predict(example.features), example.label)
 )
 new MulticlassMetrics(predictionsAndLabels)
 }
```

This function will read in the model and the test dataset, and create metrics that contain the confusion matrix mentioned earlier. It will contain model accuracy, which is one of the indicators for the classification model.

10. We define an evaluate function, which can take some tunable parameters for the Random Forest model, and do the training for the dataset:

```
def evaluate(
 trainingData: RDD[LabeledPoint],
 testData: RDD[LabeledPoint],
 numClasses: Int,
 categoricalFeaturesInfo: Map[Int,Int],
 numTrees: Int,
 featureSubsetStrategy: String,
 impurity: String,
 maxDepth: Int,
 maxBins:Int
 ) :Unit = {
val model = RandomForest.trainClassifier(trainingData, numClasses,
categoricalFeaturesInfo, numTrees, featureSubsetStrategy,impurity,
maxDepth, maxBins)
val metrics = getMetrics(model, testData)
println("Using Impurity :"+ impurity)
println("Confusion Matrix :")
println(metrics.confusionMatrix)
println("Model Accuracy: "+metrics.precision)
println("Model Error: "+ (1-metrics.precision))
 }
```

The evaluate function will read in several parameters, including the impurity type (Gini or Entropy for the model) and generate the metrics for evaluations.

11. We set the following parameters:

```
val numClasses = 2
 val categoricalFeaturesInfo = Map[Int, Int]()
 val numTrees = 3 // Use more in practice.
val featureSubsetStrategy = "auto" // Let the algorithm choose.

 val maxDepth = 4
 val maxBins = 32
```

12. We evaluate the Gini impurity first:

```
evaluate(trainingData, testData,
numClasses,categoricalFeaturesInfo,numTrees,
featureSubsetStrategy, "gini", maxDepth, maxBins)
```

From the console output:

```
Using Impurity :gini
Confusion Matrix :
118.0 1.0
4.0 59.0
Model Accuracy: 0.9725274725274725
Model Error: 0.027472527472527486
To interpret the above Confusion metrics, Accuracy is equal to
(118+ 59)/ 182 all test cases, and error is equal to 1 -
accuracy
```

13. We evaluate the Entropy impurity:

```
evaluate(trainingData, testData, numClasses,
categoricalFeaturesInfo,
  "entropy", maxDepth, maxBins)
```

From the console output:

```
Using Impurity :entropy
Confusion Matrix :
115.0   4.0
0.0     63.0
Model Accuracy: 0.978021978021978
Model Error: 0.02197802197802201
To interpret the above Confusion metrics, Accuracy is equal to
(115+ 63)/ 182 all test cases, and error is equal to 1 -accuracy
```

14. We then close the program by stopping the Spark session:

```
spark.stop()
```

How it works...

The data is the same as the data in the previous recipe, but we use Random Forest and the Multi metrics API to solve the classification problem:

- `RandomForest.trainClassifier()`
- `MulticlassMetrics()`

We have a lot of options with Random Forest Trees that we can adjust to get the right edges for classifying complex surfaces. Some of the parameters are listed here:

```
val numClasses = 2
val categoricalFeaturesInfo = Map[Int, Int]()
val numTrees = 3 // Use more in practice.
val featureSubsetStrategy = "auto" // Let the algorithm choose.
val maxDepth = 4
val maxBins = 32
```

Noteworthy is the confusion matrix in this recipe. The confusion matrix is obtained via the `MulticlassMetrics()` API call. To interpret the preceding confusion metrics, accuracy is equal to (118+ 59)/ 182 for all test cases, and error is equal to 1 -accuracy:

```
Confusion Matrix :
118.0 1.0
4.0 59.0
Model Accuracy: 0.9725274725274725
Model Error: 0.027472527472527486
```

See also

- Documentation for the constructor can be found in the following
  URLs http://spark.apache.org/docs/latest/api/scala/index.html#org.apac
  he.spark.mllib.tree.RandomForest$ and http://spark.apache.org/docs/lat
  est/api/scala/index.html#org.apache.spark.mllib.tree.model.RandomFores
  tModel

- Documentation for the Spark Matrix Evaluator can be found
  at http://spark.apache.org/docs/latest/api/scala/index.html#org.apache.
  spark.mllib.evaluation.MulticlassMetrics

Solving regression problems with Random Forest Trees in Spark 2.0

This is similar to the previous recipes, but we use Random Forest Trees to solve a regression problem (continuous). The following parameter is used to direct the algorithm to apply regression rather than classification. We again limit the number of classes to two:

```
val impurity = "variance" // USE variance for regression
```

How to do it...

1. Start a new project in IntelliJ or in an IDE of your choice. Make sure the necessary JAR files are included.

2. Set up the package location where the program will reside:

```
package spark.ml.cookbook.chapter10
```

3. Import the necessary packages from Spark:

```
import org.apache.spark.mllib.evaluation.RegressionMetrics
import org.apache.spark.mllib.linalg.Vectors
import org.apache.spark.mllib.regression.LabeledPoint
import org.apache.spark.mllib.tree.model.RandomForestModel
import org.apache.spark.rdd.RDD
import org.apache.spark.mllib.tree.RandomForest

import org.apache.spark.sql.SparkSession
import org.apache.log4j.{Level, Logger}
```

4. Create Spark's configuration and Spark session:

```
Logger.getLogger("org").setLevel(Level.ERROR)

val spark = SparkSession
.builder
.master("local[*]")
.appName("MyRandomForestRegression")
.config("spark.sql.warehouse.dir", ".")
.getOrCreate()
```

5. We read in the original raw data file:

```
val rawData =
spark.sparkContext.textFile("../data/sparkml2/chapter10/breast-
cancer-wisconsin.data")
```

6. We pre-process the dataset (see the preceding session for details):

```
val data = rawData.map(_.trim)
  .filter(text => !(text.isEmpty || text.startsWith("#") ||
text.indexOf("?") > -1))
  .map { line =>
  val values = line.split(',').map(_.toDouble)
  val slicedValues = values.slice(1, values.size)
```

```
val featureVector = Vectors.dense(slicedValues.init)
val label = values.last / 2 -1
LabeledPoint(label, featureVector)
}
```

7. We split the whole dataset into training data (70%) and test data (30%) randomly:

```
val splits = data.randomSplit(Array(0.7, 0.3))
val (trainingData, testData) = (splits(0), splits(1))
println("Training Data count:"+trainingData.count())
println("Test Data Count:"+testData.count())
```

And you will see the following on the console:

```
Training Data count:473
Test Data Count:210
```

8. We define a metrics calculation function, which utilizes the Spark `RegressionMetrics`:

```
def getMetrics(model: RandomForestModel, data: RDD[LabeledPoint]):
RegressionMetrics = {
val predictionsAndLabels = data.map(example =>
  (model.predict(example.features), example.label)
  )
new RegressionMetrics(predictionsAndLabels)
  }
```

9. We set the following parameters:

```
val numClasses = 2
val categoricalFeaturesInfo = Map[Int, Int]()
val numTrees = 3 // Use more in practice.
val featureSubsetStrategy = "auto" // Let the algorithm choose.
val impurity = "variance"
 val maxDepth = 4
val maxBins = 32
val model = RandomForest.trainRegressor(trainingData,
categoricalFeaturesInfo,
numTrees, featureSubsetStrategy, impurity, maxDepth, maxBins)
val metrics = getMetrics(model, testData)
println("Test Mean Squared Error = " + metrics.meanSquaredError)
println("My Random Forest model:\n" + model.toDebugString)
```

From the console output:

```
Test Mean Squared Error = 0.028681825568809653
My Random Forest model:
```

```
TreeEnsembleModel regressor with 3 trees
  Tree 0:
    If (feature 2 <= 3.0)
     If (feature 7 <= 3.0)
      If (feature 4 <= 5.0)
       If (feature 0 <= 8.0)
        Predict: 0.006825938566552901
       Else (feature 0 > 8.0)
        Predict: 1.0
      Else (feature 4 > 5.0)
       Predict: 1.0
     Else (feature 7 > 3.0)
      If (feature 6 <= 3.0)
       If (feature 0 <= 6.0)
        Predict: 0.0
       Else (feature 0 > 6.0)
        Predict: 1.0
      Else (feature 6 > 3.0)
       Predict: 1.0
    Else (feature 2 > 3.0)
     If (feature 5 <= 3.0)
      If (feature 4 <= 3.0)
       If (feature 7 <= 3.0)
        Predict: 0.1
       Else (feature 7 > 3.0)
        Predict: 1.0
      Else (feature 4 > 3.0)
       If (feature 3 <= 3.0)
        Predict: 0.8571428571428571
       Else (feature 3 > 3.0)
        Predict: 1.0
     Else (feature 5 > 3.0)
      If (feature 5 <= 5.0)
       If (feature 1 <= 4.0)
        Predict: 0.75
       Else (feature 1 > 4.0)
        Predict: 1.0
      Else (feature 5 > 5.0)
       Predict: 1.0
  Tree 1:
  ...
```

10. We then close the program by stopping the Spark session:

```
spark.stop()
```

How it works...

We use the dataset and Random Forest Tree to solve a regression problem with the data. The mechanics of parsing and separating remains the same, but we use the following two APIs to do the tree regression and evaluate the results:

- `RandomForest.trainRegressor()`
- `RegressionMetrics()`

Noteworthy is the definition of the `getMetrics()` function to utilize the `RegressionMetrics()` facility in Spark:

```scala
def getMetrics(model: RandomForestModel, data: RDD[LabeledPoint]):
RegressionMetrics = {
val predictionsAndLabels = data.map(example =>
 (model.predict(example.features), example.label)
 )
new RegressionMetrics(predictionsAndLabels)
}
```

We also set the impurity value to "variance" so we can use the variance for measuring errors:

```scala
val impurity = "variance" // use variance for regression
```

See also

- Documentation for the constructor can be found at the following
  URLs http://spark.apache.org/docs/latest/api/scala/index.html#org.apache.spark.mllib.tree.RandomForest$ and http://spark.apache.org/docs/latest/api/scala/index.html#org.apache.spark.mllib.tree.model.RandomForestModel
- Documentation for Spark Matrix
  Evaluator: http://spark.apache.org/docs/latest/api/scala/index.html#org.apache.spark.mllib.evaluation.RegressionMetrics

Building a classification system with Gradient Boosted Trees (GBT) in Spark 2.0

In this recipe, we will explore the Gradient Boosted Tree (GBT) classification implementation in Spark. The GBT requires more care with hyper-parameters and several tries before deciding the final outcome. One must remember that it is completely OK to grow shorter trees if using GBT.

How to do it...

1. Start a new project in IntelliJ or in an IDE of your choice. Make sure the necessary JAR files are included.

2. Set up the package location where the program will reside:

   ```
   package spark.ml.cookbook.chapter10
   ```

3. Import the necessary packages for the Spark context:

   ```
   import org.apache.spark.mllib.evaluation.MulticlassMetrics
   import org.apache.spark.mllib.linalg.Vectors
   import org.apache.spark.mllib.regression.LabeledPoint
   import org.apache.spark.mllib.tree.model.GradientBoostedTreesModel
   import org.apache.spark.rdd.RDD
   import org.apache.spark.mllib.tree.GradientBoostedTrees
   import org.apache.spark.mllib.tree.configuration.BoostingStrategy
   import org.apache.spark.sql.SparkSession
   import org.apache.log4j.{Level, Logger}
   ```

4. Create Spark's configuration and Spark session so we can have access to the cluster:

   ```
   Logger.getLogger("org").setLevel(Level.ERROR)

   val spark = SparkSession
      .builder
   .master("local[*]")
      .appName("MyGradientBoostedTreesClassification")
      .config("spark.sql.warehouse.dir", ".")
      .getOrCreate()
   ```

5. We read in the original raw data file:

```
val rawData =
spark.sparkContext.textFile("../data/sparkml2/chapter10/breast-
cancer-wisconsin.data")
```

6. We pre-process the dataset (see the preceding session for details):

```
val data = rawData.map(_.trim)
 .filter(text => !(text.isEmpty || text.startsWith("#") ||
text.indexOf("?") > -1))
 .map { line =>
val values = line.split(',').map(_.toDouble)
val slicedValues = values.slice(1, values.size)
val featureVector = Vectors.dense(slicedValues.init)
val label = values.last / 2 -1
LabeledPoint(label, featureVector)
 }
```

7. We split the whole dataset into training data (70%) and test data (30%) randomly. Please note that the random split will generate around 211 test datasets. It's approximately but NOT exactly 30% of the dataset:

```
val splits = data.randomSplit(Array(0.7, 0.3))
val (trainingData, testData) = (splits(0), splits(1))
println("Training Data count:"+trainingData.count())
println("Test Data Count:"+testData.count())
```

And you will see the on the console:

```
Training Data count:491
Test Data Count:192
```

8. We define a metrics calculation function, which utilizes the Spark `MulticlassMetrics`:

```
def getMetrics(model: GradientBoostedTreesModel, data:
RDD[LabeledPoint]): MulticlassMetrics = {
 val predictionsAndLabels = data.map(example =>
 (model.predict(example.features), example.label)
 )
 new MulticlassMetrics(predictionsAndLabels)
 }
```

9. We define an evaluate function, which can take some tunable parameters for the Gradient Boosted Trees model, and do the training for the dataset:

```
def evaluate(
  trainingData: RDD[LabeledPoint],
  testData: RDD[LabeledPoint],
  boostingStrategy : BoostingStrategy
  ) :Unit = {



  val model = GradientBoostedTrees.train(trainingData,
  boostingStrategy)

  val metrics = getMetrics(model, testData)
  println("Confusion Matrix :")
  println(metrics.confusionMatrix)
  println("Model Accuracy: "+metrics.precision)
  println("Model Error: "+ (1-metrics.precision))

}
```

10. We set the following parameters:

```
val algo = "Classification"
val numIterations = 3
val numClasses = 2
val maxDepth = 5
val maxBins = 32
val categoricalFeatureInfo = Map[Int,Int]()
val boostingStrategy = BoostingStrategy.defaultParams(algo)
boostingStrategy.setNumIterations(numIterations)
boostingStrategy.treeStrategy.setNumClasses(numClasses)
boostingStrategy.treeStrategy.setMaxDepth(maxDepth)
boostingStrategy.treeStrategy.setMaxBins(maxBins)
boostingStrategy.treeStrategy.categoricalFeaturesInfo =
categoricalFeatureInfo
```

11. We evaluate the model using the preceding Strategy parameters:

```
evaluate(trainingData, testData, boostingStrategy)
```

From the console output:

```
Confusion Matrix :
124.0 2.0
2.0 64.0
Model Accuracy: 0.9791666666666666
```

```
Model Error: 0.02083333333333337

To interpret the above Confusion metrics, Accuracy is equal to
(124+ 64)/ 192 all test cases, and error is equal to 1 -
accuracy
```

12. We then close the program by stopping the Spark session:

```
spark.stop()
```

How it works....

We skip the data ingestion and parsing since it is similar to previous recipes, but what is different is how we set up the parameters, especially the use of "classification" as a parameter that we pass into `BoostingStrategy.defaultParams()`:

```
val algo = "Classification"
 val numIterations = 3
 val numClasses = 2
 val maxDepth = 5
 val maxBins = 32
 val categoricalFeatureInfo = Map[Int,Int]()


 val boostingStrategy = BoostingStrategy.defaultParams(algo)
```

We also use the `evaluate()` function to evaluate the parameters by looking at impurity and the confusion matrix:

```
evaluate(trainingData, testData, boostingStrategy)

Confusion Matrix :
124.0 2.0
2.0 64.0
Model Accuracy: 0.9791666666666666
Model Error: 0.02083333333333337
```

There's more...

It is important to remember that the GBT is a multi-generational algorithm with the twist that we grow one tree at the time, learn from our mistakes, and then build the next tree in an iterative way.

See also

- Documentation for the constructor can be found at the following URLs http://spark.apache.org/docs/latest/api/scala/index.html#org.apache.spark.mllib.tree.GradientBoostedTrees, http://spark.apache.org/docs/latest/api/scala/index.html#org.apache.spark.mllib.tree.configuration.BoostingStrategy and http://spark.apache.org/docs/latest/api/scala/index.html#org.apache.spark.mllib.tree.model.GradientBoostedTreesModel
- Documentation for the Spark Matrix Evaluator can be found at http://spark.apache.org/docs/latest/api/scala/index.html#org.apache.spark.mllib.evaluation.MulticlassMetrics

Solving regression problems with Gradient Boosted Trees (GBT) in Spark 2.0

This recipe is similar to the GBT classification problem, but we will use regression instead. We will use `BoostingStrategy.defaultParams()` to direct the GBT to use regression:

```
algo = "Regression"
val boostingStrategy = BoostingStrategy.defaultParams(algo)
```

How to do it...

1. Start a new project in IntelliJ or in an IDE of your choice. Make sure the necessary JAR files are included.

2. Set up the package location where the program will reside:

```
package spark.ml.cookbook.chapter10.
```

3. Import the necessary packages for the Spark context:

```
import org.apache.spark.mllib.evaluation.RegressionMetrics
import org.apache.spark.mllib.linalg.Vectors
import org.apache.spark.mllib.regression.LabeledPoint
import org.apache.spark.mllib.tree.model.GradientBoostedTreesModel
import org.apache.spark.rdd.RDD
import org.apache.spark.mllib.tree.GradientBoostedTrees
import org.apache.spark.mllib.tree.configuration.BoostingStrategy

import org.apache.spark.sql.SparkSession
import org.apache.log4j.{Level, Logger}
```

4. Create Spark's configuration and Spark session:

```
Logger.getLogger("org").setLevel(Level.ERROR)

val spark = SparkSession
    .builder
    .master("local[*]")
    .appName("MyGradientBoostedTreesRegression")
    .config("spark.sql.warehouse.dir", ".")
    .getOrCreate()
```

5. We read in the original raw data file:

```
val rawData =
spark.sparkContext.textFile("../data/sparkml2/chapter10/breast-
cancer-wisconsin.data")
```

6. We pre-process the dataset (see the preceding session for details):

```
val data = rawData.map(_.trim)
  .filter(text => !(text.isEmpty || text.startsWith("#") ||
text.indexOf("?") > -1))
  .map { line =>
  val values = line.split(',').map(_.toDouble)
  val slicedValues = values.slice(1, values.size)
  val featureVector = Vectors.dense(slicedValues.init)
  val label = values.last / 2 -1
  LabeledPoint(label, featureVector)
  }
```

7. We split the whole dataset into training data (70%) and test data (30%) randomly:

```scala
val splits = data.randomSplit(Array(0.7, 0.3))
val (trainingData, testData) = (splits(0), splits(1))
println("Training Data count:"+trainingData.count())
println("Test Data Count:"+testData.count())
```

And you will see the following in the console:

```
Training Data count:469
Test Data Count:214
```

8. We define a metrics calculation function, which utilizes the Spark `RegressionMetrics`:

```scala
def getMetrics(model: GradientBoostedTreesModel, data:
RDD[LabeledPoint]): RegressionMetrics = {
 val predictionsAndLabels = data.map(example =>
 (model.predict(example.features), example.label)
 )
 new RegressionMetrics(predictionsAndLabels)
 }
```

9. We set the following parameters:

```scala
val algo = "Regression"
val numIterations = 3
val maxDepth = 5
val maxBins = 32
val categoricalFeatureInfo = Map[Int,Int]()
val boostingStrategy = BoostingStrategy.defaultParams(algo)
boostingStrategy.setNumIterations(numIterations)
boostingStrategy.treeStrategy.setMaxDepth(maxDepth)
boostingStrategy.treeStrategy.setMaxBins(maxBins)
boostingStrategy.treeStrategy.categoricalFeaturesInfo =
categoricalFeatureInfo
```

10. We evaluate the model using the preceding Strategy parameters:

```scala
val model = GradientBoostedTrees.train(trainingData, boostingStrategy)
val metrics = getMetrics(model, testData)

println("Test Mean Squared Error = " + metrics.meanSquaredError)
println("My regression GBT model:\n" + model.toDebugString)
```

From the console output:

```
Test Mean Squared Error = 0.05370763765769276
My regression GBT model:
TreeEnsembleModel regressor with 3 trees
Tree 0:
If (feature 1 <= 2.0)
If (feature 0 <= 6.0)
If (feature 5 <= 5.0)
If (feature 5 <= 4.0)
Predict: 0.0
Else (feature 5 > 4.0)
...
```

11. We then close the program by stopping the Spark session:

```
spark.stop()
```

How it works...

We used the same GBT tree as the previous recipe, but we adjusted the parameters to direct the GBT API to perform regression as opposed to classification. It is noteworthy to compare the following code with the previous recipe. "Regression" is used to direct the GBT to perform regression on the data:

```scala
val algo = "Regression"
val numIterations = 3
val maxDepth = 5
val maxBins = 32
val categoricalFeatureInfo = Map[Int,Int]()


val boostingStrategy = BoostingStrategy.defaultParams(algo)
```

We use the following API to train and evaluate the metrics from the model:

- `GradientBoostedTrees.train()`
- `getMetrics()`

The following snippet shows a typical output needed to examine the model:

```
Test Mean Squared Error = 0.05370763765769276
My regression GBT model:
Tree 0:
If (feature 1 <= 2.0)
If (feature 0 <= 6.0)
If (feature 5 <= 5.0)
If (feature 5 <= 4.0)
Predict: 0.0
Else (feature 5 > 4.0)
...
```

There's more...

GBT can capture non-linearity and variable interaction in the same manner as Random Forest and can deal with multi-class labels as well.

See also

- Documentation for the constructor can be found at the following URLs: `http://spark.apache.org/docs/latest/api/scala/index.html#org.apache.spark.mllib.tree.GradientBoostedTrees`, `http://spark.apache.org/docs/latest/api/scala/index.html#org.apache.spark.mllib.tree.configuration.BoostingStrategy`, and `http://spark.apache.org/docs/latest/api/scala/index.html#org.apache.spark.mllib.tree.model.GradientBoostedTreesModel`

- Documentation for the Spark Matrix Evaluator can be found at `http://spark.apache.org/docs/latest/api/scala/index.html#org.apache.spark.mllib.evaluation.RegressionMetrics`

11
Curse of High-Dimensionality in Big Data

In this chapter, we will cover the following topics:

- Two methods of ingesting and preparing a CSV file for processing in Spark
- **Singular Value Decomposition (SVD)** to reduce high-dimensionality in Spark
- **Principal Component Analysis (PCA)** to pick the most effective latent factor for machine learning in Spark

Introduction

The curse of dimensionality is not a new term or concept. The term was originally coined by R. Bellman when tackling problems in dynamic programming (the Bellman equation). The core concepts in machine learning refer to the problem that as we increase the number of dimensions (axes or features), the number of training data (samples) remains the same (or relatively low), which causes less accuracy in our predictions. This phenomenon is also referred to as the *Hughes Effect*, named after G. Hughes, which talks about the problem caused by rapid (exponential) increase of search space as we introduce more and more dimensions to the problem space. It is a bit counterintuitive, but if the number of samples does not expand at the same rate as you add more dimensions, you actually end up with a less accurate model!

In a nutshell, most machine learning algorithms are statistical by nature and they attempt to learn the properties of the target space by cutting up the space during training and by doing some sort of counting for the number of each classes in each subspace. The curse of dimensionality is caused by having fewer and fewer data samples, which can help the algorithm to discriminate and learn as we add more dimensions. Generally speaking, if we have N samples in a dense D dimension, then we need $(N)^D$ samples to keep the sample density constant.

For example, let us say that you have 10 patient datasets that are measured along two dimensions (height, weight). This results in 10 data points in a two-dimensional plane. What happens if we start introducing other dimensions such as region, calorie intake, ethnicity, income, and so on? In this case, we still have 10 observation points (10 patients) but in a much larger space of six dimensions. This inability for the sample data (needed for training) to expand exponentially as new dimensions are introduced is called the **Curse of Dimensionality**.

Let's look at a graphical example to show the growth of the search space versus data samples. The following figure depicts a set of five data points that are being measured in 5 x 5 (25 cells). What happens to the prediction accuracy as we add another dimension? We still have five data points in 125 3D-cells, which results in a lot of sparse subspace that cannot help the ML algorithm to learn better (discriminate) so it results in less accuracy:

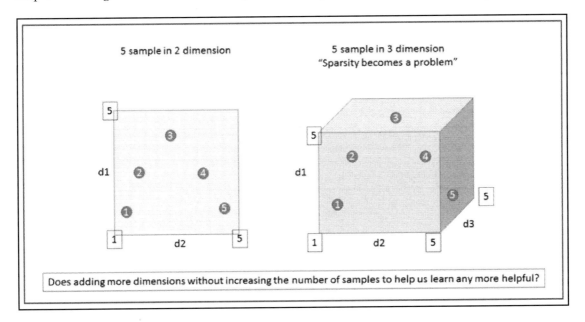

Our goal should be to strive toward a near-optimal number of features or dimensions rather than adding more and more features (maximum features or dimensions). After all, shouldn't we have a better classification error if we just add more and more features or dimensions? It seems like a good idea at first, but the answer in most cases is "no" unless you can increase the samples exponentially, which is neither practical nor possible in almost all cases.

Let us take a look at the following figure, which depicts learning error versus total number of features:

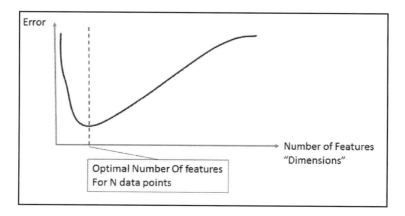

In the previous section, we examined the core concept beyond the curse of dimensionality, but we have not talked about its other side effects or how to deal with the curse itself. As we have seen previously, contrary to popular belief, it is not the dimensions themselves, but the reduction of the ratio of samples to search space which subsequently results in a less accurate forecast.

Imagine a simple ML system, as shown in the following figure. The ML system shown here takes the MNIST (http://yann.lecun.com/exdb/mnist/) type handwriting dataset and wants to train itself so it can predict what six-digit zip code is used on a parcel:

Source: MNIST

Even though the MNIST data is 20 x 20, to make the problem more visible let's assume we have a 40 x 40 pixel patch for each digit that has to be stored, analyzed, and then used for future prediction. If we assume black/white, then the *apparent* dimensionality is two (40 x 40) or 21,600, which is large. The next question that should be asked is: given the 21,600 apparent dimensions for the data, what is the actual dimension that we need to do our work? If we look at all the possible samples drawn from a 40 x 40 patch, how many of them actually look for digits? Once we look at the problem a bit more carefully, we will see that the "actual" dimensions (that is, limited to a smaller manifold subspace which is the space used by a pen stroke to make the digits. In practice, the actual subspace is much smaller and not randomly distributed across the 40 x 40 patch) are actually a lot smaller! What is happening here is that the actual data (the digits drawn by humans) exists in much smaller dimensions and most likely is confined to a small set of manifolds in the subspace (that is, the data lives around a certain subspace). To understand this better, draw 1,000 random samples from a 40 x 40 patch and visually inspect the samples. How many of them actually look alike a 3, 6, or a 5?

When we add dimensions, we can unintentionally increase the error rate by introducing noise to the system due to the fact that there would not be enough samples to predict accurately or simply act if the measurement introduces noise by itself. Common problems with adding more dimensions are as follows:

- Longer compute time
- Increased noise
- More samples needed to keep the same learning/prediction rate
- Overfitting of the data due to lack of actionable samples in sparse space

A pictorial presentation can help us understand the difference between *apparent dimensions* versus *actual dimensions* and why *less is more* in this case:

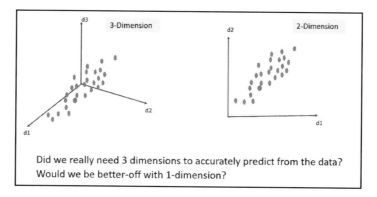

The reasons we want to reduce dimensions can be expressed as the ability to:

- Visualize data better
- Compress the data and reduce storage requirements
- Increase signal to noise ratio
- Achieve faster running time

Feature selection versus feature extraction

We have two options, feature selection and feature extraction, at our disposal for reducing the dimensions to a more manageable space. Each of these techniques is a distinct discipline and has its own methods and complexity. Even though they sound the same, they are very different and require a separate treatment.

The following figure provides a mind map, which compares the feature selection versus feature extraction for reference. While the feature selection, also referred to as feature engineering, is beyond the scope of this book, we cover the two most common feature extraction techniques (PCA and SVD) via detailed recipes:

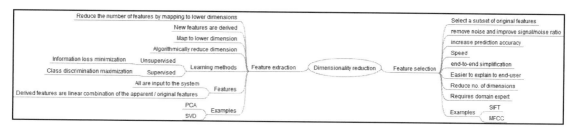

The two techniques available for picking a set of features or inputs to a ML algorithm are:

- **Feature selection**: In this technique, we use our domain knowledge to select a subset of features that best describes the variance in the data. What we are trying to do is to select the best dependent variables (features) that can help us predict the outcome. This method is often referred to as "feature engineering" and requires a data engineer or domain expertise to be effective.

   For example, we might look at 200 independent variables (dimensions, features) that are proposed for a logistics classifier to predict whether a house would sell or not in the city of Chicago. After talking to real-estate experts with 20+ years of experience in buying/selling houses in the Chicago market, we found out that only 4 of the 200 initially proposed dimensions, such as number of bedrooms, price, total square foot area, and quality of schools, are adequate for predictions. While this is great, it is usually very expensive, time-consuming, and requires a domain expert to analyze and provide direction.

- **Feature extraction**: This refers to a more algorithmic approach that uses a mapping function to map high-dimensional data to a lower-dimensional space. For example, mapping a three-dimensional space (for example, height, weight, eye color) to a one-dimensional space (for example, latent factors) that can capture almost all variances in the dataset.

   What we are trying to do here is to come up with a set of latent factors that are a combination (usually linear) of the original factor but can capture and explain the data in an accurate way. For example, we use words to describe documents which usually end in 10^6 to 10^9 space, but wouldn't it be nice to describe the documents by topics (for example, romance, war, peace, science, art, and so on) that are more abstract and high level? Do we really need to look at or include every word to do a better job with text analytics? At what cost?

   Feature extraction is about an algorithmic approach to dimensionality reduction which itself is a proxy for mapping from "apparent dimensionality" to "actual dimensionality".

Two methods of ingesting and preparing a CSV file for processing in Spark

In this recipe, we explore reading, parsing, and preparing a CSV file for a typical ML program. A **comma-separated values** (CSV) file normally stores tabular data (numbers and text) in a plain text file. In a typical CSV file, each row is a data record, and most of the time, the first row is also called the header row, which stores the field's identifier (more commonly referred to as a column name for the field). Each record consists of one or more fields, separated by commas.

How to do it...

1. The sample CSV data file is from movie ratings. The file can be retrieved at `http://files.grouplens.org/datasets/movielens/ml-latest-small.zip`.

2. Once the file is extracted, we will use the `ratings.csv` file for our CSV program to load the data into Spark. The CSV files will look like the following:

userId	movieId	rating	timestamp
1	16	4	1217897793
1	24	1.5	1217895807
1	32	4	1217896246
1	47	4	1217896556
1	50	4	1217896523
1	110	4	1217896150
1	150	3	1217895940
1	161	4	1217897864
1	165	3	1217897135
1	204	0.5	1217895786
...	...	...	...

3. Start a new project in IntelliJ or in an IDE of your choice. Make sure the necessary JAR files are included.

4. Set up the package location where the program will reside:

```
package spark.ml.cookbook.chapter11.
```

5. Import the necessary packages for Spark to get access to the cluster and `Log4j.Logger` to reduce the amount of output produced by Spark:

```
import org.apache.log4j.{Level, Logger}
import org.apache.spark.sql.SparkSession
```

6. Create Spark's configuration and Spark session so we can have access to the cluster:

```
Logger.getLogger("org").setLevel(Level.ERROR)

val spark = SparkSession
.builder
.master("local[*]")
.appName("MyCSV")
.config("spark.sql.warehouse.dir", ".")
.getOrCreate()
```

7. We read in the CSV files as a text file:

```
// 1. load the csv file as text file
val dataFile = "../data/sparkml2/chapter11/ratings.csv"
val file = spark.sparkContext.textFile(dataFile)
```

8. We process the dataset:

```
val headerAndData = file.map(line => line.split(",").map(_.trim))
val header = headerAndData.first
val data = headerAndData.filter(_(0) != header(0))
val maps = data.map(splits => header.zip(splits).toMap)
val result = maps.take(10)
result.foreach(println)
```

It should be mentioned that the `split` function here is for demonstration purposes only and a more robust tokenizer technique should be used in production.

9. First, we trim the line, remove any empty spaces, and load the CSV file into the `headerAndData` RDD since `ratings.csv` does have a header row.

10. We then read the first row as the header, and read the rest of the data into the data RDD. Any further computing could use the data RDD to perform the machine learning algorithm. For demo purposes, we mapped the header row to the data RDD and printed out the first 10 rows.

In the application console, you will see the following:

```
Map(userId -> 1, movieId -> 16, rating -> 4.0, timestamp ->
1217897793)
Map(userId -> 1, movieId -> 24, rating -> 1.5, timestamp ->
1217895807)
Map(userId -> 1, movieId -> 32, rating -> 4.0, timestamp ->
1217896246)
Map(userId -> 1, movieId -> 47, rating -> 4.0, timestamp ->
1217896556)
Map(userId -> 1, movieId -> 50, rating -> 4.0, timestamp ->
1217896523)
Map(userId -> 1, movieId -> 110, rating -> 4.0, timestamp ->
1217896150)
Map(userId -> 1, movieId -> 150, rating -> 3.0, timestamp ->
1217895940)
Map(userId -> 1, movieId -> 161, rating -> 4.0, timestamp ->
1217897864)
Map(userId -> 1, movieId -> 165, rating -> 3.0, timestamp ->
1217897135)
Map(userId -> 1, movieId -> 204, rating -> 0.5, timestamp ->
1217895786)
```

11. There is also another option to load the CSV file into Spark with the help of the Spark-CSV package.

To utilize this feature, you will need to download the following JAR file and place them on the classpath:
`http://repo1.maven.org/maven2/com/databricks/spark-csv_2.10/1.4.0/spark-csv_2.10-1.4.0.jar`

Since the Spark-CSV package is also dependent on `common-csv`, you will need to get the `common-csv` JAR file from the following location: `https://commons.apache.org/proper/commons-csv/download_csv.cgi`

We get the `common-csv-1.4-bin.zip` and extract the `commons-csv-1.4.jar` out, and put the preceding two jars on the classpath.

12. We load the CSV file using the Databricks `spark-csv` package with the following code. It will create a DataFrame object after successfully loading the CSV file:

```
// 2. load the csv file using databricks package
val df =
spark.read.format("com.databricks.spark.csv").option("header",
"true").load(dataFile)
```

13. We register a temp in-memory view named `ratings` from the DataFrame:

```
df.createOrReplaceTempView("ratings")
 val resDF = spark.sql("select * from ratings")
 resDF.show(10, false)
```

We then use a SQL query against the table and display 10 rows. In the console, you will see the following:

```
+------+-------+------+----------+
|userId|movieId|rating|timestamp |
+------+-------+------+----------+
|1     |16     |4.0   |1217897793|
|1     |24     |1.5   |1217895807|
|1     |32     |4.0   |1217896246|
|1     |47     |4.0   |1217896556|
|1     |50     |4.0   |1217896523|
|1     |110    |4.0   |1217896150|
|1     |150    |3.0   |1217895940|
|1     |161    |4.0   |1217897864|
|1     |165    |3.0   |1217897135|
|1     |204    |0.5   |1217895786|
+------+-------+------+----------+
only showing top 10 rows
```

14. Further machine learning algorithms could be performed on the DataFrame that was created previously.

15. We then close the program by stopping the Spark session:

```
spark.stop()
```

How it works...

In the older version of Spark, we needed to use a special package to read in CSV, but we now can take advantage of `spark.sparkContext.textFile(dataFile)` to ingest the file. The `Spark` which starts the statement is the Spark session (handle to cluster) and can be named anything you like via the creation phase, as shown here:

```
val spark = SparkSession
 .builder
.master("local[*]")
 .appName("MyCSV")
 .config("spark.sql.warehouse.dir", ".")
 .getOrCreate()
spark.sparkContext.textFile(dataFile)
spark.sparkContext.textFile(dataFile)
```

Spark 2.0+ uses `spark.sql.warehouse.dir` to set the warehouse location to store tables rather than `hive.metastore.warehouse.dir`. The default value for `spark.sql.warehouse.dir` is `System.getProperty("user.dir")`.

Also see `spark-defaults.conf` for more details.

Going forward, we prefer this method as opposed to obtaining the special package and the dependent JAR, as explained in step 9 of this recipe, followed by step 10:

```
spark.read.format("com.databricks.spark.csv").option("header",
"true").load(dataFile)
```

This demonstrates how to consume the file.

There's more...

The CSV file format has a lot of variations. The basic idea of separating fields with a comma is clear, but it could also be a tab, or other special character. Sometimes even the header row is optional.

A CSV file is widely used to store raw data due to its portability and simplicity. It's portable across different applications. We will introduce two simple and typical ways to load a sample CSV file into Spark, and it can be easily modified to fit your use case.

See also

- For more information regarding the Spark-CSV package, visit https://github.com/databricks/spark-csv

Singular Value Decomposition (SVD) to reduce high-dimensionality in Spark

In this recipe, we will explore a dimensionality reduction method straight out of the linear algebra, which is called **SVD (Singular Value Decomposition)**. The key focus here is to come up with a set of low-rank matrices (typically three) that approximates the original matrix but with much less data, rather than choosing to work with a large M by N matrix.

SVD is a simple linear algebra technique that transforms the original data to eigenvector/eigenvalue low rank matrices that can capture most of the attributes (the original dimensions) in a much more efficient low rank matrix system.

The following figure depicts how SVD can be used to reduce dimensions and then use the S matrix to keep or eliminate higher-level concepts derived from the original data (that is, a low rank matrix with fewer columns/features than the original):

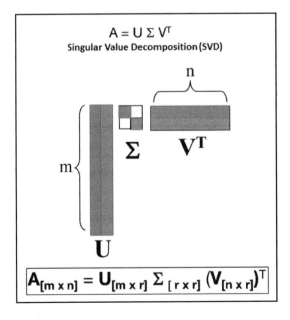

How to do it...

1. We will use the movie rating data for the SVD analysis. The movieLens 1M dataset contains around 1 million records which consist of anonymous ratings of around 3,900 movies made by 6,000 movieLens users.

 The dataset can be retrieved at:
`http://files.grouplens.org/datasets/movielens/ml-1m.zip`

The dataset contains the following files:

- `ratings.dat`: Contains the user ID, movie ID, ratings, and timestamp
- `movies.dat`: Contains the movie ID, titles, and genres
- `users.dat`: Contains the user ID, genders, ages, occupations, and zip code

2. We will use the `ratings.dat` for our SVD analysis. Sample data for the `ratings.dat` looks like the following:

```
1::1193::5::978300760
1::661::3::978302109
1::914::3::978301968
1::3408::4::978300275
1::2355::5::978824291
1::1197::3::978302268
1::1287::5::978302039
1::2804::5::978300719
1::594::4::978302268
1::919::4::978301368
1::595::5::978824268
1::938::4::978301752
```

We will use the following program to convert the data into a ratings matrix and fit it into the SVD algorithm model (in this case, we have 3,953 columns in total):

	Movie 1	Movie 2	Movie ...	Movie 3953
user 1	1	4	-	3
user 2	5	-	2	1
user ...	-	3	-	2
user N	2	4	-	5

3. Start a new project in IntelliJ or in an IDE of your choice. Make sure the necessary JAR files are included.

4. Set up the package location where the program will reside:

```
package spark.ml.cookbook.chapter11.
```

5. Import the necessary packages for the Spark session:

```
import org.apache.log4j.{Level, Logger}
import org.apache.spark.mllib.linalg.distributed.RowMatrix
import org.apache.spark.mllib.linalg.Vectors
import org.apache.spark.sql.SparkSession
```

6. Create Spark's configuration and Spark session so we can have access to the cluster:

```
Logger.getLogger("org").setLevel(Level.ERROR)

val spark = SparkSession
.builder
.master("local[*]")
.appName("MySVD")
.config("spark.sql.warehouse.dir", ".")
.getOrCreate()
```

7. We read in the original raw data file:

```
val dataFile = "../data/sparkml2/chapter11/ratings.dat"


//read data file in as a RDD, partition RDD across <partitions>
cores
val data = spark.sparkContext.textFile(dataFile)
```

8. We preprocess the dataset:

```
//parse data and create (user, item, rating) tuples
val ratingsRDD = data
    .map(line => line.split("::"))
    .map(fields => (fields(0).toInt, fields(1).toInt,
fields(2).toDouble))
```

Since we are more interested in the ratings, we extract the userId, movieId, and rating values from the data file, fields(0), fields(1), and fields(2), and create a ratings RDD based on the records.

9. We then find out how many movies are available in the ratings data and calculate the max movie index:

```
val items = ratingsRDD.map(x => x._2).distinct()
val maxIndex = items.max + 1
```

In total, we get 3,953 movies based on the dataset.

10. We put all the user movie item ratings together, using RDD's groupByKey function, so a single user's movie ratings are grouped together:

```
val userItemRatings = ratingsRDD.map(x => (x._1, ( x._2,
x._3))).groupByKey().cache()
userItemRatings.take(2).foreach(println)
```

We then print out the top two records to see the collection. Since we might have a large dataset, we cache RDD to improve performance.

In the console, you will see the following:

```
(4904,CompactBuffer((2054,4.0), (588,4.0), (589,5.0),
(3000,5.0), (1,5.0), ..., (3788,5.0)))
(1084,CompactBuffer((2058,3.0), (1258,4.0), (588,2.0),
(589,4.0), (1,3.0), ..., (1242,4.0)))
```

In the preceding records, the user ID is 4904. For the movie ID 2054, the rating is 4.0, movie ID is 588, rating is 4, and so on.

11. We then create a sparse vector to host the data:

```
val sparseVectorData = userItemRatings
  .map(a=>(a._1.toLong,
Vectors.sparse(maxIndex,a._2.toSeq))).sortByKey()

sparseVectorData.take(2).foreach(println)
```

We then convert the data into a more useful format. We use the userID as the key (sorted), and create a sparse vector to host the movie rating data.

In the console, you will see the following:

```
(1,(3953,[1,48,150,260,527,531,588,...],
[5.0,5.0,5.0,4.0,5.0,4.0,4.0...]))
(2,(3953,[21,95,110,163,165,235,265,...],[1.0,2.0,5.0,4.0,3.0,3.0,4
.0,...]))
```

In the preceding printout, for user 1, in total, there are 3,953 movies. For movie ID 1, the rating is 5.0. The sparse vector contains a `movieID` array together with a rating value array.

12. We just need the rating matrix for our SVD analysis:

```
val rows = sparseVectorData.map{
a=> a._2
}
```

The preceding code will get the sparse vector part out and create a row RDD.

13. We then create a RowMatrix based on the RDD. Once the RowMatrix object is created, we can call Spark's `computeSVD` function to compute the SVD out of the matrix:

```
val mat = new RowMatrix(rows)
val col = 10 //number of leading singular values
val computeU = true
val svd = mat.computeSVD(col, computeU)
```

14. The preceding parameters could also be adjusted to fit our needs. Once we have the SVD computed, we can get the model data out.

15. We print the singular values out:

```
println("Singular values are " + svd.s)
println("V:" + svd.V)
```

You will see the following output on the console:

From the Console output:

Singular values are
[1893.2105586893467,671.3435653757858,574.852759968471,518.0842250
224509,444.8547808167268,426.1654026154194,398.74614105343363,346.
7068453394093,335.46238645017104,316.0886024906154]

V:
-2.347441377231427E-18   -8.784853777445487E-18 ... (10 total)
0.07013713935424937   -0.020940154058955024 ...
0.023543815047740807   -0.029792454996902265 ...
0.013765839311244537   -0.01670389871069218   ...
0.0053233961967827865   -0.002962760146380113 ...
0.00971651374884698   -0.013488583341154305 ...
0.03647700692534388   -0.028836567457181495 ...
0.016502155323570307   -0.009294362577132707 ...
0.0020735701100955267   -0.0021536731391318957 ...
0.003307240697454707   -0.008420669455844697 ...
0.03226286349395502   -0.05404986818674368   ...
0.036296874437922   -0.012167583080393507 ...
0.004316939811906837   -0.005677295155360184 ...
0.003401032821348119   -0.0028903404963566883 ...
... (3953 total)

---

16. From the Spark Master (`http://localhost:4040/jobs/`), you should see the tracking as shown in the following screenshot:

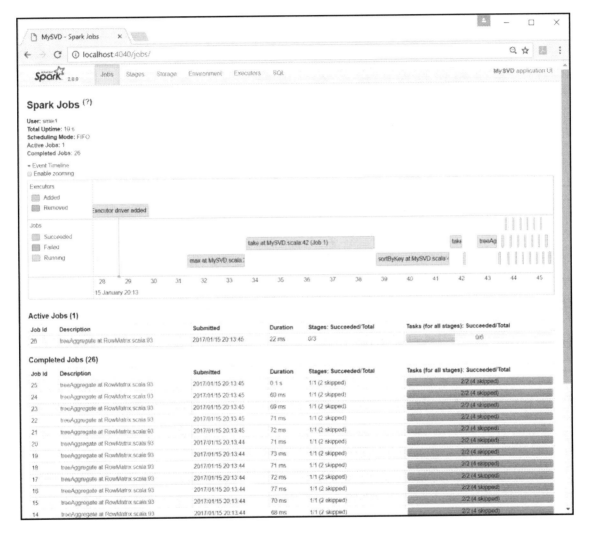

17. We then close the program by stopping the Spark session:

```
spark.stop()
```

How it works...

The core of the work gets done by declaring a `RowMatrix()` and then invoking the `computeSVD()` method to decompose the matrix into subcomponents that are much smaller, but approximate the original with uncanny accuracy:

```
valmat = new RowMatrix(rows)
val col = 10 //number of leading singular values
val computeU = true
val svd = mat.computeSVD(col, computeU)
```

SVD is a factorization technique for a real or complex matrix. At its core, it is a straight linear algebra which was actually derived from PCA itself. The concept is used extensively in recommender systems (ALS, SVD), topic modeling (LDA), and text analytics, to derive concepts from primitive high-dimensional matrices. Let's try to outline this without getting into the mathematical details of what goes in and what comes out in an SVD decomposition. The following figure depicts how this dimensionality reduction recipe and its dataset (`MovieLens`) relate to an SVD decomposition:

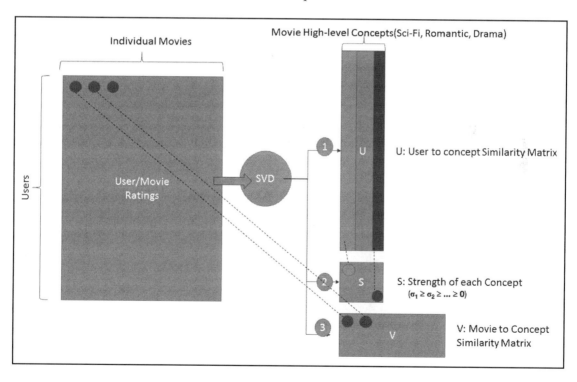

There's more...

We will end up with much more efficient (low-ranked) matrices for computation based on the original dataset.

The following equation depicts the decomposition of an array of *m x n*, which is large and hard to work with. The right-hand side of the equation helps to solve the decomposition problem which is the basis of the SVD technique.

$$A_{[m \times n]} = U_{[m \times r]} \Sigma_{[r \times r]} (V_{[n \times r]})^T$$

The following steps provides a concrete example of the SVD decomposition step by step:

- Consider a matrix of 1,000 x 1,000 which provides 1,000,000 data points (M= users, N = Movies).
- Assume there are 1,000 rows (number of observations) and 1,000 columns (number of movies).
- Let's assume we use Spark's SVD method to decompose A into three new matrices.
  - Matrix U [m x r] has 1,000 rows, but only 5 columns now (r=5; r can be thought of as concepts)
  - Matrix S [r x r] holds the singular values, which are the strength of each concept (only interested in diagonals)
  - Matrix V [n x r] has the right singular value vectors (n= Movies, r = concepts, such as romance, sci-fi, and so on)

- Let's assume that after decomposition, we end up with five concepts (romantic, sci-fi-drama, foreign, documentary, and adventure)

- How did the low rank help?

  - Originally we had 1,000,000 points of interest
  - After SVD and even before we started selecting what we want to keep using singular values (diagonals of matrix S), we ended up with total points of interest = membership in U (1,000 x 5) + S (5 x 5) + V(1,000 x 5)

- Rather than working with 1 million data points (matrix A, which is 1,000 x 1,000), we now have 5,000+25+5,000, which is about 10,000 data points, which is considerably less
- The act of selecting singular values allows us to decide how much we want to keep and how much do we want to throw away (do you really want to show the user the lowest 900 movie recommendations--does it have any value?)

See also

- Documentation for RowMatrix can be found at `http://spark.apache.org/docs/latest/api/scala/index.html#org.apache.spark.mllib.linalg.distributed.RowMatrix` and `http://spark.apache.org/docs/latest/api/scala/index.html#org.apache.spark.mllib.linalg.SingularValueDecomposition`

Principal Component Analysis (PCA) to pick the most effective latent factor for machine learning in Spark

In this recipe, we use **PCA (Principal Component Analysis)** to map the higher-dimension data (the apparent dimensions) to a lower-dimensional space (actual dimensions). It is hard to believe, but PCA has its root as early as 1901(see K. Pearson's writings) and again independently in the 1930s by H. Hotelling.

PCA attempts to pick new components in a manner that maximizes the variance along perpendicular axes and effectively transforms high-dimensional original features to a lower-dimensional space with derived components that can explain the variation (discriminate classes) in a more concise form.

The intuition beyond PCA is depicted in the following figure. Let's assume for now that our data has two dimensions (x, y) and the question we are going to ask the data is whether most of the variation (and discrimination) can be explained by only one dimension or more precisely with a linear combination of original features:

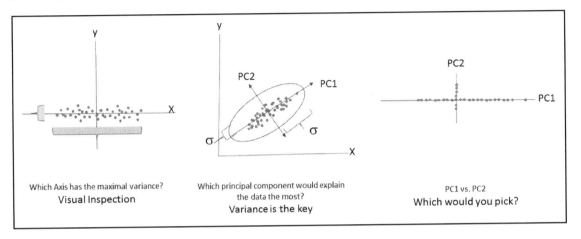

How to do it...

1. The Cleveland Heart Disease database is a published dataset used by ML researchers. The dataset contains more than a dozen fields, and experiments with the Cleveland database have concentrated on simply attempting to distinguish presence (value 1,2,3) and absence (value 0) of the disease (in the goal column, 14th column).

2. The Cleveland Heart Disease dataset is available at `http://archive.ics.uci.edu/ml/machine-learning-databases/heart-disease/processed.cleveland.data`.

3. The dataset contains the following attributes (age, sex, cp, trestbps, chol, fbs, restecg, thalach, exang, oldpeak, slope, ca, thal, num) that are depicted as the header of the table below:

For a detailed explanation on the individual attributes, refer to: `http://archive.ics.uci.edu/ml/datasets/Heart+Disease`

4. The dataset will look like the following:

age	sex	cp	trestbps	chol	fbs	restecg	thalach	exang	oldpeak	slope	ca	thal	num
63	1	1	145	233	1	2	150	0	2.3	3	0	6	0
67	1	4	160	286	0	2	108	1	1.5	2	3	3	2
67	1	4	120	229	0	2	129	1	2.6	2	2	7	1
37	1	3	130	250	0	0	187	0	3.5	3	0	3	0
41	0	2	130	204	0	2	172	0	1.4	1	0	3	0
56	1	2	120	236	0	0	178	0	0.8	1	0	3	0
62	0	4	140	268	0	2	160	0	3.6	3	2	3	3
57	0	4	120	354	0	0	163	1	0.6	1	0	3	0
63	1	4	130	254	0	2	147	0	1.4	2	1	7	2
53	1	4	140	203	1	2	155	1	3.1	3	0	7	1
57	1	4	140	192	0	0	148	0	0.4	2	0	6	0
56	0	2	140	294	0	2	153	0	1.3	2	0	3	0
56	1	3	130	256	1	2	142	1	0.6	2	1	6	2
44	1	2	120	263	0	0	173	0	0	1	0	7	0
52	1	3	172	199	1	0	162	0	0.5	1	0	7	0
57	1	3	150	168	0	0	174	0	1.6	1	0	3	0
...	...	...	...	...	...	...	...	...	...	...	...	...	...

5. Start a new project in IntelliJ or in an IDE of your choice. Make sure the necessary JAR files are included.

6. Set up the package location where the program will reside:

```
package spark.ml.cookbook.chapter11.
```

7. Import the necessary packages for the Spark session:

```
import org.apache.log4j.{Level, Logger}
import org.apache.spark.ml.feature.PCA
import org.apache.spark.ml.linalg.Vectors
import org.apache.spark.sql.SparkSession
```

8. Create Spark's configuration and Spark session so we can have access to the cluster:

```
Logger.getLogger("org").setLevel(Level.ERROR)
val spark = SparkSession
.builder
.master("local[*]")
.appName("MyPCA")
.config("spark.sql.warehouse.dir", ".")
.getOrCreate()
```

9. We read in the original raw data file and count the raw data:

```
val dataFile =
"../data/sparkml2/chapter11/processed.cleveland.data"
val rawdata = spark.sparkContext.textFile(dataFile).map(_.trim)
println(rawdata.count())
```

In the console, we get the following:

```
303
```

10. We pre-process the dataset (see the preceding code for details):

```
val data = rawdata.filter(text => !(text.isEmpty ||
text.indexOf("?") > -1))
  .map { line =>
val values = line.split(',').map(_.toDouble)

Vectors.dense(values)
}

println(data.count())

data.take(2).foreach(println)
```

In the preceding code, we filter the missing data record, and use Spark DenseVector to host the data. After filtering the missing data, we get the following count of data in the console:

```
297
```

The record print, 2, will look like the following:

```
[63.0,1.0,1.0,145.0,233.0,1.0,2.0,150.0,0.0,2.3,3.0,0.0,6.0,0.0]
[67.0,1.0,4.0,160.0,286.0,0.0,2.0,108.0,1.0,1.5,2.0,3.0,3.0,2.0]
```

11. We create a DataFrame from the data RDD, and create a PCA object for computing:

```
val df =
sqlContext.createDataFrame(data.map(Tuple1.apply)).toDF("features")
val pca = new PCA()
.setInputCol("features")
.setOutputCol("pcaFeatures")
.setK(4)
.fit(df)
```

12. The parameters for the PCA model are shown in the preceding code. We set the K value to 4. K represents the number of top K principal components that we are interested in after completing the dimensionality reduction algorithm.

13. An alternative is also available via the Matrix API:
    `mat.computePrincipalComponents(4)`. In this case, the 4 represents the top K principal components after the dimensionality reduction is completed.

14. We use the transform function to do computing and show the result in the console:

```
val pcaDF = pca.transform(df)
val result = pcaDF.select("pcaFeatures")
result.show(false)
```

The following will be displayed on the console.

What you are seeing are the four new PCA components (PC1, PC2, PC3, and PC4), which can be substituted for the original 14 features. We have successfully mapped the high-dimensional space (14 dimensions) to a lower-dimensional space (four dimensions):

```
+----------------------------------------------------------------+
|pcaFeatures                                                     |
+----------------------------------------------------------------+
|[-242.0300687784283,121.3036201521749,158.55788754696337,57.4213027823489]   |
|[-295.93413194888035,78.62237868291045,164.89404714411137,50.774221590904006] |
|[-236.95589307378614,102.81012275608082,131.81674495980488,61.776752762650545]|
|[-257.18475255366803,164.13217618694355,144.80875573077037,39.93660552917494] |
|[-211.46023940233792,148.16356844339373,145.71965730283782,42.714109070944815]|
|[-243.41916012300274,152.93562964073197,136.88231960613228,58.89077688960155] |
|[-276.6610310706115,132.24904523885735,153.00538430798025,57.91011107741793]  |
|[-361.2514826750539,139.82848436190866,128.40666628113823,54.062535428181164] |
|[-262.2329240388853,120.32509839464255,142.27376030462807,58.59450238467356]  |
|[-211.46070674857862,128.02378249384793,154.75149804635947,50.062208180745024]|
|[-200.63315592340862,120.42953701711679,154.81412810709375,53.1373395559146]  |
|[-302.3849334900374,127.06531023774065,149.7993102888494,50.159455332553186]  |
|[-263.97657591438696,116.7927409886531,140.56663969089703,50.91680644765467]  |
|[-269.9299103822257,150.554536226529,133.21451586020208,45.58110348236035]    |
|[-209.0476149186765,131.39647389196247,187.15860399038323,45.54423137717909]  |
|[-177.14287138297178,144.35605338289676,169.58339402096036,56.60456363500367] |
|[-235.6463017059383,145.5439429890641,125.0966983578342,51.110873484307696]   |
|[-247.40278654007753,133.43896522241678,153.5230149688606,50.88656791382292]  |
|[-282.63409740151326,115.76292129048788,138.0241685632812,42.10626388266632]  |
|[-273.6249269017216,146.66834495346865,143.16546461334735,48.57367552676949]  |
+----------------------------------------------------------------+
only showing top 20 rows
```

15. From the Spark Master (`http://localhost:4040/jobs`), you can also track the job, as shown in the following figure:

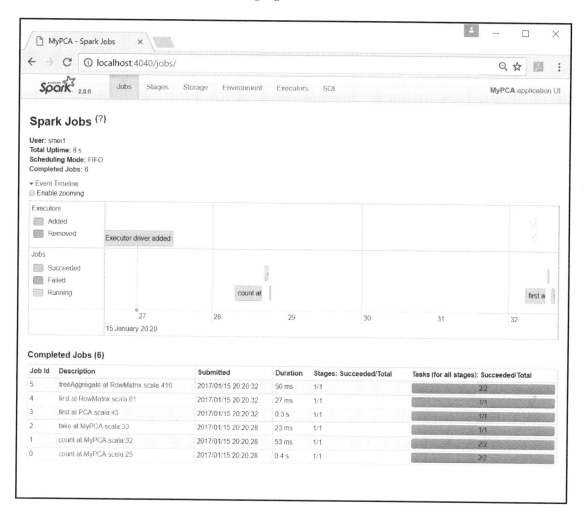

16. We then close the program by stopping the Spark session:

```
spark.stop()
```

How it works...

After loading and processing the data, the core of the work for PCA is done via the following code:

```
val pca = new PCA()
  .setInputCol("features")
  .setOutputCol("pcaFeatures")
  .setK(4)
  .fit(df)
```

The `PCA()` call allows us to select how many components we need (`setK(4)`). In the case of this recipe, we selected the first four components.

The goal is to find a lower-dimension space (a reduced PCA space) from the original higher-dimension data while preserving the structural properties (variance of data along principal component axis) in such a way that allows for maximum discrimination of labeled data without the original high-dimensional space requirement.

A sample PCA chart is shown in the following figure. After dimension reduction, it will look like the following--in this case, we can easily see that most of the variance is explained by the first four principal components. If you quickly examine the graph (red line), you see how fast the variance disappears after the fourth component. This type of knee chart (variance versus number of components) helps us to quickly pick the number of components that are needed (in this case, four components) to explain most of the variance. To recap, almost all the variance (green line) can be cumulatively attributed to the first four components, since it reaches almost 1.0 while the amount of contribution from each individual component can be traced via the red line at the same time:

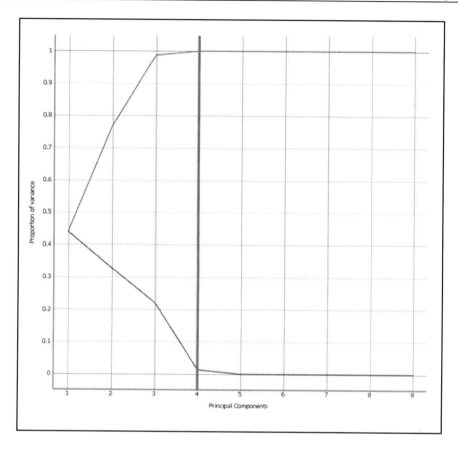

The chart above is a depiction of 'Kaiser Rule' which is the most commonly used approach to selecting the number of components. To produce the chart, one can use R to plot eigenvalues against principal components or write your own using Python.
See the following link from university of Missouri for plotting a chart in R:
http://web.missouri.edu/~huangf/data/mvnotes/Documents/pca_in_r_2.html.
As stated, the chart relates to Kaiser rule which states the more correlation variables loaded in a particular principal component, the more important that factor is in summarizing the data. The eigenvalue in this case can be thought of as a sort of index that measures how good a component is summarizing the data (in direction of maximum variance).

Using PCA is similar to other methods in which we try to learn the distribution for the data. We still need the average of each attribute and K (the number of components to keep), which is simply an estimated covariance. In short, dimension reduction occurs because we are ignoring the directions (the PCA components) that have the least variance. Keep in mind that PCA can be difficult, but you are in control of what happens and how much you keep (use knee charts to select K or the number of components to keep).

There are two methods for calculating PCA:

- Covariance method
- **Singular Value Decomposition (SVD)**

We will outline the covariance matrix method (the straight eigenvector and eigenvalue plus centering) here, but feel free to refer to the SVD recipe (*Singular Value Decomposition (SVD) to reduce high-dimensionality in Spark*) for the inner workings of SVD as it relates to PCA.

The PCA algorithm using the covariance matrix method, in a nutshell, involves the following:

1. Given a matrix of N by M:
    1. N = total number of training data
    2. M is a particular dimension (or feature)
    3. Intersection of M x N is a call with the sample value

2. Compute the mean:

$$\mu = \frac{1}{N} \sum_{i=1}^{N} x_i$$

3. Center (normalize) the data by subtracting the average from each observation:

$$\sum_{i=1}^{N} x_i - \mu$$

4. Construct the covariance matrix:

$$\frac{1}{N-1} D \times D^T$$

5. Compute eigenvectors and eigenvalues of the covariance matrix (it's straightforward, but bear in mind that not all matrices can be decomposed).
6. Pick the eigenvectors that have the largest eigenvalues.
7. The larger the eigenvalue, the more contribution to the variance of a component.

There's more...

The net result of using PCA in this recipe is that the original search space of 14 dimensions (the same as saying14 features) is reduced to 4 dimensions that explain almost all the variations in the original dataset.

PCA is not purely a ML concept and has been in use in finance for many years prior to the ML movement. At its core, PCA uses an orthogonal transformation (each component is perpendicular to the other component) to map the original features (apparent dimensions) to a set of newly derived dimensions so that most of the redundant and co-linear attributes are removed. The derived (actual latent dimension) components are linear combinations of the original attributes.

While it is easy to program PCA from scratch using RDD, the best way to learn it is to try to do PCA with a neuron network implementation and look at the intermediate result. You can do this in Café (on Spark), or just Torch, to see that it is a straight linear transformation despite the mystery surrounding it. At its core, PCA is a straight exercise in linear algebra regardless of whether you use the covariance matrix or SVD for decomposition.

Spark provides examples for PCA via source code on GitHub under both the dimensionality reduction and feature extraction sections.

See also

- Documentation for PCA can be found at `http://spark.apache.org/docs/latest/api/scala/index.html#org.apache.spark.ml.feature.PCA` and `http://spark.apache.org/docs/latest/api/scala/index.html#org.apache.spark.ml.feature.PCAModel`

Some words of caution regarding PCA usage and shortcomings:

- Some datasets are mutually exclusive so that eigenvalues do not dropoff, (every single value is needed for the matrix). For example, the following vectors (.5,0,0), (0,.5,0,0), (0,0,.5,0), and (0,0,0,.5) ...... will not allow any eigenvalue to drop.
- PCA is linear in nature and attempts to learn a Gaussian distribution by using mean and the covariance matrix.
- Sometimes two Gaussian distributions parallel to each other will not allow PCA to find the right direction. In this case, PCA will eventually terminate and find some directions and output them, but are they the best?

12
Implementing Text Analytics with Spark 2.0 ML Library

In this chapter, we will cover the following recipes:

- Doing term frequency with Spark - everything that counts
- Displaying similar words with Spark using Word2Vec
- Downloading a complete dump of Wikipedia for a real-life Spark ML project
- Using Latent Semantic Analysis for text analytics with Spark 2.0
- Topic modeling with Latent Dirichlet allocation in Spark 2.0

Introduction

Text analytics is at the intersection of machine learning, mathematics, linguistics, and natural language processing. Text analytics, referred to as text mining in older literature, attempts to extract information and infer higher level concepts, sentiment, and semantic details from unstructured and semi-structured data. It is important to note that the traditional keyword searches are insufficient to deal with noisy, ambiguous, and irrelevant tokens and concepts that need to be filtered out based on the actual context.

Ultimately, what we are trying to do is for a given set of documents (text, tweets, web, and social media), is determine what the gist of the communication is and what concepts it is trying to convey (topics and concepts). These days, breaking down a document into its parts and taxonomy is too primitive to be considered text analytics. We can do better.

Spark provides a set of tools and facilities to make text analytics easier, but it is up to the users to combine the techniques to come up with a viable system (for example, KKN clustering and topic modelling).

It is worth mentioning that many of the commercially available systems use a combination of techniques to come up with the final answer. While Spark has a sufficient number of techniques that work very well at scale, it would not be hard to imagine that any text analytics system can benefit from a graphical model (that is, GraphFrame, GraphX). The following figure is a summary of the tools and facilities provided by Spark for text analytics:

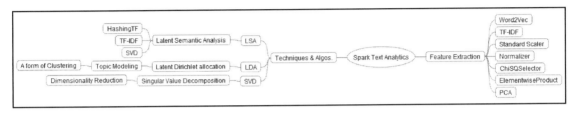

Text analytics is an upcoming and important area due to its application to many fields such as security, customer engagement, sentiment analysis, social media, and online learning. Using text analytics techniques, one can combine traditional data stores (that is, structured data and database tables) with unstructured data (that is, customer reviews, sentiments, and social media interaction) to ascertain a higher order of understanding and a more complete view of the business unit, which was not possible before. This is especially important when dealing with millennials that have chosen social media and unstructured text as their primary means of communication.

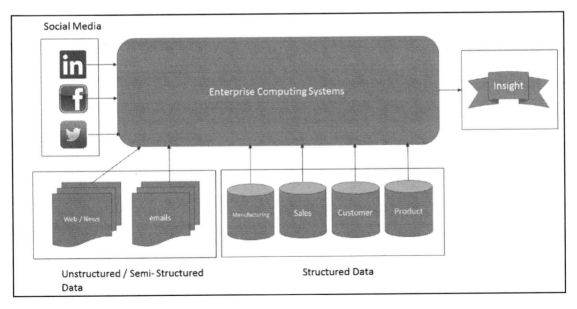

The main challenge with unstructured text is that you cannot use the traditional data platforming tools such as ETL to extract and force order on the data. We need new data wrangling, ML, and statistical methods combined with NLP techniques that can extract information and insight. Social media and customer interactions, such as transcriptions of calls in a call center, contain valuable information that can no longer be ignored without losing one's competitive edge.

We not only need text analytics to be able to address big data at rest, but must also consider big data in motion, such as tweets and streams, to be effective.

There are several approaches to deal with unstructured data. The following figure given is a depiction of the techniques in today's toolkit. While the rule-based system can be a good fit for limited text and domains, it fails to generalize due to its specific decision boundaries designed to be effective in that particular domain. The newer systems use statistical and NLP techniques to achieve better accuracy and scale.

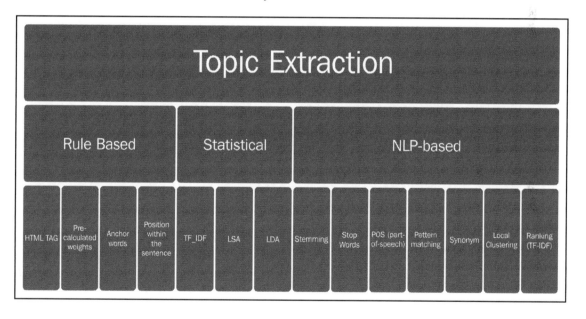

In this chapter, we cover four recipes and two real-life datasets to demonstrate Spark's facilities for handling unstructured text analytics at scale.

First, we start with a simple recipe to not only mimic the early days of web search (keyword frequency) but also to provide insight into TF-IDF in raw code format. This recipe attempts to find out how often a word or phrase occurs in a document. As unbelievable as it sounds, there was a US patent issued for this technique!

Second, we proceed with a well-known algorithm, Word2Vec, which attempts to answer the question, *if I give you a word, can you tell me the surrounding words, or what is in its neighborhood?* This is a good way to ask for synonyms inside a document using statistical techniques.

Third, we implement a **Latent Semantic Analysis (LSA)** which is a form of topic extraction. This method was invented at the University of Colorado Boulder and has been the workhorse in social sciences.

Fourth, we implement a **Latent Dirichlet Allocation (LDA)** to demonstrate topic modelling in which abstract concepts are extracted and associated with phrases or words (that is, less primitive constructs) in a scalable and meaningful way (for example, home, happiness, love, mother, family pet, children, shopping, and parties can be extracted into a single topic).

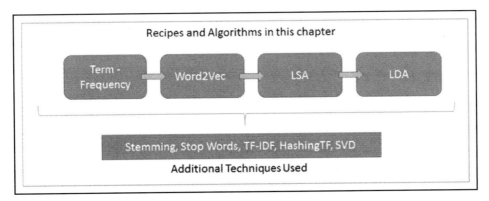

Doing term frequency with Spark - everything that counts

For this recipe, we will download a book in text format from Project Gutenberg, from `http://www.gutenberg.org/cache/epub/62/pg62.txt`.

Project Gutenberg offers over 50,000 free eBooks in various formats for human consumption. Please read their terms of use; let us not use command-line tools to download any books.

When you look at the contents of the file, you will notice the title and author of the book is *The Project Gutenberg EBook of A Princess of Mars* by Edgar Rice Burroughs.

This eBook is for the use of anyone, anywhere, at no cost, and with almost no restrictions whatsoever. You may copy it, give it away, or reuse it under the terms of the Project Gutenberg License included with this eBook online at http://www.gutenberg.org/.

We then use the downloaded book to demonstrate the classic word count program with Scala and Spark. The example may seem somewhat simple at first, but we are beginning the process of feature extraction for text processing. Also, a general understanding of counting word occurrences in a document will go a long way to help us understand the concept of TF-IDF.

How to do it...

1. Start a new project in IntelliJ or in an IDE of your choice. Make sure the necessary JAR files are included.

2. The `package` statement for the recipe is as follows:

```
package spark.ml.cookbook.chapter12
```

3. Import the necessary packages for Scala, Spark, and JFreeChart:

```
import org.apache.log4j.{Level, Logger}
import org.apache.spark.sql.SQLContext
import org.apache.spark.{SparkConf, SparkContext}
import org.jfree.chart.axis.{CategoryAxis, CategoryLabelPositions}
import org.jfree.chart.{ChartFactory, ChartFrame, JFreeChart}
import org.jfree.chart.plot.{CategoryPlot, PlotOrientation}
import org.jfree.data.category.DefaultCategoryDataset
```

4. We will define a function to display our JFreeChart within a window:

```
def show(chart: JFreeChart) {
val frame = new ChartFrame("", chart)
  frame.pack()
  frame.setVisible(true)
}
```

5. Let us define the location of our book file:

```
val input = "../data/sparkml2/chapter12/pg62.txt"
```

6. Create a Spark session with configurations using the factory builder pattern:

```
val spark = SparkSession
  .builder
  .master("local[*]")
  .appName("ProcessWordCount")
  .config("spark.sql.warehouse.dir", ".")
  .getOrCreate()
import spark.implicits._
```

7. We should set the logging level to warning, otherwise output will be difficult to follow:

```
Logger.getRootLogger.setLevel(Level.WARN)
```

8. We read in the file of stop words which will be used as a filter later:

```
val stopwords =
scala.io.Source.fromFile("../data/sparkml2/chapter12/stopwords.txt"
).getLines().toSet
```

9. The stop words file contains commonly used words which show no relevant value in matching or comparing documents, therefore they will be excluded from the pool of terms by a filter.

10. We now load the book to tokenize, analyze, apply stop words, filter, count, and sort:

```
val lineOfBook = spark.sparkContext.textFile(input)
  .flatMap(line => line.split("\\W+"))
  .map(_.toLowerCase)
  .filter( s => !stopwords.contains(s))
  .filter( s => s.length >= 2)
  .map(word => (word, 1))
  .reduceByKey(_ + _)
  .sortBy(_._2, false)
```

11. We take top the 25 words which have the highest frequency:

```
val top25 = lineOfBook.take(25)
```

12. We loop through every element in the resulting RDD, generating a category dataset model to build our chart of word occurrences:

```
val dataset = new DefaultCategoryDataset()
top25.foreach( {case (term: String, count: Int) =>
dataset.setValue(count, "Count", term) })
```

Display a bar chart of the word count:

```
val chart = ChartFactory.createBarChart("Term frequency",
 "Words", "Count", dataset, PlotOrientation.VERTICAL,
 false, true, false)

 val plot = chart.getCategoryPlot()
 val domainAxis = plot.getDomainAxis();
domainAxis.setCategoryLabelPositions(CategoryLabelPositions.DOWN_45
);
show(chart)
```

The following chart displays the word count:

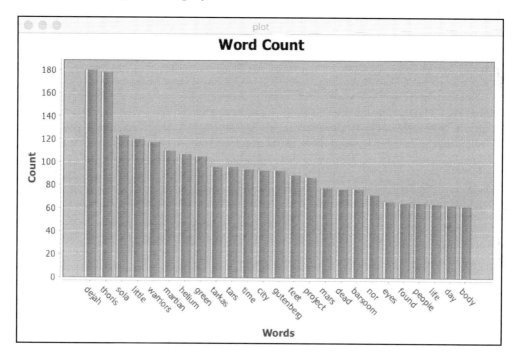

13. We close the program by stopping the SparkContext:

```
spark.stop()
```

How it works...

We began by loading the downloaded book and tokenizing it via a regular expression. The next step was to convert all tokens to lowercase and exclude stop words from our token list, followed by filtering out any words less than two characters long.

The removal of stop words and words of a certain length reduce the number of features we have to process. It may not seem obvious, but the removal of particular words based on various processing criteria reduce the number of dimensions our machine learning algorithms will later process.

Finally, we sorted the resulting word count in descending order, taking the top 25, which we displayed a bar chart for.

There's more...

In this recipe, we have the base of what a keyword search would do. It is important to understand the difference between topic modelling and keyword search. In a keyword search, we try to associate a phrase with a given document based on the occurrences. In this case, we will point the user to a set of documents that has the most number of occurrences.

See also

The next step in the evolution of this algorithm, that a developer can try as an extension, would be to add weights and come up with a weighted average, but then Spark provides a facility which we explore in the upcoming recipes.

Displaying similar words with Spark using Word2Vec

In this recipe, we will explore Word2Vec, which is Spark's tool for assessing word similarity. The Word2Vec algorithm is inspired by the *distributional hypothesis* in general linguistics. At the core, what it tries to say is that the tokens which occur in the same context (that is, distance from the target) tend to support the same primitive concept/meaning.

The Word2Vec algorithm was invented by a team of researchers at Google. Please refer to a white paper mentioned in the *There's more...* section of this recipe which describes Word2Vec in more detail.

How to do it...

1. Start a new project in IntelliJ or in an IDE of your choice. Make sure the necessary JAR files are included.

2. The `package` statement for the recipe is as follows:

   ```
   package spark.ml.cookbook.chapter12
   ```

3. Import the necessary packages for Scala and Spark:

   ```
   import org.apache.log4j.{Level, Logger}
   import org.apache.spark.ml.feature.{RegexTokenizer,
   StopWordsRemover, Word2Vec}
   import org.apache.spark.sql.{SQLContext, SparkSession}
   import org.apache.spark.{SparkConf, SparkContext}
   ```

4. Let us define the location of our book file:

   ```
   val input = "../data/sparkml2/chapter12/pg62.txt"
   ```

5. Create a Spark session with configurations using the factory builder pattern:

   ```
   val spark = SparkSession
             .builder
   .master("local[*]")
           .appName("Word2Vec App")
           .config("spark.sql.warehouse.dir", ".")
           .getOrCreate()
   import spark.implicits._
   ```

6. We should set the logging level to warning, otherwise output will be difficult to follow:

   ```
   Logger.getRootLogger.setLevel(Level.WARN)
   ```

7. We load in the book and convert it to a DataFrame:

```
val df = spark.read.text(input).toDF("text")
```

8. We now transform each line into a bag of words utilizing Spark's regular expression tokenizer, converting each term into lowercase and filtering away any term which has a character length of less than four:

```
val tokenizer = new RegexTokenizer()
 .setPattern("\\W+")
 .setToLowercase(true)
 .setMinTokenLength(4)
 .setInputCol("text")
 .setOutputCol("raw")
 val rawWords = tokenizer.transform(df)
```

9. We remove stop words by using Spark's `StopWordRemover` class:

```
val stopWords = new StopWordsRemover()
 .setInputCol("raw")
 .setOutputCol("terms")
 .setCaseSensitive(false)
 val wordTerms = stopWords.transform(rawWords)
```

10. We apply the Word2Vec machine learning algorithm to extract features:

```
val word2Vec = new Word2Vec()
 .setInputCol("terms")
 .setOutputCol("result")
 .setVectorSize(3)
 .setMinCount(0)
 val model = word2Vec.fit(wordTerms)
```

11. We find ten synonyms from the book for *martian*:

```
val synonyms = model.findSynonyms("martian", 10)
```

12. Display the results of ten synonyms found by the model:

```
synonyms.show(false)
```

```
+-----------+-------------------+
|word       |similarity         |
+-----------+-------------------+
|fool       |0.399660404463996  |
|friendships|0.3995726061226465 |
|recently   |0.399537090796303  |
|belongings |0.3995208890222543 |
|passageway |0.39947730349854393|
|dignified  |0.3993753331167374 |
|entry      |0.3993680127191416 |
|maximum    |0.3993070923891028 |
|tongue     |0.3992951179510815 |
|groundless |0.39928608744352556|
+-----------+-------------------+
```

13. We close the program by stopping the SparkContext:

```
spark.stop()
```

How it works...

Word2Vec in Spark uses skip-gram and not **continuous bag of words** (**CBOW**) which is more suitable for a **Neural Net** (**NN**). At its core, we are attempting to compute the representation of the words. It is highly recommended for the user to understand the difference between local representation versus distributed presentation, which is very different to the apparent meaning of the words themselves.

If we use distributed vector representation for words, it is natural that similar words will fall close together in the vector space, which is a desirable generalization technique for pattern abstraction and manipulation (that is, we reduce the problem to vector arithmetic).

What we want to do for a given set of words *{Word$_1$, Word$_2$, ..., Word$_n$}* that are cleaned and ready for processing, is define a maximum likelihood function (for example, log likelihood) for the sequence, and then proceed to maximize likelihood (that is, typical ML). For those familiar with NN, this is a simple multi class softmax model.

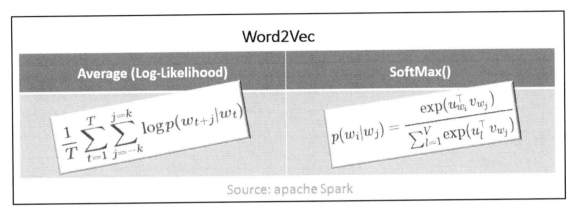

Word2Vec	
Average (Log-Likelihood)	**SoftMax()**
$$\frac{1}{T}\sum_{t=1}^{T}\sum_{j=-k}^{j=k}\log p(w_{t+j}|w_t)$$	$$p(w_i|w_j) = \frac{\exp(u_{w_i}^T v_{w_j})}{\sum_{l=1}^{V}\exp(u_l^T v_{w_j})}$$

Source: apache Spark

We start off with loading the free book into the memory and tokenizing it into terms. The terms are then converted into lowercase and we filter out any words less than four. We finally apply the stop words followed by the Word2Vec computation.

There's more...

How would you find similar words anyhow? How many algorithms are there that can solve this problem, and how do they vary? The Word2Vec algorithm has been around for a while and has a counterpart called CBOW. Please bear in mind that Spark provides the skip-gram method as the implementation technique.

The variations of the Word2Vec algorithm are as follows:

- **Continuous Bag of Words (CBOW)**: Given a central word, what are the surrounding words?
- **Skip-gram**: If we know the words surrounding, can we guess the missing word?

There is a variation of the algorithm that is called **skip-gram model with negative sampling (SGNS)**, which seems to outperform other variants.

The co-occurrence is the fundamental concept underlying both CBOW and skip-gram. Even though the skip-gram does not directly use a co-occurrence matrix, it is using it indirectly.

In this recipe, we used the *stop words* techniques from NLP to have a cleaner corpus before running our algorithm. The stop words are English words such as "*the*" that need to be removed since they are not contributing to any improvement in the outcome.

Another important concept is *stemming*, which is not covered here, but will be demonstrated in later recipes. Stemming removes extra language artefacts and reduces the word to its root (for example, *Engineering, Engineer,* and *Engineers* become *Engin* which is the root).

The white paper found at the following URL should provide deeper explanation for Word2Vec:

```
http://arxiv.org/pdf/1301.3781.pdf
```

See also

Documentation for the Word2Vec recipe:

- `Word2Vec()`: http://spark.apache.org/docs/latest/api/scala/index.html#org.apache.spark.ml.feature.Word2Vec
- `Word2VecModel()`: http://spark.apache.org/docs/latest/api/scala/index.html#org.apache.spark.ml.feature.Word2VecModel
- `StopWordsRemover()`: http://spark.apache.org/docs/latest/api/scala/index.html#org.apache.spark.ml.feature.StopWordsRemover

Downloading a complete dump of Wikipedia for a real-life Spark ML project

In this recipe, we will be downloading and exploring a dump of Wikipedia so we can have a real-life example. The dataset that we will be downloading in this recipe is a dump of Wikipedia articles. You will either need the command-line tool **curl**, or a browser to retrieve a compressed file, which is about 13.6 GB at this time. Due to the size, we recommend the curl command-line tool.

How to do it...

1. You can start with downloading the dataset using the following command:

```
curl -L -O
http://dumps.wikimedia.org/enwiki/latest/enwiki-latest-pages-articl
es-multistream.xml.bz2
```

2. Now you want to decompress the ZIP file:

```
bunzip2 enwiki-latest-pages-articles-multistream.xml.bz2
```

This should create an uncompressed file which is named `enwiki-latest-pages-articles-multistream.xml` and is about 56 GB.

3. Let us take a look at the Wikipedia XML file:

```
head -n50 enwiki-latest-pages-articles-multistream.xml
<mediawiki xmlns=http://www.mediawiki.org/xml/export-0.10/
xmlns:xsi="http://www.w3.org/2001/XMLSchema-instance"
xsi:schemaLocation="http://www.mediawiki.org/xml/export-0.10/
http://www.mediawiki.org/xml/export-0.10.xsd" version="0.10"
xml:lang="en">

  <siteinfo>
    <sitename>Wikipedia</sitename>
    <dbname>enwiki</dbname>
    <base>https://en.wikipedia.org/wiki/Main_Page</base>
    <generator>MediaWiki 1.27.0-wmf.22</generator>
    <case>first-letter</case>
    <namespaces>
      <namespace key="-2" case="first-letter">Media</namespace>
      <namespace key="-1" case="first-letter">Special</namespace>
      <namespace key="0" case="first-letter" />
      <namespace key="1" case="first-letter">Talk</namespace>
      <namespace key="2" case="first-letter">User</namespace>
      <namespace key="3" case="first-letter">User talk</namespace>
      <namespace key="4" case="first-letter">Wikipedia</namespace>
      <namespace key="5" case="first-letter">Wikipedia
talk</namespace>
      <namespace key="6" case="first-letter">File</namespace>
      <namespace key="7" case="first-letter">File talk</namespace>
      <namespace key="8" case="first-letter">MediaWiki</namespace>
      <namespace key="9" case="first-letter">MediaWiki
talk</namespace>
      <namespace key="10" case="first-letter">Template</namespace>
      <namespace key="11" case="first-letter">Template
```

```
talk</namespace>
      <namespace key="12" case="first-letter">Help</namespace>
      <namespace key="13" case="first-letter">Help talk</namespace>
      <namespace key="14" case="first-letter">Category</namespace>
      <namespace key="15" case="first-letter">Category
talk</namespace>
      <namespace key="100" case="first-letter">Portal</namespace>
      <namespace key="101" case="first-letter">Portal
talk</namespace>
      <namespace key="108" case="first-letter">Book</namespace>
      <namespace key="109" case="first-letter">Book
talk</namespace>
      <namespace key="118" case="first-letter">Draft</namespace>
      <namespace key="119" case="first-letter">Draft
talk</namespace>
      <namespace key="446" case="first-letter">Education
Program</namespace>
      <namespace key="447" case="first-letter">Education Program
talk</namespace>
      <namespace key="710" case="first-
letter">TimedText</namespace>
      <namespace key="711" case="first-letter">TimedText
talk</namespace>
      <namespace key="828" case="first-letter">Module</namespace>
      <namespace key="829" case="first-letter">Module
talk</namespace>
      <namespace key="2300" case="first-letter">Gadget</namespace>
      <namespace key="2301" case="first-letter">Gadget
talk</namespace>
      <namespace key="2302" case="case-sensitive">Gadget
definition</namespace>
      <namespace key="2303" case="case-sensitive">Gadget definition
talk</namespace>
      <namespace key="2600" case="first-letter">Topic</namespace>
    </namespaces>
  </siteinfo>
  <page>
    <title>AccessibleComputing</title>
    <ns>0</ns>
    <id>10</id>
    <redirect title="Computer accessibility" />
```

There's more...

We recommend working with the XML file in chunks, and using sampling for your experiments until you are ready for a final job submit. It will save a tremendous amount of time and effort.

See also

Documentation for Wiki download is available at `https://en.wikipedia.org/wiki/Wikipedia:Database_download`.

Using Latent Semantic Analysis for text analytics with Spark 2.0

In this recipe, we will explore LSA utilizing a data dump of articles from Wikipedia. LSA translates into analyzing a corpus of documents to find hidden meaning or concepts in those documents.

In the first recipe of this chapter, we covered the basics of the TF (that is, term frequency) technique. In this recipe, we use HashingTF for calculating TF and use IDF to fit a model into the calculated TF. At its core, LSA uses **singular value decomposition** (**SVD**) on the term frequency document to reduce dimensionality and therefore extract the most important concepts. There are other cleanup steps that we need to do (for example, stop words and stemming) that will clean up the bag of words before we start analyzing it.

How to do it...

1. Start a new project in IntelliJ or in an IDE of your choice. Make sure the necessary JAR files are included.

2. The package statement for the recipe is as follows:

    ```
    package spark.ml.cookbook.chapter12
    ```

3. Import the necessary packages for Scala and Spark:

```
import edu.umd.cloud9.collection.wikipedia.WikipediaPage
import
edu.umd.cloud9.collection.wikipedia.language.EnglishWikipediaPage
import org.apache.hadoop.fs.Path
import org.apache.hadoop.io.Text
import org.apache.hadoop.mapred.{FileInputFormat, JobConf}
import org.apache.log4j.{Level, Logger}
import org.apache.spark.mllib.feature.{HashingTF, IDF}
import org.apache.spark.mllib.linalg.distributed.RowMatrix
import org.apache.spark.sql.SparkSession
import org.tartarus.snowball.ext.PorterStemmer
```

The following two statements import the `Cloud9` library toolkit elements necessary for processing Wikipedia XML dumps/objects. `Cloud9` is a library toolkit that makes accessing, wrangling, and processing the Wikipedia XML dumps easier for developers. See the following lines of code for more detailed information:

```
import edu.umd.cloud9.collection.wikipedia.WikipediaPage
import
edu.umd.cloud9.collection.wikipedia.language.EnglishWikipediaPage
```

Wikipedia is a free body of knowledge that can be freely downloaded as a dump of XML chunks/objects via the following Wikipedia download link:

```
https://en.wikipedia.org/wiki/Wikipedia:Database_download
```

The complexity of text and its structure can be easily handled using the `Cloud9` toolkit which facilitates accessing and processing the text using the `import` statements listed previously.

The following link provides some information regarding the `Cloud9` library:

- Main page is available
  at `https://lintool.github.io/Cloud9/docs/content/wikipedia.html`.
- Source code is available
  at `http://grepcode.com/file/repo1.maven.org/maven2/edu.umd.cloud9/2.0.0/edu/umd/cloud9/collection/wikipedia/WikipediaPage.java`
  and `http://grepcode.com/file/repo1.maven.org/maven2/edu.umd.cloud9/2.0.1/edu/umd/cloud9/collection/wikipedia/language/EnglishWikipediaPage.java`.

Next, perform the following steps:

1. We define a function to parse a Wikipedia page and return the title and content text of the page:

```
def parseWikiPage(rawPage: String): Option[(String, String)] = {
 val wikiPage = new EnglishWikipediaPage()
 WikipediaPage.readPage(wikiPage, rawPage)

 if (wikiPage.isEmpty
 || wikiPage.isDisambiguation
 || wikiPage.isRedirect
 || !wikiPage.isArticle) {
 None
 } else {
 Some(wikiPage.getTitle, wikiPage.getContent)
 }
 }
```

2. We define a short function to apply the Porter stemming algorithm to terms:

```
def wordStem(stem: PorterStemmer, term: String): String = {
 stem.setCurrent(term)
 stem.stem()
 stem.getCurrent
 }
```

3. We define a function to tokenize content text of a page into terms:

```
def tokenizePage(rawPageText: String, stopWords: Set[String]):
Seq[String] = {
 val stem = new PorterStemmer()

 rawPageText.split("\\W+")
 .map(_.toLowerCase)
 .filterNot(s => stopWords.contains(s))
 .map(s => wordStem(stem, s))
 .filter(s => s.length > 3)
 .distinct
 .toSeq
 }
```

4. Let us define the location of the Wikipedia data dump:

```
val input = "../data/sparkml2/chapter12/enwiki_dump.xml"
```

5. Create a job configuration for Hadoop XML streaming:

```
val jobConf = new JobConf()
 jobConf.set("stream.recordreader.class",
"org.apache.hadoop.streaming.StreamXmlRecordReader")
 jobConf.set("stream.recordreader.begin", "<page>")
 jobConf.set("stream.recordreader.end", "</page>")
```

6. We set up the data path for Hadoop XML streaming processing:

```
FileInputFormat.addInputPath(jobConf, new Path(input))
```

7. Create a `SparkSession` with configurations using the factory builder pattern:

```
val spark = SparkSession
   .builder
.master("local[*]")
   .appName("ProcessLSA App")
   .config("spark.serializer",
"org.apache.spark.serializer.KryoSerializer")
   .config("spark.sql.warehouse.dir", ".")
   .getOrCreate()
```

8. We should set the logging level to warning, otherwise output will be difficult to follow:

```
Logger.getRootLogger.setLevel(Level.WARN)
```

9. We begin to process the huge Wikipedia data dump into article pages, taking a sample of the file:

```
val wikiData = spark.sparkContext.hadoopRDD(
 jobConf,
 classOf[org.apache.hadoop.streaming.StreamInputFormat],
 classOf[Text],
 classOf[Text]).sample(false, .1)
```

10. Next, we process our sample data into an RDD containing a tuple of title and page context text:

```
val wikiPages = wikiData.map(_._1.toString).flatMap(parseWikiPage)
```

11. We now output the number of Wikipedia articles we will process:

```
println("Wiki Page Count: " + wikiPages.count())
```

12. We load into memory the stop words for filtering the page content text:

```
val stopwords =
scala.io.Source.fromFile("../data/sparkml2/chapter12/stopwords.txt"
).getLines().toSet
```

13. We tokenize the page content text, turning it into terms for further processing:

```
val wikiTerms = wikiPages.map{ case(title, text) =>
tokenizePage(text, stopwords)  }
```

14. We use Spark's `HashingTF` class to compute term frequency of our tokenized page context text:

```
val hashtf = new HashingTF()
 val tf = hashtf.transform(wikiTerms)
```

15. We take term frequencies and compute the inverse document frequency utilizing Spark's IDF class:

```
val idf = new IDF(minDocFreq=2)
 val idfModel = idf.fit(tf)
 val tfidf = idfModel.transform(tf)
```

16. We generate a `RowMatrix` using the inverse document frequency and compute singular value decomposition:

```
tfidf.cache()
 val rowMatrix = new RowMatrix(tfidf)
 val svd = rowMatrix.computeSVD(k=25, computeU = true)

 println(svd)
```

U: The rows will be documents and the columns will be concepts.

S: The elements will be the amount variation from each concept.

V: The rows will be terms and the columns will be concepts.

17. We close the program by stopping the SparkContext:

```
spark.stop()
```

How it works...

The example starts off by loading a dump of Wikipedia XML using Cloud9 Hadoop XML streaming tools to process the enormous XML document. Once we have parsed out the page text, the tokenization phase invokes turning our stream of Wikipedia page text into tokens. We used the Porter stemmer during the tokenization phase to help reduce words to a common base form.

More details on stemming is available at `https://en.wikipedia.org/wiki/Stemming`.

The next step was to use Spark HashingTF on each page token to compute the term frequency. After this phase was completed, we utilized Spark's IDF to generate the inverse document frequency.

Finally, we took the TF-IDF API and applied a singular value decomposition to handle factorization and dimensionality reduction.

The following screenshot shows the steps and flow of the recipe:

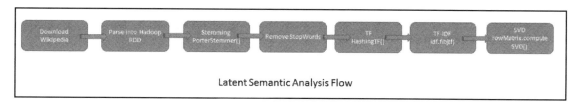

Latent Semantic Analysis Flow

The Cloud9 Hadoop XML tools and several other required dependencies can be found at:

- `bliki-core-3.0.19.jar`: http://central.maven.org/maven2/info/bliki/wiki/bliki-core/3.0.19/bliki-core-3.0.19.jar
- `cloud9-2.0.1.jar`: http://central.maven.org/maven2/edu/umd/cloud9/2.0.1/cloud9-2.0.1.jar
- `hadoop-streaming-2.7.4.jar`: http://central.maven.org/maven2/org/apache/hadoop/hadoop-streaming/2.7.4/hadoop-streaming-2.7.4.jar
- `lucene-snowball-3.0.3.jar`: http://central.maven.org/maven2/org/apache/lucene/lucene-snowball/3.0.3/lucene-snowball-3.0.3.jar

There's more...

It should be obvious by now that even though Spark does not provide a direct LSA implementation, the combination of TF-IDF and SVD will let us construct and then decompose the large corpus matrix into three matrices, which can help us interpret the results by applying the dimensionality reduction via SVD. We can concentrate on the most meaningful clusters (similar to a recommendation algorithm).

SVD will factor the term frequency document (that is, documents by attributes) to three distinct matrices that are much more efficient to extract to *N* concepts (that is, *N=27* in our example) from a large matrix that is hard and expensive to handle. In ML, we always prefer the tall and skinny matrices (that is, *U* matrix in this case) to other variations.

The following is the technique for SVD:

$$M = U\Sigma V^*$$

The primary goal of SVD is dimensionality reduction to cure desired (that is, top *N*) topics or abstract concepts. We will use the following input to get the output stated in the following section.

As input, we'll take a large matrix of *m x n* (*m* is the number of documents, *n* is the number of terms or attributes).

This is the output that we should get:

- Matrix 1 (m by n) ----> U [topics]
- Matrix 2 (n by n) ----> S [Eigenvalues are in diagonal of Matrix S]
- Matrix 3 (n by n) ------> V [proportion of contribution]

For a more detailed example and short tutorial on SVD, please see the following links:

- http://home.iitk.ac.in/~crkrish/MLT/PreRequisites/linalgWithSVD.pdf
- http://davetang.org/file/Singular_Value_Decomposition_Tutorial.pdf

You can also refer to a write up from RStudio, which is available at the following link:

http://rstudio-pubs-static.s3.amazonaws.com/222293_1c40c75d7faa42869cc59df87954
7c2b.html

See also

SVD has been covered in detail in `Chapter 11`, *Curse of High-Dimensionality in Big Data.*

For a pictorial representation of SVD, please see the recipe *Using Singular Value Decomposition (SVD) to address high-dimensionality* in `Chapter 11`, *Curse of High-Dimensionality in Big Data.*

More details on `SingularValueDecomposition()` can be found at `http://spark.apache.org/docs/latest/api/scala/index.html#org.apache.spark.mllib.linalg.SingularValueDecomposition`.

Please refer to `http://spark.apache.org/docs/latest/api/scala/index.html#org.apache.spark.mllib.linalg.distributed.RowMatrix` for more details on `RowMatrix()`.

Topic modeling with Latent Dirichlet allocation in Spark 2.0

In this recipe, we will be demonstrating topic model generation by utilizing Latent Dirichlet Allocation to infer topics from a collection of documents.

We have covered LDA in previous chapters as it applies to clustering and topic modelling, but in this chapter, we demonstrate a more elaborate example to show its application to text analytics using more real-life and complex datasets.

We also apply NLP techniques such as stemming and stop words to provide a more realistic approach to LDA problem-solving. What we are trying to do is to discover a set of latent factors (that is, different from the original) that can solve and describe the solution in a more efficient way in a reduced computational space.

The first question that always comes up when using LDA and topic modelling is *what is Dirichlet?* Dirichlet is simply a type of distribution and nothing more. Please see the following link from the University of Minnesota for details: `http://www.tc.umn.edu/~horte005/docs/Dirichletdistribution.pdf`.

How to do it...

1. Start a new project in IntelliJ or in an IDE of your choice. Make sure the necessary JAR files are included.

2. The `package` statement for the recipe is as follows:

   ```
   package spark.ml.cookbook.chapter12
   ```

3. Import the necessary packages for Scala and Spark:

   ```
   import edu.umd.cloud9.collection.wikipedia.WikipediaPage
   import edu.umd.cloud9.collection.wikipedia.language.EnglishWikipediaPage
   import org.apache.hadoop.fs.Path
   import org.apache.hadoop.io.Text
   import org.apache.hadoop.mapred.{FileInputFormat, JobConf}
   import org.apache.log4j.{Level, Logger}
   import org.apache.spark.ml.clustering.LDA
   import org.apache.spark.ml.feature._
   import org.apache.spark.sql.SparkSession
   ```

4. We define a function to parse a Wikipedia page and return the title and content text of the page:

   ```
   def parseWikiPage(rawPage: String): Option[(String, String)] = {
   val wikiPage = new EnglishWikipediaPage()
   WikipediaPage.readPage(wikiPage, rawPage)

   if (wikiPage.isEmpty
   || wikiPage.isDisambiguation
   || wikiPage.isRedirect
   || !wikiPage.isArticle) {
   None
   } else {
   Some(wikiPage.getTitle, wikiPage.getContent)
   }
   }
   ```

5. Let us define the location of the Wikipedia data dump:

   ```
   val input = "../data/sparkml2/chapter12/enwiki_dump.xml"
   ```

6. We create a job configuration for Hadoop XML streaming:

   ```
   val jobConf = new JobConf()
   ```

```
jobConf.set ("stream.recordreader.class",
"org.apache.hadoop.streaming.StreamXmlRecordReader")
jobConf.set ("stream.recordreader.begin", "<page>")
jobConf.set ("stream.recordreader.end", "</page>")
```

7. We set up the data path for Hadoop XML streaming processing:

```
FileInputFormat.addInputPath(jobConf, new Path(input))
```

8. Create a `SparkSession` with configurations using the factory builder pattern:

```
val spark = SparkSession
    .builder
.master("local[*]")
    .appName("ProcessLDA App")
    .config("spark.serializer",
"org.apache.spark.serializer.KryoSerializer")
    .config("spark.sql.warehouse.dir", ".")
    .getOrCreate()
```

9. We should set the logging level to warning, otherwise output will be difficult to follow:

```
Logger.getRootLogger.setLevel(Level.WARN)
```

10. We begin to process the huge Wikipedia data dump into article pages taking a sample of the file:

```
val wikiData = spark.sparkContext.hadoopRDD(
  jobConf,
  classOf[org.apache.hadoop.streaming.StreamInputFormat],
  classOf[Text],
  classOf[Text]).sample(false, .1)
```

11. Next, we process our sample data into an RDD containing a tuple of title and page context text to finally generate a DataFrame:

```
val df = wiki.map(_._1.toString)
  .flatMap(parseWikiPage)
  .toDF("title", "text")
```

12. We now transform the text column of the DataFrame into raw words using Spark's `RegexTokenizer` for each Wikipedia page:

```
val tokenizer = new RegexTokenizer()
  .setPattern("\\W+")
  .setToLowercase(true)
```

```
.setMinTokenLength(4)
.setInputCol("text")
.setOutputCol("raw")
val rawWords = tokenizer.transform(df)
```

13. The next step is to filter raw words by removing all stop words from the tokens:

```
val stopWords = new StopWordsRemover()
.setInputCol("raw")
.setOutputCol("words")
.setCaseSensitive(false)

val wordData = stopWords.transform(rawWords)
```

14. We generate term counts for the filtered tokens by using Spark's CountVectorizer class, resulting in a new DataFrame containing the column features:

```
val cvModel = new CountVectorizer()
.setInputCol("words")
.setOutputCol("features")
.setMinDF(2)
.fit(wordData)
val cv = cvModel.transform(wordData)
cv.cache()
```

The "MinDF" specifies the minimum number of different document terms that must appear in order to be included in the vocabulary.

15. We now invoke Spark's LDA class to generate topics and the distributions of tokens to topics:

```
val lda = new LDA()
.setK(5)
.setMaxIter(10)
.setFeaturesCol("features")
val model = lda.fit(tf)
val transformed = model.transform(tf)
```

The "K" refers to how many topics and "MaxIter" maximum iterations to execute.

16. We finally describe the top five generated topics and display:

```
val topics = model.describeTopics(5)
topics.show(false)
```

```
|topic|          termIndices|          termWeights|
+-----+--------------------+--------------------+
|    0|[712, 2706, 155, ...|[0.00156744184517...|
|    1|[0, 1991, 1, 712,...|[0.00164906709185...|
|    2|[155, 74, 56, 974...|[0.00142808800646...|
|    3|[2473, 3487, 1, 9...|[0.00121717433276...|
|    4|[712, 155, 4533, ...|[0.00145563043495...|
+-----+--------------------+--------------------+
```

17. Now display, topics and terms associated with them:

```
val vocaList = cvModel.vocabulary
topics.collect().foreach { r => {
 println("\nTopic: " + r.get(r.fieldIndex("topic")))
 val y =
r.getSeq[Int](r.fieldIndex("termIndices")).map(vocaList(_))
 .zip(r.getSeq[Double](r.fieldIndex("termWeights")))
 y.foreach(println)

 }
}
```

The console output will be as follows:

```
Topic: 0
(insurance,0.0015674418451765248)
(samba,0.0011258608853073513)
(rights,0.0010481985926593705)
(spyware,8.513540441748018E-4)
(time,8.01287339366417E-4)

Topic: 1
(american,0.0016490670918540016)
(netscape,0.0014955491401855165)
(used,9.353119763794209E-4)
(insurance,8.560486990185497E-4)
(analog,6.742308290569271E-4)

Topic: 2
(rights,0.0014280880064640189)
(human,0.001249116068564253)
(party,9.28780904037864E-4)
(labor,8.218773234641597E-4)
(mail,8.203236523858697E-4)

Topic: 3
(belarus,0.001217174332760276)
(interlingua,9.702547559148557E-4)
(used,8.767760726675688E-4)
(city,5.509786244008334E-4)
(embassy,5.30830057520273E-4)

Topic: 4
(Insurance, 0.0014556304349531235)
(rights,0.0011301614983826025)
(voight,7.854171410474698E-4)
(human,7.751093184402613E-4)
(world,6.139408988550648E-4)
```

18. We close the program by stopping the SparkContext:

```
spark.stop()
```

How it works...

We began with loading the dump of Wikipedia articles and parsed the page text into tokens using Hadoop XML leveraging streaming facilities API. The feature extraction process utilized several classes to set up the final processing by the LDA class, letting the tokens flow from Spark's `RegexTokenize`, `StopwordsRemover`, and `HashingTF`. Once we had the term frequencies, the data was passed to the LDA class for clustering the articles together under several topics.

The Hadoop XML tools and several other required dependencies can be found at:

- `bliki-core-3.0.19.jar`: http://central.maven.org/maven2/info/bliki/ wiki/bliki-core/3.0.19/bliki-core-3.0.19.jar
- `cloud9-2.0.1.jar`: http://central.maven.org/maven2/edu/umd/cloud9/2.0. 1/cloud9-2.0.1.jar
- `hadoop-streaming-2.7.4.jar`: http://central.maven.org/maven2/org/ apache/hadoop/hadoop-streaming/2.7.4/hadoop-streaming-2.7.4.jar
- `lucene-snowball-3.0.3.jar`: http://central.maven.org/maven2/org/ apache/lucene/lucene-snowball/3.0.3/lucene-snowball-3.0.3.jar

There's more...

Please see the recipe LDA to classify documents and text into topics in `Chapter 8`, *Unsupervised Clustering with Apache Spark 2.0* for a more detailed explanation of the LDA algorithm itself.

The following white paper from the *Journal of Machine Learning Research (JMLR)* provides a comprehensive treatment for those who would like to do an extensive analysis. It is a well written paper, and a person with a basic background in stat and math should be able to follow it without any problems.

Refer to the `http://www.jmlr.org/papers/volume3/blei03a/blei03a.pdf` link for more details of JMLR; an alternative link is
`https://www.cs.colorado.edu/~mozer/Teaching/syllabi/ProbabilisticModels/reading s/BleiNgJordan2003.pdf`.

See also

- Documentation for constructor is available
  at `http://spark.apache.org/docs/latest/api/scala/index.html#org.apache.spark.ml.clustering.LDA`
- Documentation for LDAModel is available at `http://spark.apache.org/docs/latest/api/scala/index.html#org.apache.spark.ml.clustering.LDAModel`

See also Spark's Scala API documentation for the following:

- DistributedLDAModel
- EMLDAOptimizer
- LDAOptimizer
- LocalLDAModel
- OnlineLDAOptimizer

13
Spark Streaming and Machine Learning Library

In this chapter, we will cover the following recipes:

- Structured streaming for near real-time machine learning
- Streaming DataFrames for real-time machine learning
- Streaming Datasets for real-time machine learning
- Streaming data and debugging with queueStream
- Downloading and understanding the famous Iris data for unsupervised classification
- Streaming KMeans for a real-time online classifier
- Downloading wine quality data for streaming regression
- Streaming linear regression for a real-time regression
- Downloading Pima Diabetes data for supervised classification
- Streaming logistic regression for an on-line classifier

Introduction

Spark streaming is an evolving journey toward unification and structuring of the APIs in order to address the concerns of batch versus stream. Spark streaming has been available since Spark 1.3 with **Discretized Stream (DStream)**. The new direction is to abstract the underlying framework using an unbounded table model in which the users can query the table using SQL or functional programming and write the output to another output table in multiple modes (complete, delta, and append output). The Spark SQL Catalyst optimizer and Tungsten (off-heap memory manager) are now an intrinsic part of the Spark streaming, which leads to a much efficient execution.

In this chapter, we not only cover the streaming facilities available in Spark's machine library out of the box, but also provide four introductory recipes that we found useful as we journeyed toward our better understanding of Spark 2.0.

The following figure depicts what is covered in this chapter:

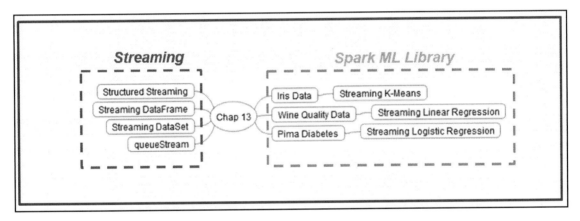

Spark 2.0+ builds on the success of the previous generation by abstracting away some of the framework's inner workings and presenting it to the developer without worrying about *end-to-end write only once* semantics. It is a journey from DStream based on RDD to a structured streaming paradigm in which your world of streaming can be viewed as infinite tables with multiple modes for output.

The state management has evolved from `updateStateByKey` (Spark 1.3 to Spark 1.5) to `mapWithState` (Spark 1.6+) to the third generation state management with structured streaming (Spark 2.0+).

A modern ML streaming system is a complex continuous application that needs to not only combine various ML steps into a pipeline, but also interact with other subsystems to provide a real-life useful, end-to-end information system.

> As we were wrapping up the book, Databricks, the company that empowers the Spark community, made the following announcement at Spark Summit West 2017 regarding the future direction of Spark streaming (not prod release yet):

> *"Today, we are excited to propose a new extension, continuous processing, that also eliminates micro-batches from execution. As we demonstrated at Spark Summit this morning, this new execution mode lets users achieve sub-millisecond end-to-end latency for many important workloads - with no change to their Spark application."*

> Source: https://databricks.com/blog/2017/06/06/simple-super-fast-streaming-engine-apache-spark.html

The following figure depicts a minimum viable streaming system that is the foundation of most streaming systems (over simplified for presentation):

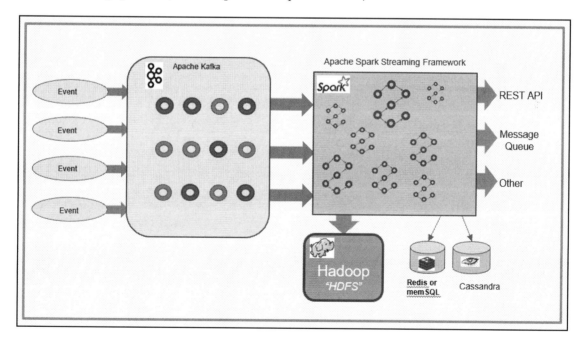

As seen in the preceding figure, any real-life system must interact with batch (for example, offline learning of the model parameters) while the faster subsystem concentrates on real-time response to external events (that is, online learning).

Spark's structured streaming full integration with ML library is on the horizon, but meanwhile we can create and use streaming DataFrames and streaming Datasets to compensate, as will be seen in some of the following recipes.

The new structured streaming has several advantages, such as:

- Unification of Batch and Stream APIs (no need to translate)
- Functional programming with more concise expressive language
- Fault-tolerant state management (third generation)
- Significantly simplified programming model:
  - Trigger
  - Input
  - Query
  - Result
  - Output
- Data stream as a unbounded table

The following figure depicts the basic concepts beyond a data stream being modeled as an infinite unbounded table:

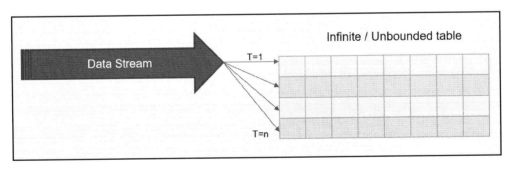

The pre-Spark 2.0 paradigm advanced the DStream construct, which modeled the stream as a set of discrete data structures (RDDs) that was very difficult to deal with when we had late arrivals. The inherent late arrival problem made it difficult to build systems that had a real-time chargeback model (very prominent in the cloud) due to the uncertainty around the actual charges.

The following figure depicts the DStream model in a visual way so it can be compared accordingly:

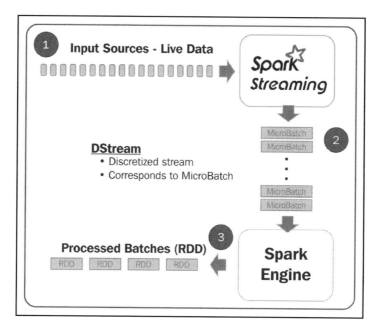

In comparison, by using the new model, there are fewer concepts that a developer needs to worry about and there is no need to translate the code from a batch model (often ETL like code) to a real-time stream model.

Currently, due to the timeline and legacy, one must know both models (DStream and structured streaming) for a while before all pre-Spark 2.0 code is replaced. We found the new structured streaming model particularly simple compared to DStream and have tried to demonstrate and highlight the differences in the four introductory recipes covered in this chapter.

Structured streaming for near real-time machine learning

In this recipe, we explore the new structured streaming paradigm introduced in Spark 2.0. We explore real-time streaming using sockets and structured streaming API to vote and tabulate the votes accordingly.

We also explore the newly introduced subsystem by simulating a stream of randomly generated votes to pick the most unpopular comic book villain.

 There are two distinct programs (VoteCountStream.scala and CountStreamproducer.scala) that make up this recipe.

How to do it...

1. Start a new project in IntelliJ or in an IDE of your choice. Make sure that the necessary JAR files are included.

2. Set up the package location where the program will reside:

    package spark.ml.cookbook.chapter13

3. Import the necessary packages for the Spark context to get access to the cluster and log4j.Logger to reduce the amount of output produced by Spark:

    ```
    import org.apache.log4j.{Level, Logger}
    import org.apache.spark.sql.SparkSession
    import java.io.{BufferedOutputStream, PrintWriter}
    import java.net.Socket
    import java.net.ServerSocket
    import java.util.concurrent.TimeUnit
    import scala.util.Random
    import org.apache.spark.sql.streaming.ProcessingTime
    ```

4. Define a Scala class to generate voting data onto a client socket:

    ```
    class CountSreamThread(socket: Socket) extends Thread
    ```

5. Define an array containing literal string values of people to vote for:

    ```
    val villians = Array("Bane", "Thanos", "Loki", "Apocalypse", "Red Skull", "The Governor", "Sinestro", "Galactus",
     "Doctor Doom", "Lex Luthor", "Joker", "Magneto", "Darth Vader")
    ```

6. Now we will override the `Threads` class `run` method to randomly simulate a vote for a particular villain:

```
override def run(): Unit = {

  println("Connection accepted")
  val out = new PrintWriter(new
BufferedOutputStream(socket.getOutputStream()))

  println("Producing Data")
  while (true) {
  out.println(villians(Random.nextInt(villians.size)))
  Thread.sleep(10)
  }

  println("Done Producing")
  }
```

7. Next, we define a Scala singleton object to accept connections on a defined port `9999` and generate voting data:

```
object CountStreamProducer {

  def main(args: Array[String]): Unit = {

  val ss = new ServerSocket(9999)
  while (true) {
  println("Accepting Connection...")
  new CountSreamThread(ss.accept()).start()
  }
  }
  }
```

8. Don't forget to start up the data generation server, so our streaming example can process the streaming vote data.

9. Set output level to ERROR to reduce Spark's output:

```
Logger.getLogger("org").setLevel(Level.ERROR)
  Logger.getLogger("akka").setLevel(Level.ERROR)
```

10. Create a `SparkSession` yielding access to the Spark cluster and underlying session object attributes such as the `SparkContext` and `SparkSQLContext`:

```
val spark = SparkSession
.builder
.master("local[*]")
.appName("votecountstream")
.config("spark.sql.warehouse.dir", ".")
.getOrCreate()
```

11. Import spark implicits, therefore adding in behavior with only an import:

```
import spark.implicits._
```

12. Create a streaming DataFrame by connecting to localhost on port 9999, which utilizes a Spark socket source as the source of streaming data:

```
val stream = spark.readStream
.format("socket")
.option("host", "localhost")
.option("port", 9999)
.load()
```

13. In this step, we group streaming data by villain name and count to simulate user votes streaming in real time:

```
val villainsVote = stream.groupBy("value").count()
```

14. Now we define a streaming query to trigger every 10 seconds, dump the whole result set into the console, and invoke it by calling the `start()` method:

```
val query = villainsVote.orderBy("count").writeStream
.outputMode("complete")
.format("console")
.trigger(ProcessingTime.create(10, TimeUnit.SECONDS))
.start()
```

The first output batch is displayed here as batch 0:

```
--------------------------------------------------
Batch: 0
--------------------------------------------------
+------------+-----+
|       value|count|
+------------+-----+
|        Bane|   57|
|   Red Skull|   58|
|      Thanos|   60|
|The Governor|   62|
|     Magneto|   68|
| Doctor Doom|   69|
|    Sinestro|   72|
| Darth Vader|   72|
|    Galactus|   75|
|  Apocalypse|   76|
|        Loki|   77|
|       Joker|   77|
|  Lex Luthor|   78|
+------------+-----+
```

An additional batch result is displayed here:

```
--------------------------------------------------
Batch: 51
--------------------------------------------------
+------------+-----+
|       value|count|
+------------+-----+
|   Red Skull| 3805|
|        Bane| 3814|
| Doctor Doom| 3830|
|        Loki| 3852|
|    Sinestro| 3880|
|       Joker| 3885|
| Darth Vader| 3886|
|  Apocalypse| 3896|
|The Governor| 3901|
|     Magneto| 3906||
|      Thanos| 3913|
|  Lex Luthor| 3923|
|    Galactus| 4021|
+------------+-----+
```

15. Finally, wait for termination of the streaming query or stop the process using the `SparkSession` API:

```
query.awaitTermination()
```

How it works...

In this recipe, we created a simple data generation server to simulate a stream of voting data and then counted the vote. The following figure provides a high-level depiction of this concept:

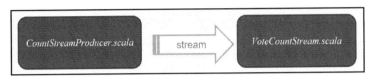

First, we began by executing the data generation server. Second, we defined a socket data source, which allows us to connect to the data generation server. Third, we constructed a simple Spark expression to group by villain (that is, bad superheroes) and count all currently received votes. Finally, we configured a threshold trigger of 10 seconds to execute our streaming query, which dumps the accumulated results onto the console.

There are two short programs involved in this recipe:

- `CountStreamproducer.scala`:
  - The producer - data generation server
  - Simulates the voting for itself and broadcasts it
- `VoteCountStream.scala`:
  - The consumer - consumes and aggregates/tabulates the data
  - Receives and count votes for our villain superhero

There's more...

The topic of how to program using Spark streaming and structured streaming in Spark is out of scope for this book, but we felt it is necessary to share some programs to introduce the concepts before drilling down into ML streaming offering for Spark.

For a solid introduction to streaming, please consult the following documentation on Spark:

- Information of Spark 2.0+ structured streaming is available
  at `https://spark.apache.org/docs/latest/structured-streaming-programmin g-guide.html#api-using-datasets-and-dataframes`
- Information of Spark 1.6 streaming is available
  at `https://spark.apache.org/docs/latest/streaming-programming-guide.htm l`

See also

- Documentation for structured streaming is available
  at `https://spark.apache.org/docs/latest/api/scala/index.html#org.apache.spark.sql.streaming.package`
- Documentation for DStream (pre-Spark 2.0) is available
  at `https://spark.apache.org/docs/latest/api/scala/index.html#org.apache.spark.streaming.dstream.DStream`
- Documentation for `DataStreamReader` is available
  at `https://spark.apache.org/docs/latest/api/scala/index.html#org.apache.spark.sql.streaming.DataStreamReader`
- Documentation for `DataStreamWriter` is available
  at `https://spark.apache.org/docs/latest/api/scala/index.html#org.apache.spark.sql.streaming.DataStreamWriter`
- Documentation for `StreamingQuery` is available
  at `https://spark.apache.org/docs/latest/api/scala/index.html#org.apache.spark.sql.streaming.StreamingQuery`

Streaming DataFrames for real-time machine learning

In this recipe, we explore the concept of a streaming DataFrame. We create a DataFrame consisting of the name and age of individuals, which we will be streaming across a wire. A streaming DataFrame is a popular technique to use with Spark ML since we do not have a full integration between Spark structured ML at the time of writing.

We limit this recipe to only the extent of demonstrating a streaming DataFrame and leave it up to the reader to adapt this to their own custom ML pipelines. While streaming DataFrame is not available out of the box in Spark 2.1.0, it will be a natural evolution to see it in later versions of Spark.

How to do it...

1. Start a new project in IntelliJ or in an IDE of your choice. Make sure that the necessary JAR files are included.

2. Set up the package location where the program will reside:

```
package spark.ml.cookbook.chapter13
```

3. Import the necessary packages:

```
import java.util.concurrent.TimeUnit
import org.apache.log4j.{Level, Logger}
import org.apache.spark.sql.SparkSession
import org.apache.spark.sql.streaming.ProcessingTime
```

4. Create a `SparkSession` as an entry point to the Spark cluster:

```
val spark = SparkSession
.builder
.master("local[*]")
.appName("DataFrame Stream")
.config("spark.sql.warehouse.dir", ".")
.getOrCreate()
```

5. The interleaving of log messages leads to hard-to-read output, therefore set logging level to warning:

```
Logger.getLogger("org").setLevel(Level.ERROR)
Logger.getLogger("akka").setLevel(Level.ERROR)
```

6. Next, load the person data file to infer a data schema without hand coding the structure types:

```
val df = spark.read
.format("json")
.option("inferSchema", "true")
.load("../data/sparkml2/chapter13/person.json")
df.printSchema()
```

From the console, you will see the following output:

```
root
|-- age: long (nullable = true)
|-- name: string (nullable = true)
```

7. Now configure a streaming DataFrame for ingestion of the data:

```
val stream = spark.readStream
.schema(df.schema)
.json("../data/sparkml2/chapter13/people/")
```

8. Let us execute a simple data transform, by filtering on age greater than 60:

```
val people = stream.select("name", "age").where("age > 60")
```

9. We now output the transformed streaming data to the console, which will trigger every second:

```
val query = people.writeStream
.outputMode("append")
.trigger(ProcessingTime(1, TimeUnit.SECONDS))
.format("console")
```

10. We start our defined streaming query and wait for data to appear in the stream:

```
query.start().awaitTermination()
```

11. Finally, the result of our streaming query will appear in the console:

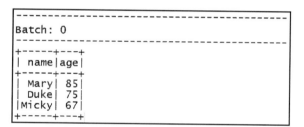

```
-------------------------------------------------
Batch: 0
-------------------------------------------------
+-----+---+
| name|age|
+-----+---+
| Mary| 85|
| Duke| 75|
|Micky| 67|
+-----+---+
```

How it works...

In this recipe, we first discover the underlying schema for a person object using a quick method (using a JSON object) as described in step 6. The resulting DataFrame will know the schema that we subsequently impose on the streaming input (simulated via streaming a file) and treated as a streaming DataFrame as seen in step 7.

The ability to treat the stream as a DataFrame and act on it using a functional or SQL paradigm is a powerful concept that can be seen in step 8. We then proceed to output the result using `writestream()` with `append` mode and a 1-second batch interval trigger.

There's more...

The combination of DataFrames and structured programming is a powerful concept that helps us to separate the data layer from the stream, which makes the programming significantly easier. One of the biggest drawbacks with DStream (pre-Spark 2.0) was its inability to isolate the user from details of the underlying details of stream/RDD implementation.

Documentation for DataFrames:

- `DataFrameReader`: https://spark.apache.org/docs/latest/api/scala/index.html#org.apache.spark.sql.DataFrameReader
- `DataFrameWriter`: https://spark.apache.org/docs/latest/api/scala/index.html#org.apache.spark.sql.DataFrameWriter

See also

Documentation for Spark data stream reader and writer:

- **DataStreamReader**: https://spark.apache.org/docs/latest/api/scala/index.html#org.apache.spark.sql.streaming.DataStreamReader
- **DataStreamWriter**: https://spark.apache.org/docs/latest/api/scala/index.html#org.apache.spark.sql.streaming.DataStreamWriter

Streaming Datasets for real-time machine learning

In this recipe, we create a streaming Dataset to demonstrate the use of Datasets with a Spark 2.0 structured programming paradigm. We stream stock prices from a file using a Dataset and apply a filter to select the day's stock that closed above $100.

The recipe demonstrates how streams can be used to filter and to act on the incoming data using a simple structured streaming programming model. While it is similar to a DataFrame, there are some differences in the syntax. The recipe is written in a generalized manner so the user can customize it for their own Spark ML programming projects.

How to do it...

1. Start a new project in IntelliJ or in an IDE of your choice. Make sure that the necessary JAR files are included.

2. Set up the package location where the program will reside:

   ```
   package spark.ml.cookbook.chapter13
   ```

3. Import the necessary packages:

   ```
   import java.util.concurrent.TimeUnit
   import org.apache.log4j.{Level, Logger}
   import org.apache.spark.sql.SparkSession
   import org.apache.spark.sql.streaming.ProcessingTime
   ```

4. Define a Scala `case class` to model streaming data:

   ```
   case class StockPrice(date: String, open: Double, high: Double,
   low: Double, close: Double, volume: Integer, adjclose: Double)
   ```

5. Create `SparkSession` to use as an entry point to the Spark cluster:

   ```
   val spark = SparkSession
   .builder
   .master("local[*]")
   .appName("Dataset Stream")
   .config("spark.sql.warehouse.dir", ".")
   .getOrCreate()
   ```

6. The interleaving of log messages leads to hard-to-read output, therefore set logging level to warning:

   ```
   Logger.getLogger("org").setLevel(Level.ERROR)
   Logger.getLogger("akka").setLevel(Level.ERROR)
   ```

7. Now, load the general electric CSV file inferring the schema:

   ```
   val s = spark.read
   .format("csv")
   .option("header", "true")
   .option("inferSchema", "true")
   .load("../data/sparkml2/chapter13/GE.csv")
   s.printSchema()
   ```

You will see the following in console output:

```
root
|-- date: timestamp (nullable = true)
|-- open: double (nullable = true)
|-- high: double (nullable = true)
|-- low: double (nullable = true)
|-- close: double (nullable = true)
|-- volume: integer (nullable = true)
|-- adjclose: double (nullable = true)
```

8. Next, we load the general electric CSV file into a dataset of type `StockPrice`:

```
val streamDataset = spark.readStream
                .schema(s.schema)
                .option("sep", ",")
                .option("header", "true")
                .csv("../data/sparkml2/chapter13/ge").as[StockPrice]
```

9. We will filter the stream for any close price greater than $100 USD:

```
val ge = streamDataset.filter("close > 100.00")
```

10. We now output the transformed streaming data to the console that will trigger every second:

```
val query = ge.writeStream
.outputMode("append")
.trigger(ProcessingTime(1, TimeUnit.SECONDS))
.format("console")
```

11. We start our defined streaming query and wait for data to appear in the stream:

```
query.start().awaitTermination()
```

12. Finally, the result of our streaming query will appear in the console:

```
-------------------------------------------------
Batch: 0
-------------------------------------------------

+-------------------+---------+---------+---------+---------+--------+---------+
|               date|     open|     high|      low|    close|  volume| adjclose|
+-------------------+---------+---------+---------+---------+--------+---------+
|2000-05-05 00:00:...|153.999996|159.999996|153.500004|158.000004|20685900|31.356408|
|2000-05-04 00:00:...|157.437504|    157.5|152.750004|153.999996|15411000|30.562573|
|2000-05-03 00:00:...|159.500004|159.999996|154.562496|156.062496|16594800|30.971894|
|2000-05-02 00:00:...|    159.0| 161.8125|158.187504|  161.0625|12725100|31.964186|
|2000-05-01 00:00:...|    159.0|    162.0|157.749996|  159.375|12486600|31.629287|
|2000-04-28 00:00:...|161.375004|    162.0| 156.5625|157.250004|14133900|31.207564|
|2000-04-27 00:00:...|    160.5|161.937504|158.187504|161.499996|20227200|32.051011|
|2000-04-26 00:00:...|  166.125|167.937504|161.312496|163.250004|21333300|32.398314|
|2000-04-25 00:00:...|162.249996|  166.3125|  160.875|165.999996|22854600|32.944073|
|2000-04-24 00:00:...|156.999996|163.937496|156.312504|162.062496|24014700|32.162643|
|2000-04-20 00:00:...|156.062496|158.499996|155.499996|158.499996|17056800|31.455636|
|2000-04-19 00:00:...|156.062496|156.812496|  154.125|155.499996|14150400|30.860261|
|2000-04-18 00:00:...| 152.8125|157.937496|151.937496|156.500004|25437900|31.058721|
|2000-04-17 00:00:...|  144.375|153.249996|143.874996|152.000004|31951500|30.165658|
|2000-04-14 00:00:...|147.999996|150.125004| 143.0625|145.749996|31645500|28.925293|
|2000-04-13 00:00:...|157.374996|157.437504|    150.0|150.500004|25497000|29.867971|
|2000-04-12 00:00:...|162.624996|163.250004|    156.0|  156.75|19443000|31.108334|
|2000-04-11 00:00:...|158.312496|  163.875|157.625004|  161.625|21002400|32.075819|
|2000-04-10 00:00:...|  159.375|161.000004| 157.875|159.437496|14234400| 31.64169|
|2000-04-07 00:00:...|157.625004|159.812496| 156.1875| 158.8125|13326600|31.517655|
+-------------------+---------+---------+---------+---------+--------+---------+
only showing top 20 rows
```

How it works...

In this recipe, we will be utilizing the market data of closing prices for **General Electric (GE)** dating back to 1972. To simplify the data, we have preprocessed for the purposes of this recipe. We use the same method from the previous recipe, *Streaming DataFrames for real-time machine learning,* by peeking into the JSON object to discover the schema (step 7), which we impose on the stream in step 8.

The following code shows how to use the schema to make the stream look like a simple table that you can read from on the fly. This is a powerful concept that makes stream programming accessible to more programmers. The schema(s.schema) and as[StockPrice] from the following code snippet are required to create the streaming Dataset, which has a schema associated with it:

```
val streamDataset = spark.readStream
        .schema(s.schema)
        .option("sep", ",")
        .option("header", "true")
        .csv("../data/sparkml2/chapter13/ge").as[StockPrice]
```

There's more...

Documentation for all the APIs available under Dataset
at `https://spark.apache.org/docs/latest/api/scala/index.html#org.apache.spark.sq l.Dataset` website.

See also

The following documentation is helpful while exploring the streaming Dataset concept:

- `StreamReader`: `https://spark.apache.org/docs/latest/api/scala/index.htm l#org.apache.spark.sql.streaming.DataStreamReader`
- `StreamWriter`: `https://spark.apache.org/docs/latest/api/scala/index.htm l#org.apache.spark.sql.streaming.DataStreamWriter`
- `StreamQuery`: `https://spark.apache.org/docs/latest/api/scala/index.html #org.apache.spark.sql.streaming.StreamingQuery`

Streaming data and debugging with queueStream

In this recipe, we explore the concept of `queueStream()`, which is a valuable tool while trying to get a streaming program to work during the development cycle. We found the `queueStream()` API very useful and felt that other developers can benefit from a recipe that fully demonstrates its usage.

We start by simulating a user browsing various URLs associated with different web pages using the program `ClickGenerator.scala` and then proceed to consume and tabulate the data (user behavior/visits) using the `ClickStream.scala` program:

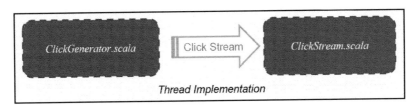

We use Spark's streaming API with `Dstream()`, which will require the use of a streaming context. We are calling this out explicitly to highlight one of the differences between Spark streaming and the Spark structured streaming programming model.

There are two distinct programs (`ClickGenerator.scala` and `ClickStream.scala`) that make up this recipe.

How to do it...

1. Start a new project in IntelliJ or in an IDE of your choice. Make sure that the necessary JAR files are included.

2. Set up the package location where the program will reside:

   ```
   package spark.ml.cookbook.chapter13
   ```

3. Import the necessary packages:

   ```
   import java.time.LocalDateTime
   import scala.util.Random._
   ```

4. Define a Scala `case class` to model click events by users that contains user identifier, IP address, time of event, URL, and HTTP status code:

   ```
   case class ClickEvent(userId: String, ipAddress: String, time:
   String, url: String, statusCode: String)
   ```

5. Define status codes for generation:

   ```
   val statusCodeData = Seq(200, 404, 500)
   ```

6. Define URLs for generation:

   ```
   val urlData = Seq("http://www.fakefoo.com",
    "http://www.fakefoo.com/downloads",
    "http://www.fakefoo.com/search",
    "http://www.fakefoo.com/login",
    "http://www.fakefoo.com/settings",
    "http://www.fakefoo.com/news",
    "http://www.fakefoo.com/reports",
    "http://www.fakefoo.com/images",
    "http://www.fakefoo.com/css",
    "http://www.fakefoo.com/sounds",
    "http://www.fakefoo.com/admin",
    "http://www.fakefoo.com/accounts"
   )
   ```

7. Define IP address range for generation:

```
val ipAddressData = generateIpAddress()
def generateIpAddress(): Seq[String] = {
 for (n <- 1 to 255) yield s"127.0.0.$n"
}
```

8. Define timestamp range for generation:

```
val timeStampData = generateTimeStamp()

def generateTimeStamp(): Seq[String] = {
val now = LocalDateTime.now()
for (n <- 1 to 1000) yield LocalDateTime.of(now.toLocalDate,
now.toLocalTime.plusSeconds(n)).toString
}
```

9. Define user identifier range for generation:

```
val userIdData = generateUserId()

def generateUserId(): Seq[Int] = {
for (id <- 1 to 1000) yield id
}
```

10. Define a function to generate one or more pseudo random events:

```
def generateClicks(clicks: Int = 1): Seq[String] = {
0.until(clicks).map(i => {
val statusCode = statusCodeData(nextInt(statusCodeData.size))
val ipAddress = ipAddressData(nextInt(ipAddressData.size))
val timeStamp = timeStampData(nextInt(timeStampData.size))
val url = urlData(nextInt(urlData.size))
val userId = userIdData(nextInt(userIdData.size))

s"$userId,$ipAddress,$timeStamp,$url,$statusCode"
})
}
```

11. Define a function to parse a pseudo random `ClickEvent` from a string:

```
def parseClicks(data: String): ClickEvent = {
val fields = data.split(",")
new ClickEvent(fields(0), fields(1), fields(2), fields(3),
fields(4))
}
```

12. Create Spark's configuration and Spark streaming context with 1-second duration:

```
val spark = SparkSession
.builder
.master("local[*]")
 .appName("Streaming App")
 .config("spark.sql.warehouse.dir", ".")
 .config("spark.executor.memory", "2g")
 .getOrCreate()
val ssc = new StreamingContext(spark.sparkContext, Seconds(1))
```

13. The interleaving of log messages leads to hard-to-read output, therefore set logging level to warning:

```
Logger.getRootLogger.setLevel(Level.WARN)
```

14. Create a mutable queue to append our generated data onto:

```
val rddQueue = new Queue[RDD[String]]()
```

15. Create a Spark queue stream from the streaming context passing in a reference of our data queue:

```
val inputStream = ssc.queueStream(rddQueue)
```

16. Process any data received by the queue stream and count the total number of each particular link users have clicked upon:

```
val clicks = inputStream.map(data =>
ClickGenerator.parseClicks(data))
 val clickCounts = clicks.map(c => c.url).countByValue()
```

17. Print out the 12 URLs and their totals:

```
clickCounts.print(12)
```

18. Start our streaming context to receive micro-batches:

```
ssc.start()
```

19. Loop 10 times generating 100 pseudo random events on each iteration and append them our mutable queue so they materialize in the streaming queue abstraction:

```
for (i <- 1 to 10) {
  rddQueue +=
ssc.sparkContext.parallelize(ClickGenerator.generateClicks(100))
  Thread.sleep(1000)
  }
```

20. We close the program by stopping the Spark streaming context:

```
ssc.stop()
```

How it works...

With this recipe, we introduced Spark Streaming using a technique many overlook, which allows us to craft a streaming application utilizing Spark's QueueInputDStream class. The QueueInputDStream class is not only a beneficial tool for understanding Spark streaming, but also for debugging during the development cycle. In the beginning steps, we set up a few data structures, in order to generate pseudo random clickstream event data for stream processing at a later stage.

It should be noted that in step 12, we are creating a streaming context instead of a SparkContext. The streaming context is what we use for Spark streaming applications. Next, the creation of a queue and queue stream is done to receive streaming data. Now steps 15 and 16 resemble a general Spark application manipulating RDDs. The next step starts the streaming context processing. After the streaming context is started, we append data to the queue and the processing begins with micro-batches.

Documentation for some of the related topics is mentioned here:

- StreamingContext and queueStream():
  https://spark.apache.org/docs/latest/api/scala/index.html#org.apache.spark.streaming.StreamingContext
- DStream: https://spark.apache.org/docs/latest/api/scala/index.html#org.apache.spark.streaming.dstream.DStream
- InputDStream: https://spark.apache.org/docs/latest/api/scala/index.html#org.apache.spark.streaming.dstream.InputDStream

See also

At its core, `queueStream()` is just a queue of RDDs that we have after the Spark streaming (pre-2.0) turns into RDD:

- Documentation for structured streaming (Spark 2.0+): `https://spark.apache.org/docs/2.1.0/structured-streaming-programming-guide.html`

- Documentation for streaming (pre-Spark 2.0): `https://spark.apache.org/docs/latest/streaming-programming-guide.html`

Downloading and understanding the famous Iris data for unsupervised classification

In this recipe, we download and inspect the well-known Iris dataset in preparation for the upcoming streaming KMeans recipe, which lets you see classification/clustering in real-time.

The data is housed on the UCI machine learning repository, which is a great source of data to prototype algorithms on. You will notice that R bloggers tend to love this dataset.

How to do it...

1. You can start by downloading the dataset using either two of the following commands:

```
wget
https://archive.ics.uci.edu/ml/machine-learning-databases/iris/iris
.data
```

You can also use the following command:

```
curl
https://archive.ics.uci.edu/ml/machine-learning-
databases/iris/iris.data -o iris.data
```

You can also use the following command:

```
https://archive.ics.uci.edu/ml/machine-learning-databases/iris/iris
.data
```

2. Now we begin our first step of data exploration by examining how the data in `iris.data` is formatted:

```
head -5 iris.data
5.1,3.5,1.4,0.2,Iris-setosa
4.9,3.0,1.4,0.2,Iris-setosa
4.7,3.2,1.3,0.2,Iris-setosa
4.6,3.1,1.5,0.2,Iris-setosa
5.0,3.6,1.4,0.2,Iris-setosa
```

3. Now we take a look at the iris data to know how it is formatted:

```
tail -5 iris.data
6.3,2.5,5.0,1.9,Iris-virginica
6.5,3.0,5.2,2.0,Iris-virginica
6.2,3.4,5.4,2.3,Iris-virginica
5.9,3.0,5.1,1.8,Iris-virginica
```

How it works...

The data is made of 150 observations. Each observation is made of four numerical features (measured in centimeters) and a label that signifies which class each Iris belongs to:

Features/attributes:

- Sepal length in cm
- Sepal width in cm
- Petal length in cm
- Petal width in cm

Label/class:

- Iris Setosa
- Iris Versicolour
- Iris Virginic

There's more...

The following image depicts an Iris flower with Petal and Sepal marked for clarity:

See also

The following link explores the Iris dataset in more detail:

https://en.wikipedia.org/wiki/Iris_flower_data_set

Streaming KMeans for a real-time on-line classifier

In this recipe, we explore the streaming version of KMeans in Spark used in unsupervised learning schemes. The purpose of streaming KMeans algorithm is to classify or group a set of data points into a number of clusters based on their similarity factor.

There are two implementations of the KMeans classification method, one for static/offline data and another version for continuously arriving, real-time updating data.

We will be streaming iris dataset clustering as new data streams into our streaming context.

How to do it...

1. Start a new project in IntelliJ or in an IDE of your choice. Make sure that the necessary JAR files are included.

2. Set up the package location where the program will reside:

```
package spark.ml.cookbook.chapter13
```

3. Import the necessary packages:

```
import org.apache.spark.mllib.linalg.Vectors
import org.apache.spark.mllib.regression.LabeledPoint
import org.apache.spark.rdd.RDD
import org.apache.spark.SparkContext
import scala.collection.mutable.Queue
```

4. We begin by defining a function to load iris data into memory, filtering out blank lines, attaching an identifier to each element, and finally returning tuple of type string and long:

```
def readFromFile(sc: SparkContext) = {
sc.textFile("../data/sparkml2/chapter13/iris.data")
.filter(s => !s.isEmpty)
.zipWithIndex()
}
```

5. Create a parser to take the string portion of our tuple and create a label point:

```
def toLabelPoints(records: (String, Long)): LabeledPoint = {
val (record, recordId) = records
val fields = record.split(",")
LabeledPoint(recordId,
Vectors.dense(fields(0).toDouble, fields(1).toDouble,
fields(2).toDouble, fields(3).toDouble))
}
```

6. Create a lookup map to convert the identifier back to the text label feature:

```
def buildLabelLookup(records: RDD[(String, Long)]) = {
records.map {
case (record: String, id: Long) => {
val fields = record.split(",")
(id, fields(4))
```

```
}
}.collect().toMap
}
```

7. Create Spark's configuration and Spark streaming context with 1-second duration:

```
val spark = SparkSession
 .builder
.master("local[*]")
 .appName("KMean Streaming App")
 .config("spark.sql.warehouse.dir", ".")
 .config("spark.executor.memory", "2g")
 .getOrCreate()

val ssc = new StreamingContext(spark.sparkContext, Seconds(1))
```

8. The interleaving of log messages leads to hard-to-read output, therefore set logging level to warning:

```
Logger.getRootLogger.setLevel(Level.WARN)
```

9. We read in the Iris data and build a lookup map to display the final output:

```
val irisData = IrisData.readFromFile(spark.sparkContext)
val lookup = IrisData.buildLabelLookup(irisData)
```

10. Create mutable queues to append streaming data onto:

```
val trainQueue = new Queue[RDD[LabeledPoint]]()
val testQueue = new Queue[RDD[LabeledPoint]]()
```

11. Create Spark streaming queues to receive data:

```
val trainingStream = ssc.queueStream(trainQueue)
 val testStream = ssc.queueStream(testQueue)
```

12. Create streaming KMeans object to cluster data into three groups:

```
val model = new StreamingKMeans().setK(3)
 .setDecayFactor(1.0)
 .setRandomCenters(4, 0.0)
```

13. Set up KMeans model to accept streaming training data to build a model:

```
model.trainOn(trainingStream.map(lp => lp.features))
```

14. Set up KMeans model to predict clustering group values:

```
val values = model.predictOnValues(testStream.map(lp => (lp.label,
lp.features)))
values.foreachRDD(n => n.foreach(v => {
println(v._2, v._1, lookup(v._1.toLong))
}))
```

15. Start streaming context so it will process data when received:

```
ssc.start()
```

16. Convert Iris data into label points:

```
val irisLabelPoints = irisData.map(record =>
IrisData.toLabelPoints(record))
```

17. Now split label point data into training dataset and test dataset:

```
val Array(trainData, test) = irisLabelPoints.randomSplit(Array(.80,
.20))
```

18. Append training data to streaming queue for processing:

```
trainQueue += irisLabelPoints
 Thread.sleep(2000)
```

19. Now we split test data into four groups and append to streaming queues for processing:

```
val testGroups = test.randomSplit(Array(.25, .25, .25, .25))
testGroups.foreach(group => {
testQueue += group
println("-" * 25)
Thread.sleep(1000)
})
```

20. The configured streaming queues print out the following results of clustered prediction groups:

```
-------------------------
(0,78.0,Iris-versicolor)
(2,14.0,Iris-setosa)
(1,132.0,Iris-virginica)
(0,55.0,Iris-versicolor)
(2,57.0,Iris-versicolor)
-------------------------
```

```
(2,3.0,Iris-setosa)
(2,19.0,Iris-setosa)
(2,98.0,Iris-versicolor)
(2,29.0,Iris-setosa)
(1,110.0,Iris-virginica)
(2,39.0,Iris-setosa)
(0,113.0,Iris-virginica)
(1,50.0,Iris-versicolor)
(0,63.0,Iris-versicolor)
(0,74.0,Iris-versicolor)
-------------------------
(2,16.0,Iris-setosa)
(0,106.0,Iris-virginica)
(0,69.0,Iris-versicolor)
(1,115.0,Iris-virginica)
(1,116.0,Iris-virginica)
(1,139.0,Iris-virginica)
-------------------------
(2,1.0,Iris-setosa)
(2,7.0,Iris-setosa)
(2,17.0,Iris-setosa)
(0,99.0,Iris-versicolor)
(2,38.0,Iris-setosa)
(0,59.0,Iris-versicolor)
(1,76.0,Iris-versicolor)
```

21. We close the program by stopping the SparkContext:

```
ssc.stop()
```

How it works...

In this recipe, we begin by loading the iris dataset and using the `zip()` API to pair data with a unique identifier to the data for generating *labeled points* data structure for use with the KMeans algorithm.

Next, the mutable queues and `QueueInputDStream` are created for appending data to simulate streaming. Once the `QueueInputDStream` starts receiving data then the streaming k-mean clustering begins to dynamically cluster data and printing out results. The interesting thing you will notice here is we are streaming the training dataset on one queue stream and the test data on another queue stream. As we append data to our queues, the KMeans clustering algorithm is processing our incoming data and dynamically generating clusters.

There's more...

Documentation for *StreamingKMeans()*:

- StreamingKMeans: `https://spark.apache.org/docs/latest/api/scala/index.html#org.apache.spark.mllib.clustering.StreamingKMeans`

- StreamingKMeansModel: `https://spark.apache.org/docs/latest/api/scala/index.html#org.apache.spark.mllib.clustering.StreamingKMeansModel`

See also

The hyper parameters defined via a builder pattern or `streamingKMeans` are:

```
setDecayFactor()
setK()
setRandomCenters(,)
```

Please refer to the *Building a KMeans classifying system in Spark* recipe in `Chapter 8`, *Unsupervised Clustering with Apache Spark 2.0* for more details.

Downloading wine quality data for streaming regression

In this recipe, we download and inspect the wine quality dataset from the UCI machine learning repository to prepare data for Spark's streaming linear regression algorithm from MLlib.

How to do it...

You will need one of the following command-line tools `curl` or `wget` to retrieve specified data:

1. You can start by downloading the dataset using either of the following three commands. The first one is as follows:

   ```
   wget
   http://archive.ics.uci.edu/ml/machine-learning-databases/wine-quali
   ty/winequality-white.csv
   ```

You can also use the following command:

```
curl
http://archive.ics.uci.edu/ml/machine-learning-databases/wine-quali
ty/winequality-white.csv -o winequality-white.csv
```

This command is the third way to do the same:

```
http://archive.ics.uci.edu/ml/machine-learning-databases/wine-quali
ty/winequality-white.csv
```

2. Now we begin our first steps of data exploration by seeing how the data in `winequality-white.csv` is formatted:

```
head -5 winequality-white.csv

"fixed acidity";"volatile acidity";"citric acid";"residual
sugar";"chlorides";"free sulfur dioxide";"total sulfur
dioxide";"density";"pH";"sulphates";"alcohol";"quality"
7;0.27;0.36;20.7;0.045;45;170;1.001;3;0.45;8.8;6
6.3;0.3;0.34;1.6;0.049;14;132;0.994;3.3;0.49;9.5;6
8.1;0.28;0.4;6.9;0.05;30;97;0.9951;3.26;0.44;10.1;6
7.2;0.23;0.32;8.5;0.058;47;186;0.9956;3.19;0.4;9.9;6
```

3. Now we take a look at the wine quality data to know how it is formatted:

```
tail -5 winequality-white.csv
6.2;0.21;0.29;1.6;0.039;24;92;0.99114;3.27;0.5;11.2;6
6.6;0.32;0.36;8;0.047;57;168;0.9949;3.15;0.46;9.6;5
6.5;0.24;0.19;1.2;0.041;30;111;0.99254;2.99;0.46;9.4;6
5.5;0.29;0.3;1.1;0.022;20;110;0.98869;3.34;0.38;12.8;7
6;0.21;0.38;0.8;0.02;22;98;0.98941;3.26;0.32;11.8;6
```

How it works...

The data is comprised of 1,599 red wines and 4,898 white wines with 11 features and an output label that can be used during training.

The following is a list of features/attributes:

- Fixed acidity
- Volatile acidity
- Citric acid
- Residual sugar

- Chlorides
- Free sulfur dioxide
- Total sulfur dioxide
- Density
- pH
- Sulphates
- Alcohol

The following is the output label:

- quality (a numeric value between 0 to 10)

There's more...

The following link lists datasets for popular machine learning algorithms. A new dataset can be chosen to experiment with as needed.

Alternative datasets are available at `https://en.wikipedia.org/wiki/List_of_datasets_for_machine_learning_research`.

We selected the Iris dataset so we can use continuous numerical features for a linear regression model.

Streaming linear regression for a real-time regression

In this recipe, we will use the wine quality dataset from UCI and Spark's streaming linear regression algorithm from MLlib to predict the quality of a wine based on a group of wine features.

The difference between this recipe and the traditional regression recipes we saw before is the use of Spark ML streaming to score the quality of the wine in real time using a linear regression model.

How to do it...

1. Start a new project in IntelliJ or in an IDE of your choice. Make sure that the necessary JAR files are included.

2. Set up the package location where the program will reside:

   ```
   package spark.ml.cookbook.chapter13
   ```

3. Import the necessary packages:

   ```
   import org.apache.log4j.{Level, Logger}
   import org.apache.spark.mllib.linalg.Vectors
   import org.apache.spark.mllib.regression.LabeledPoint
   import
   org.apache.spark.mllib.regression.StreamingLinearRegressionWithSGD
   import org.apache.spark.rdd.RDD
   import org.apache.spark.sql.{Row, SparkSession}
   import org.apache.spark.streaming.{Seconds, StreamingContext}
   import scala.collection.mutable.Queue
   ```

4. Create Spark's configuration and streaming context:

   ```
   val spark = SparkSession
   .builder
   .master("local[*]")
   .appName("Regression Streaming App")
   .config("spark.sql.warehouse.dir", ".")
   .config("spark.executor.memory", "2g")
   .getOrCreate()

   import spark.implicits._

   val ssc = new StreamingContext(spark.sparkContext, Seconds(2))
   ```

5. The interleaving of log messages leads to hard-to-read output, therefore set logging level to warning:

   ```
   Logger.getRootLogger.setLevel(Level.WARN)
   ```

6. Load the wine quality CSV using the Databricks CSV API into a DataFrame:

```
val rawDF = spark.read
  .format("com.databricks.spark.csv")
  .option("inferSchema", "true")
  .option("header", "true")
  .option("delimiter", ";")
  .load("../data/sparkml2/chapter13/winequality-white.csv")
```

7. Convert the DataFrame into an `rdd` and `zip` a unique identifier onto it:

```
val rdd = rawDF.rdd.zipWithUniqueId()
```

8. Build a lookup map to compare predicted quality against actual quality value later:

```
val lookupQuality = rdd.map{ case (r: Row, id: Long)=> (id,
r.getInt(11))}.collect().toMap
```

9. Convert wine quality into label points for use with the machine learning library:

```
val labelPoints = rdd.map{ case (r: Row, id: Long)=>
LabeledPoint(id,
  Vectors.dense(r.getDouble(0), r.getDouble(1), r.getDouble(2),
r.getDouble(3), r.getDouble(4),
  r.getDouble(5), r.getDouble(6), r.getDouble(7), r.getDouble(8),
r.getDouble(9), r.getDouble(10))
  )}
```

10. Create a mutable queue for appending data to:

```
val trainQueue = new Queue[RDD[LabeledPoint]]()
val testQueue = new Queue[RDD[LabeledPoint]]()
```

11. Create Spark streaming queues to receive streaming data:

```
val trainingStream = ssc.queueStream(trainQueue)
val testStream = ssc.queueStream(testQueue)
```

12. Configure streaming linear regression model:

```
val numFeatures = 11
 val model = new StreamingLinearRegressionWithSGD()
 .setInitialWeights(Vectors.zeros(numFeatures))
 .setNumIterations(25)
 .setStepSize(0.1)
 .setMiniBatchFraction(0.25)
```

13. Train regression model and predict final values:

```
model.trainOn(trainingStream)
val result = model.predictOnValues(testStream.map(lp => (lp.label,
lp.features)))
result.map{ case (id: Double, prediction: Double) => (id,
prediction, lookupQuality(id.asInstanceOf[Long])) }.print()
```

14. Start Spark streaming context:

```
ssc.start()
```

15. Split label point data into training set and test set:

```
val Array(trainData, test) = labelPoints.randomSplit(Array(.80,
.20))
```

16. Append data to training data queue for processing:

```
trainQueue += trainData
 Thread.sleep(4000)
```

17. Now split test data in half and append to queue for processing:

```
val testGroups = test.randomSplit(Array(.50, .50))
 testGroups.foreach(group => {
 testQueue += group
 Thread.sleep(2000)
 })
```

18. Once data is received by the queue stream, you will see the following output:

```
-----------------------------------------------
Time: 1465787342000 ms
-----------------------------------------------
(22.0,2.518480861677331E74,5)
(26.0,3.4381438546729306E74,7)
(30.0,2.643700071474678E74,7)
(42.0,2.3743054548852376E74,7)
(44.0,2.935242117306453E74,8)
(46.0,3.854792342218932E74,5)
(88.0,3.591392050188146E74,6)
(90.0,3.9063252778715705E74,7)
(98.0,3.5023649503686865E74,5)
(110.0,4.3840477190802075E74,6)
...

-----------------------------------------------
Time: 1465787344000 ms
-----------------------------------------------
(4.0,2.330551425952938E74,6)
(24.0,1.7639001479680153E74,5)
(38.0,3.141803259908679E74,5)
(50.0,5.728473063697256E74,6)
(64.0,2.397328318539249E74,6)
(68.0,4.093243263541032E74,5)
(74.0,3.2704706499920196E74,6)
(78.0,3.565065843042807E74,5)
(84.0,3.7021298012378077E74,6)
(96.0,3.7021298012378077E74,6)
...
```

19. Close the program by stopping the Spark streaming context:

```
ssc.stop()
```

How it works...

We started by loading the wine quality dataset into a DataFrame via Databrick's `spark-csv` library. The next step was to attach a unique identifier to each row in our dataset to later match the predicted quality to the actual quality. The raw data was converted to labeled points so it can be used as input for the streaming linear regression algorithm. In steps 9 and 10, we created instances of mutable queues and Spark's `QueueInputDStream` class to be used as a conduit into the regression algorithm.

We then created the streaming linear regression model, which will predict wine quality for our final results. We customarily created training and test datasets from the original data and appended them to the appropriate queue to start our model processing streaming data. The final results for each micro-batch displays the unique generated identifier, predicted quality value, and quality value contained in the original dataset.

There's more...

Documentation for
`StreamingLinearRegressionWithSGD()`: `https://spark.apache.org/docs/latest/api/scala/index.html#org.apache.spark.mllib.regression.StreamingLinearRegressionWithSGD`.

See also

Hyper parameters for `StreamingLinearRegressionWithSGD()`:

- `setInitialWeights(Vectors.zeros())`
- `setNumIterations()`
- `setStepSize()`
- `setMiniBatchFraction()`

There is also a `StreamingLinearRegression()` API that does not use the **stochastic gradient descent (SGD)** version:

`https://spark.apache.org/docs/latest/api/scala/index.html#org.apache.spark.mllib.regression.StreamingLinearAlgorithm`

The following link provides a quick reference for linear regression:

`https://en.wikipedia.org/wiki/Linear_regression`

Downloading Pima Diabetes data for supervised classification

In this recipe, we download and inspect the Pima Diabetes dataset from the UCI machine learning repository. We will use the dataset later with Spark's streaming logistic regression algorithm.

How to do it...

You will need one of the following command-line tools `curl` or `wget` to retrieve the specified data:

1. You can start by downloading the dataset using either two of the following commands. The first command is as follows:

   ```
   http://archive.ics.uci.edu/ml/machine-learning-databases/pima-india
   ns-diabetes/pima-indians-diabetes.data
   ```

   This is an alternative that you can use:

   ```
   wget
   http://archive.ics.uci.edu/ml/machine-learning-databases/pima-india
   ns-diabetes/pima-indians-diabetes.data -o pima-indians-
   diabetes.data
   ```

2. Now we begin our first steps of data exploration by seeing how the data in `pima-indians-diabetes.data` is formatted (from Mac or Linux Terminal):

   ```
   head -5 pima-indians-diabetes.data
   6,148,72,35,0,33.6,0.627,50,1
   1,85,66,29,0,26.6,0.351,31,0
   8,183,64,0,0,23.3,0.672,32,1
   1,89,66,23,94,28.1,0.167,21,0
   0,137,40,35,168,43.1,2.288,33,1
   ```

3. Now we take a look at the Pima Diabetes data to understand how it is formatted:

   ```
   tail -5 pima-indians-diabetes.data
   10,101,76,48,180,32.9,0.171,63,0
   2,122,70,27,0,36.8,0.340,27,0
   5,121,72,23,112,26.2,0.245,30,0
   1,126,60,0,0,30.1,0.349,47,1
   1,93,70,31,0,30.4,0.315,23,0
   ```

How it works...

We have 768 observations for the dataset. Each line/record is comprised of 10 features and a label value that can used for a supervised learning model (that is, logistic regression). The label/class is either a 1, meaning tested positive for diabetes, and 0 if the test came back negative.

Features/Attributes:

- Number of times pregnant
- Plasma glucose concentration a 2 hours in an oral glucose tolerance test
- Diastolic blood pressure (mm Hg)
- Triceps skin fold thickness (mm)
- 2-hour serum insulin (mu U/ml)
- Body mass index (weight in kg/(height in m)^2)
- Diabetes pedigree function
- Age (years)
- Class variable (0 or 1)

```
Label/Class:
        1 - tested positive
        0 - tested negative
```

There's more...

We found the following alternative datasets from Princeton University very helpful:

```
http://data.princeton.edu/wws509/datasets
```

See also

The dataset that you can use to explore this recipe has to be structured in a way that the label (prediction class) has to be binary (tested positive/negative for diabetes).

Streaming logistic regression for an on-line classifier

In this recipe, we will be using the Pima Diabetes dataset we downloaded in the previous recipe and Spark's streaming logistic regression algorithm with SGD to predict whether a Pima with various features will test positive as a diabetic. It is an on-line classifier that learns and predicts based on the streamed data.

How to do it...

1. Start a new project in IntelliJ or in an IDE of your choice. Make sure that the necessary JAR files are included.

2. Set up the package location where the program will reside:

   ```
   package spark.ml.cookbook.chapter13
   ```

3. Import the necessary packages:

   ```
   import org.apache.log4j.{Level, Logger}
   import
   org.apache.spark.mllib.classification.StreamingLogisticRegressionWi
   thSGD
   import org.apache.spark.mllib.linalg.Vectors
   import org.apache.spark.mllib.regression.LabeledPoint
   import org.apache.spark.rdd.RDD
   import org.apache.spark.sql.{Row, SparkSession}
   import org.apache.spark.streaming.{Seconds, StreamingContext}
   import scala.collection.mutable.Queue
   ```

4. Create a `SparkSession` object as an entry point to the cluster and a `StreamingContext`:

   ```
   val spark = SparkSession
    .builder
   .master("local[*]")
    .appName("Logistic Regression Streaming App")
    .config("spark.sql.warehouse.dir", ".")
    .getOrCreate()


   import spark.implicits._

   val ssc = new StreamingContext(spark.sparkContext, Seconds(2))
   ```

5. The interleaving of log messages leads to hard-to-read output, therefore set logging level to warning:

   ```
   Logger.getLogger("org").setLevel(Level.ERROR)
   ```

6. Load the Pima data file into a Dataset of type string:

```
val rawDS = spark.read
.text("../data/sparkml2/chapter13/pima-indians-
diabetes.data").as[String]
```

7. Build a RDD from our raw Dataset by generating a tuple consisting of the last item into a record as the label and everything else as a sequence:

```
val buffer = rawDS.rdd.map(value => {
val data = value.split(",")
(data.init.toSeq, data.last)
})
```

8. Convert the preprocessed data into label points for use with the machine learning library:

```
val lps = buffer.map{ case (feature: Seq[String], label: String) =>
val featureVector = feature.map(_.toDouble).toArray[Double]
LabeledPoint(label.toDouble, Vectors.dense(featureVector))
}
```

9. Create mutable queues for appending data to:

```
val trainQueue = new Queue[RDD[LabeledPoint]]()
val testQueue = new Queue[RDD[LabeledPoint]]()
```

10. Create Spark streaming queues to receive streaming data:

```
val trainingStream = ssc.queueStream(trainQueue)
val testStream = ssc.queueStream(testQueue)
```

11. Configure the streaming logistic regression model:

```
val numFeatures = 8
val model = new StreamingLogisticRegressionWithSGD()
.setInitialWeights(Vectors.zeros(numFeatures))
.setNumIterations(15)
.setStepSize(0.5)
.setMiniBatchFraction(0.25)
```

12. Train the regression model and predict final values:

```
model.trainOn(trainingStream)
val result = model.predictOnValues(testStream.map(lp => (lp.label,
lp.features)))
 result.map{ case (label: Double, prediction: Double) => (label,
prediction) }.print()
```

13. Start Spark streaming context:

```
ssc.start()
```

14. Split label point data into training set and test set:

```
val Array(trainData, test) = lps.randomSplit(Array(.80, .20))
```

15. Append data to training data queue for processing:

```
trainQueue += trainData
 Thread.sleep(4000)
```

16. Now split test data in half and append to the queue for processing:

```
val testGroups = test.randomSplit(Array(.50, .50))
 testGroups.foreach(group => {
 testQueue += group
 Thread.sleep(2000)
 })
```

17. Once data is received by the queue stream, you will see the following output:

```
---------------------------------------------
Time: 1488571098000 ms
---------------------------------------------
(1.0,1.0)
(1.0,1.0)
(1.0,0.0)
(0.0,1.0)
(1.0,0.0)
(1.0,1.0)
(0.0,0.0)
(1.0,1.0)
(0.0,1.0)
(0.0,1.0)
. . .
---------------------------------------------
Time: 1488571100000 ms
---------------------------------------------
```

```
(1.0,1.0)
(0.0,0.0)
(1.0,1.0)
(1.0,0.0)
(0.0,1.0)
(0.0,1.0)
(0.0,1.0)
(1.0,0.0)
(0.0,0.0)
(1.0,1.0)
...
```

18. Close the program by stopping the Spark streaming context:

```
ssc.stop()
```

How it works...

First, we loaded the Pima Diabetes Dataset into a Dataset and parsed it into a tuple by taking every element as a feature except the last one, which we used as a label. Second, we morphed the RDD of tuples into labeled points so it can be used as input to the streaming logistic regression algorithm. Third, we created instances of mutable queues and Spark's QueueInputDStream class to be used as a pathway into the logistic algorithm.

Fourth, we created the streaming logistic regression model, which will predict wine quality for our final results. Finally, we customarily created training and test datasets from original data and appended it to the appropriate queue to trigger the model's processing of streaming data. The final results for each micro-batch displays the original label and predicted label of 1.0 for testing true positive as a diabetic or 0.0 as true negative.

There's more...

Documentation for StreamingLogisticRegressionWithSGD() is available at https://spark.apache.org/docs/latest/api/scala/index.html#org.apache.spark.ml lib.classification.StreamingLogisticRegressionWithSGD

See also

The hyper parameters for the model:

- `setInitialWeights()`
- `setNumIterations()`
- `setStepSize()`
- `setMiniBatchFraction()`

Index

R

S

62536373R00369

Made in the USA
Middletown, DE
23 August 2019